Points of View

Readings in American Government and Politics

Points of View

Readings in American Government and Politics

EIGHTH EDITION

Edited by

Robert E. DiClerico
West Virginia University

Allan S. Hammock
West Virginia University

Boston   Burr Ridge, IL   Dubuque, IA   Madison, WI
New York   San Francisco   St. Louis
Bangkok   Bogotá   Caracas   Lisbon   London   Madrid   Mexico City
Milan   New Delhi   Seoul   Singapore   Sydney   Taipei   Toronto

McGraw-Hill Higher Education

A Division of The McGraw-Hill Companies

POINTS OF VIEW: READINGS IN AMERICAN GOVERNMENT AND POLITICS
EIGHTH EDITION

Published by McGraw-Hill, an imprint of The McGraw-Hill Companies, Inc., 1221 Avenue of the Americas, New York, NY 10020.

Some ancillaries, including electronic and print components, may not be available to customers outside the United States.

This book is printed on acid-free paper.

1 2 3 4 5 6 7 8 9 0 DOC/DOC 0 9 8 7 6 5 4 3 2 1 0

ISBN 0–07–232268–3

Vice president and editor-in-chief: *Thalia Dorwick*
Editorial director: *Jane E. Vaicunas*
Sponsoring editor: *Monica Eckman*
Editorial coordinator: *Hannah Glover*
Marketing manager: *Janise A. Fry*
Project manager: *Rose Koos*
Senior media producer: *Sean Crowley*
Production supervisor: *Enboge Chong*
Coordinator of freelance design: *Michelle D. Whitaker*
Cover designer: *Nathan Bahls*
Cover image: *©Paul Anderson/The Stock Illustration Source, Inc.*
Supplement coordinator: *Stacy A. Patch*
Compositor: *ElectraGraphics, Inc.*
Typeface: *10/12 Times Roman*
Printer: *R. R. Donnelley & Sons Company/Crawfordsville, IN*

Library of Congress Cataloging-in-Publication Data

Points of view : readings in American government and politics / [edited by] Robert E. DiClerico, Allan S. Hammock. — 8th ed.
　　p.　cm.
　ISBN 0–07–232268–3
　1. United States—Politics and government. I. DiClerico, Robert E. II. Hammock, Allan S., 1938–

JK21 .P59　2001
320.973—dc21
　　　　　　　　　　　　　　　　　　00–041835
　　　　　　　　　　　　　　　　　　CIP

www.mhhe.com

About the Editors

ROBERT E. DiCLERICO is Eberly Professor of Political Science at West Virginia University. An Indiana University (Bloomington) Ph.D. and a Danforth fellow, he is author of *The American President,* 5th edition (2000); co-author of *Choosing Our Choices* (2000) and *Few Are Chosen* (1984); and editor of *Political Parties, Campaigns, and Elections* (2000) and *Analyzing the Presidency* (1985).

ALLAN S. HAMMOCK is an Associate Professor and Chairman of the Department of Political Science at West Virginia University. He received his Ph.D. from the University of Virginia and is co-author of *West Virginia Politics and Government* (1996). He currently serves as chairman of the West Virginia Election Commission.

Contents

vii

Preface

Reflecting the press of events and editorial judgments, the changes made for the eighth edition of *Points of View* have been substantial. We have added three new topics. In chapter 1, "Democracy," we have added a new section, "Making Democracy Work"; in chapter 10, "Congress," we have included a new section on the filibuster; and in chapter 15, "Civil Liberties," we have added a topic dealing with the issue of student fees and freedom of speech. In addition to these changes, we have included some new selections: one on public opinion (in chapter 4), one on voting (in chapter 5), two on campaign finance (in chapter 7), and two on bureaucracy (in chapter 13). Finally, of the articles retained from the previous edition, two have been significantly updated: James L. Sundquist's article on the relationship between the president and Congress (in chapter 12) and John Kilwein's selection on crime and the courts (in chapter 14).

The basic goals of the book remain the same: namely, to provide students with a manageable number of selections that present readable, succinct, thoughtful, and diverse perspectives across a broad range of issues related to American government.

We would like to extend our thanks to a number of individuals who made valuable contributions to this project. A special debt of gratitude is owed to Wendy Nelson, who had primary editorial responsibility for this latest edition and whose keen eye for detail was instrumental in improving the style and content of the final manuscript.

We would also like to express our appreciation to the sponsoring editor, Monica Eckman, who had overall responsibility for coordinating this latest revision and did a superb job of expediting the publishing process.

In the course of revising and updating this manuscript, we repeatedly called upon the typing skills of administrative associate Lee Ann Greathouse, who cheerfully reproduced manuscripts with unfailing accuracy and in less time than we had any reason to expect.

Finally, we would like to express our deep appreciation to the following academicians who carefully read the previous edition of *Points of View* and offered the most detailed and constructive suggestions we have ever received on a revision:

Sheryl Breen—University of Minnesota

Erich G. Frankland—Casper College, Wyoming

James M. Hoefler—Dickinson College, Pennsylvania

Theodore Kamena—Western Washington University

William V. Moore—College of Charleston

C. Jonathan Moses—Flathead Valley Community College

Russell Renka—Southeast Missouri State University

Stephanie Sapiie—Brooklyn College CUNY

Robert E. DiClerico

Allan S. Hammock
Morgantown, West Virginia
March 2000

A Note to the Instructor

For some years now, both of us have jointly taught the introductory course to American government. Each year we perused the crop of existing readers, and while we adopted several different readers over this period, we were not wholly satisfied with any of them. It is our feeling that many of the readers currently on the market suffer from one or more of the following deficiencies: (1) Some contain selections which are difficult for students to comprehend because of the sophistication of the argument, the manner of expression, or both. (2) In many instances, readers do not cover all of the topics typically treated in an introductory American government course. (3) In choosing selections for a given topic, editors do not always show sufficient concern for how—or whether—one article under a topic relates to other articles under the same topic. (4) Most readers contain too many selections for each topic—indeed, in several cases the number of selections for some topics exceeds ten. Readers are nearly always used in conjunction with a textbook. Thus, to ask a student to read a lengthy chapter—jammed with facts—from a textbook and then to read anywhere from five to ten selections on the same topic from a reader is to demand that students read more than they can reasonably absorb in a meaningful way. Of course, an instructor need not assign all the selections under a given topic. At the same time, however, this approach justifiably disgruntles students who, after purchasing a reader, discover that they may only be asked to read one-half or two-thirds of it.

Instead of continuing to complain about what we considered to be the limitations of existing American government readers, we decided to try our own hand at putting one together. In doing so, we were guided by the following considerations.

Readability

Quite obviously, students will not read dull, difficult articles. As well as having something important to say, we feel that each of the articles in *Points of View* is clearly written, well organized, and free of needless jargon.

Comprehensiveness

The sixteen chapters of *Points of View* cover all the major topics of concern that are typically treated in the standard introductory course on American government.

Economy of Selections

We decided, generally, to limit the number of selections to two per topic, although we did include three selections on representation in chapter 10. The limitation on selections will maximize the possibility that students will read them. It has been our experience that when students are assigned four, five, or more selections under a given topic, they simply do not read them all. In addition, by limiting the selections for each topic, there is a greater likelihood that students will be able to associate an argument with the author who made it.

Juxtaposition

The two selections for each topic will take *opposing* or *different* points of view on some aspect of a given topic. This approach was chosen for three reasons. First, we believe that student interest will be enhanced by playing one article off against the other. Thus, the "interest" quality of a given article will derive not only from its own content, but also from its juxtaposition with the other article. Second, we think it is important to sensitize students to the fact that one's perspective on an issue will depend upon the values that he or she brings to it. Third, by having both selections focus on a particular issue related to a given topic, the student will have a greater depth of understanding about that issue. We think this is preferable to having five or six selections under a topic, with each selection focusing on a different aspect, and with the result that the student ultimately is exposed to "a little of this and a little of that"—that is, if the student even bothers to read all five or six selections.

    While the readers currently available take into account one or, in some instances, several of the considerations identified above, we believe that the uniqueness of *Points of View* lies in the fact that it has sought to incorporate *all* of them.

Robert E. DiClerico

Allan S. Hammock

Points of View

Readings in American Government and Politics

1

DEMOCRACY

Defining Democracy

*A*ny *assessment of a society's democratic character will be fundamentally determined by what the observer chooses to use as a definition of democracy. Though the concept of democracy has commanded the attention of political thinkers for centuries, the following selections by Howard Zinn and Sidney Hook serve to demonstrate that there continues to be considerable disagreement over its meaning. Each of them has scanned the American scene and reached different conclusions regarding the democratic character of our society. This difference of opinion is explained primarily by the fact that each approaches his evaluation with a different conception of what democracy is.*

For Zinn, the definition of democracy includes criteria that bear not only upon how decisions get made but also upon what results *from such decisions. Specifically, he argues that such results must lead to a certain level of human welfare within a society. In applying these criteria of human welfare to the United States, he concludes that we fall short of the mark in several areas.*

Although Sidney Hook is willing to acknowledge that democracy might indeed function more smoothly in societies where the conditions of human welfare are high, he insists that these conditions do not themselves constitute the definition of democracy. Rather, he maintains that democracy is a process—a way of making decisions. Whether such decisions lead to the conditions of human welfare that Zinn prescribes is irrelevant. The crucial test, according to Hook, is whether or not the people have the right, by majority rule, to make choices about the quality of their lives—whatever those choices might be.

How Democratic Is America?

Howard Zinn

To give a sensible answer to the question "How democratic is America?" I find it necessary to make three clarifying preliminary statements. First, I want to define "democracy," not conclusively, but operationally, so we can know what we are arguing about or at least what I am talking about. Second, I want to state what my criteria are for measuring the "how" in the question. And third, I think it necessary to issue a warning about how a certain source of bias (although not the only source) is likely to distort our judgments.

Our definition is crucial. This becomes clear if we note how relatively easy is the answer to our question when we define democracy as a set of formal institutions and let it go at that. If we describe as "democratic" a country that has a representative system of government, with universal suffrage, a bill of rights, and party competition for office, it becomes easy to answer the question "how" with the enthusiastic reply, "Very!" . . .

I propose a set of criteria for the description "democratic" which goes beyond formal political institutions, to the quality of life in the society (economic, social, psychological), beyond majority rule to a concern for minorities, and beyond national boundaries to a global view of what is meant by "the people," in that rough, but essentially correct view of democracy as "government of, by, and for the people."

Let me list these criteria quickly, because I will go on to discuss them in some detail later:

1. To what extent can various people in the society participate in those decisions which affect their lives: decisions in the political process and decisions in the economic structure?
2. As a corollary of the above: do people have equal access to the information which they need to make important decisions?
3. Are the members of the society equally protected on matters of life and death—in the most literal sense of that phrase?
4. Is there equality before the law: police, courts, the judicial process—as well as equality *with* the law-enforcing institutions, so as to safeguard equally everyone's person, and his freedom from interference by others, and by the government?
5. Is there equality in the distribution of available resources: those economic goods necessary for health, life, recreation, leisure, growth?
6. Is there equal access to education, to knowledge and training, so as to enable persons in the society to live their lives as fully as possible, to enlarge their range of possibilities?

Howard Zinn is professor emeritus of political science at Boston University. This essay was originally published in Robert A. Goldwin, ed., How Democratic Is America? *pp. 39–60 (Chicago, Rand McNally, 1971). The author revised and updated the original for* Points of View *in 1985 and again in 1997.*

7. Is there freedom of expression on all matters, and equally for all, to communicate with other members of the society?
8. Is there freedom for individuality in private life, in sexual relations, family relations, the right of privacy?
9. To minimize regulation: do education and the culture in general foster a spirit of cooperation and amity to sustain the above conditions?
10. As a final safety feature: is there opportunity to protest, to disobey the laws, when the foregoing objectives are being lost—as a way of restoring them? . . .

Two historical facts support my enlarged definition of democracy. One is that the industrialized Western societies have outgrown the original notions which accompanied their early development: that constitutional and procedural tests sufficed for the "democracy" that overthrew the old order; that democracy was quite adequately fulfilled by the Bill of Rights in England at the time of the Glorious Revolution, the Constitution of the United States, and the declaration of the Rights of Man in France. It came to be acknowledged that the rhetoric of these revolutions was not matched by their real achievements. In other words, the limitations of that "democracy" led to the reformist and radical movements that grew up in the West in the middle and late nineteenth century. The other historical note is that the new revolutions in our century, in Africa, Asia, Latin America, while rejecting either in whole or in part the earlier revolutions, profess a similar democratic aim, but with an even broader rhetoric. . . .

My second preliminary point is on standards. By this I mean that we can judge in several ways the fulfillment of these ten criteria I have listed. We can measure the present against the past, so that if we find that in 2000 we are doing better in these matters than we were doing in 1860 or 1910, the society will get a good grade for its "democracy." I would adjure such an approach because it supports complacency. With such a standard, Russians in 1910 could point with pride to how much progress they had made toward parliamentary democracy; as Russians in 1985 could point to their post-Stalin progress away from the gulag; as Americans could point in 1939 to how far they had come toward solving the problem of economic equality; as Americans in the South could point in 1950 to the progress of the southern African-American. Indeed, the American government has given military aid to brutal regimes in Latin America on the ground that a decrease in the murders by semiofficial death squads is a sign of progress.

Or, we could measure our democracy against other places in the world. Given the high incidence of tyranny in the world, polarization of wealth, and lack of freedom of expression, the United States, even with very serious defects, could declare itself successful. Again, the result is to let us all off easily; some of our most enthusiastic self-congratulation is based on such a standard.

On the other hand, we could measure our democracy against an ideal (even if admittedly unachievable) standard. I would argue for such an approach, because, in what may seem to some a paradox, the ideal standard is the pragmatic one; it affects what we *do*. To grade a student on the basis of an improvement over past performance is justifiable if the intention is to encourage someone discouraged about his ability. But if he is rather pompous about his superiority in relation to other students (and I suggest this is frequently true of Americans evaluating American "democracy"), and if in addition he is a medical student about to graduate into a world ridden with disease, it would be best to judge him by an ideal standard. That might spur him to an improvement fast enough to save lives. . . .

My third preliminary point is a caution based on the obvious fact that we make our appraisals through the prism of our own status in society. This is particularly important in assessing democracy, because if "democracy" refers to the condition of masses of people, and if we as the assessors belong to a number of elites, we will tend (and I am not declaring an inevitability, just warning of a tendency) to see the present situation in America more benignly than it deserves. To be more specific, if democracy requires a keen awareness of the condition of black people, of poor people, of young people, of that majority of the world who are not American—and we are white, prosperous, beyond draft age, and American—then we have a number of pressures tending to dull our sense of inequity. We are, if not doomed to err, likely to err on the side of complacency—and we should try to take this into account in making our judgments.

1. PARTICIPATION IN DECISIONS

We need to recognize first, that whatever decisions are made politically are made by representatives of one sort or another: state legislators, congressmen, senators, and other elected officials, governors and presidents; also by those appointed by elected officials, like Supreme Court justices. These are important decisions, affecting our lives, liberties, and ability to pursue happiness. Congress and the president decide on the tax structure, which affects the distribution of resources. They decide how to spend the monies received; whether or not we go to war; who serves in the armed forces; what behavior is considered a crime; which crimes are prosecuted and which are not. They decide what limitations there should be on our travel, or on our right to speak freely. They decide on the availability of education and health services.

If representation by its very nature is undemocratic, as I would argue, this is an important fact for our evaluation. Representative government is *closer* to democracy than monarchy, and for this reason it has been hailed as one of the great political advances of modern times; yet, it is only a step in the direction of democracy, at its best. It has certain inherent flaws—pointed out by Rousseau in the eighteenth century, Victor Considerant in the nineteenth century, Robert Michels in the beginning of the twentieth century, Hannah Arendt in our own time. No representative can adequately represent another's needs; the representative tends to become a member of a special elite; he has privileges which weaken his sense of concern at others' grievances; the passions of the troubled lose force (as Madison noted in *The Federalist 10*) as they are filtered through the representative system; the elected official develops an expertise which tends toward its own perpetuation. Leaders develop what Michels called "a mutual insurance contract" against the rest of society. . . .

If only radicals pointed to the inadequacy of the political processes in the United States, we might be suspicious. But established political scientists of a moderate bent talk quite bluntly of the limitations of the voting system in the United States. Robert Dahl, in *A Preface to Democratic Theory,* drawing on the voting studies of American political scientists, concludes that "political activity, at least in the United States, is positively associated to a significant extent with such variables as income, socio-economic status, and education." He says:

> By their propensity for political passivity the poor and uneducated disfranchise themselves. . . . Since they also have less access than the wealthy to the organizational, financial, and propaganda resources that weigh so heavily in campaigns, elections, legislative, and executive decisions, anything like equal control over government policy is triply barred to the members of Madison's unpropertied masses. They are barred by their relatively greater inactivity, by their relatively limited access to resources, and by Madison's nicely contrived system of constitutional checks.[1]

Dahl thinks that our society is essentially democratic, but this is because he expects very little. (His book was written in the 1950s, when lack of commotion in the society might well have persuaded him that no one else expected much more than he did.) Even if democracy were to be superficially defined as "majority rule," the United States would not fulfill that, according to Dahl, who says that "on matters of specific policy, the majority rarely rules."[2] After noting that "the election is the critical technique for insuring that governmental leaders will be relatively responsive to nonleaders," he goes on to say that "it is important to notice how little a national election tells us about the preferences of majorities. Strictly speaking, all an election reveals is the first preferences of some citizens among the candidates standing for office."[3] About 45 percent of the potential voters in national elections, and about 60 percent of the voters in local elections do not vote, and this cannot be attributed, Dahl says, simply to indifference. And if, as Dahl points out, "in no large nation state can elections tell us much about the preferences of majorities and minorities," this is "even more true of the interelection period." . . .

Dahl goes on to assert that the election process and interelection activity "are crucial processes for insuring that political leaders will be *somewhat* responsive to the preferences of *some* ordinary citizens."[4] I submit (the emphasized words are mine) that if an admirer of democracy in America can say no more than this, democracy is not doing very well.

Dahl tells us the election process is one of "two fundamental methods of social control which, operating together, make governmental leaders so responsive to nonleaders that the distinction between democracy and dictatorship still makes sense." Since his description of the election process leaves that dubious, let's look at his second requirement for distinguishing democracy: "The other method of social control is continuous political competition among individuals, parties, or both." What it comes down to is "not minority rule but minorities rule."[5]

If it turns out that this—like the election process—also has little democratic content, we will not be left with very much difference—by Dahl's own admission—between "dictatorship" and the "democracy" practiced in the United States. Indeed, there is much evidence on this: the lack of democracy within the major political parties, the vastly disproportionate influence of wealthy groups over poorer ones. What antismoking consumer group in the election year of 1996 could match the five million dollars donated to the Republican Party by the tobacco interests? What ordinary citizen

could have the access to President Bill Clinton that a group of bankers had in May of
that election year when they were invited to the White House?[6] All of this, and more,
supports the idea of a "decline of American pluralism" that Henry Kariel has written
about. What Dahl's democracy comes down to is "the steady appeasement of relatively
small groups."[7] If these relatively small groups turn out to be the aircraft industry far
more than the aged, the space industry far more than the poor, the Pentagon far more
than the college youth—what is left of democracy?

Sometimes the elitism of decision-making is defended (by Dahl and by others) on
the ground that the elite is enacting decisions passively supported by the mass, whose
tolerance is proof of an underlying consensus in society. But Murray Levin's studies in
The Alienated Voter indicate how much nonparticipation in elections is a result of hope-
lessness rather than approval. And Robert Wiebe, a historian at Northwestern University, talks of "consensus" becoming a "new stereotype." He approaches the question
historically.

> Industrialization arrived so peacefully not because all Americans secretly shared the
> same values or implicitly willed its success but because its millions of bitter enemies
> lacked the mentality and the means to organize an effective counterattack.[8]

Wiebe's point is that the passivity of most Americans in the face of elitist decision-
making has not been due to acquiescence but to the lack of resources for effective combat, as well as a gulf so wide between the haves and have-nots that there was no ground
on which to dispute. Americans neither revolted violently nor reacted at the polls; instead they were subservient, or else worked out their hostilities in personal ways. . . .

Presidential nominations and elections are more democratic than monarchical rule
or the procedures of totalitarian states, but they are far from some reasonable expectation of democracy. The two major parties have a monopoly of presidential power, taking turns in the White House. The candidates of minority parties don't have a chance.
They do not have access to the financial backing of the major parties, and there is not
the semblance of equal attention in the mass media; it is only the two major candidates
who have free access to prime time on national television.

More important, both parties almost always agree on the fundamentals of domestic and foreign policy, despite the election-year rhetoric which attempts to find important differences. Both parties arranged for United States intervention in Vietnam in the
1950s and 1960s, and both, when public opinion changed, promised to get out (note the
Humphrey-Nixon contest of 1968). In 1984, Democratic candidate Walter Mondale
agreed with Republican candidate Ronald Reagan that the United States (which had ten
thousand thermonuclear warheads) needed to continue increasing its arms budget, although he asked for a smaller increase than the Republicans. Such a position left Mondale unable to promise representatives of the black community (where unemployment
was over 20 percent) that he would spend even a few billion dollars for a jobs program.
Meanwhile, Democrats and Republicans in Congress were agreeing on a $297 billion
arms bill for the 1985 fiscal year.[9]

I have been talking so far about democracy in the political process. But there is another serious weakness that I will only mention here, although it is of enormous importance: the powerlessness of the American to participate in economic decision-

making, which affects his life at every moment. As a consumer, that is, as the person whom the economy is presumably intended to serve, he has virtually nothing to say about what is produced for him. The corporations make what is profitable; the advertising industry persuades him to buy what the corporations produce. He becomes the passive victim of the misallocation of resources, the production of dangerous commodities, the spoiling of his air, water, forests, beaches, cities.

2. ACCESS TO INFORMATION

Adequate information for the electorate is a precondition for any kind of action (whether electoral or demonstrative) to affect national policy. As for the voting process, Berelson, Lazarsfeld, and McPhee tell us (in their book, *Voting*) after extensive empirical research: "One persistent conclusion is that the public is not particularly well informed about the specific issues of the day." . . .

Furthermore, there are certain issues which never even reach the public because they are decided behind the scenes. . . .

Consider the information available to voters on two major kinds of issues. One of them is the tax structure, so bewilderingly complex that the corporation, with its corps of accountants and financial experts, can prime itself for lobbying activities, while the average voter, hardly able to comprehend his own income tax, stands by helplessly as the president, the Office of Management and Budget, and the Congress decide the tax laws. The dominant influences are those of big business, which has the resources both to understand and to act.

Then there is foreign policy. The government leads the citizenry to believe it has special expertise which, if it could only be revealed, would support its position against critics. At the same time, it hides the very information which would reveal its position to be indefensible. The mendacity of the government on the Bay of Pigs operation and the withholding of vital information about the Tonkin Gulf events are only two examples of the way the average person becomes a victim of government deception.*

In 1990, historian Warren Cohen resigned as adviser to the State Department in its publication of the series *Foreign Relations of the United States,* pointing out that the government was refusing to cover events less than thirty years old. And even what it did publish was not trustworthy. "The United States government is publishing blatantly fraudulent accounts of its activities in Guatemala, Iran, and Southeast Asia in the 1950s" (*World Monitor Magazine,* 1990).

When the United States invaded the tiny island of Grenada in the fall of 1983, no reporters were allowed to observe the invasion, and the American public had little opportunity to get independent verification of the reasons given by the government for the invasion. As a result, President Reagan could glibly tell the nation what even one of his own supporters, journalist George Will, admitted was a lie: that he was invading Grenada to protect the lives of American medical students on the island. He could also

---

*The Bay of Pigs operation was an unsuccessful, U.S.-backed invasion of Cuba by Cuban exiles in 1961; the Gulf of Tonkin Resolution, passed by Congress in 1965 on the occasion of an alleged attack on U.S. ships by the North Vietnamese, authorized the deployment of thousands of U.S. troops to Vietnam—*Editors.*

claim that documents found on the island indicated plans for a Cuban-Soviet takeover of Grenada; the documents showed no such thing.[10]

Furthermore, the distribution of information to the public is a function of power and wealth. The government itself can color the citizens' understanding of events by its control of news at the source: the presidential press conference, the "leak to the press," the White Papers, the teams of "truth experts" going around the country at the taxpayers' expense. As for private media, the large networks and mass-circulation magazines have the greatest access to the public mind. There is no "equal time" for critics of public policy. . . .

3. EQUAL PROTECTION

Let us go now from the procedural to the substantive, indeed to the most substantive of questions: the right of all people to life itself. Here we find democracy in America tragically inadequate. Not only Locke, one of the leading theorists of the democratic tradition, declared the ultimate right of any person to safeguard his own life when threatened by the government; Hobbes, often looked on as the foe of democratic thought, agreed. Yet, in matters of foreign policy, where the decisions involve life or death for large numbers of Americans, power rests in the hands of the president and a small group of advisers. Despite the constitutional provision that war must be declared by Congress, in reality the President can create situations (as in the Mexican War, as in both world wars) which make inevitable congressional votes for war. And in all post–World War II conflicts (Korea, Vietnam, Iraq) there was no declaration of war by Congress.

It is in connection with this most basic of rights—life itself, the first and most important of those substantive ends which democratic participation is designed to safeguard—that I would assert the need for a global view of democracy. One can at least conceive of a democratic decision for martial sacrifice by those ready to make the sacrifice; a "democratic" war is thus a theoretical possibility. But that presumption of democracy becomes obviously false at the first shot because then *others* are affected who did not decide. . . . Nations making decisions to slaughter their own sons are at least theoretically subject to internal check. The victims on the other side fall without any such chance. For the United States today, this failure of democracy is total; we have the capacity to destroy the world without giving it a chance to murmur a dissent; we did, in fact, destroy a part of southeast Asia on the basis of a unilateral decision made in Washington. There is no more pernicious manifestation of the lack of democracy in America than this single fact.

4. EQUALITY BEFORE THE LAW

Is there equality before the law? At every stage of the judicial process—facing the policeman, appearing in court, being freed on bond, being sentenced by the judge— the poor person is treated worse than the rich, the black treated worse than the white, the politically or personally odd character is treated worse than the orthodox. A defendant's poverty affects his preliminary hearing, his right to bail, the quality of his counsel. The evidence is plentiful in the daily newspapers, which inform us that an African-American boy fleeing the scene of a two-dollar theft may be shot and killed by a pursuing policeman, while a wealthy man who goes to South America after a million-dollar swindle, even if apprehended, need never fear a scratch. The wealthy price-fixer for General Motors, who costs consumers millions, will get ninety days in jail, the burglar of a liquor store will get five years. An African-American youth, or a bearded white youth poorly dressed, has much more chance of being clubbed by a policeman on the street than a well-dressed white man, given the fact that both respond with equal tartness to a question. . . .

Aside from inequality among citizens, there is inequality between the citizen and his government, when they face one another in a court of law. Take the matter of counsel: the well-trained government prosecutor faces the indigent's court-appointed counsel. Four of my students did a study of the City Court of Boston several years ago. They sat in the court for weeks, taking notes, and found that the average time spent by court-appointed counsel with his client, before arguing the case at the bench, was seven minutes.

5. DISTRIBUTION OF RESOURCES

Democracy is devoid of meaning if it does not include equal access to the available resources of the society. In India, democracy might still mean poverty; in the United States, with a Gross National Product of more than $3 trillion a year, democracy should mean that every American, working a short work-week, has adequate food, clothing, shelter, health care, education for himself and his family—in short, the material resources necessary to enjoy life and freedom. Even if only 20 percent of the American population is desperately poor . . . in a country so rich, that is an inexcusable breach of the democratic principle. Even if there is a large, prosperous middle class, there is something grossly unfair in the fact that in 1995 the richest 1 percent of the population owned over 40 percent of the total wealth, a figure that, throughout our history, has rarely been under 33 percent.

Whether you are poor or rich determines the most fundamental facts about your life: whether you are cold in the winter while trying to sleep, whether you suffocate in the summer; whether you live among vermin or rats; whether the smells around you all day are sweet or foul; whether you have adequate medical care; whether you have good teeth; whether you can send your children to college; whether you can go on vacation or have to take an extra job at night; whether you can afford a divorce, or an abortion, or a wife, or another child. . . .

6. ACCESS TO EDUCATION

In a highly industrialized society, education is a crucial determinant of wealth, political power, social status, leisure, and the ability to work in one's chosen field. Educational resources in our society are not equitably distributed. Among high-school graduates of the same IQ levels, a far higher percentage of the well-to-do go on to college than the poor.[11] A mediocre student with money can always go to college. A mediocre student without money may not be able to go, even to a state college, because he may have to work to support his family. Furthermore, the educational resources in the schools—equipment, teachers, etc.—are far superior in the wealthy suburbs than in the poor sections of the city, whether white or black.

7. FREEDOM OF EXPRESSION

Like money, freedom of expression is available to all in America, but in widely varying quantities. The First Amendment formally guarantees freedom of speech, press, assembly, and petition to all—but certain realities of wealth, power, and status stand in the way of the equal distribution of these rights. Anyone can stand on a street corner and talk to ten or a hundred people. But someone with the resources to buy loudspeaker equipment, go through the necessary red tape, and post a bond with the city may hold a meeting downtown and reach a thousand or five thousand people. A person or a corporation with $100,000 can buy time on television and reach 10 million people. A rich person simply has much more freedom of speech than a poor person. The government has much more freedom of expression than a private individual, because the president can command the airwaves when he wishes, and reach 60 million people in one night.

Freedom of the press also is guaranteed to all. But the student selling an underground newspaper on the street with a nude woman on the cover may be arrested by a policeman, while the airport newsstand selling *Playboy* and ten magazines like it will remain safe. Anyone with $10,000 can put out a newspaper to reach a few thousand people. Anyone with $10 million can buy a few newspapers that will reach a few million people. Anyone who is penniless had better have a loud voice; and then he might be arrested for disturbing the peace.

8. FREEDOM FOR INDIVIDUALITY

The right to live one's life, in privacy and freedom, in whatever way one wants, so long as others are not harmed, should be a sacred principle in a democracy. But there are hundreds of laws, varying from state to state, and sometimes joined by federal laws, which regulate the personal lives of people in this country: their marriages, their divorces, their sexual relations. Furthermore, both laws and court decisions protect policemen and the FBI in their use of secret devices which listen in on private conversations, or peer in on private conduct.

9. THE SPIRIT OF COOPERATION

The maintenance of those substantive elements of democracy which I have just sketched, if dependent on a pervasive network of coercion, would cancel out much of the benefit of that democracy. Democracy needs rather to be sustained by a spirit in society, the tone and the values of the culture. I am speaking of something as elusive as a mood, alongside something as hard as law, both of which would have to substitute co-operation tinged with friendly competition for the fierce combat of our business culture. I am speaking of the underlying drive that keeps people going in the society. So long as that drive is for money and power, with no ceiling on either, so long as ruthlessness is built into the rules of the game, democracy does not have a chance. If there is one crucial cause in the failure of American democracy—not the only one, of course, but a fundamental one—it is the drive for corporate profit, and the overwhelming influence of money in every aspect of our daily lives. That is the uncontrolled libido of our society from which the rape of democratic values necessarily follows.

The manifestations are diverse and endless: the drug industry's drive for profit has led to incredible overpricing of drugs for consumers (700 percent markup, for instance, for tablets to arthritic patients). It was disclosed in 1979 that Johns-Manville, the nation's largest asbestos manufacturer, had deliberately withheld from its workers X-ray results that showed they were developing cancer. In 1984, a company making an intrauterine birth control device—the Dalkon Shield—was found by a Minnesota court to have allowed tens of thousands of women to wear this device despite knowing that it was dangerous to their health (*Minneapolis Star and Tribune,* May 18, 1984). In the mid-1990s, it was revealed that tobacco companies had concealed information showing the narcotic nature of cigarettes. All in the interest of maximizing profit.

If these were isolated cases, reported and then eliminated, they could be dismissed as unfortunate blemishes on an otherwise healthy social body. But the major allocations of resources in our society are made on the basis of money profit rather than social use. . . .

. . . News items buttress what I have said. The oil that polluted California's beautiful beaches in the 1960s . . . was produced by a system in which the oil companies' hunger for profit has far more weight than the ordinary person's need to swim in clean water. This is not to be attributed to Republicanism overriding the concern for the little fellow of the Democratic Party. Profit is master whichever party is in power; it was the liberal Secretary of the Interior Stewart Udall who allowed the dangerous drilling to go on. . . .

In 1984, the suit of several thousand veterans against the Dow Chemical Company, claiming that they and their families had suffered terrible illnesses as a result of exposure in Vietnam to the poisonous chemical Agent Orange, was settled. The Dow corporation avoided the disclosures of thousands of documents in open court by agreeing to pay $180 million to the veterans. One thing seemed clear: the company had known that the defoliant used in Vietnam might be dangerous, but it held back the news, and blamed the government for ordering use of the chemical. The government itself, apparently wanting to shift blame to the corporation, declared publicly that Dow Chemical had been motivated in its actions by greed for profit.

10. OPPORTUNITY TO PROTEST

The first two elements in my list for democracy—decision-making and information to help make them—are procedural. The next six are substantive, dealing with the consequences of such procedures on life, liberty, and the pursuit of happiness. My ninth point, the one I have just discussed, shows how the money motive of our society corrupts both procedures and their consequences by its existence and suggests we need a different motive as a fundamental requisite of a democratic society. The point I am about to discuss is an ultimate requisite for democracy, a safety feature if nothing else—neither procedures nor consequences nor motivation—works. It is the right of citizens to break through the impasse of a legal and cultural structure, which sustains inequality, greed, and murder, to initiate processes for change. I am speaking of civil disobedience, which is an essential safeguard even in a successful society, and which is an absolute necessity in a society which is not going well.

If the institutional structure itself bars any change but the most picayune and grievances are serious, it is silly to insist that change must be mediated through the processes of that legal structure. In such a situation, dramatic expressions of protest and challenge are necessary to help change ways of thinking, to build up political power for drastic change. A society that calls itself democratic (whether accurately or not) must, as its ultimate safeguard, allow such acts of disobedience. If the government prohibits them (as we must expect from a government committed to the existent) then the members of a society concerned with democracy must not only defend such acts, but encourage them. Somewhere near the root of democratic thought is the theory of popular sovereignty, declaring that government and laws are instruments for certain ends, and are not to be deified with absolute obedience; they must constantly be checked by the citizenry, and challenged, opposed, even overthrown, if they become threats to fundamental rights.

Any abstract assessment of *when* disobedience is justified is pointless. Proper conclusions depend on empirical evidence about how bad things are at the moment, and how adequate are the institutional mechanisms for correcting them. . . .

One of these is the matter of race. The intolerable position of the African-American, in both North and South, has traditionally been handled with a few muttered apologies and tokens of reform. Then the civil disobedience of militants in the South forced our attention on the most dramatic (southern) manifestations of racism in America. The massive African-American urban uprisings of 1967 and 1968 showed that nothing less than civil disobedience (for riots and uprisings go beyond that) could make the nation see that the race problem is an American—not a southern—problem and that it needs bold, revolutionary action.

As for poverty: it seems clear that the normal mechanisms of congressional pretense and presidential rhetoric are not going to change things very much. Acts of civil disobedience by the poor will be required, at the least, to make middle-class America take notice, to bring national decisions that begin to reallocate wealth.

The war in Vietnam showed that we could not depend on the normal processes of "law and order," of the election process, of letters to the *Times,* to stop a series of especially brutal acts against the Vietnamese and against our own sons. It took a nationwide storm of protest, including thousands of acts of civil disobedience (14,000 people were arrested in one day in 1971 in Washington, D.C.), to help bring the war to an end. The role of draft resistance in affecting Lyndon Johnson's 1968 decision not to escalate the war further is told in the Defense Department secret documents of that period. In the 1980s and 1990s civil disobedience continued, with religious pacifists and others risking prison in order to protest the arms race and the plans for nuclear war.

The great danger for American democracy is not from the protesters. That democracy is too poorly realized for us to consider critics—even rebels—as the chief problem. Its fulfillment requires us all, living in an ossified system which sustains too much killing and too much selfishness, to join the protest.

NOTES

1. Robert A. Dahl, *A Preface to Democratic Theory* (Chicago: University of Chicago Press, 1963), p. 81.
2. *Ibid.,* p. 124.
3. *Ibid.,* p. 125.
4. *Ibid.,* p. 131.
5. *Ibid.,* pp. 131–32.
6. *New York Times,* January 25, 27, 1997.
7. Dahl, *A Preface to Democratic Theory,* p. 146.
8. Robert Wiebe, "The Confinements of Consensus," *TriQuarterly,* 1966, Copyright by TriQuarterly 1966. All rights reserved.
9. *New York Times,* September 25, 1984.
10. The *New York Times* reported, November 5, 1983: "There is nothing in the documents, however, that specifically indicates that Cuba and the Soviet Union were on the verge of taking over Grenada, as Administration officials have suggested."
11. See the Carnegie Council on Children study, *Small Futures,* by Richard deLore, 1979.

How Democratic Is America?
A Response to Howard Zinn

Sidney Hook

Charles Peirce, the great American philosopher, once observed that there was such a thing as the "ethics of words." The "ethics of words" are violated whenever ordinary terms are used in an unusual context or arbitrarily identified with another concept for which other terms are in common use. Mr. Zinn is guilty of a systematic violation of the "ethics of words." In consequence, his discussion of "democracy" results in a great many methodological errors as well as inconsistencies. To conserve space, I shall focus on three.

I

First of all, he confuses democracy as a political *process* with democracy as a political *product* or state of welfare; democracy as a *"free society"* with democracy as a *"good society,"* where good is defined in terms of equality or justice (or both) or some other constellation of values. One of the reasons for choosing to live under a democratic political system rather than a nondemocratic system is our belief that it makes possible a better society. That is something that must be empirically established, something denied by critics of democracy from Plato to Santayana. The equality which is relevant to democracy as a *political process* is, in the first instance, political equality with respect to the rights of citizenship. Theoretically, a politically democratic community could vote, wisely or unwisely, to abolish, retain, or establish certain economic inequalities. Theoretically, a benevolent despotism could institute certain kinds of social and even juridical equalities. Historically, the Bismarckian political dictatorship introduced social welfare legislation for the masses at a time when such legislation would have been repudiated by the existing British and American political democracies. Some of Mr. Zinn's proposed reforms could be introduced under a dictatorship or benevolent despotism. Therefore, they are not logically or organically related to democracy.

The second error in Mr. Zinn's approach to democracy is "to measure our democracy against an ideal (even if admittedly unachievable) standard . . . even if utopian . . ." without *defining* the standard. His criteria admittedly are neither necessary nor sufficient for determining the presence of democracy since he himself admits that they are applicable to societies that are not democratic. Further, even if we were to take his cri-

Sidney Hook (1902–1989) was head of the department of philosophy at New York University from 1934 to 1969 and was a senior research fellow at the Hoover Institution on War, Revolution, and Peace at Stanford University from 1973 to 1989. This essay was originally published in How Democratic Is America? *ed. Robert A. Goldwin, pp. 62–75 (Chicago, Rand McNally, 1971). The author revised and updated the original for* Points of View *in 1985.*

teria as severally defining the presence of democracy—as we might take certain physical and mental traits as constituting a definition of health—he gives no operational test for determining whether or not they have been fulfilled. For example, among the criteria he lists for determining whether a society is democratic is this: "Are the members of the society equally protected on matters of life and death—in the most literal sense of that phrase?" A moment's reflection will show that here—as well as in other cases where Zinn speaks of equality—it is impossible for all members to be equally protected on matters of life and death—certainly not in a world in which men do the fighting and women give birth to children, where children need *more* protection than adults, and where some risk-seeking adults require and deserve less protection (since resources are not infinite) than others. As Karl Marx realized, "in the most literal sense of that phrase," there cannot be absolute equality even in a classless society. . . .

The only sensible procedure in determining the absence or presence of equality from a democratic perspective is comparative. We must ask whether a culture is more or less democratic in comparison to the past with respect to some *desirable* feature of equality (Zinn ignores the fact that not all equalities are desirable). It is better for some people to be more intelligent and more knowledgeable than others than for all to be unintelligent and ignorant. There never is literally equal access to education, to knowledge and training in any society. The question is: Is there more access today for more people than yesterday, and how can we increase the access tomorrow?

Mr. Zinn refuses to take this approach because, he asserts, "it supports complacency." It does nothing of the sort! On the contrary, it shows that progress is possible, and encourages us to exert our efforts in the same direction if we regard the direction as desirable.

It will be instructive to look at the passage in which Mr. Zinn objects to this sensible comparative approach because it reveals the bias in his approach:

"With such a standard," he writes, "Russia in 1910 could point with pride to how much progress they had made toward parliamentary democracy; as Russians in 1985 could point to their post-Stalin progress away from the gulag; as Americans could point in 1939 to how far they had come in solving the problem of economic equality; as Americans in the South could point in 1950 to the progress of the southern African-American."

a. In 1910 the Russians were indeed moving toward greater progress in local parliamentary institutions. Far from making them complacent, they moved towards more inclusive representative institutions which culminated in elections to the Constituent Assembly in 1918, which was bayoneted out of existence by Lenin and the Communist Party, with a minority party dictatorship established.

b. Only Mr. Zinn would regard the slight diminution in terror from the days of Stalin to the regime of Chernenko as progress toward democracy. Those who observe the ethics of words would normally say that the screws of repression had been slightly relaxed. Mr. Zinn seems unaware that as bad as the terror was under Lenin, it was not as pervasive as it is today.* But no one with any respect for the ethics of words would

* These words and subsequent references to the Soviet Union preceded the reforms initiated under Mikhail Gorbachev and continued with greater intensity under Boris Yeltsin—*Editors.*

speak of "the progress of democracy" in the Soviet Union from Lenin to Stalin to Khrushchev to Chernenko. Their regimes were varying degrees of dictatorship and terror.

c. Americans could justifiably say that in 1939 progress had been made in giving workers a greater role, not as Mr. Zinn says in "solving the problem of economic equality" (a meaningless phrase), but in determining the conditions and rewards of work that prevailed in 1929 or previously because the existence of the Wagner Labor Relations Act made collective bargaining the law of the land. They could say this *not* to rest in complacency, but to use the organized force of their trade unions to influence further the political life of the country. And indeed, it was the organized labor movement in 1984 which in effect chose the candidate of the Democratic Party.

d. Americans in the South in 1950 could rightfully speak of the progress of the southern African-American over the days of unrestricted Jim Crow and lynching bees of the past, *not* to rest in complacency, but to agitate for further progress through the Supreme Court decision of *Brown v. Board of Education in Topeka* and through the Civil Rights Act of Congress. This has not made them complacent, but more resolved to press further to eliminate remaining practices of invidious discrimination.

Even Mr. Zinn should admit that with respect to some of his other criteria this is the only sensible approach. Otherwise we get unhistorical answers, the hallmark of the doctrinaire. He asks—criterion 1—"To what extent can various people in the society participate in those decisions which affect their lives?" and—criterion 7—"Is there freedom of expression on all matters, and equally for all, to communicate with other members of the society?" Why doesn't Mr. Zinn adopt this sensible comparative approach? Because it would lead him to inquire into the extent to which people are free to participate in decisions that affect their lives *today,* free to express themselves, free to organize, free to protest and dissent today, *in comparison with the past.* It would lead him to the judgment *which he wishes to avoid at all costs,* to wit, that despite the grave problems, gaps, and tasks before us, the United States is more democratic today than it was a hundred years ago, fifty years ago, twenty years ago, five years ago with respect to every one of the criteria he has listed. To recognize this is *not* an invitation to complacency. On the contrary, it indicates the possibility of broadening, deepening, and using the democratic political process to improve the quality of human life, to modify and redirect social institutions in order to realize on a wider scale the moral commitment of democracy to an equality of concern for all its citizens to achieve their fullest growth as persons. This commitment is to a process, not to a transcendent goal or a fixed, ideal standard.

In a halting, imperfect manner, set back by periods of violence, vigilantism, and xenophobia, the political democratic process in the United States has been used to modify the operation of the economic system. The improvements and reforms won from time to time make the still-existing problems and evils more acute in that people become more aware of them. The more the democratic process extends human freedoms, and the more it introduces justice in social relations and the distribution of wealth, the greater grows the desire for *more* freedom and justice. Historically and psychologically, it is false to assume that reforms breed a spirit of complacency. . . .

The third and perhaps most serious weakness in Mr. Zinn's view is his conception of the nature of the formal political democratic process. It suffers from several related defects. First, it overlooks the central importance of majority rule in the democratic process. Second, it denies in effect that majority rule is possible by defining democracy in such a way that it becomes impossible. . . .

"Representation by its very nature," claims Mr. Zinn, "is undemocratic." This is Rousseauistic nonsense. For it would mean that no democracy—including all societies that Mr. Zinn ever claimed at any time to be democratic—could possibly exist, not even the direct democracies or assemblies of Athens or the New England town meetings. For all such assemblies must elect officials to carry out their will. If no representative (and an official is a representative, too) can adequately represent another's needs, there is no assurance that in the actual details of governance, the selectmen, road commissioners, or other town or assembly officials will, in fact, carry out their directives. No assembly or meeting can sit in continuous session or collectively carry out the common decision. In the nature of the case, officials, like representatives, constitute an elite and their actions *may* reflect their interests more than the interests of the governed. This makes crucial the questions whether and how an elite can be removed, whether the consent on which the rule of the officials or representatives rests is free or coerced, whether a minority can peacefully use these mechanisms, by which freely given consent is registered, to win over or become a majority. The existence of representative assemblies makes democracy difficult, not impossible.

Since Mr. Zinn believes that a majority never has any authority to bind a minority as well as itself by decisions taken after free discussion and debate, he is logically committed to anarchy. Failing to see this, he confuses two fundamentally different things— the meaning or definition of democracy, and its justification.

1. A democratic government is one in which the general direction of policy rests directly or indirectly upon the freely given consent of a majority of the adults governed. Ambiguities and niceties aside, that is what democracy means. It is not anarchy. The absence of a unanimous consensus does not entail the absence of democracy.

2. One may reject on moral or religious or personal grounds a democratic society. Plato, as well as modern totalitarians, contends that a majority of mankind is either too stupid or vicious to be entrusted with self-government, or to be given the power to accept or reject their ruling elites, and that the only viable alternative to democracy is the self-selecting and self-perpetuating elite of "the wise," or "the efficient," or "the holy," or "the strong," depending upon the particular ideology of the totalitarian apologist. The only thing they have in common with democrats is their rejection of anarchy.

3. No intelligent and moral person can make an *absolute* of democracy in the sense that he believes it is always, everywhere, under any conditions, and no matter what its consequences, ethically legitimate. Democracy is obviously not desirable in a head-hunting or cannibalistic society or in an institution of the feeble-minded. But wherever and whenever a principled democrat accepts the political system of democracy, he must accept the binding authority of legislative decisions, reached

after the free give-and-take of debate and discussion, as binding upon him whether he is a member of the majority or minority. Otherwise the consequence is incipient or overt anarchy or civil war, the usual preface to despotism or tyranny. Accepting the decision of the majority as binding does not mean that it is final or irreversible. The processes of freely given consent must make it possible for a minority to urge amendment or repeal of any decision of the majority. Under carefully guarded provisions, a democrat may resort to civil disobedience of a properly enacted law in order to bear witness to the depths of his commitment in an effort *to reeducate* his fellow citizens. But in that case he must voluntarily accept punishment for his civil disobedience, and so long as he remains a democrat, voluntarily abandon his violation or noncompliance with law at the point where its consequences threaten to destroy the democratic process and open the floodgates either to the violent disorders of anarchy or to the dictatorship of a despot or a minority political party.

4. That Mr. Zinn is not a democrat but an anarchist in his views is apparent in his contention that not only must a democracy allow or tolerate civil disobedience within limits, but that "members of a society concerned with democracy must not only defend such acts, but encourage them." On this view, if southern segregationists resort to civil disobedience to negate the long-delayed but eminently just measures adopted by the government to implement the amendments that outlaw slavery, they should be encouraged to do so. On this view, any group that defies any law that violates its conscience—with respect to marriage, taxation, vaccination, abortion, education—should be encouraged to do so. Mr. Zinn, like most anarchists, refuses to generalize the principles behind his action. He fails to see that if all fanatics of causes deemed by them to be morally just were encouraged to resort to civil disobedience, even our imperfect existing political democracy would dissolve in chaos, and that civil disobedience would soon become quite uncivil. He fails to see that *in a democracy the processes of intelligence, not individual conscience, must be supreme.*

II

I turn now to some of the issues that Mr. Zinn declares are substantive. Before doing so I wish to make clear my belief that the most substantive issue of all is the procedural one by which the inescapable differences of interests among men, once a certain moral level of civilization has been reached, are to be negotiated. The belief in the validity of democratic procedures rests upon the conviction that where adult human beings have freedom of access to relevant information, they are, by and large, better judges of their own interests than are those who set themselves up as their betters and rulers, that, to use the homely maxim, those who wear the shoes know best where they pinch and therefore have the right to change their political shoes in the light of their experience. . . .

Looking at the question "How democratic is America?" with respect to the problems of poverty, race, education, etc., we must say "Not democratic enough!", but not for the reasons Mr. Zinn gives. For he seems to believe that the failure to adopt *his* solutions and proposals with respect to foreign policy, slum clearance, pollution, etc., is evidence of the failure of the democratic process itself. He overlooks the crucial difference between the procedural process and the substantive issues. When he writes that democracy is devoid of meaning if it does not include "equal access to the available resources of the society," he is simply abusing language. Assuming such equal access is desirable (which some might question who believe that access to *some* of society's resources—for example, to specialized training or to scarce supplies—should go not equally to all but to the most needful or sometimes to the most qualified), a democracy may or may not legislate such equal access. The crucial question is whether the electorate has the power to make the choice, or to elect those who would carry out the mandate chosen. . . .

When Mr. Zinn goes on to say that "in the United States . . . democracy should mean that every American, working a short work-week, has adequate food, clothing, shelter, health care, . . ." he is not only abusing language, he is revealing the fact that the procedural processes that are essential to the meaning of democracy, in ordinary usage, are not essential to his conception. He is violating the basic ethics of discourse. If democracy "should mean" what Zinn says it should, then were Huey Long or any other dictator to seize power and introduce a "short work-week" and distribute "adequate food, clothing, shelter, health care" to the masses, Mr. Zinn would have to regard his regime as democratic.

After all, when Hitler came to power and abolished free elections in Germany, he at the same time reduced unemployment, increased the real wages of the German worker, and provided more adequate food, clothing, shelter, and health care than was available under the Weimar Republic. On Zinn's view of what democracy "should mean," this made Hitler's rule more democratic than that of Weimar. . . .

Not surprisingly, Mr. Zinn is a very unreliable guide even in his account of the procedural features of the American political system. In one breath he maintains that not enough information is available to voters to make intelligent choices on major political issues like tax laws. (The voter, of course, does not vote on such laws but for representatives who have taken stands on a number of complex issues.) "The dominant influences are those of big business, which has the resources both to understand and to act." In another breath, he complains that the electorate is at the mercy of the propagandist. "The propagandist does not need to lie; he overwhelms the public with so much information as to lead it to believe that it is all too complicated for anyone but the experts."

Mr. Zinn is certainly hard to please! The American political process is not democratic because the electorate hasn't got enough information. It is also undemocratic because it receives too much information. What would Zinn have us do so that the public gets just the right amount of information and propaganda? Have the government control the press? Restrict freedom of propaganda? But these are precisely the devices of totalitarian societies. The evils of the press, even when it is free of government control, are many indeed. The great problem is to keep the press free and responsible. And as defective as the press and other public media are today, surely it is an exaggeration to say that with respect to tax laws "the dominant influences are those of big business." If they were, how can we account for the existence of the income tax laws? If the influence of big business on the press is so dominant and the press is so biased, how can we account for the fact that although 92 percent of the press opposed Truman's candidacy in 1948, he was reelected? How can we account for the profound dissatisfaction of Vice President Agnew with the press and other mass media?* And since Mr. Zinn believes that big business dominates our educational system, especially our universities, how can we account for the fact that the universities are the centers of the strongest dissent in the nation to public and national policy, that the National Association of Manufacturers bitterly complained a few years ago that the economics of the free enterprise system was derided, and often not even taught, in most Departments of Economics in the colleges and universities of the nation?

Mr. Zinn's exaggerations are really caricatures of complex realities. Far from being controlled by the monolithic American corporate economy, American public opinion is today marked by a greater scope and depth of dissent than at any time in its history, except for the days preceding the Civil War. The voice and the votes of Main Street still count for more in a democratic polity than those of Wall Street. Congress has limited, and can still further limit, the influence of money on the electoral process by federal subsidy and regulations. There are always abuses needing reforms. By failing to take a comparative approach and instead focusing on some absolute utopian standard of perfection, Mr. Zinn gives an exaggerated, tendentious, and fundamentally false picture of the United States. There is hardly a sentence in his essay that is free of some serious flaw in perspective, accuracy, or emphasis. Sometimes they have a comic effect, as when Mr. Zinn talks about the lack of "equal distribution of the right of freedom of expression." What kind of "equal distribution" is he talking about? Of course, a person with more money can talk to more people than one with less, although this does not mean that more persons will listen to him, agree with him, or be influenced by him. But a person with a more eloquent voice or a better brain can reach more people than you or I. What shall we do to insure equal distribution of the right of freedom of expression? Insist on equality of voice volume or pattern, and equality of brain power? More money gives not only greater opportunity to talk to people than less money but the ability to do thousands of things barred to those who have less money. Shall we then decree that all people have the same amount of money all the time and forbid anyone from depriving anyone else of any of his money even by fair means? "The government," writes Mr. Zinn, "has much more freedom of expression than a private individual because the president can command the airwaves when he wishes, and reach 60 million people in one night."

Alas! Mr. Zinn is not joking. Either he wants to bar the president or any public official from using the airwaves or he wants all of us to take turns. One wonders what country Mr. Zinn is living in. Nixon spoke to 60 million people several times, and so did Jimmy Carter. What was the result? More significant than the fact that 60 million people hear the president is that 60 million or more can hear his critics, sometimes right after he speaks, and that no one is compelled to listen.

Mr. Zinn does not understand the basic meaning of equality in a free, open democratic society. Its philosophy does not presuppose that all citizens are physically or intellectually equal or that all are equally gifted in every or any respect. It holds that all

---

* Spiro Agnew, former governor of Maryland and vice president of the United States before being forced to resign in 1973 during the second term of President Richard Nixon, was a frequent and vociferous critic of the "liberal" press—*Editors.*

enjoy a *moral* equality, and that therefore, as far as is practicable, given finite resources, the institutions of a democratic society should seek to provide an equal opportunity to all its citizens to develop themselves to their full desirable potential.

Of course, we cannot ever provide complete equal opportunity. More and more is enough. For one thing, so long as children have different parents and home environments, they cannot enjoy the same or equal opportunities. Nonetheless, the family has compensating advantages for all that. Let us hope that Mr. Zinn does not wish to wipe out the family to avoid differences in opportunity. Plato believed that the family, as we know it, should be abolished because it did not provide equality of opportunity, and that all children should be brought up by the state.

Belief in the moral equality of men and women does not require that all individuals be treated identically or that equal treatment must be measured or determined by equality of outcome or result. Every citizen should have an equal right to an education, but that does not mean that, regardless of capacity and interest, he or she should have the same amount of schooling beyond the adolescent years, and at the same schools, and take the same course of study. With the increase in national wealth, a good case can be made for an equal right of all citizens to health care or medical treatment. But only a quack or ideological fanatic would insist that therefore all individuals should have the same medical regimen no matter what ails them. This would truly be putting all human beings in the bed of Procrustes.

This conception of moral equality as distinct from Mr. Zinn's notions of equality is perfectly compatible with intelligent recognition of human inequalities and relevant ways of treating their inequalities to further both the individual and common good. Intelligent and loving parents are equally concerned with the welfare of all their children. But precisely because they are, they may provide different specific strategies in health care, education, psychological motivation, and intellectual stimulation to develop the best in all of them. The logic of Mr. Zinn's position—although he seems blissfully unaware of it—leads to the most degrading kind of egalitarian socialism, the kind which Marx and Engels in their early years denounced as "barracks socialism."

It is demonstrable that democracy is healthier and more effective where human beings do not suffer from poverty, unemployment, and disease. It is also demonstrable that to the extent that property gives power, private property in the means of social production gives power over the lives of those who must live by its use, and, therefore, that such property, whether public or private, should be responsible to those who are affected by its operation. Consequently one can argue that political democracy depends not only on the extension of the franchise to all adults, not only on its active exercise, but on programs of social welfare that provide for collective bargaining by free trade unions of workers and employees, unemployment insurance, minimum wages, guaranteed health care, and other social services that are integral to the welfare state. It is demonstrable that although the existing American welfare state provides far more welfare than was ever provided in the past—my own lifetime furnishes graphic evidence of the vast changes—it is still very far from being a genuine welfare state. Political democracy can exist without a welfare state, but it is stronger and better with it.

The basic issue that divides Mr. Zinn from others no less concerned about human welfare, but less fanatical than he, is how a genuine welfare state is to be brought about.

My contention is that this can be achieved by the vigorous exercise of the existing democratic process, and that by the same coalition politics through which great gains have been achieved in the past, even greater gains can be won in the future.

For purposes of economy, I focus on the problem of poverty, or since this is a relative term, hunger. If the presence of hunger entails the absence of the democratic political process, then democracy has never existed in the past—which would be an arbitrary use of words. Nonetheless, the existence of hunger is always a *threat* to the continued existence of the democratic process because of the standing temptation of those who hunger to exchange freedom for the promise of bread. This, of course, is an additional ground to the even weightier moral reasons for gratifying basic human needs.

That fewer people go hungry today in the United States than ever before may show that our democracy is better than it used to be but not that it is as good as it can be. Even the existence of one hungry person is one too many. How then can hunger or the extremes of poverty be abolished? Certainly not by the method Mr. Zinn advises: "Acts of civil disobedience by the poor will be required, at the least, to make middle-class America take notice, to bring national decisions that begin to reallocate wealth."

This is not only a piece of foolish advice, it is dangerously foolish advice. Many national decisions to reallocate wealth have been made through the political process—what else is the system of taxation if not a method of reallocating wealth?—without resort to civil disobedience. Indeed, resort to civil disobedience on this issue is very likely to produce a backlash among those active and influential political groups in the community who are aware that normal political means are available for social and economic reform. The refusal to engage in such normal political processes could easily be exploited by demagogues to portray the movement towards the abolition of hunger and extreme poverty as a movement towards the confiscation and equalization of all wealth.

The simplest and most effective way of abolishing hunger is to act on the truly revolutionary principle, enunciated by the federal government, that it is responsible for maintaining a standard of relief as a minimum beneath which a family will not be permitted to sink. . . .

For reasons that need no elaboration here, the greatest of the problems faced by American democracy today is the race problem. Although tied to the problems of poverty and urban reconstruction, it has independent aspects exacerbated by the legacy of the Civil War and the Reconstruction period.

Next to the American Indians, African-Americans have suffered most from the failure of the democratic political process to extend the rights and privileges of citizenship to those whose labor and suffering have contributed so much to the conquest of the continent. The remarkable gains that have been made by African-Americans in the last twenty years have been made primarily through the political process. If the same rate of improvement continues, the year 2000 may see a rough equality established. The growth of African-American suffrage, especially in the South, the increasing sense of responsibility by the white community, despite periodic setbacks resulting from outbursts of violence, opens up a perspective of continuous and cumulative reform. The man and the organization he headed chiefly responsible for the great gains made by African-Americans, Roy Wilkins and the NAACP, were convinced that the democratic political process can be more effectively used to further the integration of African-Americans into our national life than by reliance on any other method. . . .

The only statement in Mr. Zinn's essay that I can wholeheartedly endorse is his assertion that the great danger to American democracy does not come from the phenomena of protest as such. Dissent and protest are integral to the democratic process. The danger comes from certain modes of dissent, from the substitution of violence and threats of violence for the mechanisms of the political process, from the escalation of that violence as the best hope of those who still have grievances against our imperfect American democracy, and from views such as those expressed by Mr. Zinn which downgrade the possibility of peaceful social reform and encourage rebellion. It is safe to predict that large-scale violence by impatient minorities will fail. It is almost as certain that attempts at violence will backfire, that they will create a climate of repression that may reverse the course of social progress and expanded civil liberties of the last generation. . . .

It is when Mr. Zinn is discussing racial problems that his writing ceases to be comic and silly and becomes irresponsible and mischievous. He writes:

> The massive African-American urban uprisings of 1967 and 1968 showed that nothing less than civil disobedience (for riots and uprisings go beyond that) could make the nation see that the race problem is an American—not a southern—problem and that it needs bold, revolutionary action.

First of all, every literate person knows that the race problem is an American problem, not exclusively a southern one. It needs no civil disobedience or "black uprisings" to remind us of that. Second, the massive uprisings of 1967 and 1968 were violent and uncivil, and resulted in needless loss of life and suffering. The Civil Rights Acts, according to Roy Wilkins, then head of the NAACP, were imperiled by them. They were adopted despite, not because, of them. Third, what kind of "revolutionary" action is Mr. Zinn calling for? And by whom? He seems to lack the courage of his confusions. Massive civil disobedience when sustained becomes a form of civil war.

Despite Mr. Zinn and others, violence is more likely to produce reaction than reform. In 1827 a resolution to manumit slaves by purchase (later, Lincoln's preferred solution) was defeated by three votes in the House of Burgesses of the State of Virginia. It was slated to be reintroduced in a subsequent session with excellent prospects of being adopted. Had Virginia adopted it, North Carolina would shortly have followed suit. But before it could be reintroduced, Nat Turner's rebellion broke out. Its violent excesses frightened the South into a complete rejection of a possibility that might have prevented the American Civil War—the fiercest and bloodiest war in human history up to that time, from whose consequences American society is still suffering. Mr. Zinn's intentions are as innocent as those of a child playing with matches.

III

One final word about "the global" dimension of democracy of which Mr. Zinn speaks. Here, too, he speaks sympathetically of actions that would undermine the willingness and capacity of a free society to resist totalitarian aggression.

The principles that should guide a free democratic society in a world where dictatorial regimes seek to impose their rule on other nations were formulated by John Stuart

Mill, the great defender of liberty and representative government, more than a century ago:

> To go to war for an idea, if the war is aggressive not defensive, is as criminal as to go to war for territory or revenue, for it is as little justifiable to force our ideas on other people, as to compel them to submit to our will in any other aspect. . . . *The doctrine of non-intervention, to be a legitimate principle of morality, must be accepted by all governments.* The despots must consent to be bound by it as well as the free states. Unless they do, the profession of it by free countries comes but to this miserable issue, that the wrong side may help the wrong side but the right may not help the right side. Intervention to enforce non-intervention is always right, always moral *if not always prudent.* Though it may be a mistake to give freedom (or independence—S.H.) to a people who do not value the boon, it cannot be right to insist that if they do value it, they shall not be hindered from the pursuit of it by foreign coercion (*Fraser's Magazine,* 1859, emphasis mine).

Unfortunately, these principles were disregarded by the United States in 1936 when Hitler and Mussolini sent troops to Spain to help Franco overthrow the legally elected democratic Loyalist regime. The U.S. Congress, at the behest of the administration, adopted a Neutrality Resolution which prevented the democratic government of Spain from purchasing arms here. This compelled the Spanish government to make a deal with Stalin, who not only demanded its entire gold supply but the acceptance of the dread Soviet secret police, the NKVD, to supervise the operations. The main operation of the NKVD in Spain was to engage in a murderous purge of the democratic ranks of anti-Communists which led to the victory of Franco. The story is told in George Orwell's *Homage to Catalonia.* He was on the scene.

The prudence of American intervention in Vietnam may be debatable but there is little doubt that [UN ambassador] Adlai Stevenson, sometimes referred to as the liberal conscience of the nation, correctly stated the American motivation when he said at the UN on the very day of his death: "My hope in Vietnam is that resistance there may establish the fact that changes in Asia are not to be precipitated by outside force. This was the point of the Korean War. This is the point of the conflict in Vietnam."

. . . Mr. Zinn's remarks about Grenada show he is opposed to the liberal principles expressed by J. S. Mill in the passage cited above. His report of the facts about Grenada is as distorted as his account of present-day American democracy. On tiny Grenada, whose government was seized by Communist terrorists, were representatives of every Communist regime in the Kremlin's orbit, Cuban troops, and a Soviet general. I have read the documents captured by the American troops. They conclusively establish that the Communists were preparing the island as part of the Communist strategy of expansion.[1]

It is sad but significant that Mr. Zinn, whose heart bleeds for the poor Asians who suffered in the struggle to prevent the Communist takeover in Southeast Asia, has not a word of protest, not a tear of compassion for the hundreds of thousands of tortured, imprisoned, and drowned in flight after the victory of the North Vietnamese "liberators," not to mention the even greater number of victims of the Cambodian and Cuban Communists.

One summary question may be asked whose answer bears on the issue of how democratic America is. Suppose all the iron and bamboo and passport curtains of the world were lifted today, in what direction would freedom loving and democratic people move? Anyone is free to leave the United States today, except someone fleeing from the law, but in [some of] the countries arrayed against the United States people are penned in like animals and cannot cross a boundary without risking death. Has this no significance for the "global" aspect of our question?

NOTE

1. *The Grenada Papers: The Inside Story of the Grenadian Revolution—and the Making of a Totalitarian State as Told in Captured Documents* (San Francisco: Institute of Contemporary Studies, 1984).

Making Democracy Work: Civic Involvement

In this second pair of articles, we turn our attention from the question of how democracy should be defined to the matter of how to make it work. In this connection, there is a considerable amount of evidence to suggest that democracy functions more effectively in societies characterized by a high level of civic participation; that is to say, where citizens join with others in pursuit of some community-related goal or purpose. Although the propensity for Americans to form and join civic associations has long been remarked upon as a salient feature of our society, Robert Putnam, in the first selection, argues that serveral indicators point to a significant decline in civic engagement over the last 25 years. He then identifies what he believes to be the major factor responsible for producing this decline, and explains why it has had this effect.

Michael Schudson, however, is unpersuaded by Putnam's analysis. In response, he asserts that the alleged decline in civic participation might not be real at all, but rather an artifact of how Putnam defines civic participation, how he measures it, and what he selects as a baseline for comparison. Moreover, even if we assume for the sake of argument that there has been such a decline, the culprit that Putnam points to does not fit his own evidence very well; and besides, there are, according to Schudson, other culprits that are equally plausible.

Tuning In, Tuning Out
The Strange Disappearance of Social Capital in America
Robert D. Putnam

BOWLING ALONE: AMERICA'S DECLINING SOCIAL CAPITAL

Many students of the new democracies that have emerged over the past decade and a half have emphasized the importance of a strong and active civil society to the consolidation of democracy. Especially with regard to the postcommunist countries, scholars and democratic activists alike have lamented the absence or obliteration of traditions of independent civic engagement and a widespread tendency toward passive reliance on the state. To those concerned with the weakness of civil societies in the developing or postcommunist world, the advanced Western democracies and above all the United States have typically been taken as models to be emulated. There is striking evidence, however, that the vibrancy of American civil society has notably declined over the past several decades.

Ever since the publication of Alexis de Tocqueville's *Democracy in Ameria,* the United States has played a central role in systematic studies of the links between democracy and civil society. Although this is in part because trends in American life are often regarded as harbingers of social modernization, it is also because America has traditionally been considered unusually "civic" (a reputation that, as we shall later see, has not been entirely unjustified).

When Tocqueville visited the United States in the 1830s, it was the Americans' propensity for civic association that most impressed him as the key to their unprecedented ability to make democracy work. "Americans of all ages, all stations in life, and all types of disposition," he observed, "are forever forming associations. There are not only commercial and industrial associations in which all take part, but others of a thousand different types—religious, moral, serious, futile, very general and very limited,

Robert D. Putnam is Clarence Dillon Professor of International Affairs and director of the Center for International Affairs at Harvard University. He is author of the recently published book Bowling Alone: The Collapse and Revival of American Community (May 2000). *This article is a composite of two articles written by Robert D. Putnam. The first section of the article, "Bowling Alone: America's Declining Social Capital," is from Robert D. Putnam, "Bowling Alone: America's Declining Social Capital,"* Journal of Democracy *(January, 1995), pp. 65–78; the second section, beginning with "Bowling Alone: Trends in Civic Engagement," is from Robert D. Putnam, "Tuning In, Tuning Out: The Strange Disappearance of Social Capital in America,"* PS: Political Science & Politics *(December, 1995), pp. 664–666, 677–683. Notes and references have been changed to correspond with edited text.*

immensely large and very minute. . . . Nothing, in my view, deserves more attention than the intellectual and moral associations in America."

Recently, American social scientists of a neo-Tocquevillean bent have unearthed a wide range of empirical evidence that the quality of public life and the performance of social institutions (and not only in America) are indeed powerfully influenced by norms and networks of civic engagement. Researchers in such fields as education, urban poverty, unemployment, the control of crime and drug abuse, and even health have discovered that successful outcomes are more likely in civically engaged communities. Similarly, research on the varying economic attainments of different ethnic groups in the United States has demonstrated the importance of social bonds within each group. These results are consistent with research in a wide range of settings that demonstrates the vital importance of social networks for job placement and many other economic outcomes. . . .

The norms and networks of civic engagement also powerfully affect the performance of representative government. That, at least, was the central conclusion of my own 20-year, quasi-experimental study of subnational governments in different regions of Italy. Although all these regional governments seemed identical on paper, their levels of effectiveness varied dramatically. Systematic inquiry showed that the quality of governance was determined by longstanding traditions of civic engagement (or its absence). Voter turnout, newspaper readership, membership in choral societies and football clubs—these were the hallmarks of a successful region. In fact, historical analysis suggested that these networks of organized reciprocity and civic solidarity, far from being an epiphenomenon of socioeconomic modernization, were a precondition for it.

No doubt, the mechanisms through which civic engagement and social connectedness produce such results—better schools, faster economic development, lower crime, and more effective government—are multiple and complex. . . . Social scientists in several fields have recently suggested a common framework for understanding these phenomena, a framework that rests on the concept of *social capital*. By analogy with notions of physical capital and human capital—tools and training that enhance individuals productivity—"social capital" refers to features of social organization such as networks, norms, and social trust that facilitate coordination and cooperation for mutual benefit.

Civic Engagement

For a variety of reasons life is easier in a community blessed with a substantial stock of social capital. In the first place, networks of civic engagement foster sturdy norms of generalized reciprocity and encourage the emergence of social trust. Such networks facilitate coordination and communication, amplify reputations, and thus allow dilemmas of collective action to be resolved. When economic and political negotiation is embedded in dense networks of social interaction, incentives for opportunism are reduced. At the same time, networks of civic engagement embody past success at collaboration, which can serve as a cultural template for future collaboration. Finally, dense networks of interaction probably broaden the participants' sense of self developing the "I". . . into the "we." . . .

*   *   *

BOWLING ALONE: TRENDS IN CIVIC ENGAGEMENT

Evidence from a number of independent sources strongly suggests that America's stock of social capital has been shrinking for more than a quarter century.

- Membership records of such diverse organizations as the PTA, the Elks club, the League of Women Voters, the Red Cross, labor unions, and even bowling leagues show that participation in many conventional voluntary associations has declined by roughly 25 percent to 50 percent over the last two to three decades (Putnam 1995, 1996).
- Surveys of the time budgets of average Americans in 1965, 1975, and 1985, in which national samples of men and women recorded every single activity undertaken during the course of a day, imply that the time we spend on informal socializing and visiting is down (perhaps by one quarter) since 1965, and that the time we devote to clubs and organizations is down even more sharply (probably by roughly half) over this period.[1]
- While Americans' interest in politics has been stable or even growing over the last three decades, and some forms of participation that require moving a pen, such as signing petitions and writing checks, have increased significantly, many measures of collective participation have fallen sharply (Rosenstone and Hansen 1993; Putnam 1996), including attending a rally or speech (off 36 percent between 1973 and 1993), attending a meeting on town or school affairs (off 39 percent), or working for a political party (off 56 percent).
- Evidence from the General Social Survey demonstrates, at all levels of education and among both men and women, a drop of roughly one-quarter in group membership since 1974 and a drop of roughly one-third in social trust since 1972.[2] . . . slumping membership has afflicted all sorts of groups, from sports clubs and professional associations to literary discussion groups and labor unions.[3] Only nationality groups, hobby and garden clubs, and the catch-all category of "other" seems to have resisted the ebbing tide. Furthermore, Gallup polls report that church attendance fell by roughly 15 percent during the 1960s and has remained at that lower level ever since, while data from the National Opinion Research Center suggests that the decline continued during the 1970s and 1980s and by now amounts to roughly 30 percent (Putnam 1996). . . .

A fuller audit of American social capital would need to account for apparent countertrends.[4] Some observers believe, for example, that support groups and neighborhood watch groups are proliferating, and few deny that the last several decades have witnessed explosive growth in interest groups represented in Washington. The growth of "mailing list" organizations, like the American Association of Retired People or the Sierra Club, although highly significant in political (and commercial) terms, is not really a counterexample to the supposed decline in social connectedness, however, since these are not really associations in which members meet one another. Their members' ties are to common symbols and ideologies, but not to each other. These organizations are sufficiently different from classical "secondary" associations as to deserve a new rubric—perhaps "tertiary" associations. Similarly, although most secondary associations are not-for-profit, most prominent nonprofits (from Harvard University to the Metropolitan Opera) are bureaucracies, not secondary associations, so the growth of the "Third Sector" is not tantamount to a growth in social connectedness. With due regard to various kinds of counterevidence, I believe that the weight of the available evidence confirms that Americans today are significantly less engaged with their communities than was true a generation ago.

Of course, lots of civic activity is still visible in our communities. American civil society is not moribund. Indeed, evidence suggests that America still outranks many other countries in the degree of our community involvement and social trust (Putnam 1996). But if we compare ourselves, not with other countries but with our parents, the best available evidence suggests that we are less connected with one another.

This prologue poses a number of important questions that merit further debate:

- Is it true that America's stock of social capital has diminished?
- Does it matter?
- What can we do about it?

The answer to the first two questions is, I believe, "yes," but I cannot address them further in this setting. Answering the third question—which ultimately concerns me most—depends, at least in part, on first understanding the *causes* of the strange malady afflicting American civic life. This is the mystery I seek to unravel here: Why, beginning in the 1960s and accelerating in the 1970s and 1980s, did the fabric of American community life begin to fray? Why are more Americans bowling alone?

Explaining the Erosion of Social Capital

Many possible answers have been suggested for this puzzle:

- Busyness and time pressure
- Economic hard times (or, according to alternative theories, material affluence)
- Residential mobility
- Suburbanization
- The movement of women into the paid labor force and the stresses of two-career families
- Disruption of marriage and family ties
- Changes in the structure of the American economy, such as the rise of chain stores, branch firms, and the service sector
- The sixties (most of which actually happened in the seventies), including
  –Vietnam, Watergate, and disillusion with public life
  –The cultural revolt against authority (sex, drugs, and so on)
- Growth of the welfare state
- The civil rights revolution
- Television, the electronic revolution, and other technological changes

*   *   *

The Puzzle Reformulated

To say that civic disengagement in contemporary America is in large measure generational merely reformulates our central puzzle. We . . . know that much of the cause of our lonely bowling probably dates to the 1940s and 1950s, rather than to the 1960s and 1970s. What could have been the mysterious anti-civic "X-ray" that affected Americans who came of age after World War II and whose effects progressively deepened at least into the 1970s?[5] . . .

I have discovered only one prominent suspect against whom circumstantial evidence can be mounted, and in this case, it turns out, some directly incriminating evidence has also turned up. This is not the occasion to lay out the full case for the prosecution, nor to review rebuttal evidence for the defense. However, I want to illustrate the sort of evidence that justifies indictment. The culprit is television.

First, the timing fits. The long civic generation was the last cohort of Americans to grow up without television, for television flashed into American society like lightning in the 1950s. In 1950 barely 10 percent of American homes had television sets, but by 1959, 90 percent did, probably the fastest diffusion of a technological innovation ever recorded. The reverberations from this lightning bolt continued for decades, as viewing hours per capita grew by 17–20 percent during the 1960s and by an additional 7–8 percent during the 1970s. In the early years, TV watching was concentrated among the less educated sectors of the population, but during the 1970s the viewing time of the more educated sectors of the population began to converge upward. Television viewing increases with age, particularly upon retirement, but each generation since the introduction of television has begun its life cycle at a higher starting point. By 1995, viewing per TV household was more than 50 percent higher than it had been in the 1950s.[6]

Most studies estimate that the average American now watches roughly four hours per day.[7] Robinson (1990b), using the more conservative time-budget technique for determining how people allocate their time, offers an estimate closer to three hours per day, but concludes that as a primary activity, television absorbs 40 percent of the average American's free time, an increase of about one-third since 1965. Moreover, multiple sets have proliferated; by the late 1980s, three-quarters of all U.S. homes had more than one set (Comstock 1989), and these numbers too are rising steadily, allowing ever more private viewing. In short, as Robinson and Godbey 1995 conclude, "television is the 800-pound gorilla of leisure time." This massive change in the way Americans spend our days and nights occurred precisely during the years of generational civic disengagement.

Evidence of a link between the arrival of television and the erosion of social connections is, however, not merely circumstantial. The links between civic engagement and television viewing can instructively be compared with the links between civic engagement and newspaper reading. The basic contrast is straightforward: newspaper reading is associated with high social capital, TV viewing with low social capital. . . .

. . . [E]ach hour spent viewing television is associated with less social trust and less group membership, while each hour reading a newspaper is associated with more. An increase in television viewing of the magnitude that the United States has experienced in the last four decades might directly account for as much as one-quarter to one-half of the total drop in social capital, even without taking into account, for example, the indirect effects of television viewing on newspaper readership or the cumulative effects of "life-time" viewing hours.[8]

How might television destroy social capital?

- *Time displacement.* Even though there are only 24 hours in everyone's day, most forms of social and media participation are positively correlated. People who listen to lots of classical music are more likely, not less likely, than others to attend Cubs games. Television is the principal exception to this generalization—the only leisure activity that seems to inhibit participation outside the home. TV watching comes at expense of nearly every social activity outside the home, especially social gatherings and informal conversations (Comstock et al. 1978; Comstock 1989; Bower 1985; and Robinson and Godbey 1995). TV viewers are homebodies.

  Most studies that report a negative correlation between television watching and community involvement . . . are ambiguous with respect to causality, because they merely compare different individuals at a single time. However, one important quasi-experimental study of the introduction of television in three Canadian towns (Williams 1986) found the same pattern at the aggregate level across time: a major effect of television's arrival was the reduction in participation in social, recreational, and community activities among people of all ages. In short, television is privatizing our leisure time.

- *Effects on the outlooks of viewers.* An impressive body of literature, gathered under the rubric of the "mean world effect," suggests that heavy watchers of TV are unusually skeptical about the benevolence of other people—overestimating crime rates, for example. This body of literature has generated much debate about the underlying causal patterns, with skeptics suggesting that misanthropy may foster couch-potato behavior rather than the reverse. While awaiting better experimental evidence, however, a reasonable interim judgment is that heavy television watching may well increase pessimism about human nature (Gerbner et al. 1980; Dobb and MacDonald 1979; Hirsch 1980; Hughes 1980; and Comstock 1989, 265–69). Perhaps, too, as social critics have long argued, both the medium and the message have more basic effects on our ways on interacting with the world and with one another. Television may induce passivity, as Postman (1985) has claimed, and it may even change our fundamental physical and social perceptions, as Meyrowitz (1985) has suggested.

- *Effects on children.* TV occupies an extraordinary part of children's lives—consuming about 40 hours per week on average. Viewing is especially high among pre-adolescents, but it remains high among younger adolescents: time-budget studies (Carnegie Council on Adolescent Development 1993, 5, citing Timmer et al. 1985) suggest that among youngsters aged 9–14 television consumes as much time as *all other discretionary activities combined,* including playing, hobbies, clubs, outdoor activities, informal visiting, and just hanging out. The effects of television on childhood socialization have, of course, been hotly debated for more than three decades. The most reasonable conclusion from a welter of sometimes conflicting results appears to be that heavy television watching probably increases aggressiveness (although perhaps not actual violence), that it probably reduces school achievement, and that it is statistically associated with "psychosocial malfunctioning," although how much of this effect is self-selection and how much causal remains much debated (Condry 1993). The evidence is, as I have said, not yet enough to convict, but the defense has a lot of explaining to do.

Conclusion

Ithiel de Sola Pool's posthumous book, *Technologies Without Borders* (1990), is a prescient work, astonishingly relevant to our current national debates about the complicated links among technology, public policy, and culture. Pool defended what he called "soft technological determinism." Revolutions in communications technologies have profoundly affected social life and culture, as the printing press helped bring on the Reformation. Pool concluded that the electronic revolution in communications technology, whose outlines he traced well before most of us were even aware of the impending changes, was the first major technological advance in centuries that would have a profoundly decentralizing and fragmenting effect on society and culture.

Pool hoped that the result might be "community without contiguity." As a classic liberal, he welcomed the benefits of technological change for individual freedom, and, in part, I share that enthusiasm. Those of us who bemoan the decline of community in contemporary America need to be sensitive to the liberating gains achieved during the same decades. We need to avoid an uncritical nostalgia for the Fifties. On the other hand, some of the same freedom-friendly technologies whose rise Pool predicted may indeed be undermining our connections with one another and with our communities. I suspect that Pool would have been open to that argument, too, for one of Pool's most talented protégés, Samuel Popkin (1991, 226–31) has argued that the rise of television and the correlative decline of social interaction have impaired American political discourse. The last line in Pool's last book (1990, 262) is this: "We may suspect that [the technological trends that we can anticipate] will promote individualism and will make it harder, not easier, to govern and organize a coherent society."

Pool's technological determinism was "soft" precisely because he recognized that social values can condition the effects of technology. In the end this perspective invites us not merely to consider how technology is privatizing our lives—if, as it seems to me, it is—but to ask whether we entirely like the result, and if not, what we might do about it. But that is a topic for another day.

NOTES

1. The 1965 sample, which was limited to nonretired residents of cities between 30,000 and 280,000 population, was not precisely equivalent to the later national samples, so appropriate adjustments need to be made to ensure comparability. For the 1965–1975 comparison, see Robinson (1981, 125). For the 1975–1985

      comparison (but apparently without adjustment for the 1965 sampling peculiarities), see Cutler (1990). Somewhat smaller declines are reported in Robinson and Godbey (1995), although it is unclear whether they correct for the sampling differences. Additional work to refine these cross-time comparisons is required and is currently underway.

2. Trust in political authorities—and indeed in many social institutions—has also declined sharply over the last three decades, but that is conceptually a distinct trend. As we shall see later, the etiology of the slump in social trust is quite different from the etiology of the decline in political trust.

3. . . . [*C*]*ontrolling* for the respondent's education level.

4. Some commentaries on "Bowling Alone" have been careless, however, in reporting apparent membership growth. *The Economist* (1995, 22), for example, celebrated a recent rebound in total membership in parent-teacher organizations, without acknowledging that this rebound is almost entirely attributable to the growing number of children. The fraction of parents who belong to PTAs has regained virtually none of the 50 percent fall that this metric registered between 1960 and 1975. Despite talk about the growth of "support groups," another oft-cited counterexample, I know of no statistical substantiation for this claim. One might even ask whether the vaunted rise in neighborhood watch groups might not represent only a partial, artificial replacement for the vanished social capital of traditional neighborhoods—a kind of sociological Astroturf, suitable only where you can't grow the real thing. See also Glenn (1987, S124) for survey evidence of "an increased tendency for individuals to withdraw allegiance from . . . anything outside of themselves."

5. I record here one theory attributed variously to Robert Salisbury (1985), Gerald Gamm, and Simon and Garfunkel. Devotees of our national pastime will recall that Joe Dimaggio signed with the Yankees in 1936, just as the last of the long civic generation was beginning to follow the game, and he turned center field over to Mickey Mantle in 1951, just as the last of "the suckers" reached legal maturity. Almost simultaneously, the Braves, the Athletics, the Browns, the Senators, the Dodgers, and the Giants deserted cities that had been their homes since the late nineteenth century. By the time Mantle in turn left the Yankees in 1968, much of the damage to civic loyalty had been done. This interpretation explains why Mrs. Robinson's plaintive query that year about Joltin' Joe's whereabouts evoked such widespread emotion. A deconstructionist analysis of social capital's decline would highlight the final haunting lamentation, "our nation turns its *lonely* eyes to you" [emphasis added].

6. For introductions to the massive literature on the sociology of television, see Bower (1985), Comstock et al. (1978), Comstock (1989), and Grabner (1993). The figures on viewing hours in the text are from Bower (1985, 33) and *Public Perspective* (1995, 47). Cohort differences are reported in Bower 1985, 46.

7. This figure excludes periods in which television is merely playing in the background. Comstock (1989, 17) reports that "on any fall day in the late 1980s, the set in the average television owning household was on for about eight hours.")

8. Newspaper circulation (per household) has dropped by more than half since its peak in 1947. To be sure, it is not clear which way the tie between newspaper reading and civic involvement works, since disengagement might itself dampen one's interest in community news. But the two trends are clearly linked.

REFERENCES

Bower, Robert T. 1985. *The Changing Television Audience in America.* New York: Columbia University Press.

Carnegie Council on Adolescent Development. 1993. *A Matter of Time: Risk and Opportunity in the Nonschool House: Executive Summary.* New York: Carnegie Corporation of New York.

Coleman, James. 1990. *Foundations of Social Theory.* Cambridge, MA: Harvard University Press.

Comstock, George, Steven Chaffee, Natan Katzman, Maxwell McCombs, and Donald Roberts, 1978. *Television and Human Behavior.* New York: Columbia University Press.

Comstock, George. 1989. *The Evolution of American Television.* Newbury Park, CA: Sage.

Condry, John. 1993. "Thief of Time. Unfaithful Servant: Television and the American Child," *Daedalus* 122 (Winter): 259–78.

Cutler, Blaine. 1990. "Where Does the Free Time Go?" *American Demographics* (November): 36–39.

Dobb, Anthony N., and Glenn F. Macdonald, 1979. "Television Viewing and Fear of Victimization: Is the Relationship Causal?" *Journal of Personality and Social Psychology* 37: 170–79.

Gerbner, George, Larry Gross, Michael Morgan, and Nancy Signorielli. 1980. "The 'Mainstreaming' of America: Violence Profile No. 11," *Journal of Communication* 30 (Summer): 10–29.

Glenn, Norval D. 1987. "Social Trends in the United States: Evidence from Sample Surveys." *Public Opinion Quarterly* 51: S109–S126.

Grabner, Doris A. 1993. *Mass Media and American Politics.* Washington, D.C.: CQ Press.

Hirsch, Paul M. "The 'Scary World' of the Nonviewer and Other Anomalies: A Reanalysis of Gerbner et al.'s Findings on Cultivation Analysis. Part I." *Communication Research* 7 (October): 403–56.

Hughes, Michael. 1980. "The Fruits of Cultivation Analysis: A Re-examination of the Effects of Television Watching on Fear of Victimization, Alienation, and the Approval of Violence." *Public Opinion Quarterly* 44: 287–303.

Meyrowitz, Joshua. 1985. *No Sense of Place: The Impact of Electronic Media on Social Behavior.* New York: Oxford University Press.

Pool, Ithiel de Sola. 1990. *Technologies Without Boundaries: On Telecommunications in a Global Age.* Cambridge, MA: Harvard University Press.

Popkin, Samuel L. 1991. *The Reasoning Voter.* Chicago: University of Chicago Press.

Postman, Neil. 1985. *Amusing Ourselves to Death: Public Discourse in the Age of Show Business.* New York: Viking-Penguin Books.

Putnam, Robert D. 1993. *Making Democracy Work: Civic Traditions in Modern Italy.* Princeton, NJ: Princeton University Press.

Putnam, Robert D. 1995. "Bowling Alone. Revisited." *The Responsive Community* (Spring): 18–33.

Putnam, Robert D. 1996. "Bowling Alone: Democracy in America at the End of the Twentieth Century," forthcoming in a collective volume edited by Axel Hadenius, New York: Cambridge University Press.

Robinson, John. 1981. "Television and Leisure Time: A New Scenario." *Journal of Communication* 31 (Winter): 120–30.

Robinson, John. 1990b. "I Love My TV." *American Demographics* (September): 24–27.

Robinson, John, and Geoffrey Godbey. 1995. *Time for Life.* College Park, MD: University of Maryland. Unpublished manuscript.

Rosenstone, Steven J., and John Mark Hansen. 1993. *Mobilization Participation and Democracy in America.* New York: Macmillan.

Salisbury, Robert H. 1985. "Blame Dismal World Conditions on . . . Baseball." *Miami Herald* (May 18): 27A.

Timmer, S. G., J. Eccles, and I. O'Brien. 1985. "How Children Use Time." In *Time, Goods, and Well-Being,* ed. F. T. Juster and F. B. Stafford. Ann Arbor: University of Michigan, Institute for Social Research.

Williams, Tannis Macbeth, ed. 1986. *The Impact of Television: A Natural Experiment in Three Communities.* New York: Academic Press.

What If Civic Life Didn't Die?

Michael Schudson

Robert Putnam's important and disturbing work on civic participation . . . (*TAP* Winter 1996) has led him to conclude that television is the culprit behind civic decline. But lest we be *too* disturbed, we ought to consider carefully whether the data adequately measure participation and justify his conclusions and whether his conclusions fit much else that we know about recent history. I suggest that his work has missed some key contrary evidence. If we could measure civic participation better, the decline would be less striking and the puzzle less perplexing. If we looked more carefully at the history of civic participation and the differences among generations, we would have to abandon the rhetoric of decline. And if we examined television and recent history more closely, we could not convict TV of turning off civic involvement.

Consider, first, the problem of measuring whether there has been civic decline. Putnam has been ingenious in finding multiple measures of civic engagement, from voter turnout to opinion poll levels of trust in government to time-budget studies on how people allocate their time to associational membership. But could it be that even all of these measures together mask how civic energy is deployed?

Data collected by Sidney Verba, Kay Lehman Schlozman, and Henry Brady suggest the answer is yes. In 1987, 34 percent of their national sample reported active membership in a community problem-solving organization compared to 31 percent in 1967; in 1987, 34 percent reported working with others on a local problem compared to 30 percent in 1967. Self-reports should not be taken at face value, but why does this survey indicate a slight increase in local civic engagement? Does it capture something Putnam's data miss?

Putnam's measures may, in fact, overlook several types of civic activity. First, people may have left the middling commitment of the League of Women Voters or the PTA for organized activity both much less and much more involving. As for much more: Churches seem to be constantly reinventing themselves, adding a variety of groups and activities to engage members, from singles clubs to job training to organized social welfare services to preschools. An individual who reports only one associational membership—say, a church or synagogue—may be more involved in it and more "civic" through it than someone else who reports two or three memberships.

Second, people may have left traditional civic organizations that they used for personal and utilitarian ends for commercial organizations. If people who formerly joined the YMCA to use the gym now go to the local fitness center, Putnam's measures will show a decrease in civic participation when real civic activity is unchanged.

Michael Schudson is professor of communication and sociology, University of California–San Diego. Reprinted from Michael Schudson, "What If Civic Life Didn't Die?" Reprinted with permission from The American Prospect *25 March–April Copyright 1995.* The American Prospect, *P.O. Box 772, Boston, MA 02102-0772. All rights reserved.*

Third, people may be more episodically involved in political and civic activity as issue-oriented politics grows. For instance, in California, motorcycle riders have become influential political activists since the 1992 passage of a law requiring bikers to wear helmets. According to the *San Diego Union,* of 800,000 licensed motorcyclists, 10,000 are now members of the American Brotherhood Aimed Toward Education (ABATE), which has been credited as decisive in several races for the state legislature. Members do not meet on a regular basis, but they do periodically mobilize in local political contests to advance their one legislative purpose. Would Putnam's data pick up on this group? What about the intense but brief house-building activity for Habitat for Humanity?

Fourth, Putnam notes but leaves to the side the vast increase in Washington-based mailing list organizations over the past 30 years. He ignores them because they do not require members to do more than send in a check. This is not Tocquevillian democracy, but these organizations may be a highly efficient use of civic energy. The citizen who joins them may get the same civic payoff for less personal hassle. This is especially so if we conceive of politics as a set of public policies. The citizen may be able to influence government more satisfactorily with the annual membership in the Sierra Club or the National Rifle Association than by attending the local club luncheons.

Of course, policy is a limited notion of government. Putnam assumes a broader view that makes personal investment part of the payoff of citizenship. Participation is its own reward. But even our greatest leaders—Jefferson, for one—complained about the demands of public life and, like Dorothy in liberating Oz, were forever trying to get back home. Getting government off our backs was a theme Patrick Henry evoked. And who is to say that getting back home is an unworthy desire?

The concept of politics has broadened enormously in 30 years. Not only is the personal political (the politics of male-female relations, the politics of smoking and not smoking), but the professional or occupational is also political. A woman physician or accountant can feel that she is doing politics—providing a role model and fighting for recognition of women's equality with men—every time she goes to work. The same is true for African American bank executives or gay and lesbian military officers.

The decline of the civic in its conventional forms, then, does not demonstrate the decline of civic-mindedness. The "political" does not necessarily depend on social connectedness: Those membership dues to the NRA are political. Nor does it even depend on organized groups at all: Wearing a "Thank you for not smoking" button is political. The political may be intense and transient: Think of the thousands of people who have joined class action suits against producers of silicone breast implants or Dalkon shields or asbestos insulation.

Let us assume, for argument's sake, that there has been a decrease in civic involvement. Still, the rhetoric of decline in American life should send up a red flag. For the socially concerned intellectual, this is as much off-the-rack rhetoric as its mirror opposite, the rhetoric of progress, is for the ebullient technocrat. Any notion of "decline" has to take for granted some often arbitrary baseline. Putnam's baseline is the 1940s and 1950s when the "long civic generation"—people born between 1910 and 1940—came into their own. But this generation shared the powerful and unusual experience of four years of national military mobilization on behalf of what nearly everyone came to accept as a good cause. If Putnam had selected, say, the 1920s as a baseline, would he have given us a similar picture of decline?

Unlikely. Intellectuals of the 1920s wrung their hands about the fate of democracy, the decline of voter turnout, the "eclipse of the public," as John Dewey put it or "the phantom public" in Walter Lippmann's terms. They had plenty of evidence, particularly in the record of voter turnout, so low in 1920 and 1924 (49 percent each year) that even our contemporary nadir of 1988 (50.3 percent) [48.9% in 1996—Editors] does not quite match it. Putnam himself reports that people born from 1910 to 1940 appear more civic than those born before as well as those born after. There is every reason to ask why this group was so civic rather than why later groups are not.

The most obvious answer is that this group fought in or came of age during World War II. This is also a group that voted overwhelmingly for Franklin D. Roosevelt and observed his leadership in office over a long period. Presidents exercise a form of moral leadership that sets a norm or standard about what kind of a life people should lead. A critic has complained that Ronald Reagan made all Americans a little more stupid in the 1980s—and I don't think this is a frivolous jibe. Reagan taught us that even the president can make a philosophy of the principle, "My mind's made up, don't confuse me with the facts." He taught us that millions will pay deference to someone who regularly and earnestly confuses films with lived experience.

The "long civic generation" had the advantages of a "good war" and a good president. Later generations had no wars or ones about which there was less massive mobilization and much less consensus—Korea and, more divisively, Vietnam. They had presidents of dubious moral leadership—notably Nixon, whom people judged even in the glow of his latter-day "rehabilitation" as the worst moral leader of all post–World War II presidents. So if there has been civic disengagement in the past decades, it may be not a decline but a return to normalcy.

If the rhetoric of decline raises one red flag, television as an explanation raises another. Some of the most widely heralded "media effects" have by now been thoroughly discredited. The yellow press had little or nothing to do with getting us into the Spanish-American War. Television news had little or nothing to do with turning Americans against the Vietnam War. Ronald Reagan's mastery of the media did not make him an unusually popular president in his first term (in fact, for his first 30 months in office he was unusually unpopular).

Indeed, the TV explanation doesn't fit Putnam's data very well. Putnam defines the long civic generation as the cohort born from 1910 to 1940, but then he also shows that the downturn in civic involvement began "rather abruptly" among people "born in the early 1930s." In other words, civic decline began with people too young to have served in World War II but too old to have seen TV growing up. If we take 1954 as a turning-point year—the first year when more than half of American households had TV sets—Americans born from 1930 to 1936 were in most cases already out of the home and the people born the next four years were already in high school by the time TV is likely to have become a significant part of their lives. Of course, TV may have influenced this group later, in the 1950s and early 1960s when they were in their twenties and thirties. But this was a time when Americans watched many fewer hours of television, averaging five hours a day rather than the current seven, and the relatively benign TV fare of that era was not likely to induce fearfulness of the outside world.

All of my speculations here and most of Putnam's assume that one person has about the same capacity for civic engagement as the next. But what if some people have decidedly more civic energy than others as a function of, say, personality? And what if these civic spark plugs have been increasingly recruited into situations where they are less civically engaged?

Putnam accords this kind of explanation some attention in asking whether women who had been most involved in civic activities were those most likely to take paying jobs, "thus lowering the average level of civic engagement among the remaining home-makers and raising the average among women in the workplace." Putnam says he "can find little evidence" to support this hypothesis, but it sounds plausible.

A similar hypothesis makes sense in other domains. Since World War II, higher education has mushroomed. Of people born from 1911 to 1920, 13.5 percent earned college or graduate degrees; of those born during the next decade, 18.8 percent; but of people born from 1931 to 1950, the figure grew to between 26 and 27 percent. A small but increasing number of these college students have been recruited away from their home communities to elite private colleges; some public universities also began after World War II to draw from a national pool of talent. Even colleges with local constituencies increasingly have recruited faculty nationally, and the faculty have shaped student ambitions toward national law, medical, and business schools and corporate traineeships. If students drawn to these programs are among the people likeliest in the past to have been civic spark plugs, we have an alternative explanation for civic decline.

Could there be a decline? Better to conceive the changes we find as a new environment of civic and political activity with altered institutional openings for engagement. Television is a part of the ecology, but in complex ways. It is a significant part of people's use of their waking hours, but it may be less a substitute for civic engagement than a new and perhaps insidious form of it. TV has been more politicized since the late 1960s than ever before. In 1968, *60 Minutes* began as the first moneymaking entertainment news program, spawning a dozen imitators. *All In The Family* in 1971 became the first prime-time sitcom to routinely take on controversial topics, from homosexuality to race to women's rights. *Donahue* was first syndicated in 1979, *Oprah* followed in 1984, and after them, the deluge.

If TV does nonetheless discourage civic engagement, what aspect of TV is at work? Is it the most "serious," civic-minded, and responsible part—the news? The latest blast at the news media, James Fallow's *Breaking the News,* picks up a familiar theme that the efforts of both print and broadcast journalists since the 1960s to get beneath the surface of events has led to a journalistic presumption that no politician can be trusted and that the story behind the story will be invariably sordid.

All of this talk needs to be tempered with the reminder that, amidst the many disappointments of politics between 1965 and 1995, this has been an era of unprecedented advances in women's rights, gay and lesbian liberation, African American opportunity, and financial security for the elderly. It has witnessed the first consumers' movement since the 1930s, the first environmental movement since the turn of the century, and public health movements of great range and achievement, especially in antismoking. It has also been a moment of grassroots activism on the right as well as on the left, with the pro-life movement and the broad-gauge political involvement both locally and nationally of the Christian right. Most of this activity was generated outside of political parties and state institutions. Most of this activity was built on substantial "grassroots" organizing. It is not easy to square all of this with an account of declining civic virtue.

Robert Putnam has offered us a lot to think about, with clarity and insight. Still, he has not yet established the decline in civic participation, let alone provided a satisfying explanation for it. What he has done is to reinvigorate inquiry on a topic that could scarcely be more important.

2

THE CONSTITUTION

Of the many books that have been written about the circumstances surrounding the creation of our Constitution, none generated more controversy than Charles Beard's An Economic Interpretation of the Constitution of the United States *(1913). An historian by profession, Beard challenged the belief that our Constitution was fashioned by men of democratic spirit. On the contrary, in what appeared to be a systematic marshaling of evidence, Beard sought to demonstrate (1) that the impetus for a new constitution came from individuals who saw their own economic interests threatened by a growing trend in the population toward greater democracy; (2) that the Founding Fathers themselves were men of considerable "personalty" (i.e., holdings other than real estate), who were concerned not so much with fashioning a democratic constitution as they were with protecting their own financial interests against the more democratically oriented farming and debtor interests within the society; and, finally, (3) that the individuals charged with ratifying the new Constitution also represented primarily the larger economic interests within the society. Although space limitations prevent a full development of Beard's argument, the portions of his book that follow should provide some feel for both the substance of his argument and his method of investigation.*

Beard's analysis has been subject to repeated scrutiny over the years. The most systematic effort in this regard came in 1956 with the publication of Robert Brown's Charles Beard and the Constitution: A Critical Analysis of "An Economic Interpretation of the Constitution." *Arguing that the rigor of Beard's examination was more apparent than real, Brown accuses him of citing only the facts that supported his case while ignoring those that did not. Moreover, he contends that even the evidence Beard provided did not warrant the interpretation he gave to it. Brown concludes that the best evidence now available does not support the view that "the Constitution was put over undemocratically in an undemocratic society by personal property."*

An Economic Interpretation of the Constitution of the United States

Charles A. Beard

Suppose it could be shown from the classification of the men who supported and opposed the Constitution that there was no line of property division at all; that is, that men owning substantially the same amounts of the same kinds of property were equally divided on the matter of adoption or rejection—it would then become apparent that the Constitution had no ascertainable relation to economic groups or classes, but was the product of some abstract causes remote from the chief business of life—gaining a livelihood.

Suppose, on the other hand, that substantially all of the merchants, money lenders, security holders, manufacturers, shippers, capitalists, and financiers and their professional associates are to be found on one side in support of the Constitution and that substantially all or the major portion of the opposition came from the nonslaveholding farmers and the debtors—would it not be pretty conclusively demonstrated that our fundamental law was not the product of an abstraction known as "the whole people," but of a group of economic interests which must have expected beneficial results from its adoption? Obviously all the facts here desired cannot be discovered, but the data presented in the following chapters bear out the latter hypothesis, and thus a reasonable presumption in favor of the theory is created.

Of course, it may be shown (and perhaps can be shown) that the farmers and debtors who opposed the Constitution were, in fact, benefited by the general improvement which resulted from its adoption. It may likewise be shown, to take an extreme case, that the English nation derived immense advantages from the Norman Conquest and the orderly administrative processes which were introduced, as it undoubtedly did; nevertheless, it does not follow that the vague thing known as "the advancement of general welfare" or some abstraction known as "justice" was the immediate, guiding purpose of the leaders in either of these great historic changes. The point is, that the direct, impelling motive in both cases was the economic advantages which the beneficiaries expected would accrue to themselves first, from their action. Further than this, economic interpretation cannot go. It may be that some larger world process is working through each series of historical events: but ultimate causes lie beyond our horizon. . . .

Charles A. Beard (1874–1948) was professor of history and political science at Columbia University and former president of the American Political Science Association. This selection is reprinted with the permission of Simon & Schuster from An Economic Interpretation of the Constitution of the United States *by Charles A. Beard, pp. 16–18, 149–151, 268–270, 288–289, 324–325. Copyright 1935 by Macmillan Publishing Company, copyright renewed © 1963 by William Beard and Miriam Beard Vagts.*

THE FOUNDING FATHERS: AN ECONOMIC PROFILE

A survey of the economic interests of the members of the Convention presents certain conclusions:

A majority of the members were lawyers by profession.

Most of the members came from towns, on or near the coast, that is, from the regions in which personalty was largely concentrated.

Not one member represented in his immediate personal economic interests the small farming or mechanic classes.

The overwhelming majority of members, at least five-sixths, were immediately, directly, and personally interested in the outcome of their labors at Philadelphia, and were to a greater or less extent economic beneficiaries from the adoption of the Constitution.

1. Public security interests were extensively represented in the Convention. Of the fifty-five members who attended no less than forty appear on the Records of the Treasury Department for sums varying from a few dollars up to more than one hundred thousand dollars. . . .

    It is interesting to note that, with the exception of New York, and possibly Delaware, each state had one or more prominent representatives in the Convention who held more than a negligible amount of securities, and who could therefore speak with feeling and authority on the question of providing in the new Constitution for the full discharge of the public debt. . . .

2. Personalty invested in lands for speculation was represented by at least fourteen members. . . .

3. Personalty in the form of money loaned at interest was represented by at least twenty-four members. . . .

4. Personalty in mercantile, manufacturing, and shipping lines was represented by at least eleven members. . . .

5. Personalty in slaves was represented by at least fifteen members. . . .

It cannot be said, therefore, that the members of the Convention were "disinterested." On the contrary, we are forced to accept the profoundly significant conclusion that they knew through their personal experiences in economic affairs the precise results which the new government that they were setting up was designed to attain. As a group of doctrinaires, like the Frankfort assembly of 1848, they would have failed miserably; but as practical men they were able to build the new government upon the only foundations which could be stable: fundamental economic interests.[1] . . .

RATIFICATION

New York

There can be no question about the predominance of personalty in the contest over the ratification in New York. That state, says Libby, "presents the problem in its simplest form. The entire mass of interior counties . . . were solidly Anti-federal, comprising the agricultural portion of the state, the last settled and the most thinly populated. There were however in this region two Federal cities (not represented in the convention [as such]), Albany in Albany county and Hudson in Columbia county. . . . The Federal area centred about New York city and county: to the southwest lay Richmond county (Staten Island); to the southeast Kings county, and the northeast Westchester county; while still further extending this area, at the northeast lay the divided county of Dutchess, with a vote in the convention of 4 to 2 in favor of the Constitution, and at the southeast were the divided counties of Queens and Suffolk. . . . These radiating strips of territory with New York city as a centre form a unit, in general favorable to the new Constitution; and it is significant of this unity that Dutchess, Queens, and Suffolk counties, broke away from the anti-Federal phalanx and joined the Federalists, securing thereby the adoption of the Constitution."[2]

Unfortunately the exact distribution of personalty in New York and particularly in the wavering districts which went over to the Federalist party cannot be ascertained, for the system of taxation in vogue in New York at the period of the adoption of the Constitution did not require a state record of property.[3] The data which proved so fruitful in Massachusetts are not forthcoming, therefore, in the case of New York; but it seems hardly necessary to demonstrate the fact that New York City was the centre of personalty for the state and stood next to Philadelphia as the great centre of operations in public stock.

This somewhat obvious conclusion is reinforced by the evidence relative to the vote on the legal tender bill which the paper money party pushed through in 1786. Libby's analysis of this vote shows that "no vote was cast against the bill by members of counties north of the county of New York. In the city and county of New York and in Long Island and Staten Island, the combined vote was 9 to 5 against the measure. Comparing this vote with the vote on the ratification in 1788, it will be seen that of the Federal counties 3 voted against paper money and 1 for it; of the divided counties 1 (Suffolk) voted against paper money and 2 (Queens and Dutchess) voted for it. Of the anti-Federal counties none had members voting against paper money. The merchants as a body were opposed to the issue of paper money and the Chamber of Commerce adopted a memorial against the issue."[4]

Public security interests were identified with the sound money party. There were thirty members of the New York constitutional convention who voted in favor of the ratification of the Constitution and of these no less than sixteen were holders of public securities. . . .

South Carolina

South Carolina presents the economic elements in the ratification with the utmost simplicity. There we find two rather sharply marked districts in antagonism over the Constitution. "The rival sections," says Libby, "were the coast or lower district and the upper, or more properly, the middle and upper country. The coast region was the first settled and contained a larger portion of the wealth of the state; its mercantile and commercial interests were important; its church was the Episcopal, supported by the state." This region, it is scarcely necessary to remark, was overwhelmingly in favor of the Constitution. The upper area, against the Constitution, "was a frontier section, the last to receive settlement; its lands were fertile and its mixed population was largely small farmers. . . . There was no established church, each community supported its own church and there was a great variety in the district."[5]

A contemporary writer, R. G. Harper, calls attention to the fact that the lower country, Charleston, Beaufort, and Georgetown, which had 28,694 white inhabitants, and about seven-twelfths of the representation in the state convention, paid £28,081:5:10 taxes in 1794, while the upper country, with 120,902 inhabitants, and five-twelfths of the representation in the convention, paid only £8390:13:3 taxes.[6] The lower districts in favor of the Constitution therefore possessed the wealth of the state and a disproportionate share in the convention—on the basis of the popular distribution of representation.

These divisions of economic interest are indicated by the abstracts of the tax returns for the state in 1794 which show that of £127,337 worth of stock in trade, faculties, etc. listed for taxation in the state, £109,800 worth was in Charleston, city and county—the stronghold of Federalism. Of the valuation of lots in towns and villages to the amount of £656,272 in the state, £549,909 was located in that city and county.[7]

The records of the South Carolina loan office preserved in the Treasury Department at Washington show that the public securities of that state were more largely in the hands of inhabitants than was the case in North Carolina. They also show a heavy concentration in the Charleston district.

At least fourteen of the thirty-one members of the state-ratifying convention from the parishes of St. Philip and Saint Michael, Charleston (all of whom favored ratification) held over $75,000 worth of public securities. . . .

Conclusions

At the close of this long and arid survey—partaking of the nature of catalogue—it seems worthwhile to bring together the important conclusions for political science which the data presented appear to warrant.

The movement for the Constitution of the United States was originated and carried through principally by four groups of personalty interests which had been adversely affected under the Articles of Confederation: money, public securities, manufactures, and trade and shipping.

The first firm steps toward the formation of the Constitution were taken by a small and active group of men immediately interested through their personal possessions in the outcome of their labors.

No popular vote was taken directly or indirectly on the proposition to call the Convention which drafted the Constitution.

A large propertyless mass was, under the prevailing suffrage qualifications, excluded at the outset from participation (through representatives) in the work of framing the Constitution.

The members of the Philadelphia Convention which drafted the Constitution were, with a few exceptions, immediately, directly, and personally interested in, and derived economic advantages from, the establishment of the new system.

The Constitution was essentially an economic document based upon the concept that the fundamental private rights of property are anterior to government and morally beyond the reach of popular majorities.

The major portion of the members of the Convention are on record as recognizing the claim of property to a special and defensive position in the Constitution.

In the ratification of the Constitution, about three-fourths of the adult males failed to vote on the question, having abstained from the elections at which delegates to the state conventions were chosen, either on account of their indifference or their disfranchisement by property qualifications.

The Constitution was ratified by a vote of probably not more than one-sixth of the adult males.

It is questionable whether a majority of the voters participating in the elections for the state conventions in New York, Massachusetts, New Hampshire, Virginia, and South Carolina, actually approved the ratification of the Constitution.

The leaders who supported the Constitution in the ratifying conventions represented the same economic groups as the members of the Philadelphia Convention; and in a large number of instances they were also directly and personally interested in the outcome of their efforts.

In the ratification, it became manifest that the line of cleavage for and against the Constitution was between substantial personalty interests on the one hand and the small farming and debtor interests on the other.

The Constitution was not created by "the whole people" as the jurists have said; neither was it created by "the states" as southern nullifiers long contended; but it was the work of a consolidated group whose interests knew no state boundaries and were truly national in their scope.

NOTES

1. The fact that a few members of the Convention, who had considerable economic interests at stake, refused to support the Constitution does not invalidate the general conclusions here presented. In the cases of Yates, Lansing, Luther Martin, and Mason, definite economic reasons for their action are forthcoming; but this is a minor detail.
2. O. G. Libby, *Geographical Distribution of the Vote of the Thirteen States on the Federal Constitution*, p. 18. Libby here takes the vote in the New York convention, but that did not precisely represent the popular vote.
3. *State Papers: Finance*, vol. 1, p. 425.
4. Libby, *Geographical Distribution*, p. 59.
5. *Ibid.*, pp. 42–43.
6. "Appius," *To the Citizens of South Carolina* (1794), Library of Congress, Duane Pamphlets, vol. 83.
7. *State Papers: Finance*, vol. 1, p. 462. In 1783 an attempt to establish a bank with $100,000 capital was made in Charleston, S.C., but it failed. "Soon after the adoption of the funding system, three banks were established in Charleston whose capitals in the whole amounted to twenty times the sum proposed in 1783." D. Ramsey, *History of South Carolina* (1858 ed.), vol. 2, p. 106.

Charles Beard and the Constitution
A Critical Analysis

Robert E. Brown

At the end of Chapter XI [of *An Economic Interpretation of the Constitution of the United States*], Beard summarized his findings in fourteen paragraphs under the heading of "Conclusions." Actually, these fourteen conclusions merely add up to the two halves of the Beard thesis. One half, that the Constitution originated with and was carried through by personalty interests—money, public securities, manufactures, and commerce—is to be found in paragraphs two, three, six, seven, eight, twelve, thirteen, and fourteen. The other half—that the Constitution was put over undemocratically in an undemocratic society—is expressed in paragraphs four, five, nine, ten, eleven, and fourteen. The lumping of these conclusions under two general headings makes it easier for the reader to see the broad outlines of the Beard thesis.

Before we examine these two major divisions of the thesis, however, some comment is relevant on the implications contained in the first paragraph. In it Beard characterized his book as a long and arid survey, something in the nature of a catalogue. Whether this characterization was designed to give his book the appearance of a coldly objective study based on the facts we do not know. If so, nothing could be further from reality. As reviewers pointed out in 1913, and as subsequent developments have demonstrated, the book is anything but an arid catalogue of facts. Its pages are replete with interpretation, sometimes stated, sometimes implied. Our task has been to examine Beard's evidence to see whether it justifies the interpretation which Beard gave it. We have tried to discover whether he used the historical method properly in arriving at his thesis.

If historical method means the gathering of data from primary sources, the critical evaluation of the evidence thus gathered, and the drawing of conclusions consistent with this evidence, then we must conclude that Beard has done great violation to such method in this book. He admitted that the evidence had not been collected which, given the proper use of historical method, should have precluded the writing of the book. Yet he nevertheless proceeded on the assumption that a valid interpretation could be built on secondary writings whose authors had likewise failed to collect the evidence. If we accept Beard's own maxim, "no evidence, no history," and his own admission that the data had never been collected, the answer to whether he used historical method properly is self-evident.

Neither was Beard critical of the evidence which he did use. He was accused in 1913, and one might still suspect him, of using only that evidence which appeared to support his thesis. The amount of realty in the country compared with the personalty, the vote in New York, and the omission of the part of *The Federalist,* No. 10, which did not fit his thesis are only a few examples of the uncritical use of evidence to be found in the book. Sometimes he accepted secondary accounts at face value without checking them with the sources; at other times he allowed unfounded rumors and traditions to color his work.

Finally, the conclusions which he drew were not justified even by the kind of evidence which he used. If we accepted his evidence strictly at face value, it would still not add up to the fact that the Constitution was put over undemocratically in an undemocratic society by personalty. The citing of property qualifications does not prove that a mass of men were disfranchised. And if we accept his figures on property holdings, either we do not know what most of the delegates had in realty and personalty, or we know that realty outnumbered personalty three to one (eighteen to six). Simply showing that a man held public securities is not sufficient to prove that he acted only in terms of his public securities. If we ignore Beard's own generalizations and accept only his evidence, we have to conclude that most of the country, and that even the men who were directly concerned with the Constitution, and especially Washington, were large holders of realty.

Perhaps we can never be completely objective in history, but certainly we can be more objective than Beard was in this book. Naturally, the historian must always be aware of the biases, the subjectivity, the pitfalls that confront him, but this does not mean that he should not make an effort to overcome these obstacles. Whether Beard had his thesis before he had his evidence, as some have said, is a question that each reader must answer for himself. Certain it is that the evidence does not justify the thesis.

So instead of the Beard interpretation that the Constitution was put over undemocratically in an undemocratic society by personal property, the following fourteen paragraphs are offered as a possible interpretation of the Constitution and as suggestions for future research on that document.

1. The movement for the Constitution was originated and carried through by men who had long been important in both economic and political affairs in their respective states. Some of them owned personalty, more of them owned realty, and if their property was adversely affected by conditions under the Articles of Confederation, so also was the property of the bulk of the people in the country, middle-class farmers as well as town artisans.
2. The movement for the Constitution, like most important movements, was undoubtedly started by a small group of men. They were probably interested personally in the outcome of their labors, but the benefits which they expected were not confined to personal property or, for that matter, strictly to things economic. And if their own interests would be enhanced by a new government, similar interests of other men, whether agricultural or commercial, would also be enhanced.
3. Naturally there was no popular vote on the calling of the convention which drafted the Constitution. Election of delegates by state legislatures was the constitutional method under the Articles of Confederation, and had been the method long established in this country. Delegates to the Albany Congress, the Stamp Act Congress,

the First Continental Congress, the Second Continental Congress, and subsequent congresses under the Articles were all elected by state legislatures, not by the people. Even the Articles of Confederation had been sanctioned by state legislatures, not by popular vote. This is not to say that the Constitutional Convention should not have been elected directly by the people, but only that such a procedure would have been unusual at the time. Some of the opponents of the Constitution later stressed, without avail, the fact that the Convention had not been directly elected. But at the time the Convention met, the people in general seemed to be about as much concerned over the fact that they had not elected the delegates as the people of this country are now concerned over the fact that they do not elect our delegates to the United Nations.

4. Present evidence seems to indicate that there were no "propertyless masses" who were excluded from the suffrage at the time. Most men were middle-class farmers who owned realty and were qualified voters, and, as the men in the Convention said, mechanics had always voted in the cities. Until credible evidence proves otherwise, we can assume that state legislatures were fairly representative at the time. We cannot condone the fact that a few men were probably disfranchised by prevailing property qualifications, but it makes a great deal of difference to an interpretation of the Constitution whether the disfranchised comprised 95 percent of the adult men or only 5 percent. Figures which give percentages of voters in terms of the entire population are misleading, since less than 20 percent of the people were adult men. And finally, the voting qualifications favored realty, not personalty.

5. If the members of the Convention were directly interested in the outcome of their work and expected to derive benefits from the establishment of the new system, so also did most of the people of the country. We have many statements to the effect that the people in general expected substantial benefits from the labors of the Convention.

6. The Constitution was not just an economic document, although economic factors were undoubtedly important. Since most of the people were middle class and had private property, practically everybody was interested in the protection of property. A constitution which did not protect property would have been rejected without any question, for the American people had fought the Revolution for the preservation of life, liberty, and property. Many people believed that the Constitution did not go far enough to protect property, and they wrote these views into the amendments to the Constitution. But property was not the only concern of those who wrote and ratified the Constitution, and we would be doing a grave injustice to the political sagacity of the Founding Fathers if we assumed that property or personal gain was their only motive.

7. Naturally the delegates recognized that protection of property was important under government, but they also recognized that personal rights were equally important. In fact, persons and property were usually bracketed together as the chief objects of government protection.

8. If three-fourths of the adult males failed to vote on the election of delegates to ratifying conventions, this fact signified indifference, not disfranchisement. We must not confuse those who could *not* vote with those who *could* vote but failed to

exercise their right. Many men at the time bewailed the fact that only a small portion of the voters ever exercised their prerogative. But this in itself should stand as evidence that the conflict over the Constitution was not very bitter, for if these people had felt strongly one way or the other, more of them would have voted.

Even if we deny the evidence which I have presented and insist that American society was undemocratic in 1787, we must still accept the fact that the men who wrote the Constitution believed that they were writing it for a democratic society. They did not hide behind an iron curtain of secrecy and devise the kind of conservative government that they wanted without regard to the views and interests of "the people." More than anything else, they were aware that "the people" would have to ratify what they proposed, and that therefore any government which would be acceptable to the people must of necessity incorporate much of what was customary at the time. The men at Philadelphia were practical politicians, not political theorists. They recognized the multitude of different ideas and interests that had to be reconciled and compromised before a constitution would be acceptable. They were far too practical, and represented far too many clashing interests themselves, to fashion a government weighted in favor of personalty or to believe that the people would adopt such a government.

9. If the Constitution was ratified by a vote of only one-sixth of the adult men, that again demonstrates indifference and not disfranchisement. Of the one-fourth of the adult males who voted, nearly two-thirds favored the Constitution. Present evidence does not permit us to say what the popular vote was except as it was measured by the votes of the ratifying conventions.

10. Until we know what the popular vote was, we cannot say that it is questionable whether a majority of the voters in several states favored the Constitution. Too many delegates were sent uninstructed. Neither can we count the towns which did not send delegates on the side of those opposed to the Constitution. Both items would signify indifference rather than sharp conflict over ratification.

11. The ratifying conventions were elected for the specific purpose of adopting or rejecting the Constitution. The people in general had anywhere from several weeks to several months to decide the question. If they did not like the new government, or if they did not know whether they liked it, they could have voted *no* and there would have been no Constitution. Naturally the leaders in the ratifying conventions represented the same interests as the members of the Constitutional Convention— mainly realty and some personalty. But they also represented their constituents in these same interests, especially realty.

12. If the conflict over ratification had been between substantial personalty interests on the one hand and small farmers and debtors on the other, there would not have been a constitution. The small farmers comprised such an overwhelming percentage of the voters that they could have rejected the new government without any trouble. Farmers and debtors are not synonymous terms and should not be confused as such. A town-by-town or county-by-county record of the vote would show clearly how the farmers voted.

13. The Constitution was created about as much by the whole people as any government could be which embraced a large area and depended on representation rather

than on direct participation. It was also created in part by the states, for as the *Records* show, there was strong state sentiment at the time which had to be appeased by compromise. And it was created by compromising a whole host of interests throughout the country, without which compromises it could never have been adopted.

14. If the intellectual historians are correct, we cannot explain the Constitution without considering the psychological factors also. Men are motivated by what they believe as well as by what they have. Sometimes their actions can be explained on the basis of what they hope to have or hope that their children will have. Madison understood this fact when he said that the universal hope of acquiring property tended to dispose people to look favorably upon property. It is even possible that some men support a given economic system when they themselves have nothing to gain by it. So we would want to know what the people in 1787 thought of their class status. Did workers and small farmers believe that they were lower class, or did they, as many workers do now, consider themselves middle class? Were the common people trying to eliminate the Washingtons, Adamses, Hamiltons, and Pinckneys, or were they trying to join them?

As did Beard's fourteen conclusions, these fourteen suggestions really add up to two major propositions: the Constitution was adopted in a society which was fundamentally democratic, not undemocratic; and it was adopted by a people who were primarily middle-class property owners, especially farmers who owned realty, not just by the owners of personalty. At present these points seem to be justified by the evidence, but if better evidence in the future disproves or modifies them, we must accept that evidence and change our interpretation accordingly.

After this critical analysis, we should at least not begin future research on this period of American history with the illusion that the Beard thesis of the Constitution is valid. If historians insist on accepting the Beard thesis in spite of this analysis, however, they must do so with the full knowledge that their acceptance is founded on "an act of faith," not an analysis of historical method, and that they were indulging in a "noble dream," not history.

3

FEDERALISM

The Tenth Amendment to the U.S. Constitution states: "The powers not delegated to the United States by the Constitution, nor prohibited by it to the States, are reserved to the States respectively, or to the people." Although this brief amendment, containing just slightly more than 25 words, seems simple and uncomplicated, it has, in fact, consti-tuted the basis for one of the more protracted debates in U.S. history—namely, the de-bate over the extent of the national government's powers in relation to those of the states.

A modern manifestation of this debate is to be found in the controversy over "un-funded federal mandates." Unfunded mandates are those laws passed by Congress that require states to carry out national regulations without *federal government funding. Examples are the Clean Water Act of 1972, the Americans with Disabilities Act of 1990, and the National Voter Registration Act of 1993. Although noble in purpose, these acts have frequently been criticized as interfering with the powers and financial responsi-bilities of the states in violation of the spirit, if not the letter, of the constitutional divi-sion of powers between the national government and the states.*

In the selections that follow, unfunded mandates are debated by two members of Congress. In the first selection, U.S. Senator Spencer Abraham (R-Mich.) develops the case for limiting the number of federal mandates and requiring Congress to conduct a full review of the costs of any mandate. Senator Abraham's arguments against unfunded mandates are grounded in the belief that the national government should not impose on the states financial burdens for programs to which the states have not agreed; nor should Congress seek to bypass its own responsibility in fiscal matters by passing along to the states the costs of federal programs.

In the second selection, U.S. Representative George Miller (D-Cal.) makes the case for keeping the system of federal mandates, both funded and unfunded. Representative Miller rests his case both on the good that has come from such mandates and also on the continuing unwillingness or inability of the states to solve pressing social, eco-nomic, and environmental problems on their own.

Unfunded Mandates
The Negative Effects

Spencer Abraham

Mr. President, I rise in support of S.1, which, of course, addresses the problem of unfunded Federal mandates. S.1 would significantly limit the Federal Government's ability to require State or local governments to undertake affirmative activities or comply with Federal standards unless the Federal Government was also prepared to reimburse the costs of such activities or compliance. As with direct Federal expenditures, the financial burdens of such mandates fall squarely upon the middle-class taxpayer. . . .

Perhaps nothing better reflects contemporary trends in government than the enormous growth in the level of unfunded Federal mandates over the past two decades. An unfunded mandate arises when the Federal Government imposes some responsibility or obligation upon a State or local government to implement a program or carry out an action without, at the same time, providing the State or local government with the necessary funding. Several recent illustrations of unfunded mandates include obligations imposed on States and localities to establish minimum voter registration procedures in the Motor Vehicle Voter Registration Act; obligations imposed on States and localities to conduct automobile emissions testing programs under the Clean Air Act; and obligations imposed on States and localities to monitor water systems for contaminants under the Safe Drinking Water Act. These examples, however, are only the smallest tip of the iceberg.

While there is virtually no area of public activity in which Federal mandates are absent, such mandates are most visible in the area of environmental legislation. Of the 12 most costly mandates identified by the National Association of Counties in a 1993 survey, 7 of them involve environmental programs such as the Resource Conservation and Recovery Act, the Endangered Species Act, the Safe Drinking Water Act, and the Superfund Act.

The negative effect of unfunded Federal mandates are at least fivefold: First, such mandates camouflage the full extent of Federal Government spending by placing an increasingly significant share of that spending off-budget, in the form of costs imposed upon other levels of government. While it is extraordinarily difficult to assess the dollar costs of unfunded mandates, a sense of their magnitude is evidenced by a 3-month study done earlier this year by the State of Maryland, in which they concluded that approximately 24 percent of their total budget was committed to meeting legal requirements mandated by Congress. Assuming the rough accuracy of this estimation, and assuming that Maryland is not subject to extraordinary levels of mandates, this would amount to approximately $80 to $85 billion imposed nationally upon all State

Spencer Abraham is a Republican U.S. Senator from the state of Michigan. Excerpted from a speech delivered in the U.S. Senate, Congressional Record, *Proceedings and Debates of the 104th Congress, 1st Session, Senate, January 19, 1995, vol. 141, No. 11, S1183–S1184.*

governments. This figure does not include mandates imposed upon local governments. To calculate the true burden of Federal spending, the costs of these mandates must be added to an already bloated Federal budget. The Federal government consumes the limited resources of the people every bit as much when it compels State or local governments to do something as when it directly does something itself.

Second, the impact of the unfunded Federal mandate is to distort the cost-benefit analysis that Congress undertakes in assessing individual pieces of legislation. The costs imposed by the Congress upon States and localities are rarely considered, much less estimated with any accuracy. As a result, the presumed benefits of legislative measures are not viewed in the full context of their costs. Legislative benefits tend consistently to be overestimated and legislative costs tend consistently to be underestimated.

Third, unfunded Federal mandates burden State and local governments with spending obligations for programs which they have never chosen to incur while requiring them to reduce spending obligation for programs which they have chosen to incur. For the options are clear when mandates are imposed by Washington: Either State and local governments must raise taxes—since they do not have the same access to deficit spending as the Federal Government—or they must reorder their budget by reducing or terminating programs which had already been determined to merit public resources. With State balanced budget requirements and with taxpayers already burdened to the hilt by government demands for a share of their income, State and local governments are forced into a zero-sum analysis by unfunded mandates; every new Federal mandate must be compensated for directly by a reduction in another area of State or local spending. Further, every Federal mandate must effectively be treated as the number one spending priority by State and local governments, notwithstanding the sense of their community and the judgment of their elected officials. Such governments must first budget whatever is necessary to pay for the mandates and only afterwards evaluate the level of resources remaining for other spending measures.

Which leads to the fourth impact of the unfunded Federal mandate. An increasing proportion of State and local budgets is devoted to spending measures deemed to be important not by the elected representatives in those jurisdictions, but rather by decisionmakers in Washington. In 1993, for example, compliance with Federal Medicaid mandates cost the State of Michigan $95.3 million, which exceeded by $7 million the combined expenses of the Michigan Departments of State, Civil Rights, Civil Services, Attorney General, and Agriculture. Although the Supreme Court in recent years has reduced the 10th Amendment to effective insignificance, I believe nevertheless that there are constitutional implications to this trend. It is lamentable enough that the Federal budget has grown at the pace that we have witnessed over the past generation; for Washington additionally to be determining the budgetary priorities of Michigan and Texas and Pennsylvania is for it to trespass upon the proper constitutional prerogatives of the States. To the extent that the States are straitjacketed in their ability to determine the composition of their own budgets, their sovereignty has been undermined.

Indeed, the Constitution aside, it is difficult to understand how a reasoned assessment of the efficacy of Federal Government programs over the past several decades would encourage anyone in the notion that Washington had any business instructing other governments how best to carry out their responsibilities.

Finally, unfunded Federal mandates erode the accountability of government generally. The average citizen now finds that his State and local representatives disavow responsibility for spending measures resulting from Federal mandates, while his Washington representatives also claim not to be responsible. Lines of accountability are
simply too indirect and too convoluted where Federal mandates are involved. The result
is that the citizenry come to feel that no one is clearly responsible for what government
is doing, and that they have little ability to influence its course.

I am particularly supportive of S.1 because I believe that it will result in governments at all levels thinking more seriously about the proper scope of government. In
truth, unfunded mandates are but one symptom of the more fundamental problem that
the Federal Government has lost sight of the proper scope of its functions. While there
are some mandates that are reasonable, Congress should be prepared to reimburse the
States for the costs attendant to such mandates. In cases where the wisdom of mandates
is more dubious, S.1 would force upon Congress a more balanced and a sober decision-
making process. Instead of neglecting the hidden pass-the-buck costs entailed in unfunded mandates, Congress instead would be forced to make hard-headed decisions
about the costs and benefits of new programs. In at least some of these cases, I am confident that the legislative balance will be drawn differently than that we have consistently seen over recent decades. I am confident that the virtues of federalism will be recognized more readily when new programs are no longer free but must be explicitly
accounted for in the Federal budget. The one-size-fits-all mentality which tends to underlie most Federal mandates may also be reconsidered in the process.

At the same time, State and local officials will also have to make difficult decisions.
With Congress likely to curtail or terminate altogether some mandates when confronted
with the requirement that they have to pay for them, State and local governments will
have to determine whether they are willing to support such programs on their own. No
longer will they be able to enjoy the benefits of such programs while being able to di-
vert responsibility for their costs to the Federal Government. Rather, they will have to
make equally hard decisions as those that will have to be made by Washington lawmakers about the relative merits of public programs.

Perhaps the greatest long-term benefit of the present legislation is that it will force
more open and honest decision making and budgeting upon all levels of government.
When greater governmental accountability is achieved, the public will be better posi-
tioned to punish and reward public officials for actions. As a result, government will be
more responsive to the electorate in its spending decisions. Government, in short, will
be made more representative by this legislation. . . .

Unfunded Mandates
Laws That Bind Us Together

George Miller

Mr. Chairman, this legislation strikes at the very heart of the body of laws that bind us together as a progressive society, and with the highest standard of living in the world; the body of law that ensures that no matter where you live in this country, you can enjoy clean water: that no matter where you live in this country, local government and the private sector are working every day to improve the air that you breathe, so we no longer have to send our children indoors because it is too smoggy out. We no longer have to tell our senior citizens they cannot go out for a walk because the air quality is too bad, or we cannot drive to work because they do not want the automobiles on the road.

These are the laws that accomplished those successes. These are laws that said "Yes, if you take money from the Federal Government, we are going to put onto you an obligation to educate the handicapped children of this Nation," because before that was the law, the handicapped children of this Nation could not get an education in the public school systems run by the States and localities that we now say are so ready to do the job.

But for that law, tens of thousands of handicapped children, because they have cerebral palsy, because they have Downs syndrome, would not be allowed in our public schools, but that is a Federal mandate. Yes, we pay part of the freight, but this law would say "Unless the Federal Government presents 100 percent of it, no school district would be required to educate that handicapped child. Unless the Federal Government spends 100 percent of the money to clean up the local water supply, the local sewage treatment, the city would have no obligation."

What happens along the Mississippi River in Indiana or Minnesota if they choose, or in Ohio, if they choose not to clean up the municipal sewage because the Federal Government will not pay 100 percent? That means the people in Mississippi and Louisiana have to inherit that sewage.

An unfunded mandate upstream is untreated sewage downstream. What does that mean to the fishermen, to the commercial enterprises, and to the tourist industry in those States? It means they suffer. That is why we have national laws.

When I was a young man you could smell San Francisco Bay before you could see it, but now we require all of the cities, not just the town that I live in, not just the oil industry, not just the chemical industry, but the cities upstream and downstream [to clean up]. Some of them, we had to take them to court to tell them to clean it up. Today San Francisco Bay is a tourist attraction. Commercial fishing is back. People can use it for recreation.

George Miller is a Democratic U.S. Representative from the state of California. Excerpted from a speech delivered in the U.S. House of Representatives, Congressional Record, *Proceedings and Debates of the 104th Congress, 1st Session, House of Representatives, January 19, 1996, vol. 141, No. 11, H355–H356.*

That is what these mandates have done. Yes, we have not paid 100 percent, but we have put billions and billions and billions of dollars into helping local communities make airports safe so they could become international airports, so people would have confidence in going to those cities. We have cleaned up their water and air. We have made it safe to drink. That is what this legislation is an assault on.

Mr. Chairman, the proponents of this legislation would have us believe this is a simple and straightforward initiative: Congress should mandate the States and local governments to do nothing that Congress is not willing to pay for in its entirety.

In fact, this legislation strikes at the very heart of the entire concept on which our Government is based. Government does not have the responsibility to require that those in our societies—private individuals, businesses, and State and local governments—meet certain responsibilities.

Even the drafters of this legislation recognize that some mandates need not be paid for. They are ideologues of convenience. They do not require we pay for compliance with civil rights and disability laws. But they would compel funding for actions relating to public health and safety, protection of the environment, education of children, medical services to our elderly, safeguards to our workers.

And they would require that we pay only when that burden is imposed on entities of government. Private industry, many of which compete with State and local government in the provision of services, is accorded no relief. And those who work for Government, performing exactly the same services as those in the private sector, are potentially denied such basic protections as minimum wages, worker right to know about hazardous substances, and OSHA protections.

Never mind that the same State and local governments to whose aid we are rushing impose precisely the same unfunded mandates on lower levels of government.

So, I think this clearly demonstrates what is going on here: this is not about unfunded mandates: It is about undermining this Nation's environmental, education, health and labor laws, and wrapping the attack in the flag of unfunded mandates.

The last time we tried this deceptive tactic—cutting away at the basic role of Government in the name of cost savings—we tripled the national debt in 8 years.

But let me take issue with the very name of this concept—unfunded mandates.

Unfunded? Really?

We have spent tens of billions of dollars helping States and local communities meet these mandates by improving water systems, upgrading drinking water supplies, building and improving transportation systems, improving education programs, and on and on.

Have we funded every mandate fully? No. Should the Federal Government have to pay States and local communities to protect their employees, their environment and their public health and safety? Because let's remember: A lot of them were not protecting those people and those resources before the Federal mandates came along.

No, we haven't funded every dollar. But have we covered 50, 75, 90 percent of the cost of many of these projects? Time and time again.

And have we provided these same State and local governments with hundreds of billions of dollars to build, expand and improve highways, rapid transit and harbors and to respond to disasters—even when there was no Federal responsibility to provide a dollar? Have we provided money to assure that communities are safe from nuclear power plants and hazardous waste sites? Have we provided money to educate the handicapped, to train the jobless, and to house tens of millions of Americans?

I have little doubt that those who champion this legislation fully expect that its passage would have no effect on our willingness to fund their future actions in these areas. They are very wrong. Every State and community should be aware that the appetite of the Congress for funding local projects and programs that fail to meet a Federal standard of quality and protection and performance is going to be very minimal, particularly in light of the coming effort for a balanced budget amendment that would slash Federal spending radically.

So I think we should proceed with some caution here. If the States and local communities don't want the mandates, don't expect the Federal dollars either.

I find it somewhat ironic that in my own State of California, for example, the Governor has failed to come up with his promise of matching funds for the $5 billion in Federal disaster aid following last year's Northridge earthquake. Now he wants more Federal money for earthquake assistance; and he will want more still for the flooding, and he'll probably throw in a few billion dollars' worth of dams and other infrastructure from Federal taxpayers.

Yet he is one of the biggest proponents of this unfunded mandates legislation—and at the same time that he forces unfunded mandates down the throat of every county and city in California.

We see that kind of hypocrisy in the legislation before us today.

In case you didn't read the fine print, this mandate ban neglects to include the dozens of new unfunded Federal mandates contained in the Republicans' Contract With America. Just the mandates in the welfare bill alone could bring the States to their knees. But all those new mandates are exempted, even though none of them have yet been enacted into law. So much for being honest with the American people.

Let's be very clear what this legislation is going to do to some of the most important laws this Congress has passed and has spent billions of dollars helping States and local communities implement.

Safe drinking water. We have upgraded the water supply across this Nation, virtually eliminating disease, contamination and danger. Much of that has been paid for by Federal dollars. Which local community would like to have taken on that task without Federal assistance? Which Americans want to put the future and the consistency of our safe drinking water at risk through this legislation?

Clean water. You used to be able to smell San Francisco Bay before you could see it. You used to need a battery of shots if you stuck your toe in the Potomac River. The sewage and waste water of 80 million Americans from a score of States flows out of the mouth of the Mississippi River, and for years contaminated the commercial fishing areas. A few years before the Clean Water Act was passed, the Cuyohoga River in Cleveland was burning. Want to go back to those days? You tell me which financially strapped city and State will take on that burden without Federal assistance?

Nuclear safety. Should nuclear power plants and generators of radioactive wastes—which exist in every large city and many small ones—be able to ignore Federal safety standards for operations and waste disposal?

Deadbeat parents. We are collecting hundreds of millions of dollars a year from parents who have ignored their financial responsibilities to their children, thanks to Federal law. Should we just abandon that program?

The list of inequities goes on and on. What happens to reauthorizations of existing laws? What if those reauthorizations are delayed for years by obstructive tactics in Congress? The answer is: We don't know. And the reason we are legislating in the dark here is because this complex bill, which would fundamentally alter the entire nature of Federal-State relations, was drafted in haste, denied public comment and public hearings, and marked up in a haphazard and manipulated process that made thoughtful review all but impossible.

Of course we should examine whether Federal funding of mandates has been adequate. In fact, that process was begun last year. . . .

But let us not rush to pass a deeply flawed, confusing, and deceptive bill, . . . a bill that misrepresents not only the need for mandates, but ignores the billions of dollars we have given to States and communities to help meet those mandates.

4

PUBLIC OPINION

At a time when a substantial number of Americans see government as increasingly remote and excessively influenced by organized interests, it is not surprising that "reformers" are seeking new ways to reconnect the American people to their government. Some reformers have turned to new technology to help provide that connection. Computer enthusiasts, for example, foresee the use of the Internet as a means to energize citizens, to get them to vote, and to get them to express their opinions on a whole range of issues. Thus, in the year 2000, candidates for president communicated directly with voters via the Internet, and Democratic primary elections in Arizona were held online. If this trend continues, no doubt, voting on policy issues will be online and the potential for the Internet to provide citizens with information on a whole array of topics will be virtually unlimited.

In the two selections that follow, contrasting arguments are presented on the potential for using the new computer technology to improve the public discourse and government decision making. In the first selection, political consultant Dick Morris sees the Internet as revolutionizing politics. An unabashed advocate of the Internet, Morris views the technology of cyberspace as a means to energize the electorate and to connect citizens to their government in a way not possible with any other medium. Indeed, in his judgment politics via the Internet is about as close as one can get to direct democracy, literally allowing millions of Americans to express their opinions one-on-one with representatives and with each other. In the second selection, two Washington, D.C., commentators, Norman Ornstein and Amy Schenkenberg, raise very serious questions about the new technology and the role the public should play in our representative system of government. Ornstein and Schenkenberg ask: Will "cyberdemocracy" improve our system of representation? Will voters take seriously their responsibilities in this new system of direct participation? Moreover, what controls, if any, will be placed on these new systems? And, most importantly, do we really want a sometimes disinterested and ill-formed public to exert that much control over policymaking? These are profound questions that once again cause us to reflect on the proper role of citizens in our still evolving democracy.

Vox Populi in Cyberspace

Dick Morris

Thomas Jefferson would have loved to see the Internet. His utopian vision of a democracy based on town meetings and direct popular participation is about to become a reality. In the era of the Fifth Estate, the massive, uncontrolled, and unregulated interaction of tens of millions of people will be the central political reality. Ideas, opinions, viewpoints, and perspectives will race back and forth over the Internet instantly and continuously, weaving together to create new national fabric of democracy.

Input from a multiplicity of sources will make it impossible for any organization or agency to control the flow of information or the shaping of opinion. As Matt Drudge, the Internet investigative reporter, puts it, "Everybody will be a publisher, disseminating his views to all who choose to log on to read them." News organizations and opinion leaders will spring up all over in a wonderfully chaotic and anarchic freedom. Limitations imposed by capital, paper, and ink, or the unavailability of bands and frequencies, will no longer screen out the opinions of the less connected and less powerful.

Only a few years ago, the voting records of our elected officials were inaccessible, the identities of large campaign donors were obscured, and the expenditures by government and by campaigns were concealed by layers of bureaucracy. Only by joining one of the few public interest organizations, such as Public Interest Research Group (PIRG) or Common Cause, could we find some of this data. Even then, it was slow to reach us through monthly newsletters, annual reports, or pre-election mailings. All of that is in the past. Now we are able to get instantaneous and comprehensive reports of the activities of political figures. Through a wide array of documents placed on the Internet by organizations, individuals, and the press, we are inundated with the tools of effective citizenship.

The incredible speed and interactivity of the Internet will inevitably return our country to a de facto system of direct democracy by popular referendums. The town-meeting style of government will become a national reality. Eventually the 1990s contrived "town meetings" popularized by Bill Clinton will be obsolete, as voters will reject the idea of specially handpicked, agreeable participants who, in fact, don't reflect our towns. Instead, the real town meetings will occur on the Internet, with real people, and the politicians will have to listen.

Ad hoc, nonbinding voting over the Internet is starting to transform our democracy. A proliferation of political Web sites soon will offer voters the chance to be heard at the instant that an issue becomes important. Whether it is in response to a random act of violence such as Columbine, the death of an American icon like John F. Kennedy Jr., or a court decision such as O. J. Simpson's acquittal, American voters are already finding an outlet for their emotions and political views that has never before been available.

Dick Morris is a political consultant, TV commentator for Fox News Channel, *and newspaper columnist for the* New York Post. *Copyright © 1999 by Eileen McGann from* VOTE.com *by Dick Morris. Reprinted by permission of Renaissance Books. Los Angeles, California.*

Through interactive political and news Web sites, people will be able to vote on any issue they wish. We will all be more like the citizens in California and other states where voters can take matters into their own hands through direct referendums and initiatives in each year's balloting. Internet referendums will not, in the beginning, have any legally binding effect, but they will be politically binding. As the number of people participating in these votes grows from the thousands well into the millions, they will acquire a political force that will compel our elected representatives, anxious to keep their jobs, to heed their message. No congressman, senator, or president would dare fly in the face of so massive an expression of public sentiment.

In all likelihood these Internet referendums will be staged without the slightest government participation. Private Web sites like Vote.com will provide the ballot boxes. Financed by advertising, these nongovernmental means of expressing voter opinion, in effect, mean the end of a government monopoly on the process of registration and voting.

When will voters be consulted on important issues? Whenever they want to be. Anytime enough Internet users want to have a referendum they will simply have one. There will likely be hundreds of referendums each year. Of course only a few will attract the attention of enough voters to matter politically, but, by the self-correcting increase or decrease in turnout, voters will indicate how important they feel a given issue to be. Some issues will arouse sufficient public attention to generate a huge outpouring of public opinion and tens of millions of votes. These referendums, on the key issues of the day, will have an enormous impact on governmental decision-making at all levels. Others will, undoubtedly, be flaky or unimportant. Then few will vote or participate and they will be ignored.

Elections will still be run by government bureaucracies. We'll still choose our president and Congress by the old election system, but the influence the public can bring to bear will make it far less important whom we elect. It is the public's will, not theirs, that will most often be controlling.

Is this a good thing? Our legislators and leaders, with their addiction to special-interest money and power, have forfeited their right to our trust. A little direct democracy might dilute the power of these self-interested and well-funded organizations and restore a measure of popular sovereignty. The insider system, with its focus on partisan combat and subservience to powerful lobbyists, could use a bit of fresh air now and then. Thomas Jefferson recommended a revolution every twenty years to "refresh . . . the tree of liberty." As revolutions go, this one is likely to be both more pacific and more constructive than most.

Of course voters make mistakes and are often turned from good sense by racism, bigotry, and prejudice. Demagogues make a good living off the gullible. Ultimately our experience with direct democracy will lead voters to see the wisdom of ceding back to those who are more experienced a measure of the power the Internet has given the general public. Eventually, chastened and humbled, our elected leaders may find the pendulum swinging back in their direction. But not anytime soon.

Whether direct Internet democracy is good or bad is, however, quite beside the point. It is inevitable. It is coming and we had better make our peace with it. We have to better educate ourselves so that we can make good decisions. Restricting the power of the people is no longer a viable option. The Internet made it obsolete.

People are yearning for some way to express their views on political issues, beyond talking back to an unresponsive television screen or muttering into their coffee over the morning newspaper. (As we shall see, this frustration with the limited opportunities for political self-expression is a basic reason for the popularity of talk radio's call-in format.)

How popular would Internet referendums become? An April 1999 survey by Dresner, Wickers and Associates, taken for the Vote.com Web site, predicts that upwards of 40 percent of people over sixteen years of age would be interested in participating. The survey asked respondents on which issues they would like to vote. The answer is that significant numbers would like to vote on practically anything.

Interest in Voting on the Internet

| | % of Internet Users Who Are Interested | | |
Topic	Very	Somewhat	Total
General interest in participating in referendums	25	19	44
. . . In presidential primaries	35	19	54
How should budget surplus be spent?	48	20	68
Should Hillary run for the senate?	20	9	29
Should the U.S. grant more trade concessions to China?	20	14	34
Should sales over the Internet be taxed?	24	12	36

Source: Dresner, Wickers and Associates Survey, April 1999. 1,000 Internet users.

How are we to reconcile this predicted quantum leap in voter interest with the depressing spectacle of annually dropping election-day turnout? While turnout has indeed decreased, the falloff is more illusory than real. As political consultant Richard Dresner puts it, the drop in voter turnout is "more a generational thing than anything else." Dresner notes that turnout among those reared during the Depression and amid World War II has always been very high, higher than that of any other generation. "Much of the drop in turnout," Dresner says, "is due to this generation dying out. Turnout among all other generations has been roughly the same over the past twenty or thirty years." The sole exception, he notes, is that there is a very low turnout among young adults who have not been to college.

As turnout drops, how will participation through the Internet rise? Will the X Generation, skilled in the Internet but indifferent to politics, remain ouline but continue to ignore the ballot box? Probably this is exactly what will happen.

Participation is a simple matter of logging on. There is no trip through the rain to the polling place. No authority-figure inspectors are there to look up your name in the Doomsday Book to verify your status as a legal voter.

Internet users may not elect public officials, but they will tell those officials what to do. Indeed, referendum voting over the Internet will likely become as habitual as reading a newspaper or using e-mail. Instantly the voter will see his or her vote counted and can log on to follow the progress of the referendum. Those who vote will soon learn how their representative in Congress, the state legislature, or the city council voted on the issue at hand. Feedback will be instantaneous and responsive.

Will the resulting vote-count truly mirror the opinions of those who will really vote to select their senators and congressmen on election day? At first, probably not. But in a society where only about half of voting-age adults actually participates in presidential elections, and only about 40 percent in off-year congressional contests, why should this national canvass of opinion exclude the other half to two-thirds? Indeed, as nonvoters get used to voting over the Internet, they will find themselves more involved in the political process and may well become interested enough to make the journey to the polls on election day.

*   *   *

Internet use is disproportionately concentrated among those under fifty, but contrary to popular wisdom, its use among minorities is extensive. While the proportion of Internet users who are Black or Hispanic is somewhat less than that of the general population, it does approximate their proportion of those who actually vote. The following table compares the proportion of Internet users from each age and race group with their percentage of the general population.

Internet Use by Age and Race

Age or Racial Group	% of Net Users	% of Population over 16
16–30	39	27
31–50	46	40
51–65	11	17
Over 65	4	16
Black	11	12
Hispanic	5	11

Only Hispanics and those over sixty-five are grossly underrepresented on the Internet. The former is likely due, in part, to linguistic problems, which will be overcome as the years pass. As Internet use grows, the participation of Americans over sixty-five is certain to increase. The Internet population is more and more likely to be a reflection of America.

Obviously, a fair number of people under the age of eighteen will also vote in Internet referendums. While these young people would not be able to vote in actual elections, they will likely still want to use the Internet to send messages to the adult leadership of their country. As teen habits go, voting is relatively less pernicious than smoking, drinking, or drug use, so why not encourage it? The Internet will redefine citizenship.

Will Internet voting be subject to fraud or abuse? Technology can, or soon will, likely be able to stop multiple voting. Every once in a while, a dedicated hacker will be up to the challenge of invading the system and recording multiple votes, but systems can be put in place to prevent any substantial abuse of the process. The validity of an Internet referendum will depend mainly on the verification system of the Web site.

As Internet voting becomes widespread and the turnout for Internet referendum mounts, the energies of our political system will flow into the Internet and further increase its impact. Candidates will campaign over the Internet. Lobbying groups will use Internet voting to animate their positions. Special-interest organizations will adapt themselves to using Internet referendums to make their political points. A new arena will be created that will absorb more and more of the kinetic energy of our political process.

The Promise and Perils
of Cyberdemocracy

Norman Ornstein and Amy Schenkenberg

In 1992, Ross Perot promised that if elected president he would use electronic town hall meetings to guide national decisions. Perot lost the election (and never made clear how those meetings would operate), but the idea of "cyberdemocracy" aroused much interest and is spreading quickly as technology advances. Every U.S. senator and 190 representatives currently have World Wide Web pages, as do all . . . major . . . presidential contenders. In 1995, the Library of Congress, under the leadership of Newt Gingrich, established an on-line system offering all legislation considered and passed by Congress.

On the local level, the city government of Colorado Springs has a non-commercial electronic bulletin board called Citylink. Established in 1990 to allow citizens to communicate with city managers and city council members, it's available free of charge. In 1994, the Minnesota Electronic Democracy Project conducted on-line debates among candidates in the gubernatorial and senate races.

States have begun fashioning their governmental processes around this direct-democracy ideal. Twenty-four states permit citizen initiatives that place legislation or constitutional amendments on the ballot. Oregon has held local vote-by-mail elections since 1981, and in 1995 initiated its first state-wide mail ballot to replace Senator Bob Packwood. North Dakota's 1996 presidential primary [was conducted] by mail ballot.

All this may be just the beginning. As new technologies emerge, many futurists paint rosy scenarios of more direct roles for individuals in law-making. Some prophesy that legislators will vote and debate from their home state through computers and televisions, eliminating the need for the actual houses of Congress in Washington. Lawrence Grossman, former president of PBS and NBC, imagines Congress evolving into a body that discusses issues and disseminates information, but only makes decisions after being instructed by the public. Futurist Christine Slaton questions the need for elected legislators at all. She envisions using technology to create a participatory democracy where representatives are selected by lot and rotated regularly. Alvin and Heidi Toffler of "third wave" fame predict that today's political parties will disappear, replaced by fluid coalitions that vary according to changing legislative interests. The Tofflers also envision representatives chosen by lot, or at a minimum, elected officials

Norman Ornstein is a resident scholar and Amy Schenkenberg Mitchell is a former re-search associate at the American Enterprise Institute, a government and public policy research organization in Washington, D.C. Reprinted from Norman Ornstein and Amy Schenkenberg, "The Promise & Perils of Cyberdemocracy," American Enterprise, *March/April 1996, pp. 53–54. Reprinted with the permission of The American Enterprise Institute for Public Policy Research, Washington D.C.*

casting 50 percent of a vote and a random sampling of the public casting the other 50 percent. In this scenario, individuals will not only vote on more things than they do now, they'll vote on more complex questions, as simple yes/no votes are replaced by if-then referenda. Nor will voters have to inconvenience themselves by traveling to the local polling station. They probably won't even have to lick a stamp. Instead, voters will simply punch in their vote from their TV remote control, never leaving the house, never having to speak with another individual, not even having to spend more than a few seconds thinking about their choice.

Enchanting as these innovations may sound to Americans grown weary of Washington ways, several questions arise: Would cyberdemocracy in fact be more representative? Would voters take seriously their new responsibilities? Would they even be interested? Who will determine the exact questions the public will decide? And most importantly, what sort of deliberation, if any, will exist under this new regime?

A cyberdemocracy based on personal computers and upscale television systems will not be equally open to all citizens. Twenty-two percent of college graduates go on line at least weekly, while only 1 percent of those with a high school diploma do, a recent Times Mirror survey reports. Men are twice as likely as women to be daily on-line users. Twenty-seven percent of families with incomes of $50,000 or greater have gone on line, but only 6 percent of those with incomes under $20,000 have. Indeed, the Colorado Springs information systems manager reported that in 1995 there were only 250 active Citylink users in a city of over 300,000. No doubt the popularity of comparable information systems will increase substantially over time, and costs will come down, but a skew toward the highly educated and well-to-do is inevitable.

Even if the technology were made available to everyone equally, how would interest be sustained? Lloyd Morrisett, president of the Markle Foundation, recently wrote that he envisions the early fascination with cyberdemocracy ebbing until cybervoting falls into the same predicament as current voting rights: treasured but not necessarily used. Studying California's experience with referenda, Morrisett found that "the ballot has become so loaded with complex initiatives that it seems to discourage people from going to the polls, rather than motivating them to express their judgment." If the average voter tuned out complex items flashing across his screen, "voting" would be much less representative than it is today.

Cyberdemocracy's greatest danger lies in the way it would diminish deliberation in government. Everyone applauds technology's capacity to inform voters and to improve communications between them and their representatives. But we must also recall that the Founders expressly rejected "pure" democracies where citizens "assemble and administer the government in person," because they usually end in the tyranny of the majority. The Constitution instead establishes a republic where voters select representatives to make and execute the laws. The Founders designed this process to produce a public *judgment,* enlarging upon and refining popular opinions. That judgment, as opposed to public emotions, can only arise through deliberation. In the slow process of debate, give-and-take, and face-to-face contact among representatives, all perspectives and interests can be considered. The need to persuade an informed group of representatives with diverse concerns should, the Founders thought, result in decisions that are more just and more likely to meet the test of time with citizens.

Deliberation even figures in our political campaigns. Over weeks and months, campaigns provide a larger deliberative canvas, an opportunity for voters to consider issues, governing philosophies, and questions of leadership, resulting in a great appreciation of the choices that will face Congress and the President. Of course, our governing system does not always live up to the challenges of serious deliberation, but it still remains our foundation.

What happens to deliberation with the ascent of cyberdemocracy? Consider elections. For all the understandable criticism of never-ending campaigns, negative advertising, and demagoguery, campaigns still work, at least sometimes, as deliberative processes. Voters' initial inclination, not to mention their priorities on issues, often change as they receive more information. Early polls rarely reflect the actual voting. Citizens striving for informed judgments usually make them in the final, most intense days of a campaign. Instantaneous electronic voting would destroy whatever is left of this deliberative process. In Oregon most voters return their mail ballots within five days, casting their votes well before the final days (or even weeks) of intense campaigning.

Mail or electronic balloting also removes the symbolic quality of voting as an act where voters make a private judgment in a public place, surrounded by their fellow citizens, acknowledging simultaneously our individuality and our collective responsibility and common purpose. Compare standing in line at a polling place, going into a private booth, and making individual choices with the alternative of vote-by-mail—the political equivalent of filling out a Publishers Clearing House ballot—or electronic voting, where elections would resemble the Home Shopping Network.

Voting by mail or electronically is only one challenge cyberpolitics presents to deliberative democracy. Consider the difference between laws passed by referenda and laws passed in legislatures. Legislative deliberation encourages informed debate among somewhat-informed individuals with different interests. It allows a proposal to change, often dramatically, as it goes through the gantlet of hearings, floor debate, and amendment in both houses of Congress.

To be sure, some debate can occur during a state referendum campaign, through ads and media analysis, but that is no substitute for face-to-face debate involving not just two sides, but sometimes dozens or hundreds, reflected in representatives from various areas and constituencies. Mail or electronic balloting would short-circuit campaigns even further. And referenda have no amendment process, no matter how complex the issue. Their outcome relies on voters who have many other things to do besides study the issues, much less read the bills or provisions.

Could electronic town meetings provide a popular equivalent to traditional legislating? Theoretically, a broad mass of voters could be part of a different deliberative process. That's the thesis of political scientist James Fishkin, whose "deliberative poll" brought a random sample of 600 citizens together in late January [1996] at considerable expense for three days of expert-guided discussion in Austin, Texas. Even if the Fishkin experiment were scrupulously fair, such enterprises generally seem susceptible to undemocratic manipulation by "experts" and agenda-setters. And "deliberative polls" are unlikely to win out over the allure of a quick, trigger-like vote on the TV or computer. Cyberdemocratic meetings would likely turn into fancier versions of "Talk Back Live." And most deliberation would be reduced—as now in California and other initiative-prone states—to high-tech public relations campaigns by powerful interests with the re-sources to put their issues on the ballot—making for more special interest influence, not more democracy.

Cyberspace offers wonderful possibilities for citizens to discuss issues. New electronic alliances based on similar interests can be enjoyed. And every day, citizens and legisla-tors can download more information. But the combination of cynical distrust of politi-cal institutions, a rising tide of populism glorifying "pure" democracy, and the in-creased speed of information technology, is a highly dangerous one. While Newt Gingrich has benefited from the political cynicism and populism that drove voters in 1994, he knows the dangers facing deliberative democracy. As he told one of his col-lege classes, "Direct democracy says, Okay, how do we feel this week? We all raise our hand. Let's rush off and do it. The concept of republican representation, which is very clear in the Founding Fathers, is you hire somebody who you send to a central place. . . . They, by definition, learn things you don't learn, because you don't want to—you want to be able to live your life. They are supposed to use their judgment to represent you. . . . [The Founders] feared the passion of the moment."

Newt is right. But preserving the Founders' vision as the "third wave" of cy-bertechnology approaches won't be easy.

5

VOTING

Despite the fact that our population is better educated and faces fewer procedural impediments to voting than ever before, a significant portion of the American electorate does not participate in elections. Indeed, from 1960 through 1996 voting turnout in presidential elections declined some 14 percentage points, and the turnout figure of just over 49 percent in 1996 was the lowest in 72 years.

To many observers, these are alarming statistics. Low voter turnout, it is argued, is just one more sign of a general deterioration in the quality of political life in the United States as citizens increasingly opt out of the political system. Indeed, citizen trust in government is at an all-time low just as voting for president has slipped below the 50 percent mark.

Should we be alarmed by the decline in voting? In the selections below, two distinguished political commentators address this question. In the first selection, a former president of the American Political Science Association, Arend Lijphart, argues that low voter turnout is indeed a serious problem about which citizens ought to be concerned, for the level of voter participation has important implications for the legitimacy of government, as well as its policies. Indeed, so concerned is Lijphart about low voter turnout in the United States that he proposes what some might regard as a radical solution—compulsory voting.

The author of the second article, political scientist Austin Ranney, argues that we need not fear the fact that many persons choose not to vote. Ranney bases his argument on two main propositions: First, he contends that because voters and nonvoters do not differ significantly in policy and candidate preferences, no great harm is done to our system of representation if a sizable percentage of people do not vote; and second, nonvoting does not offend any basic democratic principle, for the right not to vote is every bit as precious as the right to vote.

Compulsory Voting Is the Best Way to Keep Democracy Strong

Arend Lijphart

Voting is the commonest and most basic way of participating in a democracy, but far too many citizens do not exercise their right to vote, especially in the United States. In the 1988 and 1992 Presidential elections, the turnout of registered voters was only 50 and 55 percent, respectively, and in the midterm Congressional elections in 1990 and 1994, it was only 33 and 36 percent. Four years later, the turnout in the Presidential election was 49 percent, while for the 1998 off-year Congressional election it was 36 percent.

This is a serious problem for two reasons. One is democratic legitimacy: Can a government that has gained power in a low-turnout election really claim to be a representative government? For instance, some Americans questioned President Clinton's mandate because he received only 43 percent of the votes cast and because only 55 percent of those registered to vote actually did so—which meant that he received the support of fewer than 25 percent of all eligible voters in 1992. The other, even more serious problem is that low turnout almost inevitably means that certain groups vote in greater numbers than other groups and hence gain disproportionate influence on the government and its policies.

The only way to solve these problems is to maximize turnout. It may not be realistic to expect everyone to vote, but a turnout of, say, 90 percent is a feasible goal, as the experience of quite a few democracies shows.

On the basis of studies ranging from the 1920s work of Harold F. Gosnell at the University of Chicago to the 1990s research of Robert W. Jackman of the University of California at Davis and Mark N. Franklin of the University of Houston, we know a great deal about the institutional mechanisms that can increase turnout. They include voter-friendly registration procedures; voting on the weekend instead of during the week; easy access to absentee ballots; proportional representation, with multiple lawmakers representing electoral districts instead of the current U.S. system of winner-takes-all elections; and scheduling as many elections as possible—national, state, and local—on the same day.

The evidence suggests that using all of these measures together can produce a voter turnout of around 90 percent. But adopting all of them is a tall order. Only a handful of states have even managed to introduce the minor reform of allowing citizens to register to vote on the same day as the election.

Fortunately, one other reform, by itself, can maximize turnout as effectively as all of the other methods combined: compulsory voting. In Australia, Belgium, Brazil,

Arend Lijphart is a professor of political science at the University of California at San Diego and a former president of the American Political Science Association. From "Compulsory Voting Is the Best Way to Keep Democracy Strong," The Chronicle of Higher Education, *October 18, 1996, B3–4.*

Greece, Italy, Venezuela, and several other Latin American democracies, mandatory voting has produced near-universal voter turnout.

It is somewhat surprising that making voting compulsory is so effective, because the penalties for failing to vote are typically minor, usually involving a fine roughly equal to that for a parking violation. Moreover, enforcement tends to be very lax; because of the large numbers of people involved, compulsory voting simply cannot be strictly enforced. (Parking rules tend to be enforced much more strictly.)

For instance, with 10 million eligible voters in Australia, even a typical turnout of 95 percent means that half a million people did not vote, and it obviously is not practical to issue such a large number of fines. Australia is actually among the strictest enforcers of compulsory voting, but even there, only about 4 percent of nonvoters end up having to pay the small fines. In Belgium, fewer than one-fourth of 1 percent of nonvoters are fined.

Mandatory-voting requirements produce large turnouts, however, even though a government technically cannot compel an actual vote. A government can require citizens to show up at the polls, or even to accept a ballot and then drop it into the ballot box, but it cannot require its citizens to cast a valid vote; secret ballots mean that nobody can be prevented from casting an invalid or blank one.

It is worth emphasizing why low voter turnout is such a serious problem for democracies—one that deserves our attention. Low turnout typically means that privileged citizens (those with better education and greater wealth) vote in significantly larger numbers than less-privileged citizens. This introduces a systematic bias in favor of well-off citizens, because, as the old adage has it, "If you don't vote, you don't count." The already-privileged citizens who vote are further rewarded with government policies favoring their interests.

The socio-economic bias in voter turnout is an especially strong pattern in the United States, where turnout is extremely low. In Presidential elections from 1952 to 1988, turnout among the college-educated was 26 percentage points higher than that among the population as a whole; the turnout for people without a high-school diploma was 16 percentage points lower. Unless turnout is very high—about 90 percent—socio-economic biases in voting tend to be a major problem. For instance, low and unequal voter turnout is a major reason why politicians find it so much easier to reduce government aid to the poor than to cut entitlement programs that chiefly benefit the middle class.

The low levels of voter turnout in the United States are often contrasted with turnouts as high as 95 percent in a few other countries. But when we measure turnout in other democracies in the way we usually measure it in the United States—as a percentage of *the voting-age population,* rather than as a percentage of *the registered electorate*—we find very few countries with turnouts above 90 percent, and most of those nations have compulsory voting. According to a study by G. Bingham Powell of the University of Rochester, half of the world's democracies have turnout levels below about 75 percent of the voting-age population. This half includes most of the larger democracies; not only the United States, but also Britain, France, Japan, and India, none of which require citizens to vote.

Even these figures cast turnouts in a deceptively favorable light, because they measure voting in what political scientists call first-order elections—that is, national-level parliamentary or presidential elections. But the vast majority of elections are second-order elections—for lesser posts—which attract less attention from citizens and lower turnouts. In the United States, only Presidential elections produce turnouts of more than 50 percent of the voting-age population; turnout in midterm Congressional elections has been only about 35 percent in recent years, and in local elections is closer to 25 percent.

Low turnout is typical for second-order elections in other countries, too. For local elections in Britain, it is only about 40 percent. Even in Australia, it is only about 35 percent, because voting at the local level is not mandatory, as it is for national elections. In the 1994 elections for the European Parliament, another example of a second-order contest, the average turnout in the 12 nations of the European Union was 58 percent. The power of mandatory voting is highlighted by the fact that when it is applied to local elections—as it is in all nations with compulsory voting except Australia—turnout levels are almost the same as those for presidential and parliamentary contests.

It is time that we paid more attention to the issue of voter turnout, because the already low levels of voting in many countries around the world are declining even more. In the United States, voting in Presidential elections has fallen to 50 to 55 percent of the voting-age population in the 1980s and '90s, from 60 to 65 percent during the 1950s and '60s. . . .

The biggest advantage of compulsory voting is that, by enhancing voter turnout, it equalizes participation and removes much of the bias against less-privileged citizens. It also has two other significant advantages. One is that mandatory voting can reduce the role of money in politics, since it does away with the need for candidates and political parties to spend large sums on getting voters to the polls. Second, it reduces the incentives for negative advertising.

As the political scientists Stephen Ansolabehere of the Massachusetts Institute of Technology and Shanto Iyengar of the University of California at Los Angeles have shown in *Going Negative: How Attack Ads Shrink and Polarize the Electorate* (Free Press, 1995), attack ads work—indeed, they work all too well. They are effective not because they persuade people to vote *for* the candidate making the attack and *against* the candidate attacked in the ads, but because they raise enough doubts in voters' minds that they decide not to vote at all. So the candidate making the attack has lowered his or her opponent's total vote.

Moreover, attack ads breed general distrust of politicians and cynicism about politics and government. Under mandatory voting, it would be so much harder for attack ads to depress turnout that I believe they would no longer be worth the effort.

The main objection to compulsory voting is that it violates the individual's freedom—the freedom not to vote. This was the main reason it was abolished in the Netherlands in 1970, for example. It is unlikely, however, that the Dutch would have made this decision had they foreseen the disastrous plunge in their voter turnouts, from about 90 percent in all elections to only 50 percent and 36 percent, respectively, in the most recent elections for provincial offices and for seats in the European Parliament.

In any case, the individual-freedom argument is extremely weak, because—as I've noted—compulsory voting does not actually require a citizen to cast a valid ballot. Besides, mandatory voting entails an extremely small decrease in freedom compared with many other, more onerous tasks that democracies require their citizens to perform, such as serving on juries, paying taxes, and serving in the military.

Some scholars argue that U.S. courts might rule compulsory voting unconstitutional because it restricts individual freedom. Richard L. Hasen, of the Chicago-Kent College of Law at the Illinois Institute of Technology, . . . has argued, in "Voting Without Law?" (*University of Pennsylvania Law Review,* May 1996), that the only plausible ground for such a ruling would be the First Amendment's guarantee of freedom of speech. But the Supreme Court has explicitly rejected the notion that voting can be regarded as a form of speech. For instance, in 1992, in *Burdick v. Takushi,* the Court upheld Hawaii's ban on write-in votes, ruling against a voter's claim that the ban deprived him of the right to cast a protest vote for Donald Duck. The Court said an election is about choosing representatives, not about expressing oneself. Of course, even if mandatory voting were to be found unconstitutional, a constitutional amendment permitting it could be adopted—a difficult, but not impossible, prospect.

Probably the most important practical obstacle to compulsory voting in countries that do not have it is the opposition of conservative parties, like the Republican Party in the United States. High turnout is clearly not in their partisan self-interest, because unequal turnout favors privileged voters, who tend to be conservative. But conservative parties generally were also opposed to universal suffrage, which eventually was accepted by all democracies, because it was recognized to be a basic democratic principle. Compulsory voting should be seen as an extension of universal suffrage—which we now all take for granted.

Nonvoting Is Not a Social Disease

Austin Ranney

In 1980 only 53 percent of the voting-age population in the United States voted for president, and in 1982 only 38 percent voted for members of the House. [The 1996 presidential election turnout was 49 percent; the 1994 congressional election turnout was 37 percent—*Editors.*] As the statistics are usually presented, this rate is, on the average, from 10 to 40 points lower than in the democratic nations of Western Europe, Scandinavia, and the British Commonwealth—although such numbers involve major technical problems of which we should be aware.[1] We also know that the level of voter participation has [declined] since the early 1960s.

All forms of *in*voluntary nonvoting—caused by either legal or extralegal impediments—are violations of the most basic principles of democracy and fairness. Clearly it is a bad thing if citizens who want to vote are prevented from doing so by law or intimidation. But what about *voluntary* nonvoters—the 30 percent or so of our adult citizens who *could* vote if they were willing to make the (usually minimal) effort, but who rarely or never do so? What does it matter if millions of Americans who could vote choose not to?

We should begin by acknowledging that suffrage and voting laws, extralegal force, and intimidation account for almost none of the nonvoting. A number of constitutional amendments, acts of Congress, and court decisions since the 1870s—particularly since the mid-1960s—have outlawed all legal and extralegal denial of the franchise to African-Americans, women, Hispanics, people over the age of 18, and other groups formerly excluded. Moreover, since the mid-1960s most states have changed their registration and voting laws to make casting ballots a good deal easier. Many states, to be sure, still demand a somewhat greater effort to register than is required by other democratic countries. But the best estimates are that even if we made our voting procedures as undemanding as those in other democracies, we would raise our average turnouts by only nine or so percentage points. That would still leave our voter participation level well below that of all but a handful of the world's democracies, and far below what many people think is the proper level for a healthy democracy.

Throughout our history, but especially in recent years, many American scholars, public officials, journalists, civic reformers, and other people of good will have pondered our low level of voting participation and have produced a multitude of studies, articles, books, pamphlets, manifestoes, and speeches stating their conclusions. On one

Austin Ranney is professor emeritus of political science at the University of California–Berkeley and a former president of the American Political Science Association. This selection was adapted from a paper delivered to the ABC/Harvard Symposium on Voter Participation on October 1, 1983. From Austin Ranney, "Nonvoting Is Not a Social Disease," Public Opinion, October/November 1983, pp. 16–19. Reprinted with permission of American Enterprise Institute for Public Policy Research, Washington, D.C.

point they agree: All start from the premise that voluntary, as well as involuntary, nonvoting is a bad thing for the country and seek ways to discourage it. Yet, despite the critical importance of the question, few ask *why* voluntary nonvoting is a bad thing.

Voluntary nonvoting's bad name stems from one or a combination of three types of arguments or assumptions. Let us consider these arguments in turn.

WHAT HARM DOES IT DO?

One of the most often-heard charges against nonvoting is that it produces unrepresentative bodies of public officials. After all, the argument runs, if most of the middle-class WASPs vote and most of the African-Americans, Hispanics, and poor people do not, then there will be significantly lower proportions of African-Americans, Hispanics, and poor people in public office than in the general population. Why is that bad? For two reasons. First, it makes the public officials, in political theorist Hanna Pitkin's term, "descriptively unrepresentative." And while not everyone would argue that the interests of African-Americans are best represented by African-American officials, the interests of women by women officials, and so on, many people believe that the policy preferences of the underrepresented groups will get short shrift from the government. Second, this not only harms the underrepresented groups but weakens the whole polity, for the underrepresented are likely to feel that the government cares nothing for them and they owe no loyalty to it. Hence it contributes greatly to the underclasses' feelings of alienation from the system and to the lawlessness that grows from such alienation.

This argument seems plausible enough, but a number of empirical studies comparing voters with nonvoters do not support it. They find that the distributions of policy preferences among nonvoters are approximately the same as those among voters, and therefore the pressures on public officials by constituents for certain policies and against others are about the same as they would be if everyone, WASPs and minorities, voted at the same rate.

Moreover, other studies have shown that the level of cynicism about the government's honesty, competence, and responsiveness is about the same among nonvoters as among voters, and an increased level of nonvoting does not signify an increased level of alienation or lawlessness. We can carry the argument a step further by asking if levels of civic virtue are clearly higher and levels of lawlessness lower in Venezuela (94 percent average voting turnout), Austria (94 percent), and Italy (93 percent) than in the United States (58 percent), Switzerland (64 percent), and Canada (76 percent). If the answer is no, as surely it is, then at least we have to conclude that there is no clear or strong relationship between high levels of voting turnout and high levels of civic virtue.

Another argument concerns future danger rather than present harm to the Republic. Journalist Arthur Hadley asserts that our great and growing number of "refrainers" (his term for voluntary nonvoters) constitutes a major threat to the future stability of our political system. In his words:

> These growing numbers of refrainers hang over the democratic process like a bomb, ready to explode and change the course of our history as they have twice in our past. . . . Both times in our history when there have been large numbers of refrainers,

sudden radical shifts of power have occurred. As long as the present gigantic mass of refrainers sits outside of our political system, neither we nor our allies can be certain of even the normally uncertain future. This is why creating voters, bringing the re-frainers to the booth, is important.

Hadley's argument assumes that if millions of the present nonvoters suddenly voted in some future election, they would vote for persons, parties, and policies radically different from those chosen by the regular voters. He asserts that that is what happened in 1828 and again in 1932, and it could happen again any time. Of course, some might feel that a sudden rush to the polls that produces another Andrew Jackson or Franklin Roosevelt is something to be longed for, not feared, but in any case his assumption is highly dubious. We have already noted that the policy preferences of nonvoters do not differ greatly from those of voters, and much the same is true of their candidate preferences. For example, a leading study of the 1980 presidential election found that the five lowest voting groups were African-Americans, Hispanics, whites with family incomes below $5,000 a year, whites with less than high school educations, and working-class white Catholics. The study concluded that if all five groups had voted at the same rate as the electorate as a whole, they would have added only about one-and-a-half percentage points to Carter's share of the vote, and Reagan would still have been elected with a considerable margin. So Hadley's fear seems, at the least, highly exaggerated.

WHAT SOCIAL SICKNESS DOES NONVOTING MANIFEST?

Some writers take the position that, while a high level of voluntary nonvoting may not in itself do harm to the nation's well-being, it is certainly a symptom of poor civic health. Perhaps they take their inspiration from Pericles, who, in his great funeral oration on the dead of Marathon, said:

> . . . Our ordinary citizens, though occupied with the pursuits of industry, are still fair judges of public matters; for, unlike any other nation, regarding him who takes no part in these duties not as unambitious but as useless. . . .

One who holds a 20th-century version of that view is likely to believe that our present level of voluntary nonvoting is a clear sign that millions of Americans are civically useless—that they are too lazy, too obsessed with their own selfish affairs and interests, and too indifferent to the welfare of their country and the quality of their government to make even the minimum effort required to vote. A modern Pericles might ask, How can such a nation hope to defend itself in war and advance the public welfare in peace? Are not the lassitude and indifference manifested by our high level of nonvoting the root cause of our country's declining military strength and economic productivity as well as the growing corruption and bungling of our government?

Perhaps so, perhaps not. Yet the recent studies of nonvoters have shown that they do not differ significantly from voters in the proportions who believe that citizens have a civic duty to vote or in the proportions who believe that ordinary people have a real say in what government does. It may be that nonvoters are significantly less patriotic citizens, poorer soldiers, and less productive workers than voters, but there is no evidence to support such charges. And do we accept the proposition that the much higher turnout rates for the Austrians, the French, and the Irish show that they are significantly better on any or all of these counts than the Americans? If not, then clearly there is no compelling reason to believe that a high level of nonvoting is, by itself, a symptom of sickness in American society.

WHAT BASIC PRINCIPLES DOES IT OFFEND?

I have asked friends and colleagues whether they think that the high level of voluntary nonvoting in America really matters. Almost all of them believe that it does, and when I ask them why they usually reply not so much in terms of some harm it does or some social illness it manifests but rather in terms of their conviction that the United States of America is or should be a democracy, and that a high level of voluntary nonvoting offends some basic principles of democracy.

Their reasoning goes something like this: The essential principle of democratic government is government by the people, government that derives its "just powers from the consent of the governed." The basic institution for ensuring truly democratic government is the regular holding of free elections at which the legitimate authority of public officials to govern is renewed or terminated by the sovereign people. Accordingly, the right to vote is the basic right of every citizen in a democracy, and the exercise of that right is the most basic duty of every democratic citizen.

Many have made this argument. For example, in 1963 President John F. Kennedy appointed an 11-member Commission on Registration and Voting Participation. Its report, delivered after his death, began:

> Voting in the United States is the fundamental act of self-government. It provides the citizen in our free society the right to make a judgment, to state a choice, to participate in the running of his government. . . . The ballot box is the medium for the expression of the consent of the governed.

In the same vein the British political philosopher Sir Isaiah Berlin declares, "Participation in self-government is, like justice, a basic human requirement, *an end in itself.*"

If these views are correct, then any nominal citizen of a democracy who does not exercise this basic right and fulfill this basic duty is not a full citizen, and the larger the proportion of such less-than-full citizens in a polity that aspires to democracy, the greater the gap between the polity's low realities and democracy's high ideals.

Not everyone feels this way, of course. The late Senator Sam Ervin, for example, argues:

> I'm not going to shed any real or political or crocodile tears if people don't care enough to vote. I don't believe in making it easy for apathetic, lazy people. I'd be extremely happy if nobody in the United States voted except for the people who thought about the issues and made up their own minds and wanted to vote. No one else who votes is going to contribute anything but statistics, and I don't care that much for statistics.

The issues between these two positions are posed most starkly when we consider proposals for compulsory voting. After all, if we are truly convinced that voluntary nonvoting is a violation of basic democratic principles, and a major social ill, then why not follow the lead of Australia, Belgium, Italy, and Venezuela and enact laws *requiring* people to vote and penalizing them if they do not?

The logic seems faultless, and yet most people I know, including me, are against compulsory voting laws for the United States. All of us want to eradicate all vestiges of *in*voluntary nonvoting, and many are disturbed by the high level of voluntary nonvoting. Yet many of us also feel that the right to abstain is just as precious as the right to vote, and the idea of legally compelling all citizens to vote whether they want to or not is at least as disturbing as the large numbers of Americans who now and in the future probably will not vote without some compulsion.

THE BRIGHT SIDE

In the light of the foregoing considerations, then, how much should we worry about the high level of voluntary nonvoting in our country? At the end of his magisterial survey of voting turnout in different democratic nations, Ivor Crewe asks this question and answers, "There are . . . reason[s] for *not* worrying—too much."

I agree. While we Americans can and probably should liberalize our registration and voting laws and mount register-and-vote drives sponsored by political parties, civic organizations, schools of government, and broadcasting companies, the most we can realistically hope for from such efforts is a modest increase of 10 or so percentage points in our average turnouts. As a college professor and political activist for 40 years, I can testify that even the best reasoned and most attractively presented exhortations to people to behave like good democratic citizens can have only limited effects on their behavior, and most get-out-the-vote drives by well-intentioned civic groups in the past have had disappointingly modest results.

An even more powerful reason not to worry, in my judgment, is that we are likely to see a major increase in our voting turnouts to, say, the 70 or 80 percent levels, only if most of the people in our major nonvoting groups—African-Americans, Hispanics, and poor people—come to believe that voting is a powerful instrument for getting the government to do what they want it to do. The . . . register-and-vote drives by the NAACP and other African-American-mobilization organizations have already had significant success in getting formerly inactive African-American citizens to the polls. . . . Organizations like the Southern Voter Registration Education Project have had some success with Hispanic nonvoters in Texas and New Mexico and may have more. Jesse Helms and Jerry Falwell may also have success in their . . . efforts to urge more conservatives to register and vote. But hard evidence that voting brings real benefits, not exhortations to be good citizens, will be the basis of whatever success any of these groups enjoy.

If we Americans stamp out the last vestiges of institutions and practices that produce *in*voluntary nonvoting, and if we liberalize our registration and voting laws and procedures to make voting here as easy as it is in other democracies, and if the group-mobilization movements succeed, then perhaps our level of voting participation may become much more like that of Canada or Great Britain. (It is unlikely ever to match the levels in the countries with compulsory voting or even those in West Germany or the Scandinavian countries.)

But even if that does not happen, we need not fear that our low voting turnouts are doing any serious harm to our politics or our country, or that they deprive us of the right to call ourselves a democracy.

NOTE

1. European and American measures of voting and nonvoting differ significantly. In all countries the numerator for the formula is the total number of votes cast in national elections. In most countries the denominator is the total number of persons on the electoral rolls—that is, people we would call "registered voters"—which includes almost all people legally eligible to vote. In the United States, on the other hand, the denominator is the "voting-age population," which is the estimate by the Bureau of the Census of the number of people in the country who are 18 or older at the time of the election. That figure, unlike its European counterpart, includes aliens and inmates of prisons and mental hospitals as well as persons not registered to vote. One eminent election analyst, Richard M. Scammon, estimates that if voting turnout in the United States were computed by the same formula as that used for European countries, our average figures would rise by 8 to 10 percentage points, a level that would exceed Switzerland's and closely approach those of Canada, Ireland, Japan, and the United Kingdom.

6
CAMPAIGNS AND THE MEDIA

Probably nothing has so revolutionized American politics as the emergence of television as the principal means of communicating with the voters. What used to be the experience of only a few people—hearing and seeing a candidate at a campaign rally, for example—is now an experience shared by many millions of Americans. Because television enables political candidates to be seen and heard in every living room in the country, it is no wonder that politicians devote so much time and so many resources to producing television advertisements and other political programming.

The advent of TV advertising also has led to shorter and shorter campaign spots, in which candidates in 30-second or shorter sound and picture bites "bash" their opponents or attempt to communicate key word messages to the sometimes uninformed, unsuspecting, and undecided voters. These political advertisements are most often referred to as "negative ads," but they need not be.

The 30-second campaign TV spot has prompted a great deal of attention from both political scientists and the popular press. One of the more serious and thoughtful critics of the current mode of TV political advertising is political scientist Darrell M. West, a professor at Brown University and the author of Air Wars, *an important book on campaign advertising. Portions of Professor West's book are reprinted as the first selection in this chapter. West argues that today's TV ads are harmful not only because they frequently misrepresent candidates' views but also because they tend to be divisive, often emphasizing issues that pit one social group (racial, gender, economic) against another. Although West does not believe that we should do away with such ads, he argues that the mass media ought to serve as the "watchdog" of campaign ads, holding the sponsors of such ads to ever-stricter standards of truth and honesty.*

Still, there are those who defend TV spots and argue that political ads actually are highly useful. Such a point of view is presented by the authors of our second selection—Stephen Bates and Edwin Diamond. Bates and Diamond, while recognizing that TV spots have their negative aspects, are not convinced that such spots are as bad as the critics allege. Indeed, they see such ads as contributing greatly to political "discourse," leaving the voter better informed than would otherwise be the case. To Bates and Diamond, then, reforming TV campaigns spots is like trying to remove politics from campaigns. TV is the modern medium of politics; it cannot and should not be "turned off" for the sake of satisfying the critics.

Advertising and Democratic Elections
What Can Be Done?

Darrell M. West

DIFFERENT ARENAS, DIFFERENT THREATS

The susceptibility of voters to advertising appeals has long generated despair from po-litical observers. McGinniss's book, *The Selling of the President,* and Spero's volume, *The Duping of the American Voter,* express common fears about the dangers of adver-tisements.[1] But these authors failed to recognize that not all electoral arenas are subject to the same threat. The visibility of the setting makes a big difference.

The major threat in highly visible arenas, such as presidential general election cam-paigns, is substantive manipulation. The 1988 general election gave a textbook illustra-tion of this danger, as the relatively unknown Dukakis saw his entire campaign shat-tered by Bush's successful efforts to move the campaign from past performance to flags, furloughs, and patriotism. Bush used advertising on tax and spending matters as well as crime that year to fill in the public profile of the relatively unknown Dukakis. The vice president was able to dominate the campaign because few voters knew much about the Massachusetts governor, 1988 was a year with a fluid policy agenda, and Dukakis did not successfully defend himself. Bush painted a portrait of the Massachusetts governor that many observers considered grossly exaggerated; Bush pictured an unrepentant lib-eral who was soft on crime and out of touch with the American people. Combined with uncritical coverage for the media, Bush's ads in this election had consequences that were both substantial and quite disturbing.

Less visible electoral arenas, such as presidential nomination campaigns, are more vulnerable to strategic manipulation. Because they are less visible contests that are heavily influenced by campaign dynamics, they contain fewer of the countervailing forces than are present in presidential general elections. Democrats compete against Democrats and Republicans against Republicans in a sequential nominating process.[2] In this situation, party identification is not central to vote choice. The setting limits the power of long-term forces and makes it possible for short-term factors, such as adver-tising and media coverage, to dominate.

Senate races share some features with nominating races. These contests are sus-ceptible to ad appeals because relatively unknown candidates compete in races that resemble roller-coaster rides. There often are wild swings in electoral fortunes during the course of the campaign. The absence of prior beliefs about the candidates makes

Darrell M. West is professor of political science at Brown University. From Darrell M. West, "Advertising and Democratic Elections," Air Wars: Television Advertising in Election Campaigns, 1952–1992 *(Washington, D.C.: Congressional Quarterly, 1993), pp. 154–60. Reprinted with the permission of Congressional Quarterly, Inc. Notes have been renumbered to correspond with edited text.*

advertising influential.³ It is easier to create a new political profile (for yourself or the opponent) than to alter a well-defined image. Candidates who are the least known are the most able to use advertisements to influence the public. But they also are the most susceptible to having an opponent create an unfair image of themselves through television.

SLICING AND DICING THE ELECTORATE

Campaign advertisements also pose problems for democratic elections on the systemic level. Even if ads influence voting behavior only in certain circumstances, they have consequences for the way in which the campaign is viewed. Advertisements are one of the primary means of communication, and much of how people feel about the electoral system is a product of how campaign battles are contested.

In contemporary elections it is common for political consultants to divide voters into advertising segments based on public opinion polls and focus groups: the committed (those who are for you), the hopeless (those who are against you and about whom little can be done), and the undecided (those who could vote either way). The last group, of course, is the central target of campaign tactics.

Ads are developed to stir the hopes and fears of the 20 to 30 percent of the electorate that is undecided, not the 70 to 80 percent that is committed or hopeless. Narrow pockets of support are identified and targeted appeals are made. Many Americans complain that campaign discussions do not reflect their concerns. Their complaints are legitimate. With advertising appeals designed for the small group of voters who are undecided, it is little wonder many voters feel left out.

In this system of segmentation and targeted appeals, candidates have clear incentives to identify pockets of potential support and find issues that will move these voters. Whether it is the backlash against affirmative action among white rural dwellers in North Carolina (one of the winning issues for [U.S. Senator Jesse] Helms in 1990) or Bush's attacks on Clinton for his 1969 antiwar demonstrations (which did not save the election for Bush), the current electoral system encourages candidates to find divisive issues that pit social group against social group.

It is not surprising in this situation that Americans feel bad at the end of election campaigns. Candidates engage in an electronic form of civil war not unlike what happens in divided societies. The battleground issues often touch on race, lifestyle, and gender, which are among the most contentious topics in America. Ads and sound bites are the weapons of choice in these confrontations.

The long-run dangers from the electronic air wars are ill feelings and loss of a sense of community. Bill Clinton addressed these fears in his [1992] nomination acceptance speech. Long before his patriotism had been challenged, Clinton warned about the danger of divisiveness and the importance of community: "The New Covenant is about more than opportunities and responsibilities for you and your families. It's also about our common community. Tonight every one of you knows deep in your heart that we are too divided. It is time to heal America. . . . Look beyond the stereotypes that blind us. We need each other . . . this is America. There is no them. There is only us."⁴

WHAT CAN BE DONE?

The controversies that have arisen concerning television commercials have generated heartfelt pleas for fundamental changes in U.S. campaigns. Following the example of Australia, and until recently West Germany, some have called for an outright ban on televised campaign ads in the United States. Others have suggested the application of the rule followed in France, where ads are banned during the closing weeks of the campaign.[5] These calls undoubtedly reflect deep frustration over the uses of advertisements in the United States.[6] But it is far too simple to blame ads for electoral deficiencies. The problem of political commercials is as much a function of campaign structure and voters' reactions as of candidates' behavior. Structural and attitudinal changes have loosened the forces that used to restrain elite strategies. The rise of a mass-based campaign system at a time when candidates have powerful means of influencing viewers rewards media-centered campaigns.

At the same time, voters are vulnerable to candidates' messages because the forces that used to provide social integration have lost their influence. Intermediary organizations no longer organize political reality. Consensus has broken down on key domestic and foreign policy questions. Voters are bombarded with spot ads precisely because of their proven short-term effectiveness, as has been evident in recent races.

Recent court rulings make an outright ban on campaign commercials unlikely. Most court decisions have treated candidates' expenditures on advertisements as tantamount to free speech.[7] Since ads are a form of expression, they are subject to constitutional protection and are thereby quite difficult to restrict. Most attempts at direct regulation have been resisted as unconstitutional encroachments upon free speech.[8] Self-monitoring efforts, such as those proposed by the National Association of Political Consultants, are of limited value.

However, there is an informal mechanism in the advertising area which when combined with regulatory reform, promises more success: the media. In the case of candidates' advertising, government regulation clearly would be inadequate without direct and effective media oversight. Reporters have the power to make or break the regulation of advertising by how they cover spot commercials.

For example, follow-up reporting by the news media would enable viewers to link ad sponsorship to responsibility. Journalists who aggressively focused on negative commercials would help the public hold candidates accountable for ads that crossed the threshold of acceptability. This attention would alter the strategic environment of campaigns and create clear disincentives for the excessive or unfair use of attack ads.

Currently, advertising coverage falls far short of what would be needed to uphold democratic elections. Reporters devote plenty of attention to candidates' ads, but not necessarily in a way that furthers citizens' knowledge. They are more likely, for example, to use ads to discuss the horse race than the policy views of the candidates.

But with a different approach to ad coverage, television could become an enlightening force in American elections. Journalists in the United States have an unusually high credibility with the public. American reporters are seen as being more fair and trustworthy than in other countries. A recent comparative study of five countries illustrates this point. Whereas 69 percent of the Americans surveyed had great confidence in the media, only 41 percent of Germans and 38 percent of the British gave high ratings to journalists.[9]

What is needed in the United States is a "truth in political advertising" code which would feature a prominent oversight role for the media. Both [Kathleen Hall] Jamieson and David Broder have suggested that journalists should exercise their historic function of safeguarding the integrity of the election process.[10] The media could use their high public credibility to improve the functioning of the political system.

There are several tenets to this code that would improve the quality of electoral discourse. Reporters must use Ad Watches to evaluate the accuracy of candidates' claims. Candidates periodically make exaggerated claims in their efforts to win votes. Journalists need to look into their claims and report to voters on their accuracy. The 1992 race was notable because journalists made detailed assessments of candidates' claims. Newspapers routinely printed the text of commercials in Ad Watches, with sentence-by-sentence evaluations of their honesty. In addition, television reporters reviewed videos of commercials with an eye toward false claims, exaggerated promises, or unrealistic commitments.[11]

These efforts are valuable, but journalists must go beyond fact checking to true oversight. Commercials have become the major strategic tool for the contesting of American elections. Candidates devote the largest portion of their overall campaign budgets to advertising. Their ads feature their own appeals as well as comments about their opposition. Arbitrators are needed to ensure that ads are not misused and that the electronic battle is fought fairly. Almost every election now features claims and counter claims regarding the fairness of television ads. Voters are not usually in a position to assess these claims, and the Federal Election Commission has chosen not to adjudicate them.

The media are left with the responsibility to expose manipulation, distortion, and deception, not just inaccurate use of facts. Candidates who exceed the boundaries of fair play should be brought to task by reporters. Unfair tactics or misleading editing needs to be publicized. Commercials that engage in obvious appeals to racism, for example, should be condemned. Media pressure could protect the airwaves, as happened when the "Daisy" ad was condemned in 1964. [The "Daisy" ad showed a nuclear bomb explosion superimposed on a young girl holding a daisy. The ad was directed at the so-called reckless policy statements on nuclear weapons by the Republican candidate for president, Barry Goldwater. The ad was withdrawn after severe criticism.—*Editors*]

Television has a special obligation because it is the medium through which most Americans receive their political news. The Cable News Network pioneered the Ad Watch technique of broadcasting the spot in a smaller square on the side of the screen so that the ad would not overpower the analysis. This valuable innovation should become a model for the rest of the electronic media.

Aggressive Ad Watches are especially important in spots involving race, lifestyle issues, gender, or other topics with emotional overtones.[12] The danger in focusing on such commercials is that viewers will remember the candidate's message, not the critique. Since ads on "hot button" issues using well-recognized codewords are becoming quite common, reporters need to check candidates' messages to limit manipulatory appeals.

These actions will help protect the integrity of the electoral process. Reporters are the only major group with the credibility vis-à-vis the American public to arbitrate electoral advertising. In fact, a 1985 Gallup poll revealed that citizens would like the media to undertake an aggressive watchdog role.[13] Government regulators at the Federal Communications Commission or the Federal Election Commission would not be as effective in such a role. Nor would political elites be seen as credible because they are associated with partisan politics.

There is some danger for the media in openly assuming this role. Many Americans already are concerned about what they believe is excessive influence and bias on the part of the news media.[14] If journalists aggressively challenge candidates' statements, they may be viewed as part of the problem rather than the solution. There are increasing signs of a backlash against the media, and reporters could become subject to more stringent criticism regarding their overall influence and objectivity.

In 1991, for example, Louisiana gubernatorial candidate [David] Duke tried to foster antipathy to the media through a last-minute ad directly criticizing coverage of his campaign: "Have you ever heard such weeping and gnashing of teeth? The news media have given up any pretense of fair play. The liberals have gone ballistic. The special interests have gone mad. The politicians who play up to them are lining up on cue. Principles lie abandoned and hypocrisy rules the day. I raise issues that must be discussed, and get back venom instead. Try a little experiment. Next time you hear them accuse me of intolerance and hatred, notice who is doing the shouting."[15] Bush also attempted to build support for his 1992 reelection in his slogan: "Annoy the media: re-elect Bush."

Local surveys conducted in Los Angeles during the fall 1992 race revealed that 44 percent rated the media as having done a fair or poor job of covering the presidential campaign while 54 percent thought the media had done an excellent or good job. In the fall campaign, 43 percent felt reporters had been biased against particular candidates and 49 percent said they had not been. When asked to identify which campaigner had received the most biased coverage, 43 percent named Bush, 32 percent named Clinton, 21 percent named Perot, and 4 percent cited other candidates. Content analysis from the Center for Media and Public Affairs reveals that Bush earned the highest percentage of negative comments (71 percent) from network evening newscasts, compared with Clinton (48 percent) and Perot (55 percent). The content analysis also fits with evidence that reporters were more likely to report Democratic leanings in 1992 than in earlier years.[16]

Despite the drawbacks, oversight by the media is vital enough to the political system to warrant the risk of backlash. The quality of information presented during elections is important enough to outweigh the practical difficulties facing the fourth estate. Nothing is more central to democratic elections than electoral discourse. Without informative material, voters have little means of holding leaders accountable or engaging in popular consent.[17] By encouraging candidates to address the substantive concerns of the electorate, media watchdogs will raise the caliber of the political process and help voters make meaningful choices.

NOTES

1. Joe McGinniss, *The Selling of the President* (New York: Simon and Schuster, 1969); and Robert Spero, *The Duping of the American Voter* (New York: Lippincott and Crowell, 1980).
2. J. Gregory Payne, John Marlier, and Robert Baukus, "Polispots in the 1988 Presidential Primaries," *American Behavioral Scientist* 32 (1989): 375.
3. Where strong prior beliefs are present, the danger of advertising goes down dramatically. But, of course, in a rapidly changing world where traditional moorings are disappearing—witness the collapse of communism on the world scene—even prior assumptions are being challenged. For a discussion of constraints on ad influence, see Elizabeth Kolbert, "Ad Effect on Vote Slipping," *New York Times,* March 22, 1992, "Week in Review," 4.
4. The Clinton quote comes from the text of his acceptance speech as printed in *Congressional Quarterly Weekly Report,* July 18, 1992, 2130.
5. Klaus Schoenbach, "The Role of Mass Media in West German Election Campaigns," *Legislative Studies Quarterly* 12 (1987): 373–94. For a review of the experience of other countries, see Howard Penniman and Austin Ranney, "The Regulation of Televised Political Advertising in Six Selected Democracies" (Paper prepared for the Committee for the Study of the American Electorate, Washington, D.C., undated).
6. Critics have also complained about the effectiveness of ad targeting on underage youths by tobacco companies. Research reported in the December 11, 1991, issue of the *Journal of the American Medical Association* has shown that the cartoon figure Old Joe Camel, used to advertise Camel cigarettes, has been a huge hit among youths aged twelve to nineteen years. Compared with adults in general, students were much more likely to indicate that they recognized Old Joe, liked him as a friend, and thought the ads looked cool. See Walecia Konrad, "I'd Toddle a Mile for a Camel," *Business Week,* December 23, 1991, 34.
7. The classic Supreme Court ruling in the campaign area was *Buckley v. Valeo* in 1976. This case struck down a number of finance regulations as unconstitutional encroachments. See Clarke Caywood and Ivan Preston, "The Continuing Debate on Political Advertising: Toward a Jeopardy Theory of Political Advertising as Regulated Speech," *Journal of Public Policy and Marketing* 8 (1989): 204–26. For other reviews of newly emerging technologies, see Jeffrey Abramson, Christopher Arterton, and Gary Orren, *The Electronic Commonwealth* (New York: Basic Books, 1988), and Erwin Krasnow, Lawrence Longley, and Herbert Terry, *The Politics of Broadcast Regulation,* 3d ed. (New York: St. Martin's, 1982).
8. A more extended discussion of reform proposals can be found in Darrell West, "Reforming Campaign Ads," *PS: Political Science and Politics* 24 (1992): 74–77.
9. Laurence Parisot, "Attitudes about the Media: A Five-Country Comparison," *Public Opinion* 10 (1988): 18–19, 60. However, viewers do see differences in the helpfulness of television and newspapers. A May 1992 survey of Los Angeles residents revealed that those who followed Ad Watches in newspapers were much more

likely (35 percent) to see them as being very helpful than those who relied on television (16 percent).

10. Kathleen Hall Jamieson, "For Televised Mendacity, This Year Is the Worst Ever," *Washington Post,* October 30, 1988, C1; and David Broder, "Five Ways to Put Some Sanity Back in Elections," *Washington Post,* January 14, 1990, B1.

11. Media scholar Jamieson has been instrumental in encouraging these Ad Watch efforts. According to personal correspondence from her, 42 campaigns in 1990 were subjected to detailed critiques. For example, television stations airing discussions of particular ads included WFAA in Dallas, KVUE in Austin, WCVB in Boston, KRON in San Francisco, WBBM in Chicago, and WCCO in Minneapolis. Newspapers that followed ad campaigns closely were the *New York Times, Washington Post, Los Angeles Times, Chicago Sun-Times, Dallas Morning News, Houston Chronicle, Cleveland Plain-Dealer, Akron Beacon-Journal,* and *Louisville Courier-Journal.*

12. Race, of course, has been a controversial subject in many areas of American life. For a discussion of controversial rapper Ice Cube, see Craig McCoy, "Korean-American Merchants Claim Victory against Rapper Ice Cube," *Boston Globe,* November 28, 1991, A35. Also see Edward Carmines and James Stimson, *Issue Evolution: Race and the Transformation of American Politics* (Princeton: Princeton University Press, 1989).

13. Quoted by Kathleen Jamieson and Karlyn Kohrs Campbell in *The Interplay of Influence,* 2d ed. (Belmont, Calif.: Wadsworth, 1988), 55.

14. For an example of this thinking, see L. Brent Bozell and Brent Baker, eds., *And That's the Way It Isn't* (Alexandria, Va.: Media Research Center, 1990). Also see Lynda Lee Kaid, Rob Gobetz, Jane Garner, Chris Leland, and David Scott, "Television News and Presidential Campaigns: The Legitimization of Televised Political Advertising," *Social Science Quarterly* 74 (June 1993), 274–85, and Elizabeth Kolbert, "As Political Campaigns Turn Negative, the Press Is Given a Negative Rating," *New York Times,* May 1, 1992, A18.

15. Text is quoted from Robert Suro, "In Louisiana, Both Edwards and Duke Are Sending a Message of Fear," New York Times, November 15, 1991, A20.

16. The media rating was in response to an October 1992 question in our Los Angeles County survey: "So far this year, would you say the news media have done an excellent, good, fair, or poor job of covering this presidential campaign?" The press bias question also was asked in the October survey: "In your opinion, has news coverage of this year's fall presidential campaign been biased against any individual candidate? If so, which candidate received the most biased coverage?" The figures on television coverage come from Howard Kurtz, "Networks Stressed the Negative in Comments about Bush, Study Finds," *Washington Post,* November 15, 1992, A7. The longitudinal evidence on the party leanings of reporters is discussed by William Glaberson in "More Reporters Leaning Democratic, Study Says," *New York Times,* November 18, 1992, A20. Also see Elizabeth Kolbert, "Maybe the Media Did Treat Bush a Bit Harshly," *New York Times,* November 22, 1992, "Week in Review," 3.

17. Jeffrey Tulis, *The Rhetorical Presidency* (Princeton: Princeton University Press, 1987).

Damned Spots
A Defense of Thirty-Second Campaign Ads

Stephen Bates and Edwin Diamond

. . . [E]veryone denounc[es] 30-second spots as demeaning, manipulative, and responsible for all that's wrong with American politics. David Broder, the mandarin of the op-ed page, admits he's "a crank on the subject." Otherwise staunch First Amendment champions, including *Washington Monthly* and, yes, *The New Republic,* want Congress to restrict the content of political ads. In fact, such commercials are good for the campaign, the voter, and the republic.

To cite the most common complaints:

1. TV Spots Make Campaigns Too Expensive.   The problem is nearly as old as television itself. William Benton, an ad-agency founder and a U.S. senator from Connecticut, talked of the "terrifying" cost of TV back in 1952. Campaign spending has risen sharply since then, and television advertising has contributed disproportionately. Whereas total political spending, adjusted for inflation, has tripled since 1952, the amount spent on television has increased at least fivefold. In some races, nine out of ten campaign dollars go to TV.

The important question is what candidates get in return. Quite a lot: a dollar spent on TV advertising may reach as many voters as $3 worth of newspaper ads or $50 worth of direct mail. Banning spots would probably *increase* campaign spending, by diverting candidates to less efficient forms of communication. In addition, spots reach supporters, opponents, and fence-sitters alike. This mass auditing imposes a measure of accountability that other media, particularly direct mail, lack.

2. A Candidate Can't Say Anything Substantive in 30 Seconds.   Referring to sound bites as well as spots, Michael Dukakis [1988 Democratic candidate for president] sourly concluded that the 1988 campaign was about "phraseology," not ideology. But a lot can be said in thirty seconds. John Lindsay's 1972 presidential campaign broadcast a 30-second spot in Florida that gave the candidate's positions on, among other issues, gun control (for), abortion rights (for), and school prayer (against). Lindsay's media manager, David Garth, later joked that the spot "probably lost the entire population of Florida."

A candidate can even make his point in 10 seconds. In California's 1992 Republican primary for U.S. Senate, one spot said simply: "I'm Bruce Herschensohn. My opponent, Tom Campbell, was the only Republican congressman opposing the 1990

Stephen Bates is a Senior Fellow with the Annenberg Washington Program in Communication Policy Studies, Washington, D.C. Edwin Diamond is professor of journalism at New York University and a media columnist for the New Yorker *magazine.* *From "Damned Spots,"* New Republic, *September 7 and 14, 1992, pp. 14–18. Reprinted by permission of the* New Republic, © *1992, The New Republic, Inc.*

anti-crime bill. He's liberal and wrong." Campbell replied in kind: "Bruce Herschen-sohn is lying, Tom Campbell voted to extend the death penalty to twenty-seven crimes, and was named Legislator of the Year by the California Fraternal Order of Police."

Though hardly encyclopedic, these spots reveal something about the candidates' priorities. They assert facts that can be checked and conclusions that can be challenged. If nothing else, they improve on what may have been the first ten-second spot, broadcast in 1954: "Minnesota needs a wide-awake governor! Vote for Orville Freeman and bring wide-awake action to Minnesota's problems!"

Brief ads do have one shortcoming. In 30 seconds, a candidate cannot hope to answer a half-true attack spot. In Bush's [Wille Horton] "revolving door" prison ad of 1988, for instance, the voice-over says that Dukakis "gave weekend furloughs to first-degree murderers not eligible for parole," while the text on the screen tells viewers that "268 escaped" and "many are still at large." But as reporters discovered, only 4 of the 268 escapees were first-degree murderers, and only three escapees—none of them a murderer—were still at large. The Willie Horton example was an aberration.

This point might have been hard for the Dukakis team to convey in 30 seconds. What kept them from responding to Hortonism, however, was not the constraints of brevity; it was their decision to try to get public attention off the furlough program—a subject that, even without the Bush campaign's factual finagling, was bound to cost them votes. No sensible candidate will defend himself by saying he's only half as bad as his opponent charges.

Just as short spots aren't invariably shallow, long telecasts aren't invariably thoughtful. The 1960 John F. Kennedy campaign aired a two-minute spot with a bouncy jingle; it conveyed youth and vitality, but scarcely any information (except for a musical reference to Kennedy's Catholicism: "Can you deny to any man/The right he's guaranteed/To be elected president/No matter what his creed?"). As Ross Perot demonstrated, a candidate determined to be evasive can do so in a 30-second spot or in a two-hour live Q&A session.

3. Political Ads Are Responsible for the Low-Down-and-Dirty State of Political Discourse.   According to Arthur Schlesinger Jr., television is "draining content out of campaigns." But that assertion romanticizes the past. In the 1890s James Bryce, a Briton, decried American political campaigns in 1990s terms. Campaigns devote less attention to issues, he fretted, than to "questions of personal fitness," such as any "irregularity" in the candidate's relations with women. These issueless campaigns diminish the "confidence of the country in the honor of its public men."

Sleazy ads hardly raise the level of political discourse, but they aren't the super-weapon that critics claim. "When a client of ours is attacked," boasts Democratic consultant Bob Squier, "the people of that state are going to get some kind of response the next day." These responses are invariably revealing. In a 1988 Dukakis ad, the candidate watches a TV set showing a Bush ad. "I'm fed up with it," Dukakis says. "Never seen anything like it in twenty-five years of public life—George Bush's negative television ads, distorting my record. . . ." But instead of presenting a sharp reply, Dukakis only turns off the set—a metaphor for his entire campaign.

4. TV Ads Keep the Potatoes on the Couch.   Barely half of eligible citizens voted in 1988, the lowest turnout in 40 years [Turnout in 1996 was even lower—49 percent. —*Editors*]. In fact, turnout has declined steadily since 1960. During the same period campaign-TV expenditures have tripled in constant dollars. Many of the TV dollars have been diverted from doorbell pushing, rallies, and other activities that involve citizens in politics. And, according to critics, simplistic, unfair spots discourage people from voting.

It is nearly impossible to untangle the factors that influence voter turnout. Some consultants, like Republican Eddie Mahe, argue that the decline in voting is a passing consequence of demographics. In the 1960s and 1970s the baby-boom generation reached voting age and lowered voting figures (so did the 26th Amendment, which changed the voting age from 21 to 18). No surprises there: turnout is traditionally lower among the young. So, as the boomer generation ages, turnout will increase.

As for how spots affect turnout in particular elections, the evidence goes both ways. In the 1990 race for U.S. Senate in North Carolina, early polls showed blue-collar whites inclined to stay home. But many of them turned out to vote for Jesse Helms after his anti-quotas spot received heavy air play and news coverage.

Are spots, then, blameless for the parlous state of voter participation? Well, no. Even if they don't cloud the mind, they may in some sense sap the political will. To the extent that spots resemble lifestyle commercials—It's Miller Time, It's Morning in America—they may be taken no more seriously than other TV advertising. This is especially so when no other campaign is visible to the viewer. Today's political rally, as Democratic consultant Robert Shrum has said, consists of three people around the TV set.

But the doomsayers' solution—to try to divorce politics from TV—won't work. Since the 1950s the voting classes have increasingly stayed home to be entertained, a trend encouraged by demographics (the suburban migration), by new at-home options (cable, VCRs), and at least partly by fear (crime in the streets). Banning political spots, as some cranks in the press and Congress would do, wouldn't bring voters outdoors. It would deprive the couch-potato/citizen of a sometimes abused but ultimately unmatched source of electoral information. As Dukakis discovered, melodramatically turning off the TV resolves nothing.

7

ELECTIONS

Campaign Finance

It was the magnitude of money scandals in the 1972 presidential election that spurred Congress to act, producing by 1974 the most comprehensive campaign finance reforms enacted in our nation's history. These included contribution limits, spending limits, public financing, more rigorous disclosure requirements, and a newly created Federal Election Commission to oversee the financing of federal elections. The 1996 presidential election, however, brought with it renewed concern about the role of money in elections as unprecedented sums were raised and spent—much of it legal, some not. In the 2000 race for the presidential nomination, the issue of financing campaigns continued to receive considerable attention, not only because it appeared that spending levels would outdistance even the record set in 1996, but also because presidential candidates spoke to the issue. The parties' two nominees, Al Gore and George W. Bush, went on record as favoring some changes in the current law, and Senator John McCain (R-Az.) went so far as to make campaign finance reform the very centerpiece of his unsuccessful bid for the Republican presidential nomination.

In the first selection, however, Robert Samuelson views with a jaundiced eye efforts to legislate still more restrictions on campaign contributions and spending. In his judgment, contributors will continue to find ways around legal restrictions, just like water does when it encounters an obstacle. Furthermore, not only does Samuelson see many reform proposals as running afoul of First Amendment guarantees of free speech, but he also rejects as greatly exaggerated the claim that we spend too much on elections, and the charge that money has corrupting influence on the decisions of government.

Jack Hitt, on the other hand, is convinced that we do need to take further steps to curb the role of big money in elections and government. The reform he discusses, however, is startlingly different from others. Rather than providing for more disclosure, his proposal calls for no disclosure at all; and instead of placing further limits on contributions, it removes limits altogether. Hitt also maintains that this reform, in contrast to many others now circulating, will pass the test of constitutionality.

Campaign Finance Hysteria

Robert J. Samuelson

Few subjects inspire more intellectual conformity than "campaign finance reform." All "right-thinking" people "know" that election spending is "out of control," that the present system of campaign finance is corrupt and that only reactionaries block "reform." Who cares if these common beliefs are either wrong or wildly exaggerated—or that most "reforms" would do more damage to democracy than any harm they might cure? The case against "reform" is almost impossible to make, because people's minds are closed.

It is easier to think that vast flows of tainted money clog the legislative process— and frustrate the "public interest"—than to acknowledge the actual sources of division: conflicting goals (higher spending vs. lower taxes); differences over values and desirable policy (on, say, abortion or the minimum wage); legitimate rivalry among interest groups (involving, for example, parts of the computer industry); and the insecurity of politicians, who avoid anything that risks unpopularity. Campaign finance serves as a respectable diversion. This is worth remembering as the Senate prepares to debate "reform."

Campaign spending is said to be "excessive" and exploding. Not really. The 1996 elections—at all levels, from city council to president—cost about $4 billion. This was one-twentieth of one percent of the national income then, $7.66 trillion. It's a small price for democracy. In 1998 winning House candidates spent an average of $675,478. After adjusting for inflation, this was 28 percent higher than in 1986—hardly an explosion. Congressional districts average slightly more than 600,000 people; spending is about $1 per person. For the Senate, the average winning candidate in 1998 spent $4,660,847; after inflation, this was only 3.9 percent higher than in 1986.

It is true that politicians devote a huge amount of time to fund-raising and that many loathe the process. The difficulty of raising money may also deter some good potential candidates from seeking office. But these problems result mostly from the 1974 post-Watergate campaign finance reform law, which hampered fund-raising by imposing tight limits on contributions. In federal elections, an individual can give only $1,000 to any candidate (per election) and $20,000 to national political parties or committees (per year). An individual's total contributions cannot exceed $25,000 a year.

After 25 years, inflation has eroded the purchasing power of these permitted contributions by about two thirds. Inevitably, politicians have invented new ways to raise money, which—given the costs of TV, direct mail, consultants, Internet sites—is essential for any campaign. Also inevitably, these new methods violate the spirit of campaign finance laws, though not the letter. "Soft money" is the latest evasion.

It obliterates contribution limits; almost anyone can give a soft money donation of any size to a political party or committee. The reason is that the activities that soft

Robert J. Samuelson is a contributing editor of Newsweek *magazine and columnist for* Washington Post. *From Robert J. Samuelson, "Campaign Finance Hysteria,"* Washington Post, *October 8, 1999, A25.*

money finances—state-party voter drives and "issue" ads that don't ask people to vote for or against specific candidates—are not legally defined as "federal" election activities. Therefore, they aren't covered by federal election laws. Campaign reform advocates argue that this legal distinction makes no practical sense. On this, they are correct. But it does not follow that soft money should be banned, as the House has voted, and the Senate will consider.

The trouble is that if this source of contributions is closed, new sources will emerge. The history of "campaign finance reform" is that every limit inspires new evasions. One possibility is that interest groups will finance more independent campaigns (TV ads, direct mailings) to elect or defeat targeted candidates. "Reformers" view such "issue ads" (praising or condemning candidates without telling people how to vote) as shams. And so, the next step would be to curb such advertising, even if curbs flout the First Amendment.

"Any effort to reform issue advocacy spending in connection with federal elections must strike a regulatory balance between protecting political speech and protecting the integrity of our electoral process," says one reform group. By contrast, the First Amendment says that Congress "shall make no law . . . abridging the freedom of speech." There's no mention of "regulatory balance," and if elections and "issue ads" aren't about political speech, what are they about? "Right thinking" people minimize the conflict between "campaign finance reform" and free speech, because it's inconvenient.

Their justification is the allegedly undue influence of campaign contributions on government policy. This is vastly overstated. No doubt money buys some access and favors. But the bigger the issue, the less the influence. The total size of giving and the number of donors dilute the influence of individual contributors.

Stories "proving" the opposite are often distorted. Roger Tamraz, a businessman who gave $300,000 in soft money to the Democrats, bragged about his "access" to the White House. But it did not buy him what he wanted: administration support for his pipeline project. Or consider the tobacco industry. Its big contributions (so the story goes) thwarted anti-smoking legislation. What actually happened was very different.

In June 1997 the industry and state attorneys general reached an agreement requiring companies to pay $368 billion over 25 years in return for some protection against lawsuits. A powerful industry could have persuaded Congress to approve something like the agreement. Instead, congressional committees raised the cost by about 40 percent and eliminated many legal protections. The industry then gave up and launched a $40 million ad campaign against the legislation. Its defeat probably owed less to the ads than to the bill's complexity and some Republican hostility to a huge back-door increase in the cigarette tax.

As long as we have the First Amendment, the effort to regulate elections—under the guise of "campaign finance reform"—is futile, self-defeating and undesirable. The hysteria about money's corrupting power worsens the very problem that "reformers" claim to deplore: public cynicism. But right-thinking people are oblivious to evidence or logic. They're at ease with their own respectable conformity.

Real Campaign Finance Reform

Jack Hitt

George W. Bush Jr. has raised the most money of any Presidential candidate in history: $36 million and counting [$84 million by May, 2000—*Editors*]. Much of it was gathered by only 200 people, super-fund-raisers whom Bush has dubbed "Pioneers." Should Bush get elected President next year, it is not caviling to say that those 200 people are more likely to get a phone call through, and possibly even get a favor returned, than, say, I will. So who are these very special people? Bush's campaign advisers have decided it is not in our interest to know, and there is no legal means to compel them to tell.

Outrageous? Well, is it any more upsetting than Al Gore's notorious visit to the Buddhist temple? Or the afternoon in 1995 when Representative John Boehner of Ohio, the G.O.P. Conference chairman, was spotted on the House floor cheerfully tossing out checks from tobacco lobbyists like daisies? How about when Trent Lott and Bill Clinton conspired in a fit of midnight *fraternité* to sneak through a $50 billion tax loophole for the tobacco companies? Does *anyone* disagree that our campaign-finance system has lapsed into legalized corruption?

For closeted campaign-finance wonks like myself, the real news every Presidential election is not who is running but what fresh scheme has been devised by the high-finance shamans to exploit the newest loophole. This year's twist: George W.'s $36 million is composed of direct contributions to his campaign, or "hard money." The focus of reformers over the last few election cycles, of course, has been "soft money"—contributions to the national party, which comes into play only after party nominations are official. The McCain-Feingold bill, . . . forced onto the Senate by John McCain, another Republican Presidential candidate, . . . deals almost exclusively with soft money. Why? Because Bill Clinton's scheme in the last two elections was to artfully co-opt the soft-money coffers of the Democratic National Committee to his own use. (Today, for example, the national chairman of the D.N.C. is Steven Grossman, a man, in all likelihood, you have never heard of. But he's a very good friend of Al Gore's. Coincidence?)

Every poll taken reveals that voters strongly favor reform. But when pressed for details of what might work, folks appear overwhelmed by the complexity. It seems like some public policy Rubik's cube for think-tank nerds to solve, with all that talk of spending caps, soft-money restrictions, limits on political action committees and Federal Election Commission reporting requirements. Even most expert commentary is little more than frustration venting. In a recent Op-Ed article, George McGovern lamented the "vexing" problem of "big money in politics. Thoughtful members of both parties are stymied by this issue."

What everyone seems to agree on, and has for decades, is that the problem boils

Jack Hitt is a contributing writer for New York Times Magazine, Harper's Magazine, *and the public radio program,* This American Life. *From Jack Hitt, "Real Campaign Finance Reform,"* New York Times Magazine, *July 25, 1999, 36–37.*

down to "too much money" and the solution unquestionably involves "restrictions" and "fuller disclosure."

Actually, not *everyone* agrees about this. There are other would-be reformers out there who describe the problem differently. To see the world their way is to see the limitations of fixes inspired by conventional wisdom. And to see how a radically different solution might not only solve our predicament quite elegantly but also profoundly change the way elections are conducted in the process.

The current crop of labored patches to the system—like the McCain-Feingold bill and its bouquet of technical fixes—is trying to end-run a 23-year-old Supreme Court decision that reasonably warned reformers that the voters' right to give money to candidates is inextricably bound up with the voters' right to free speech, expression and peaceable assembly. The brain teaser is this: How do you allow voters to freely donate money to the candidates and parties without permitting the easy money of special interests to crowd the rest of us out? Or, vice versa, how do you restrict the special interests without hobbling the necessary expression of voters in a robust election?

The official big fix that Beltway reformers are at least willing to acknowledge is "clean money," or public financing, which solves the riddle by asking candidates to voluntarily forgo all donated money in exchange for a stream of revenue from the state. Again, it is fundamentally about limiting money. The proposal has some support in cozy small-d democratic states like Maine and Vermont, liberal Massachusetts and the libertarian outpost of Arizona. But Government-financed elections are unlikely to find much of a reception in states as heterogeneous as New York or as angry as South Carolina.

One night not long ago, at dinner in New Haven, I met Prof. Bruce Ackerman of Yale, who has a provocative plan indeed: he proposes to create a dedicated form of election currency and positively flood the system with it. At election time, every registered voter would receive, say, 100 "patriot dollars" via a digital credit card. The voters could donate this money any way they saw fit—to a party, a union, to Tom DeLay's PAC or to People for the American Way. While the last Presidential election cost roughly $400 million, Patriot dollars would marginalize all greenbacks by sluicing $13 billion into the system. Since the viable candidates could get money only directly from voters, voters are who they'd have to campaign to. Patriot dollars bring to fund-raising the equality inherent in voting. One man, one vote? One vote, a hundred bucks.

This has its charms, but does seem a little unwieldy. Then, at another dinner, I learned that a friend had a plan that shares one of the assumptions of Ackerman's scheme—that limiting money is the wrong way to go. Prof. Ian Ayres of Yale and a co-author, Jeremy Bulow of Stanford, have published a law-review article detailing their idea to allow anybody or any institution to give as much campaign money as they want. But with one key proviso: the candidate cannot find out who the donors are.

All campaign donations would be funneled through a blind trust. The candidate still gets the money. He just can't know to whom he owes, or doesn't owe, a favor. Anyone could claim to be a donor with the same impunity that each of us can safely claim to have "voted" for the politician. This idea questions reform's most basic assumption—that more and fuller disclosure is the only answer. "Instead of limiting money," the authors write, "we might limit information."

The constitutionality of such a plan would be difficult to question. It is modeled on something seemingly more fundamental than even free-speech concerns: the secret ballot. Just as a voter goes into a booth and votes secretly, the donor would go into what the authors call, metaphorically, a "donation booth" and donate. In both cases, the voters know for whom they voted (donated to), but the candidates do not. The Supreme Court would be hard pressed to explain why a secret ballot is constitutional and a secret donation is not. And politicians would be equally challenged to come up with a convincing answer to this question: Why do you need to know the identity of your donors?

It turns out the secret ballot was invented for the precise reason the authors suggest the donation booth. In the 19th century, voting in America was shockingly corrupt. Party bosses organized voters and drove them to the voting stations like cattle. The ballots for opposing candidates were published on different colored paper. The bosses typically checked on their vote-buying by forcing voters into single-file lines and demanding that they physically wave their paid-for ballots over their heads. This practice came to an end when the "Australian ballot"—the secret ballot was invented there—came to America. Masssachusetts was the first state to adopt the secret ballot, in 1888. South Carolina was the last . . . in 1950.

By and large, the secret ballot pretty much eliminated vote-buying; perhaps a donation booth would have a similar effect. It neatly solves the PAC problem, which is a dark mutation of mandatory disclosure. Today, the PAC can "bundle" bags of legal checks for the candidates and explain precisely where they came from. With donation booths, PACs would wither.

So, perhaps, would a lot of campaign contributions. After the secret ballot went into effect, voting dropped off nearly 7 percent. The authors themselves worry that their reform would "shift money toward less accountable 'issue advocacy' expenditures and may be so effective in disrupting the market for influence that it cripples candidates' ability to raise funds."

Just how far you think donations might plunge is almost a Rorschach test of how deeply corrupt you believe the system to be. I don't know about you, but I am comforted by the fact that voting fell only 7 percent. Would donations dip only a bit, suggesting that most contributors want little more than the election of a generally like-minded individual? Or would they crash, revealing that donors want specific quid for quo, or nothing? Either outcome of the donation booth would be radical, in the sense that it would completely upend the system we currently have in place. But would anyone really miss it?

Perhaps the candidates would just become shuttlecocks battered amid a riot of citizen-financed issue ads. Would that be so bad? And if candidates could not afford to saturate television with either feel-good commercials Vaselined with slo-mo family values or with negative ads predicting moral decay in stentorian voice-over, perhaps they would have to work the streets for votes and fashion clever speeches to attract free media exposure.

It would be utopian to think that any of these solutions would restore us to some Jeffersonian democracy of high-minded yeomen. (That never existed anyway.) But now we tolerate a system in which we routinely hear stories about, say, the presence of corporate campaign donors at Congressional staff meetings to draw up new environmental laws. In a truly transformed system, it just might be that our politicians would, from time to time, find themselves contemplating the affairs of their voters as a coherent whole instead of the concerns of their most generous fund-raisers. Imagine that.

The Electoral College

At least once every four years, as the nation approaches the election of the president, political commentators raise the issue of the electoral college mechanism for electing the president, claiming that something ought to be done to correct it. One such critic, political scientist Lawrence Longley, in the first of the two selections in this section, argues that the electoral college is both undemocratic and politically dangerous: undemocratic because voters and votes are treated unequally; dangerous because there exists the possibility that it could lead to a major disruption of the normal electoral process.

In the second selection, another political scientist, Robert Weissberg, takes the view that we should retain the electoral college. While acknowledging that the present arrangement is not perfect, he maintains that the defects of the electoral college are not as serious as critics would have us believe. Moreover, he argues that several positive features associated with the electoral college more than compensate for its shortcomings, not the least of which is that it works.

The Electoral College Should Be Abolished

Lawrence D. Longley

The American electoral college is a deplorable political institution. Obscure and even unknown to the average citizen, it nevertheless serves as a crucial mechanism for transforming popular votes cast for president into electoral votes that actually elect the president. If the electoral college were only a neutral and sure means for counting and aggregating votes, it would be the subject of little controversy. The electoral college, however, is neither certain in its operations nor neutral in its effects. It may fail to produce a winner, in which case an extraordinarily awkward contingency procedure comes into play. Even when it operates relatively smoothly, it does not just tabulate popular votes in the form of electoral votes. Instead, it is an institution that works with noteworthy inequality—it favors some interests and hurts others. In short, the electoral college is a flawed means of determining the president. Its workings at best are neither smooth nor fair, and at worse contain the potential for constitutional crisis. Yet it continues to exist as the constitutional mechanism for electing the people's president. It must be abolished. . . .

THE FLAWS OF THE CONTEMPORARY ELECTORAL COLLEGE

The shortcomings of the contemporary electoral college are many, but five major flaws stand out. These are the faithless elector, the winner-take-all system, the "constant two" electoral votes, the uncertainty of the winner winning, and the contingency election procedure.

1. The Faithless Elector

The first of these flaws or problems of the contemporary electoral college arises out of the fact that the electoral college today is not the gathering of wise and learned elders as envisioned by its creators, but is rather little more than a motley state-by-state collection of political hacks and fat cats usually selected because of their past loyalty and support for their party. Neither in the quality of the electors nor in law is there any assurance that the electors will vote as expected by those who voted for them. State laws requiring electors to vote for their party's candidate are in practice unenforceable—and

Lawrence D. Longley is professor of political science at Lawrence University, Appleton, Wisconsin. Reprinted from Lawrence D. Longley, "Yes, The Electoral College Should Be Abolished," Controversial Issues in Presidential Selection. *Second Edition edited by Gary L. Rose by permission of the State University of New York Press. © 1994.*

almost certainly unconstitutional. The language of the Constitution directs that "the electors shall vote"—which suggests that they have discretion as to how they cast their votes. As a result, personal pledges—backed up by party and candidate loyalty together with a certain lack of imagination—can be seen as the only basis of elector voting consistent with the will of a state's electorate.

The problem of the "faithless elector" is neither theoretical nor unimportant. Following the 1968 election, Republican elector Doctor Lloyd W. Bailey of North Carolina decided to vote for George Wallace rather than for his pledged candidate, Richard Nixon—after deciding that Republican nominee Nixon was a communist. Another Republican elector Roger MacBride of Virginia, likewise deserted Nixon in 1972 to vote instead for Libertarian Party candidate John Hospers. In the 1976 election, once again there was a faithless elector—and curiously enough once again a deviant Republican elector. Mike Padden, in the state of Washington, decided six weeks after the November election that he preferred not to support Republican nominee Gerald Ford because President Ford had not been forthright enough in denouncing abortion. Instead Padden cast his electoral vote that year for Ronald Reagan, four years before Reagan won the Republican nomination and was elected president. Another variant electoral vote was cast in 1988 by West Virginia Democratic elector Margaret Leach, who cast her presidential vote not for Democratic presidential nominee Michael Dukakis but for vice-presidential nominee Lloyd Bentsen as a protest against the electoral college system. Other defections from voter expectations also occurred in 1948, 1956, and 1960, or in other words, in 7 of the 13 most recent U.S. presidential elections. Even more important is that the likelihood of such deviations occurring on a multiple basis would be greatly heightened should an electoral vote majority rest on only one or two votes, a real possibility in any close presidential election.

In fact, when one looks at the election return for the most recent close U.S. election, 1976, one can observe that if about 5,560 votes had switched from Jimmy Carter to Gerald Ford in the single state of Ohio, Carter would have lost that state and thus had but 272 electoral votes, only two more than the absolute minimum needed of 270. In that case, two or three Democratic individual electors seeking personal recognition or attention to a pet cause could withhold—or threaten to withhold—their electoral votes from Carter, and thus make the election outcome very uncertain.

Republican 1976 vice-presidential nominee Robert Dole provided evidence of the possibilities inherent in such a close presidential contest. Testifying before the U.S. Senate Judiciary Committee on January 17, 1977, in *favor* of abolishing the electoral college, Senator Dole remarked that during the 1976 election night vote count:

> We were looking around on the theory that maybe Ohio might turn around because they had an automatic recount. We were shopping—not shopping, excuse me. Looking around for electors. Some took a look at Missouri, some were looking at Louisiana, some in Mississippi, because their laws are a little bit different. And we might have picked up one or two in Louisiana. There were allegations of fraud maybe in Mississippi, and something else in Missouri. We [would] need to pick up three or four after Ohio. So that may happen in any event. But it just seems to me that the temptation is there for that elector in a very tight race to really negotiate quite a bunch.

2. The Winner-Take-All System

The second problem of the contemporary electoral college system lies in the almost universal state statutory provisions (the only exceptions being the states of Maine and Nebraska) giving *all* of a state's electoral votes to the winner of a state's popular vote plurality (not even a majority). This extraconstitutional practice, gradually adopted by all states during the 19th century as a means of enhancing state power, can lead to bizarre results—such as in Arkansas in 1968 where major party nominees Hubert Humphrey and Richard Nixon together divided slightly over 61 percent of the popular vote, while third-party candidate George Wallace, with less than 39 percent popular support in Arkansas, received 100 percent of the state's electoral votes. Similarly, in the 1992 election, three-way popular vote divisions among George Bush, Bill Clinton, and Ross Perot resulted in a number of states having their blocs of electoral votes decided on the basis of remarkably small pluralities. President Bush won the electoral votes of the Arizona and Kansas with but 39 percent of the popular vote, while Bill Clinton received all the electoral votes of Maine and New Hampshire with 39 percent and Montana and Nevada on the basis of only 38 percent of these states' popular vote. Ross Perot, with fully 30 percent of the popular vote in Maine, was only nine percentage points behind the state's winner, Bill Clinton, and thus came relatively close to winning electoral votes in that state (a goal actually easier because of Maine's unusual district-based determination of two of its four electoral votes).

Even more significant, however, is the fact that the winner-take-all determination of slates of state electors tends to magnify tremendously the relative voting power of residents of the largest states. Each of their voters might, by a vote cast, decide not just one popular vote, but how a bloc of 33 or 54 electoral votes are cast—if electors are faithful. As a result, the electoral college has a major impact on candidate strategy—as shown by the concern of Carter and Ford strategists, in the final weeks of the very close and uncertain 1976 campaign, with the nine big electoral vote states, which together that year had 245 of the 270 electoral votes necessary to win. The vote in seven of these nine megastates proved to be exceedingly close, with both major party candidates that year receiving at least 48 percent. Similarly in 1992, presidential candidates Clinton, Bush, and Perot focused their campaigns generally on the ten largest electoral vote states, which in the 1990s have fully 257 of the 270 electoral votes needed to win; these states are seen as determinants of any presidential contest's outcome.

In short, the electoral college does not treat voters alike—a thousand voters in Scranton, Pennsylvania, are far more important strategically than a thousand voters in Wilmington, Delaware. This inequity also places a premium on the support of key political leaders in large electoral vote states—as can be observed in any presidential election in the candidates' desperate wooing of the mayors of such cities as Philadelphia, Chicago, and Los Angeles. These political leaders are seen as possibly playing a major role in determining the electoral outcome in the large states of Pennsylvania, Illinois, and California, and thus as important to winning those large blocs of electoral votes. The electoral college treats political leaders as well as voters unequally—those in large marginal states are vigorously courted.

The electoral college also encourages fraud—or at least fear and rumor of fraud. In 1976, for example, New York, by itself had more than enough electoral votes to determine the winner of the presidential contest, and that state went to Carter by 290,000 popular votes. Claims of voting irregularities and calls for a recount were made on election night, but were later withdrawn because of Carter's clear national popular vote win. *If* fraud was present in New York, only 290,000 votes determined the 1976 presidential election; under a national direct election plan, at least 1,700,000 votes would have had to have been irregular in the same election to have changed the outcome.

The electoral college at times also provides even relatively minor third-party candidates the opportunity to exercise magnified political influence in the election of the president when they can gather votes in large, closely balanced states. In 1976, third-party candidate Eugene McCarthy, with less than 1 percent of the popular vote, came close to tilting the presidential election through his strength in close pivotal states. In four states (Iowa, Maine, Oklahoma, and Oregon) totaling 26 electoral votes, McCarthy's relatively small popular vote exceeded the margin by which Ford defeated Carter. In those states, McCarthy's candidacy *may* have swung those states to Ford. Even more significantly, had McCarthy been on the New York ballot (he had been ruled off at the last moment on technical grounds), it is likely Ford would have carried that state with its 41 electoral votes, and with it the election—despite Carter's overall national vote majority and lead of well over one and one-half million votes.

3. The "Constant Two" Electoral Votes

A third flaw of the electoral college system lies in the apportionment of electoral votes among the states. The constitutional formula is simple: one vote per state per senator and representative. Another distortion from equality appears here because of the "constant two" electoral votes, regardless of population, which correspond to each state's two senators. Because of this, inhabitants of the smallest states are advantaged to the extent that they "control" three electoral votes (two for the state's two senators and one for the representative) while their small population might otherwise entitle them to but one or two votes. This is weighing by states, not by population—however, the importance of this feature is greatly outweighed by the previously mentioned winner-take-all system. Nevertheless, the constant two feature of the electoral college—as the winner-take-all system—is yet another distorting factor in the election of the president. These structural features of the electoral college ensure that it can never be a neutral counting device and that it instead contains a variety of biases dependent solely upon the state in which voters cast their ballots. The contemporary electoral college is not just an archaic mechanism for counting the votes for president; it is also an institution that aggregates popular votes in an inherently imperfect manner.

4. The Uncertainty of the Winner Winning

The fourth flaw of the contemporary electoral college system is that under the present system there is no assurance that the winner of the popular vote will win the election. This problem is a fundamental one—can an American president operate effectively if he or she clearly has received fewer votes than the loser? I would suggest that the effect upon the legitimacy of a contemporary American presidency would be disastrous if a president were elected by an obscure electoral college after losing in the popular vote.

An American "divided verdict" election, however, *can* happen and *has* in fact occurred two or three times in American history, the most recent undisputable case (the election of 1960 being undeterminable) being the election of 1888, when the 100,000 popular vote lead of Grover Cleveland was turned into a losing 42 percent of the electoral vote. Was there a real possibility of such a divided verdict in the last truly close U.S. election, that of 1976? An analysis of the election results shows that if 9,245 votes had shifted to Ford in Ohio and Hawaii, *Ford* would have been instead elected president with 270 electoral votes, the absolute minimum, despite Carter's 51 percent of the national popular vote and lead of 1.7 million votes.

One hesitates to contemplate the political and constitutional consequences had a nonelected president, such as Ford, been inaugurated for four more years after having been rejected by a majority of the American voters in his only presidential election.

5. The Contingency Election Procedure

Besides the four aspects of the electoral college system so far discussed, one last problem should also be examined: an aspect of the electoral college system that is both probably the most complex and also the most dangerous for the stability of the American political order. The Constitution provides that if no candidate receives an absolute majority of the electoral votes—in recent years 270 electoral votes—the House of Representatives chooses the president from among the top three candidates. Two questions need to be asked: Is such an electoral college deadlock likely to occur in contemporary politics? And would the consequences be likely to be disastrous? A simple answer to both questions is yes.

In some illustrative examples, in 1960 a switch of less than 9,000 popular votes from John Kennedy to Richard Nixon in the two states of Illinois and Missouri would have prevented either man from receiving an electoral college majority. Similarly, in 1968, a 53,000 vote shift in New Jersey, Missouri, and New Hampshire would have resulted in an electoral college deadlock, with Nixon then receiving 269 votes—one short of a majority. Finally, in the close 1976 election, if some 11,950 popular votes in Delaware and Ohio had shifted from Carter to Ford, Ford would have carried these two states. The result of the 1976 election would then have been—*an exact tie* in electoral votes, 269–269! The presidency would have been decided not on election night, but through deals or switches at the electoral college meetings the following December 13, or alternatively by means of the later uncertainties of the House of Representatives.

What specifically might happen in the case of an election night apparent electoral college nonmajority or deadlock? A first possibility, of course, would be that a faithless elector or two, pledged to one candidate, might switch at the time of the actual meetings of the electoral college six weeks later, so as to create a majority for the presidential candidate leading in electoral votes. Such an action might resolve the crisis, although it would be sad to think of the president's mandate as based on such a thin reed of legitimacy as faithless electors.

If, however, no deals or actions at the time of the mid-December meetings of the electoral college were successful in forming a majority, then the action would shift to the newly elected House of Representatives, meeting at noon on January 6, only 14 days before the constitutionally scheduled Inauguration Day for the new president. The House of Representatives contingency procedure, which would now be followed, is, as discussed earlier, an awkward relic of the compromises of the writing of the new Constitution. Serious problems of equity would exist, certainly, in following the constitutionally prescribed one-vote-per-state procedure. In the 1990s, for example, the seven Representatives from the seven single member smallest states could outvote the 177 House members from the six largest states. The voters of the District of Columbia would be without any representation at all in the election of the president. Beyond these noteworthy problems of fairness lurks an even more serious problem—what if the House itself should deadlock and be unable to agree on a president?

In a two-candidate race, this would unlikely be a real problem; however, in a three-candidate contest, such as 1968, 1980, or 1992, there might well be enormous difficulties in getting a majority of states behind one candidate as House members agonized over choosing between partisan labels and support for the candidate (such as George Wallace, John Anderson, or Ross Perot) who might have carried their district. The result, in 1968, 1980, or 1992, might well have been no immediate majority forthcoming of 26 states, and political uncertainty and chaos as the nation approached Inauguration Day uncertain as to who was to be the president.

CONCLUSION

The electoral college has disturbing potential as an institution threatening the certainty of U.S. elections and the legitimacy of the American president. But even beyond these considerations, the electoral college inherently—by its very nature—is a distorted counting device for turning popular votes into electoral votes. It can never be a faithful reflection of the popular will, and will always stand between the citizen's and the people's president.

It is for these reasons that substantial efforts have been made in recent years to reform or abolish the electoral college, especially following the close and uncertain presidential elections of 1968 and 1976. The first of these "hairbreadth elections" resulted in a constitutional amendment to abolish the electoral college being overwhelmingly passed by the House of Representatives in 1969, only to be filibustered to death in the U.S. Senate in 1970. Similar constitutional proposals were debated by the Senate once again following the close 1976 election, during the period of 1977 to 1979, prior to failing in that chamber in July 1979 for want of the necessary two-thirds vote. In the early 1990s, electoral college reform proposals were once again before Congress and were the subject of national televised U.S. Senate hearings in 1992.

Inertia, institutional conservatism, and the self-interest of senators from states perceived as advantaged by the existing electoral college, served to preserve the electoral college during the debates of the 1970s, despite the concerted efforts of well-organized and persistent electoral reformers. The politics of electoral college reform are kindled by

close U.S. presidential elections, which demonstrate the inadequacies of the electoral college as a means of electing the president. Should . . . subsequent presidential election[s] prove to be uncertain in outcome or unfairly determined by the special characteristics of the electoral college, that institution will become once again a major target of reformers' efforts. Until that time, the electoral college will continue as an important aspect of American politics, shaping and determining the election of the U.S. president.

The problems inherent in the contemporary electoral college are numerous and should be dealt with *prior* to the nightmares and night sweats of a problem election. They cannot be dealt with by patchwork reforms such as abolishing the office of elector to solve solely the problem of the faithless elector. Rather, the distorted and unwieldy counting device of the electoral college must be abolished, and the votes of the American people—wherever cast—must be counted directly and equally in determining who shall be president of the United States: the people's president.

In Defense of the Electoral College

Robert Weissberg

Defending the electoral college is like defending sin. Almost every responsible person is against it; defenders are rare, yet it somehow survives. However, while sin may be beyond eradication, the electoral college is not deeply rooted in human nature. The electoral college can be abolished just as we abolished other archaic portions of the Constitution. Clearly, then, a defense of this system of selecting our President must be defended on grounds other than its inevitability. Our defense will be divided into two parts. We shall first show that its alleged defects are not as serious as some critics would have us believe. Second, we shall argue that there are in fact several virtues of this electoral arrangement, which the American Bar Association has characterized as "archaic, undemocratic, complex, ambiguous, and dangerous"!

CRITICISMS OF THE ELECTORAL COLLEGE

Criticisms of the electoral college basically fall into two groups. The first emphasize the unpredictable and unintended outcomes that are conceivable under the present system. In a nutshell, from the perspective of these critics, here is what *could* have happened in the 1996 presidential election: Bill Clinton wins a plurality of the popular vote but, thanks to a handful of states narrowly going to Ross Perot, fails to win a majority in the Electoral College. Meanwhile, a few Electors refuse to honor their Dole pledges and cast their ballots for Harry Brown, the Libertarian Party candidate. After a six-month-long acrimonious debate, Ross Perot is selected as president by the GOP dominated House with the promise to serve only a single term and pass a balanced budget.

The second basic criticism accuses the electoral college of overvaluing some votes at the expense of other votes. Some disagreement occurs over just who benefits from these distortions, but most experts claim that voters in populous states, especially members of certain urban ethnic and racial groups, are overrepresented. Would-be presidents pay more attention to some New York and California voters at the expense of votes in places like North Dakota.

THE NIGHTMARE OF UNINTENDED CONSEQUENCES

These are serious charges. Let us first consider what may be called the nightmare of unintended political outcomes. Two points may be made concerning this criticism. First, the odds of any one of these events occurring is remote. Only once in U.S. history—in 1888—has the undisputed winner of the popular vote lost the electoral college vote.

Robert Weissberg is professor of political science at the University of Illinois at Urbana-Champaign. This article was written especially for Points of View *in 1983 and revised and updated by the author in 1997.*

Electors have voted contrary to their popular instructions, but this has been extremely rare, and most important, such "unfaithful electors" have never affected who won and have almost never tried to influence the election's outcome (their actions were largely symbolic in a clearly decided contest). Nor has the last 160 years seen a presidential election decided by the House, despite some efforts by minor-party candidates to bring this about. All in all, the odds of any one event happening are low, and the odds of several such events occurring and making a difference in the same election are remote.

A second rejoinder to this nightmare of unintended, undesirable consequences is that hypothetical catastrophes are possible under *any* electoral system. Take, for example, a direct popular election with the provision for a runoff in the event no candidate receives a majority. It is conceivable that the initial election brings forth a wide range of candidates. A large number of moderate candidates each gets 5 or 7 percent from the middle of the political spectrum, and for the runoff, the public faces a contest between two unpopular extremists who together received 25 percent of the vote in the first election. *All* electoral mechanisms contain so-called time bombs waiting to go off.

MISREPRESENTATION CAUSED BY THE ELECTORAL COLLEGE

This alleged defect of misrepresentation derives from both the electoral college as stated in the Constitution plus individual state nonconstitutional requirements that all of a state's electoral votes go to the candidate receiving the largest number of votes (though Maine and Nebraska allow a division of their electoral vote). The effect of this unit voting is that to win the presidency a candidate must win in several populous states. New York, California, Texas, Illinois, and a few other big states are the valuable prizes in the election and thus a few thousand New Yorkers have more electoral clout than a few thousand voters in South Dakota. It supposedly follows, then, that the desires of these strategically placed voters are given greater attention by those seeking the presidency.

Four points can be made in response to this inequality-of-voters argument. First, it is far from self-evident just who those overadvantaged voters are and whether these big groups can be the cornerstone of electoral victory. It has been said, for example, that since there are many African-Americans in New York, the African-American vote can determine who carries New York. However, New York, like all populous states, has a varied population, so in principle the same argument can be applied to farmers, young people, white Protestants, middle-class suburbanites—any group comprising at least 10 percent of the electorate. This "key-voting-bloc-in-a-key-state" argument is largely the creation of statistical manipulation. Of course, it makes considerable sense for a group to *claim* that its vote, given its strategic position, put a candidate in the White House.

Second, it is a great exaggeration to assert that these strategically placed, "overrepresented" voters can exert control or significantly influence the election. Let's suppose that a candidate said that to win the presidency one must win the big states; to win the big states one must do very well among African-Americans, Jews, and union workers because these groups are overrepresented in these big states. Not only might it be difficult to appeal to all groups simultaneously (promising jobs to African-Americans may anger union workers), but also, even if one's appeals are successful, these "key" votes alone are not enough. The idea of certain well-situated minorities running the electoral show via the electoral college ignores the problems of creating large, diverse voting coalitions and the relatively small size of these "key" groups. At best, the electoral college may provide a disproportionate influence to voters—not a specific group—in large states in close elections (and since World War II national elections have been close only about half the time).

Third, the relationship between overrepresentation caused by the electoral college and disproportionate government benefits has never been demonstrated. The relationship has appeared so reasonable and been mentioned so often that it is now reiterated as if it were a truism. Actual evidence, however, has never been marshaled. Obviously, presidents have endorsed some policies favorable to supposed key groups in large states, but presidents have also opposed policies favorable to these same groups. It may be true that presidents have occasionally taken the operation of the electoral college into account in their policy calculations, but such action has not been sufficiently blatant to draw widespread attention.

Finally, the electoral system embodied in the electoral college may be biased in favor of some voters, but bias is part of *every* system of election. To reject a system because it is somehow "unfair" makes sense only if some perfectly fair system did exist. In fact, no such system does exist. As we did before, let us take as an example the simple majority rule plus a runoff system commonly advocated by opponents of the electoral college. This seemingly "pure" system is "unfair" for several reasons. Unlike the systems of proportional representation used by many European democracies, it provides no representation to citizens whose candidate received less than a majority—49.9 percent of all voters may get nothing. Moreover, it can be easily demonstrated that by allowing each citizen only one yes or no vote, the system does not allow citizens to rank candidates so that the candidate most acceptable to the most people is selected. In other words, a candidate who is not the first choice of a majority, but is still highly acceptable to almost everyone, is shut out under a simple majority system. In short, the issue is not one of "fair" versus "unfair," but what type of unfairness will be present.

DEFENDING THE ELECTORAL COLLEGE

Thus far we have argued that the major criticisms against the electoral college either rest on exaggerations and misunderstandings or are simply unproven. Is there, however, anything positive to be said for the frequently maligned system? At least four virtues of the electoral college seem reasonably clear and are probably advantageous to most people: (1) it is a proven, workable system; (2) it makes campaigns more manageable; (3) it discourages election fraud; and (4) it preserves a moderate two-party system.

The first virtue—*it is a proven, workable system*—is basically a conservative argument. Conservatives believe that when something works, though somewhat imperfectly, it should not be easily abandoned for the promise of perfection. That is, on paper almost every alternative to the electoral college is without defect. However, as anyone familiar with the success rates of proposed reforms knows well, political changes do not always work as intended. The nightmare and inequalities of the status quo are hypothetical and alleged: a change might bring real and consequential problems despite promises of perfection. Constitutional changes should be made only if the real costs of the electoral college are heavy.

The second virtue—*it makes campaigns more manageable*—derives from two facts. First, in terms of time, money, and energy, the present electoral system is already very demanding on candidates. Running for president is so exhausting physically that some have said, half jokingly, that only the mentally unbalanced are attracted to this activity. Second, the electoral college, plus the "winner-take-all" role in 48 of the 50 states plus the District of Columbia, means that some votes are not as important as others. Swaying a few thousand uncommitted voters in a closely divided populous state is much more important than an appeal to the same number of voters in a small, one-party-dominated state. Obviously, then, without some division of voters into important and unimportant voters, campaigning for president would become even more hectic and overwhelming than ever. A rational candidate might even lock himself in a television studio rather than attempt the impossible task of trying to wage an effective nationwide personal campaign.

The third virtue—*it discourages election fraud*—also derives from the present system's divisions of votes into important and less important. In a state with a relatively small number of electoral votes, where the outcome is not in much doubt, little incentive exists for widespread election fraud. Such manipulation is only worthwhile in big states like New York or Illinois where presidential elections tend to be close and a large bloc of electoral votes may hinge on a few thousand votes. Under a direct popular election system, however, all votes are equally valuable and thus equally worth manipulating. Practices such as multiple voting, voting the dead, and intimidating the opposition, which were once limited to a few localities, might very well become national in scope.

The fourth and final virtue—*it preserves a moderate two-party system*—is perhaps the most important. Under the existing system, winning the presidency means winning numerous electoral votes. Since to win electoral votes you must win pluralities in many states, it takes a formidable political organization to win these big prizes. A group that won, say, 5 to 10 percent of the vote in a few states would be doomed. Even an organization that wins a few million votes usually comes up with very little where the prizes are big blocs of electoral votes. In contemporary politics, the only organizations capable of such a massive electoral undertaking are large, diverse, compromise-oriented political parties such as the Democratic and Republican parties.

To appreciate this contribution of the existing electoral college system, imagine presidential campaigns *without* the two major parties. Instead of two major candidates and a dozen or two inconsequential candidates, there would be numerous hopefuls with some reasonable chance of success. These candidates would likely draw most of their support from relatively small segments of the population. There might be an anti-abortion candidate, a strong civil rights candidate, an anti-school-busing candidate, and a few others closely associated with one or two specific issues. The incentive to create broad-based coalitions to capture a majority in 20 or 30 states would be considerably reduced and thus the two major parties would virtually disappear.

This type of campaign politics would suffer from several problems. The narrow basis of candidate appeal would likely generate much sharper conflict and deepen group antagonism (for example, African-Americans might see for the first time in modern times an explicitly anti–civil rights candidate who could win). Perhaps most important, postelection governance would become difficult. Not only would a president have a much smaller base of popular support, but he or she would likely have to deal with a Congress composed of people with no party attachment whose primary purpose was to advance a particular group or regional interest. Of course, the present system of Democratic and Republican party politics does not eliminate the advancement of narrow interests and interbranch conflict. However, the situation would probably be even worse if numerous single-issue groups replaced the present two major political parties. In short, the electoral college, plus the winner-take-all-system, encourages the current two-party system, and this system moderates conflict and promotes effective postelection governance.

We began by noting that defending the electoral college is like defending sin. We have argued that, as some have said of sin, it is not nearly as bad as is claimed, and it may even be beneficial. We have not argued that the present system is beyond reproach. The system has been modified numerous times since its inception, and future changes are certainly possible. It is a serious mistake, however, to believe that abolishing the electoral college will be as beneficial as finally ridding ourselves of sin.

8

POLITICAL PARTIES

For something that was unintended by the founders of this nation, political parties have been a remarkably stable feature of the American political landscape. Parties were alive and kicking in the 1790s, and they are alive and kicking as the nation enters the new millennium. Just as remarkably, the U.S. political party system has featured competition between two major parties—the Democratic and Republican parties—for at least 130 years. True, there have been periods in our history where one party has been fairly dominant (winning most offices, including the presidency and Congress, for example, over a long period of time), but the two-party pattern remains well established.

The 1992 and 1996 presidential elections, however, presented a challenge to this persistent two-party pattern. Third-party candidate Ross Perot mounted extremely well financed and organized campaigns for the presidency, and although ultimately unsuccessful, he nevertheless threw a scare into the two major parties. Indeed, it was Ross Perot who, in the 1992 election, was able to dominate the airwaves and force the major-party candidates to open up the presidential debates to three viable candidates instead of two.

The emergence of Perot's third party—"United We Stand America" in 1992 and the "Reform Party" in 1996 and 2000—has prompted a debate within the academic and political communities over (1) the extent to which Perot's two candidacies constituted significant challenges to the two-party system; and (2) the extent to which Perot's or any other third party represents a positive development in American politics.

In the selections that follow, the third-party question is addressed first by Theodore J. Lowi, a professor of political science at Cornell University. Lowi argues that the 1992 election was "the beginning of the end of America's two-party system" and the emergence of the Perot party provided a healthy jolt to the political system. Contending that the two major parties are "brain dead," Lowi believes that a viable third party is just the medicine the country needs to encourage parties that address issues instead of focusing on images, and that generate enthusiasm and greater participation instead of apathy and cynicism.

In the second selection, political scientist Paul S. Herrnson of the University of Maryland takes strong exception to Lowi's point of view. Herrnson develops his counterargument on principally two grounds: first, there is too much tradition and institutional bias in favor of the two-party system for it to be cast aside lightly; and second, while third parties have in the past made important contributions to politics and policy, they should not be further encouraged because they only contribute to more division and fragmentation in our political system—a system that is already so overloaded with both that government finds it difficult to act to solve critical national problems.

117

The Party Crasher
The Need for a Third Party

Theodore J. Lowi

. . . [H]istorians will undoubtedly focus on 1992 as the beginning of the end of America's two-party system. The extraordinary rise of Ross Perot and the remarkable outburst of enthusiasm for his ill-defined alternative to the established parties removed all doubt about the viability of a broad-based third party. Republicans, Democrats and independents alike have grasped the essential point that the current incumbents will not, and cannot, reform a system that drastically needs overhauling.

A third party would do more than shock the powers that be into a few reforms. Its very existence—never mind its specific policies—would break the institutional gridlock that has paralyzed Washington for most of the past 20 years. Ultimately, it would give us a more parliamentary style of government, in keeping, it seems to me, with what the Founding Fathers had in mind. Perot demonstrated the possibility. It now falls to the rest of us to make the breakthrough to a three-party system. The New Party, self-defined as "broadly Social Democratic," which has been gathering strength. . . ; the John Anderson crowd from the 1980s, of which I am one; the perennial Libertarian Party—we are going to have to get together.

One of the best-kept secrets in American politics is that the two-party system has long been brain dead—kept alive by support systems like state electoral laws that protect the established parties from rivals and by Federal subsidies and so-called campaign reform. The two-party system would collapse in an instant if the tubes were pulled and the IV's were cut.

Back when the Federal Government was smaller and less important, the two parties could be umbrella parties—organizing campaigns, running elections and getting the vote out—without much regard to ideology or policy. But with the New Deal and the rise of the welfare state, the federal government became increasingly vulnerable to ideological battles over policy. None of this was particularly noticeable while the government and the economy were expanding, but in the early 1970's class and ideological conflicts began to emerge more starkly.

Thus were born the familiar "wedge" issues—crime, welfare, prayer, economic regulation, social regulation, taxes, deficits and anti-Communism. No matter what position party leaders took on such issues, they were bound to alienate a substantial segment of their constituency. While the Democrats were the first to feel the cut of wedge issues, particularly concerning race, Republicans are now having their own agonies

Theodore J. Lowi is John L. Senior Professor of American Institutions, Cornell University and a former president of the American Political Science Association. From Theodore J. Lowi, "The Party Crasher: The Need for a Third Party," New York Times Magazine, *August 23, 1992, pp. 28–33. Copyright © 1992 by the New York Times Company. Reprinted by permission.*

over abortion, foreign policy and budget deficits. Wedge issues immobilize party leadership, and once parties are immobilized the government is itself immobilized.

The parties have also atrophied because both have been in power too long. In theory, a defeated party becomes vulnerable to new interests because it is both weaker and more willing to take risks. But for nearly 40 years, both parties have in effect been majority parties. Since each party has controlled a branch of government for much of that time, neither is eager to settle major policy issues in the voting booth. A very important aspect of the corruption of leadership is the tacit contract between the two parties to avoid taking important issues to the voters and in general to avoid taking risks.

Party leaders have responded to gridlock not with renewed efforts to mobilize the electorate but with the strategy of scandal. An occasional exposure of genuine corruption is a healthy thing for democracy, but when scandal becomes an alternative to issues, leaving the status quo basically unaltered, it is almost certain that all the lights at the crossroads are stuck on red. In fact, the use of scandal as a political strategy has been so effective that politicians have undermined themselves by demonstrating to the American people that the system itself is corrupt.

The Perot candidacy differed fundamentally from past independent presidential candidacies, which were basically single-issue appeals. Perot tapped into a genuinely unprecedented constituency—moderates disgusted with the two major parties, regardless of the nominees. Two major polls completed in May and June [1992] found that about 60 percent of Americans favored the establishment of a new political party.

Predictably, the two-party system defenders have devoted considerable energy to shooting down any suggestion that the status quo can be improved upon. They have produced all sorts of scenarios about how a third party could throw presidential elections into the Congress, with the House of Representatives choosing the president and the Senate choosing the vice president—not only delaying the outcome but producing a Bush-Gore, a Clinton-Quayle, or, God forbid, a Quayle-Who-Knows administration. Worse yet, if it survived to future elections, a third party would hold the balance of power and, as a result, wield an influence far out of proportion to its electoral size. It might, by its example, produce a fourth or a fifth party. And if it elected members to Congress, it might even inconvenience congressional leaders in their allocation of committee assignments.

In fact, genuine third parties have been infrequent in the United States, but wherever they have organized they have had significant, generally positive effects. One of these is providing a halfway house for groups wedged out of the two larger parties. In 1924, the progressive movement succeeded in forming the Progressive Party in Wisconsin and other midwestern states, which nominated Robert M. La Follette for president. In the 1930s, the Farmer-Labor Party flourished in Minnesota, where it eventually fused with an invigorated Democratic Party. In the process, both of these third parties provided the channel through which many dissident and alienated groups found their way back into politics, and their influence lingered long after the parties themselves. Similarly, wherever the Dixiecrats organized as a party, that state was later transformed to a genuinely competitive two-party state.

With three parties, no party needs to seek a majority or pretend that it is a majority. What a liberating effect this would have on party leaders and candidates, to go after constituencies composed of 35 percent rather than 51 percent of the voters. A three-party system would be driven more by issues, precisely because parties fighting for pluralities can be clearer in their positions. Third parties have often presented constructive and imaginative programs, which have then been ridiculed by leaders of the two major parties, who point out that third-party candidates can afford to be intelligent and bold since they can't possibly win. In a three-party system, even the two major parties would have stronger incentives to be more clearly programmatic, because their goal is more realistic and their constituency base is simpler.

Flowing directly from this, voting would increase, as would other forms of participation. Virtually our entire political experience tells us that more organized party competition produces more participation. And we already know that genuine three-party competition draws people into politics—not merely as voters but as petition gatherers, door knockers, envelope lickers and $5 contributors—making the three-party system an antidote to the mass politics that virtually everybody complains about nowadays.

Even defenders of the two-party system criticize the reliance of candidates on television, computerized voter lists, mass mailings and phone banks—which dehumanize politics, discourage participation, replace discourse with 15-second sound bites and reduce substantive alternatives to subliminal imagery and pictorial allusion. And the inordinate expense of this mass politics has led to a reliance on corporate money, particularly through the political action committees, destroying any hope of collective party responsibility.

These practices and their consequences cannot be eliminated by new laws—even if the laws didn't violate the First Amendment. A multiparty system would not immediately wipe out capital-intensive mass politics, but it would eliminate many of the pressures and incentives that produce its extremes, because of the tendency of third parties to rely on labor-intensive politics. Third parties simply do not have access to the kind of financing that capital-intensive politics requires. But more than that, there is an enthusiasm about an emerging party that inspires people to come out from their private lives and to convert their civic activity to political activity.

Finally, a genuine three-party system would parliamentarize the presidency. Once a third party proves that it has staying power, it would increase the probability of presidential elections being settled in the House of Representatives, immediately making Congress the primary constituency of the presidency. Congress would not suddenly "have power over" the presidency. It has such power already, in that the Constitution allows it complete discretion in choosing from among the top three candidates. But if Congress were the constituency of the president, the president would have to engage Congress in constant discourse. The president might under those circumstances have even more power than now, but he would have far less incentive to go over the head of Congress to build a mass following.

Even now, with two parties based loosely on mythical majorities, a president cannot depend on his party to provide a consistent congressional majority. The whole idea of a mandate is something a victorious president claims but few members of Congress accept, even for the length of the reputed honeymoon. Thus, current reality already involves the president in bargains with members of the opposition party.

Confronting three parties in Congress, each of whose members is elected on the basis of clear policy positions, the president's opportunities for bargaining for majority support would be more fluid and frequent. In our two-party environment, issues are bargained out within the ranks of each party and often never see the light of day, particularly during the session prior to a presidential election. A third party with a small contingent of members of Congress would insure a more open and substantive atmosphere for bargaining to take place—*after* the election.

A third party would play the role of honest broker and policy manager, because it would hold a balance of power in many important and divisive issues. There would be little fear of the tail wagging the dog, because, unlike European parties, Democrats and Republicans are not ideologically very far apart—they have simply not been cooperating with each other. The presence of a third-party delegation gives the President an alternative for bargaining, but if the new party raised its price too high it would simply give the President a greater incentive to bargain with the other major party.

The point here is that the third party is a liberating rather than a confining force, a force for open debate on politics. Another important myth in the United States is that policy making is a matter of debate between the affirmative and the negative. But simple yea versus nay on clearly defined alternatives is a very late stage in any policy-making process. In sum, just as the rise of the two-party system fundamentally altered the constitutional structure of our government appropriately for the 19th century, so a three-party system would alter the structure appropriately for the 21st century.

Immediately, one must add an important proviso: A genuine third party must be built from the bottom up. It must be an opportunist party, oriented toward the winning of elections. It must nominate and campaign for its own candidates at all levels and not simply run somebody for president. And it must attract regular Democrats and Republicans by nominating some of them to run as candidates with the third-party nomination as well as that of their own party. Joint sponsorship has been practiced by the Liberal and Conservative Parties in New York for decades. Being listed on two lines on the ballot is a powerful incentive for regular Democrats and Republicans to cooperate with a new party, if not to switch over. About 40 states have laws preventing or discouraging this practice, but their provisions will probably not stand up to serious litigation.

By whatever means, the new party must have enough organizational integrity to last beyond one election. Running candidates for office in every election is the only way to secure organizational integrity. And a new, third political party is the best moderate means of breaking the institutional impasse in American politics.

Ross Perot was never the issue. The issue is a third party, and this is a call to arms, not a dispassionate academic analysis. A third party could, it just could, turn the switches at the crossroads from red to green.

The Reform Party
Fizzle or Crash and Burn?

Paul S. Herrnson

Presidential candidate Ross Perot burst onto the political scene in 1992 like a meteor in a clear night sky and then crashed and skidded along the ground, leaving behind only fragments of an ill-fated candidacy. In 1996 his sun never rose. Perot's entrance, disappearance, and reemergence in the 1992 presidential campaign did little to dissuade most Americans from turning to some familiar choices. His stewardship of the newly created Reform Party in 1996 produced similar results. By the time election day came around in both years, most voters were ready to cast their ballots for one of the major parties' two candidates.

Previous independent or minor-party candidacies have also been largely unsuccessful. It is these results and the persistence of the two-party system that are the most important stories behind the 1992 and 1996 presidential elections. Those who argue that Perot's candidacies will lead to a new permanent minor party just plain have it wrong. Those who believe that the development of a multiparty system would improve American politics are equally mistaken.

Perot's bids for the presidency were built on the discontent that many voters felt toward the major parties and the political system in general. Whatever successes Perot enjoyed at the polls were more a reflection of the disenchantment that the American people had with the performance of the federal government and the two major parties than an endorsement of the candidate's beliefs.

Scandal, gridlock, and the major parties' failure to deal with the nation's sagging economy led to the middle-class frustrations that provided the foundation for Perot's campaigns. The degree to which the major parties deal with these issues in the future will be more influential in determining the survival of Perot's Reform Party than the efforts of Perot himself. This is typical of most of the independent and minor-party presidential candidacies that have occurred in the United States during the 20th century.

IMPEDIMENTS TO MINOR PARTIES

There are a number of reasons that most minor parties fail to root themselves firmly in the American landscape. Institutional impediments rank high among them. The Constitution is hostile to minor parties and party politics in general. Single-member simple-plurality elections, of which the electoral college is a peculiar variant, make it very difficult for minor parties to have much of an impact on the political process. These

Paul S. Herrnson is professor of political science at the University of Maryland and executive director of the Committee for Party Renewal. This article was written especially for Points of View *in 1994 and updated by the author in 1997.*

winner-take-all systems deprive any candidate or party that does not win an election a share of elected offices, even when they come in second place. This is especially harmful to minor-party candidates, who usually consider themselves to have been successful when they come in second at the polls. Other electoral systems, like the proportional multimember representation systems used in much of Europe, on the other hand, virtually guarantee at least some legislative seats to any party—no matter how small, transient, or geographically confined—that wins a threshold of votes. These seats result in minor parties receiving both institutional recognition and political legitimacy.

Institutional recognition also gives the Democratic and Republican parties some critical advantages over minor parties. Because they receive automatic placement on the ballot, federal subsidies for their national conventions, and full funding for their presidential candidates, the two major parties are able to focus most of their energies on winning the support of voters. Minor-party and independent candidates, to the contrary, can obtain full access to the ballot only after they have collected thousands of signatures and met other requirements that have been established by each of the 50 states and the District of Columbia.

Moreover, it is difficult for minor-party and independent presidential candidates to obtain federal funding. Newly emergent minor parties can only qualify for federal subsidies retroactively. Those that do well in a given election are rewarded with campaign subsidies, but these funds are provided too late to have any impact on the election. Minor parties that have made a good showing in a previous election are automatically entitled to some campaign subsidies in advance, but these parties get only a fraction of the money that is made available to the Democrats and the Republicans. Of course, neither money nor ballot access difficulties provided serious obstacles to Ross Perot in 1992, and Perot qualified for federal matching funds in 1996.

Institutional impediments, however, are not the only hurdles that must be cleared in order for minor parties to survive. Americans' moderate views about politics deprive minor parties and their candidates of the bases of support that exist for minor parties in most other modern democracies. The fact that the vast majority of Americans hold opinions that are close to the center of a fairly narrow ideological spectrum means that most elections, particularly those for the presidency, are primarily contests to capture the "middle ground." At their very essence, Democratic strategies involve piecing together a coalition of moderates and voters on the left, and Republican strategies dictate holding their party's conservative base while attracting the support of voters at the center. The distribution of public opinion, particularly the association that each of the major parties has with an ideological pole, leaves little room for a minor party to develop a sizable base of reliable supporters. Democracies whose citizens have a broader array of ideological perspectives or have higher levels of class or ethnic solidarity generally provide more fertile ground for minor-party efforts.

The career paths of the politically ambitious are extremely important in explaining the weakness and short-term existence of most minor-party movements in the United States. Budding politicians learn early in their careers that the Democratic and Republican parties can provide them with useful contacts, expertise, some financial assistance, and an orderly path of entry into electoral politics. Minor parties and independent candidacies simply do not offer these same benefits. As a result, the two parties tend to attract the most talented among those interested in a career in public service. A large part of the parties' hegemony can be attributed to their advantages in candidate recruitment.

Voters are able to discern differences in the talents of minor-party and major-party candidates and, not surprisingly, they hesitate to cast their votes for minor-party contestants for the presidency or other public offices. Even voters who are willing to publicly declare their support for a minor-party or independent candidate early in the election cycle often balk at casting their ballot for one of these candidates on election day. Major-party candidates and their supporters prey upon Americans' desire to go with a winner—or at least affect the election outcome—when they discourage citizens from "throwing away" their votes on fringe candidates.

Finally, mainstream politicians are not stupid. When a minor-party or independent candidate introduces an issue that proves to be popular, Democratic and Republican leaders are quick to co-opt it. In 1992 Ross Perot proclaimed himself to be an agent of change and was championed as someone who would make the tough choices needed to reform the political system and get America's sagging economy moving again. When that proved popular, many major-party candidates, including President George Bush in 1992 and President Bill Clinton in 1996, staked out similar positions. There is nothing disingenuous about these conversions. By adopting positions espoused in popular movements, party leaders are able to better represent their constituents as well as attract votes. Such strategic adjustments are commonplace in American history. By robbing minor party and independent movements of their platforms the two major parties ensure the longevity of the two-party system.

PEROT—PARTY LEADER OR SELF-AGGRANDIZER?

The preceding institutional and structural barriers apply to minor parties equally, but some forces that will impede the transformation of Perot's bids for the presidency into an enduring minor party originate from within the Perot movement itself. American politics have produced two types of enduring minor-party efforts. United We Stand America (UWSA), the vehicle for Perot's 1992 candidacy, and the Reform Party, his vehicle for 1996, resemble neither.

The first type of minor party, which includes the Communist and Libertarian parties, adheres to narrow ideologies and principally pursues educational goals. These parties survive because their supporters are strongly committed to an ideological cause. Their support for a cause is usually stronger than their desire to elect a winning candidate. Freed from electoral imperatives beyond actually fielding a contestant, these parties do not need to moderate their views in order to survive. Indeed, the ideological purity that is largely responsible for their survival tends to render them electorally inconsequential.

The other type of enduring minor party, which was more common in the 19th than the 20th centuries, possesses most of the characteristics of the major parties. These parties, which include the Liberty Party of the 1840s, the Know Nothing (or American)

Party of the 1850s, and the Populist (or People's) Party of the 1880s, began as grass-roots movements, fielded candidates for state and local office, experienced contested nominations, hosted conventions, took stands on a broad range of issues, and were led by well-respected and established politicians. They persisted for several election cycles because they functioned like existing parties rather than independent candidacies.

UWSA and the Reform Party, and Perot's two presidential candidacies, bear little resemblance to either type of minor party. They differ from the first type in that Perot's, UWSA's, and the Reform Party goals were electorally oriented, not ideologically or educationally motivated. Perot has expressed no interest in leading a cause designed to persuade Americans to support an extremist ideology. His goal in both 1992 and 1996 was clearly to win votes.

UWSA, the Reform Party, and Perot's two campaigns also differed significantly from the other type of enduring minor party. Unlike those parties, Perot's campaigns were built entirely around one person who was their sole focus. The Perot campaigns did not originate as grassroots efforts, nor were they bottom-up phenomena. In 1992 Perot publicly offered himself as a candidate for office, stating he would run if the voters had his name placed on every state ballot. He then hired Ed Rollins and Frank Luntz—two high-powered political consultants—to run his campaign, and had "paid" and "real" volunteers make sure he made it onto the ballot. In 1996 Perot and his followers created the Reform Party to serve as a vehicle for Perot's aspirations.

Perot's tightly controlled, high-tech bids for office, which relied primarily on "infomercials" to propagate his message, are probably closer to the model of future protest candidacies than the decentralized, grassroots minor-party campaigns that existed prior to the development of the electronic media and the rise of modern public relations technology. In fact, modern campaign technology, suburban sprawl, and other systemic developments associated with the rise of a mass society and the decline of grassroots party organizations made independent campaigns like Perot's possible.

Unlike either type of minor party, and both major parties, Perot's followers did not encourage state and local candidates to run under either UWSA's or the Reform Party's label. In 1992 UWSA's charter prohibited them from doing so. In 1996 the Reform Party endorsed several major-party candidates for Congress and other offices and did virtually nothing to help Reform Party candidates wage their campaigns.

UWSA's and the Reform Party's operations also differed from those of traditional minor or major parties in other ways. UWSA held secretive strategy meetings and eschewed public conventions. The closed meetings may have been useful for shutting off debate and allowing Perot to dominate party proceedings, but they were not useful for attracting public support or providing the foundation for a broad-based political movement.

The Reform Party has also differed from other parties in the degree to which it has been dominated by one person. First, Perot's money, roughly $6.7 million, was the overwhelming source of the party's revenue in 1996. Second, the party's nomination process was designed to provide a coronation for Perot rather than to select a nominee from among competing aspirants. The balloting process was poorly carried out. Many party members received their ballots late. Others, including such prominent Reform

Party members as Perot's opponent for the nomination, former Colorado Governor Richard Lamm, never received a ballot. Still others received several ballots. Flawed balloting procedures and a lack of interest among Reform Party members resulted in less than 5 percent of all Reform Party members participating in the process.

The nomination process also denied Lamm the opportunity to compete on a level playing field. Perot was the only Reform Party candidate who had access to the party's supporter list, and he benefited from a direct-mail piece that featured his but not Lamm's picture. The Reform Party's decision to stack the deck so heavily in favor of Perot suggests that it will have difficulty making the transition from a movement dominated by a single charismatic leader to an enduring comprehensive party. This transition would require the party to develop a formal governing body that is independent of Perot, an independent source of financing, and a routinized system of candidate selection. It would also require the party to nominate candidates for state, local, and congressional office and to develop a permanent organization capable of assisting its candidates with their general election campaigns.

In short, Perot's efforts never really grew beyond his own aspirations. Perot's candidacies began as a one-person, anti-Washington crusade that tapped into the deep-seated frustrations that many Americans felt toward their government and the dissatisfaction that they felt toward the two major parties and their nominees. The 1992 Perot campaign gained some legitimacy when it published an economic program written by some respected national leaders, faltered when the candidate dropped out of and then back into the race, and then suffered immensely when the media began to subject Perot and his running mate to the same level of scrutiny to which all major-party candidates are subjected. After the election, UWSA further harmed its prospects when it resorted to closed-door strategy sessions and decided against fielding candidates in the 1994 elections. Other activities, such as collecting $1,000 contributions from doctors in order to pay a team of researchers to write a health care plan, did little to fuel a populist-style movement.

Perot's 1996 bid for the presidency suffered difficulties from the start. The lack of evenhandedness in how it conducted its nomination caused the Reform Party to lose some of its credibility with its reform-oriented base and other voters. Perot's inability to attract a respected and recognizable running mate posed a second major problem. Economist Pat Choate was unknown in elite political and journalistic circles, did not register with the general public, and did little to strengthen the Perot ticket's vote-getting power. Perot's decision to accept federal matching funds for his general election campaign limited the party's spending to roughly half of that given to the two major parties, hampering its ability to communicate with voters. The Presidential Debate Commission's decision to deny Perot a place in the presidential debates denied the candidate's lackluster campaign a springboard from which it might take off. The decision also reinforced the widely held belief among voters that a vote for a minor-party candidate is a wasted vote. Finally, the fact that the American economy was growing stronger during the Clinton presidency did not bode well for Perot and, at least in the short term, does not bode well for other minor-party or independent candidacies that hope to use economic issues to attract political support.

IS A MULTIPARTY SYSTEM DESIRABLE?

Throughout its history, the United States has had a two-party system that has been punctuated by the appearance of minor parties. The Civil War, the depression of the 1890s, the Great Depression, the Civil Rights era, and the 1992 election are just a few of the many times in which political instability or public dissatisfaction with the existing two parties have given rise to significant minor-party or independent presidential candidacies. These candidacies, including Perot's, have introduced new ideas, raised some issues that the two major parties might have otherwise ignored, altered the policy debate, and in some cases led to major changes in public policy. They have also acted as safety valves, providing peaceful outlets for public discontent. These are all important political functions.

The question remains, "Should Americans want a permanent three- or multiparty system?" The answer I offer is probably not. Just as minor parties and independent candidacies rise and fall in response to voter dissatisfaction, permanent minor parties are likely to contribute to that dissatisfaction. The American system of checks and balances—with its separation of powers, bicameralism, and federal structure—complicates the political process tremendously. By making each federal, state, and local elected official responsible for his or her own tenure in office, it does little to encourage teamwork across different policy-making bodies. More than anything else, the fragmentation of power between an independent executive and separately elected members of Congress has led to a lack of collective responsibility and the political gridlock and public frustration that often accompanies it.

The introduction of one or more permanent minor parties would make majority rule even more difficult to achieve. These parties would probably draw significant votes away from the victor in a presidential race, cutting into the president's popular majority or policy mandate. They would also probably divide opposition, making it easier for an incumbent, even an unpopular one, to win reelection.

If minor-party candidates were able to elect significant numbers of representatives and senators, they could also change the dynamics in Congress. The majority party in the legislature would have to compromise with more than one minor party in order to enact its policies. Legislators from one or more parties could prevent the majority party from dealing with important issues and escape accountability by blaming that party or one or another for not compromising enough. Increasing the number of parties would fragment power more than the framers of the Constitution intended and lead to greater gridlock, not result in the development of the parliamentary style of government—which they vigorously opposed in the first place.

CONCLUSION

With but a few exceptions, the American political system has had a history of two major parties nominating the most qualified candidates and presenting voters with the most meaningful policy choices. The two major parties have also provided most voters with their electoral decision-making cues. Once the election is over, these parties have organized the government, promoted majority rule, translated public opinion into public policy, helped to centralize power within a fragmented political system, worked to sustain a moderate and inclusive style of politics, and provided a measure of political accountability to voters. The parties have also acted as stabilizing and socializing forces in politics.

The dynamics of the American two-party system are such that when independent or minor-party candidates succeed in tapping into public sentiment, majority party candidates usually rob them of their issue and their movement's *raison d'être,* leaving these candidates and their movements to falter. Ironically, the major contributions that minor-party and independent candidacies make to American politics are to shore up the two-party system. United We Stand America has disappeared from the political universe. And, the Reform Party will probably fizzle out—as have most of its predecessors—that is, if it, too, doesn't crash and burn under Perot's leadership first.

9
INTEREST GROUPS

*O*ne of the most significant political developments over the last 25 years has been the emergence and spectacular growth of political action committees, or PACs. PACs are specially organized political campaign finance groups, functioning outside the traditional political parties, whose primary purpose is to raise and spend money on behalf of candidates running for office. Modern PACs, with members numbering in the thousands, represent all sorts of special interests, from organized labor, to professional and business organizations, to liberal and conservative ideological groups.

Although PACs clearly have every right to exist in a democratic political system and contribute significantly to our free system of elections, there are those who allege that PACs have come to exercise too much political and governmental power—that they affect electoral and legislative outcomes far more than they should, often to the detriment of the public interest.

Among the critics is Philip M. Stern, for many years an "insider" in politics and more recently a forceful critic of the cozy relationship between PACs and members of Congress. Stern's point of view on PACs is revealed by the title of his book, Still the Best Congress Money Can Buy, *from which we have excerpted several passages. From first-hand accounts of members of Congress, as well as his own analysis, Stern gives us a pretty lamentable view of the corrupting influence of money and PACs in Congress—a view that is deeply disturbing to those who think elected representatives ought to be above reproach, neither soliciting nor accepting campaign funds from special interests.*

The selection offered in rebuttal to Stern is written by political scientist Larry Sabato, considered one of the nation's leading authorities on PACs. While admitting some faults with PACs, Professor Sabato strongly defends their existence and the contributions they make to our system of democracy. In Sabato's view, PACs have been the victim of a bum rap, neither causing the current excesses in campaign finance nor unduly influencing individual legislators or the Congress as a whole.

Still the Best Congress Money Can Buy
A PAC Primer

Philip M. Stern

. . . PACs . . . have introduced into modern American politics two phenomena that distort traditional concepts of representative democracy.

First, they have re-introduced "carpetbagging" into American politics, for the first time since Reconstruction. That is, to the extent candidates and lawmakers derive their funds from PACs, they are receiving their money from entities *outside* their state or district, essentially, from people *who are not allowed to vote for them on election day.*[1]

The second distortion of democracy is the new meaning with which this newfound money-built connection between interest groups and legislative committees has altered the word "constituency." Constituents used to be citizens within a candidate's district or state who were entitled to vote for him or her. Voters. That was all. Today, PACs have introduced a new definition: members of Congress now represent—first, their voters, and second (what may be more important to them), their legislative or economic constituencies as well—who may or may not be (probably are not) part of their voting constituency. For example, the members of the Armed Services Committees and Defense Appropriations Subcommittees have as their natural economic "constituents" the defense contractors. Similarly, members of the Telecommunications Subcommittees of the House and Senate have as their legislative and economic "constituents," broadcasters, telephone companies, the cable industry, and others affected by government regulation of communications.

It's an ugly, undemocratic new concept.

How much influence do the PACs *really* have? Do they actually sway votes? Do they even win preferential access for their lobbyists?

. . . [D]efenders of the PACs argue that PAC donations have a minimal influence on the outcome of legislation. Lawmakers themselves—the recipients of the PACs' largess —indignantly protest that the PACs' influence is virtually nil. The typical refrain is, "I spent $500,000 on my last campaign. It's absolutely preposterous to suggest I would sell my vote for $1,000—or even $5,000—just one percent of my campaign budget!"

There are several counterarguments: the first—and most self-evidently powerful— is the raw evidence of the steady increases in PAC donations to candidates which have risen, on average, 40 percent annually since 1974. Evidently, the PACs think they are getting something for their money. After all, they are not charities. Here are the statistics:

Philip M. Stern, author of many books on government reform, is a former newspaper reporter and research director of the Democratic party. From Still the Best Congress Money Can Buy *by Philip M. Stern, pp. 44–48, 49, 129–134, 145–146, 148–149. Copyright © 1992 by Regnery Gateway. All rights reserved. Reprinted by special permission of Regenery Publishing, Inc., Washington, D.C.*

Year	Number of PACs	PAC Gifts to Congressional Candidates
1974	608	$ 12.5 million
1978	1,653	$ 35.2 million
1982	3,371	$ 83.6 million
1986	4,157	$135.2 million
1990	4,681	$150.5 million

Second, many legislators acknowledge that money influences their votes. In a 1987 survey of 27 senators and 87 House members, the non-partisan Center for Responsive Politics found that 20 percent of surveyed members told the interviewers that political contributions have affected their votes. An additional 30 percent were "not sure."[2]

Third, there are examples of how contributions influence members of Congress:

- Former Republican Senator Rudy Boschwitz, of Minnesota, after receiving $30,000 from the manufacture of pesticides, pushed an amendment on behalf of the Chemical Specialties Manufacturers Association (CSMA) to block states from writing regulations stiffer than federal requirements. Prior to its consideration by the Senate Agriculture Committee, the Boschwitz amendment was "widely referred to" as the "CSMA" amendment, according to *The Nation.*

- Republican Senator Orrin Hatch, of Utah, received $30,000 from company officials and PACs of the major Health Industry Manufacturers Association (HIMA) members (Eli Lilly, Bristol-Meyers and Pfizer) for his 1988 campaign. After receiving those contributions, Hatch successfully blocked a measure intended to better regulate such items as pacemakers, incubators and X-ray machines.

A more dramatic example is that of a massive campaign by the privately owned utilities to postpone repayment of $19 billion collected from consumers.

Over a period of years utilities collected money from consumers as a reserve from which to pay federal income taxes. But the 1986 tax reform act lowered the corporate tax rate from 46 to 34 percent, thus reducing the utilities' taxes by $19 billion, a savings the companies owed consumers. (The utilities owed the typical residential customer around $100.)

But how quickly should the utilities be required to repay consumers? Ordinarily that question would be left up to state regulators, but in 1986 Congress passed a special provision allowing the refunds in all states to be paid out over as long as a 30-year period.

The following year, North Dakota Democrat Byron Dorgan introduced a bill calling for a faster refund of the $19 billion. Initially, 48 other Democrats and nine Republicans were signed as co-sponsors.

Immediately the utilities responded by stepping up their political contributions. During 1987, 1988, and 1989, PACs sponsored by utilities and their trade associations gave over $5 million to sitting House members. Five hundred and ten thousand of that went to members of the tax-writing House Ways and Means Committee, through which Dorgan's bill had to pass.

The utilities' honoraria increased as well, totaling $446,000 in the years 1987 and 1988.

Slowly, supporters of the Dorgan bill changed their minds. Some examples:

- Missouri Democrat Richard Gephardt, an original co-sponsor of the Dorgan bill, withdrew his co-sponsorship after the utilities donated over $46,000 to his 1988 campaign.
- South Carolina Democrat Butler Derrick switched his position on the Dorgan bill after the utility industry lavished him with trips, honoraria and campaign contributions. Derrick told the *Wall Street Journal* that the money and trips had "nothing to do with [his decision not to renew co-sponsorship of the Dorgan bill]."
- Eight of the nine representatives who formally repudiated the Dorgan bill after co-sponsoring it received campaign donations from utility PACs averaging $13,000 each.

The original Dorgan bill died without a vote in the House Ways and Means Committee at the end of 1988. . . .

PAC proponents strenuously debate the question: how much influence do PACs really have? Do their contributions actually buy lawmakers' *votes?*

Former Wisconsin Senator William Proxmire, a legislator with 31 years experience, says the influence need not be that direct. He has written of the various subtle ways money can influence a legislator's behavior:

> It [the influence of a campaign contribution] may not come in a vote. It may come in a speech not delivered. The PAC payoff may come in a colleague not influenced. It may come in a calling off of a meeting that otherwise would result in advancing legislation. It may come in a minor change in one paragraph in a 240-page bill. It may come in a witness not invited to testify before a committee. It may come in hiring a key staff member for a committee who is sympathetic to the PAC. Or it may come in laying off or transferring a staff member who is unsympathetic to a PAC. . . .

. . . I interviewed several current and former members of Congress. Here is what they told me:

FORMER CONGRESSMAN MICHAEL BARNES OF MARYLAND

Mike Barnes came to national attention when, as the beneficiary of a liberal revolt on the House Foreign Affairs Committee, he became the chairman of the Western Hemisphere Subcommittee and a principal spokesman against the Reagan Administration's policies in Central America.

From 1978 to 1986, Barnes represented Montgomery County, Maryland, a bedroom suburb of Washington, D.C. In 1986, he ran unsuccessfully for the U.S. Senate. Barnes has a mild-mannered bespectacled mien ("I'm criticized by my friends for not being more flamboyant," he once said). But he displays great passion, especially when speaking about the urgent need for campaign finance reform. His convictions on this subject were solidified by his 1986 experience as a senatorial candidate, during which money-raising was a constant preoccupation. ("There was never a waking moment that I was not either raising money or feeling guilty that I was not.")

Barnes practices law in Washington.

As I spoke to political consultants, they all said I should not even consider running for the Senate if I weren't prepared to spend 80 or 90 percent of my time raising money. It turned out that they were absolutely correct. That's an absolute outrage because the candidates should be talking about the issues and meeting with constituents and voters and working on policy questions.

As a congressman, I had plenty of phone calls from political directors of PACs in which the conversation went something like this:

"Mike, we're getting ready to make our next round of checks out, and I just want to let you know that you're right up there at the top. We really think we can help you with a nice contribution."

"Gee, that's great. Really appreciate it. Grateful to have your help."

"Oh, by the way, Mike, have you been following that bill in Ways and Means that's going to be coming to the floor next week? It's got an item in there we're concerned about—the amendment by Congressman Schwartz. You know, we'll be supporting that and we hope you'll be with us on that one. Hope you'll take a good look at it, and if you need any information about it, we'll send that up to you."

That conversation is perfectly legal under the current laws of the United States, and it probably takes place daily in Washington, D.C. It is an absolute outrage!

You know, if that conversation took place with someone in the executive branch, someone would go to jail.

I regard it as really demeaning to both people—the guy who gets the phone call and the guy who has to make it. It's just a terrible, terrible blight on our political process.

I remember standing on the floor of the House one night when we were voting on the issue of regulations affecting the funeral industry that were, in my view, eminently reasonable. The funeral industry was opposed to this regulation. I remember the evening it was voted on; a rumor swept across the floor of the House that anybody who voted against the regulation would get $5,000 from the industry PAC for his or her upcoming campaign. I don't know if that rumor was true or not, but it flew around the place. Everybody was sort of laughing about this. There's not a doubt in my mind that that rumor had an effect on votes. I was standing next to a guy who, as he put his card in the machine [that registers representatives' votes in the House], said, "You know, I was going to vote against the industry on this thing, but what the hell, I can use the $5,000."

During the months preceding an election, I would say that more than half the conversations between congressmen relate to fundraising. "How are you doing with your fundraising? Will you stop by my fundraiser? God, I'm having a tough time getting money out of X—do you know anybody over there that could help? Do you have access to a rock group or a movie star that could help me with my fundraising?"

More often than not the question is not "Who's your opponent?" or "What are the issues in your race?" It's "How much money have you raised?" Money permeates the whole place.

You have to make a choice. Who are you going to let in the door first? You get back from lunch. You got fourteen phone messages on your desk. Thirteen of them are from constituents you've never heard of, and one of them is from a guy who doesn't live in your district, and is therefore not a constituent, but who just came to your fundraiser two weeks earlier and gave you $2,000. Which phone call are you going to return first?

Money just warps the democratic process in ways that are very sad for the country. You have otherwise responsible, dedicated public servants grubbing for money and having to spend inordinate amounts of their time raising money rather than addressing the issues that they came to Washington to deal with. And you have people trying to present their cases on the merits feeling they have no choice but to buy access to the people who will make the decisions. It demeans both sides in ways that are very sad. You've got good people on both sides, a lot of dedicated lobbyists in Washington who are trying in a responsible way to present their points of view and get forced into becoming fundraisers and contributors in a way that's really outrageous.

FORMER CONGRESSMAN TOBY MOFFETT OF CONNECTICUT

Toby Moffett was 30 years old when, as a former Naderite (he was the first director of the Connecticut Citizen Action Group, one of Ralph Nader's early grass-roots organizations), he was elected to Congress as a member of the post-Watergate class of 1974.

He soon won a seat on the House Energy and Commerce Committee, one of the PAC hot-spots, handling legislation regulating the oil, chemical, broadcasting, and health industries.

An unalloyed liberal (he might prefer the term "progressive") with prodigious energy, he initially chafed at the need, in Congress, for compromise and accommodation. As a new congressman, he observed, "After you stay in the House for a while, all the square edges get rounded off, and you get to look like all the other congressmen." Later, though, he took pleasure in the legislative skills he developed, in "working the system."

In 1982, 1984 and 1990, he ran unsuccessfully for, respectively, U.S. Senate, governor, and U.S. representative.

> There was always pressure to raise more and spend more, and build up your margin. If you win by 58 percent, it's one heck of a big difference from winning by 52 percent—in terms of what you have to face next time. So the goal is always to try and get yourself up over 60 or 62 and then 64 percent, and then, in many states, if you get up over 70 or 75, maybe you'll be unopposed. That's the dream, to be unopposed. So as a result, you go to where you have to go to get the money to build up that margin.
>
> I remember during the Carter years, right in the middle of the hospital-cost-control vote—the hospitals and the AMA were just throwing money at the [House Commerce] Committee [which was handling the bill] as fast as they could. It was coming in wheelbarrows.
>
> Our committee was a prime target, because the Commerce Committee had clean-air legislation, we had all the health bills, we had all the energy stuff—you know, natural gas pricing and that sort of stuff. We had all the communications stuff. So there was a lot of PAC money aimed at neutralizing the Committee. The PACs took those ten or fifteen [swing] votes, and they really went to work on 'em. It was just no secret. Everybody in the room knew it.

You're sitting next to a guy on the Committee and you're trying to get his vote on a clean-air amendment, and you suddenly realize that the night before he had a fundraiser, and all the people who were lobbying against the bill were at the fundraiser. Ways and Means members used to boast about the timing of their fundraisers. What kind of system is that?

In my 1982 Senate race, we had some fundraising people, the kinds of people that you bring on when you've got to raise a lot of money—I mean, very cold-blooded. You know, never mind the issues, let's get the money in. And I remember very, very well their telling me in, maybe, September, that we had to come up with $25,000 immediately for a down payment on a television buy. And I remember sitting down with a member of the House from the farm states, and he said, "How's it going?" I said, "Horrible, I've got to come up with $25,000." He said, "How about some dairy money?" And I said, "Oh, no! I can't do that." Remember, in the seventies, dairy money had a pretty bad name.[3]

He said, "Well, I can get you ten or fifteen thousand." I said, "Really?" He said, "Yeah. You know, your record has been pretty good on those issues. I think I can do it." Well, I went back to him the next day and said, "Let's do it."

By the time I got to the last month of the campaign, I was telling my wife and my close friends that here I was, somebody who took less PAC money, I think, than anybody running that year, but I felt strongly that I wasn't going to be the kind of senator that I had planned on being when I started out. I felt like they were taking a piece out of me and a piece out of my propensity to be progressive and aggressive on issues. I felt like, little by little, the process was eating away at me. One day it was insurance money, the next day it was dairy money. . . .

CONGRESSMAN JIM LEACH OF IOWA

Congressman Leach is one of a handful of House members who refuse to take campaign money from PACs, and is at the forefront of the campaign-reform movement in the House. In 1985 and 1986, he joined with Democratic Representative Mike Synar of Oklahoma in sponsoring a bill to limit the amount of PAC money any House candidate could receive in an election.

Although listed as a Republican, Jim Leach sides with the Democrats in the House on issues such as arms control, the cessation of chemical-warfare weapons production, sanctions against South Africa and denying funds for the Contra forces in Central America.

I argue that what you have in a campaign contribution is an implicit contract with the person who gave. If you listen carefully to that group's concerns, and abide by them, there is an implicit promise of another contribution for the next election.

What you've done is turn upside-down the American premise of government, which is the idea that people are elected to represent people. Officeholders should be indebted to the individuals that cast the ballots. Today candidates are becoming increasingly indebted to the people that *influence* the people who cast the ballots. It's a one-step removal. And so we're having an indirect, secondary kind of democracy—one that is increasingly group oriented and financially influenced.

If I had my way, I would eliminate all group giving to campaigns. Prohibit group giving, period. I'd make all contributions individual. I would also prohibit giving from outside the state. That is, why allow an Iowan to influence a Nebraskan or a New Yorker to influence a Californian? That's why in my own campaigns I don't accept PACs and I also don't accept out-of-state gifts.

We have $10 or $20 receptions throughout the district. We have hog roasts, we have barbecues in which we seek small contributions. But it's very time-consuming and difficult as contrasted with the people around Washington. Every night of the week, here, there's a reception at the Capitol Hill Club for candidates, and they can raise $10,000 to $150,000. That takes me three weeks. Twenty events. But on the other hand, my way gets more people involved in the process. And I think it makes them feel a little bit more part of it. For example, how much a part of a campaign is someone going to feel if they give $10 to a candidate who just got $10,000 from ten different unions? Or ten different businesses?

There's always an argument that PACs get more people involved. I've never seen it. I think it's exactly the reverse. Not having PACs forces candidates to go to the voters. I don't raise near as much as other candidates. But I raise over $100,000 and sometimes $150,000. That should be adequate to run a campaign in a state like Iowa. The fact that others in our state spend two to four to five times as much is an indication of how sick the system has become. In part, one side raises all that money because the other side does. It amounts to an arms race. What you need is a domestic SALT agreement. . . .

GOVERNOR AND FORMER SENATOR LAWTON CHILES OF FLORIDA

In 1970, an unknown state senator running for the U.S. Senate pulled on a pair of khaki trousers and hiking boots and spent 92 days hiking across Florida. His thousand-mile trek transformed his long-shot candidacy into a seat in the U.S. Senate.

One of his trademarks in the Senate became "sunshine government"—conducting the processes of government out in the open rather than behind closed doors, and subjecting officeholders' personal financial statements and the activities of lobbyists to public disclosure requirements.

In his next campaign, in 1976, Senator Chiles limited contributions to $10 and refused to accept contributions from out-of-state donors. In 1982, when the Republican Party promised to underwrite his opponent heavily, he apologetically raised the donor ceiling to $100, but added a new restriction: he would not accept contributions from political action committees. Much to the frustration of his fundraisers, he retained all of those limits for his would-be 1988 reelection campaign.

In late 1987, Chiles announced he would not seek a fourth Senate term in 1988. But he returned to politics in 1990, winning the governorship after a hard-fought campaign in which he once again limited contributions to $100 and refused to accept out-of-state contributions.

Today, PACs are running in packs, where segments of industry or segments of labor, or segments of this group, get together with multiple PACs and decide how they are going to contribute. Sometimes you're talking about $250,000 for a campaign. Overall I think they're distorting the electoral system and what I sense is, very strong, that your John Q. Public is saying, "I don't count any more. My vote doesn't count, I can't contribute enough money to count. No one is going to listen to me."

I'm looking at congressmen 50 percent of whom, I don't know exactly, but around half, that get half of their money or more by PACs. They don't even have to come home. Their money is raised at [Washington] cocktail parties.

At the same time, when I sit down with my fellow senators, they say, "The bane of our existence is fund-raising. We're having to do it over six years and we're having to go to Chicago, Los Angeles, New York, Florida. A lot of us spend a lot of time there. But that's what I have to do at night. That's what I have to do on weekends. And, of course, for these big, big PACs, I have to be pretty careful about what my voting record is going to be."

I think if out-of-state contributions were prohibited, you'd have a better chance of those people in your state making the decision based on the merit of the candidate. I think if one candidate, who usually would be an incumbent, can go raise all kinds of out-of-state money, I think he can [distort] his record very much.

A lot of people seem to think that somebody gives you a PAC contribution, then they come in and say, "I expect you to vote for this." It never happens that way. All that person wants you to do is to take and take and take, and then when he comes in, he never says, "I expect." It's always on the basis of, "This is a big one for me, and maybe my job's on the line." He doesn't need to say anything more than that because the hook is already in you and if you've taken it, you know it, and you *know* you know it. . . .

NOTES

1. I consider all PACs to be "outside" PACs unless (a) the decision as to how the PAC's money is distributed is made *within the state or district* of the particular candidate or lawmaker; or (b) unless the PAC's procedures provide for donors from a given district or state to earmark their funds for the local candidate. Many PACs and PAC defenders dispute this line of reasoning, arguing that in instances where a given PAC represents a company that has large plants and many employees in, say, the Fourth District of North Carolina, it is wrong to label that company's PAC an "outside" PAC. I maintain, however, that if that PAC is headquartered in, say, Pittsburgh, and if the decisions as to how that PAC's money is distributed nationwide are made there rather than in North Carolina, it is wrong to say that those decisions are made with the interests of the people of the Fourth District of North Carolina primarily in mind, no matter how many plants or employees that company may have in that district.
2. In addition, two-thirds of the senators and 87 percent of their staff members said that raising money affected the time they spent on legislative work. Forty-three percent of members participating in the survey said that PACs had a "largely or somewhat negative" influence on the political process. *Not a single one of the 115 staff members surveyed said that PACs had a positive impact* (Emphasis mine).
3. Because of the dairy lobby's offer of $2 million to the 1972 Nixon campaign in exchange for a higher government dairy subsidy.

The Misplaced Obsession with PACs

Larry J. Sabato

The disturbing statistics and the horror stories about political action committees seem to flow like a swollen river, week after week, year in and year out. Outrage extends across the ideological spectrum: the liberal interest group Common Cause has called the system "scandalous," while conservative former senator Barry Goldwater (R-Ariz.) has bluntly declared, "PAC money is destroying the election process. . . ."[1]

PAC-bashing is undeniably a popular campaign sport,[2] but the "big PAC attack" is an opiate that obscures the more vital concerns and problems in campaign finance. PAC excesses are merely a symptom of other serious maladies in the area of political money, but the near-obsessive focus by public interest groups and the news media on the PAC evils has diverted attention from more fundamental matters. The PAC controversy, including the charges most frequently made against them, can help explain why PACs are best described as agents of pseudo corruption.[3]

THE PAC ERA

While a good number of PACs of all political persuasions existed prior to the 1970s, it was during that decade of campaign reform that the modern PAC era began. Spawned by the Watergate-inspired revisions of the campaign finance laws, PACs grew in number from 113 in 1972 to 4,196 in 1988 [4,599 in 1998—*Editors*], and their contributions to congressional candidates multiplied more than fifteenfold, from $8.5 million in 1971–72 to $130.3 million in 1985–86 [$243 million in 1998—*Editors*].

The rapid rise of PACs has engendered much criticism, yet many of the charges made against political action committees are exaggerated and dubious. While the widespread use of the PAC structure is new, special interest money of all types has always found its way into politics. Before the 1970s it simply did so in less traceable and far more disturbing and unsavory ways. And while, in absolute terms, PACs contribute a massive sum to candidates, it is not clear that there is proportionately more interest-group money in the system than before. As political scientist Michael Malbin has argued, we will never know the truth because the earlier record is so incomplete.[4]

The proportion of House and Senate campaign funds provided by PACs has certainly increased since the early 1970s, but individuals, most of whom are unaffiliated with PACs, together with the political parties, still supply about three-fifths of all the money spent by or on behalf of House candidates and three-quarters of the campaign expenditures for Senate contenders. So while the importance of PAC spending has grown,

Larry Sabato is professor of political science at the University of Virginia. From Chapter 1, Larry J. Sabato, Paying for Elections: The Campaign Finance Thicket, *A Twentieth Century Fund Paper. © 1989 by the Twentieth Century Fund, New York. Used with permission of the Twentieth Century Fund, New York.*

PACs clearly remain secondary as a source of election funding. PACs, then, seem rather less awesome when considered within the entire spectrum of campaign finance.

Apart from the argument over the relative weight of the PAC funds, PAC critics claim that political action committees are making it more expensive to run for office. There is some validity to this assertion. Money provided to one candidate funds the purchase of campaign tools that the other candidate must match in order to stay competitive.

In the aggregate, American campaign expenditures seem huge. In 1988, the total amount spent by all U.S. House of Representatives candidates taken together was about $256 million, and the campaign cost of the winning House nominee averaged over $392,000. Will Rogers's 1931 remark has never been more true: "Politics has got so expensive that it takes lots of money to even get beat with."

Yet $256 million is far less than the annual advertising budgets of many individual commercial enterprises. These days it is expensive to communicate, whether the message is political or commercial. Television time, polling costs, consultants' fees, direct-mail investment, and other standard campaign expenditures have been soaring in price, over and above inflation.[5] PACs have been fueling the use of new campaign techniques, but a reasonable case can be made that such expenses are necessary, and that more and better communication is required between candidates and an electorate that often appears woefully uninformed about politics. PACs therefore may be making a positive contribution by providing the means to increase the flow of information during elections.

PACs are also accused of being biased toward the incumbent, and except for the ideological committees, they do display a clear and overwhelming preference for those already in office. But the same bias is apparent in contributions from individuals, who ask the same reasonable, perhaps decisive, economic question: Why waste money on contenders if incumbents almost always win? On the other hand, the best challengers—those perceived as having fair-to-good chances to win—are usually generously funded by PACs. Well-targeted PAC challenger money clearly helped the GOP win a majority in the U.S. Senate in 1980, for instance, and in turn aided the Democrats in their 1986 Senate takeover.

The charge that PACs limit the number of strong challengers is true, because by giving so much money so early in the race to incumbents, they deter potential opponents from declaring their candidacies. On the other hand, the money that PACs channel to competitive challengers late in the election season may actually help increase the turnover of officeholders on election day. PAC money also tends to invigorate competitiveness in open-seat congressional races where there is no incumbent. . . .

PAC MONEY AND CONGRESSIONAL "CORRUPTION"

The most serious charge leveled at PACs is that they succeed in buying the votes of legislators on issues important to their individual constituencies. It seems hardly worth arguing that many PACs are shopping for congressional votes and that PAC money buys access, or opens doors, to congressmen. But the "vote-buying" allegation is generally not supported by a careful examination of the facts.[6] PAC contributions do make a difference, at least on some occasions, in securing access and influencing the course of events, but those occasions are not nearly as frequent as anti-PAC spokesmen, even congressmen themselves, often suggest.

PACs affect legislative proceedings to a decisive degree only when certain conditions prevail. First, the less visible the issue, the more likely that PAC funds can change or influence congressional votes. A corollary is that PAC money has more effect in the early stages of the legislative process, such as agenda setting and votes in subcommittee meetings, than in later and more public floor deliberations. Press, public, and even "watchdog" groups are not nearly as attentive to initial legislative proceedings.

PAC contributions are also more likely to influence the legislature when the issue is specialized and narrow, or unopposed by other organized interests. PAC gifts are less likely to be decisive on broad national issues such as American policy in Nicaragua or the adoption of a Star Wars missile defense system. But the more technical measures seem tailor-made for the special interests. Additionally, PAC influence in Congress is greater when large PACs or groups of PACs (such as business and labor PACs) are allied. In recent years, despite their natural enmity, business and labor have lobbied together on a number of issues, including defense spending, trade policy, environmental regulation, maritime legislation, trucking legislation, and nuclear power.[7] The combination is a weighty one, checked in many instances only by a tendency for business and labor in one industry (say, the railroads) to combine and oppose their cooperating counterparts in another industry (perhaps the truckers and teamsters).

It is worth stressing, however, that most congressmen are not unduly influenced by PAC money on most votes. The special conditions simply do not apply to most legislative issues, and the overriding factors in determining a legislator's votes include party affiliation, ideology, and constituents' needs and desires. Much has been made of the passage of large tax cuts for oil and business interests in the 1981 omnibus tax package. The journalist Elizabeth Drew said there was a "bidding war" to trade campaign contributions for tax breaks benefiting independent oil producers.[8] Ralph Nader's Public Citizen group charged that the $280,000 in corporate PAC money accepted by members of the House Ways and Means Committee helped to produce a bill that "contained everything business ever dared to ask for, and more."[9] Yet as Robert Samuelson has convincingly argued, the "bidding war" between Democrats and Republicans was waged not for PAC money but for control of a House of Representatives sharply divided between Reaganite Republicans and liberal Democrats, with conservative "boll weevil" Democrats from the southern oil states as the crucial swing votes.[10] The Ways and Means Committee actions cited by Nader were also more correctly explained in partisan terms. After all, if these special interests were so influential in writing the 1981 omnibus tax package, how could they fail so completely to derail the much more important (and, for them, threatening) tax reform legislation of 1986?

If party loyalty can have a stronger pull than PAC contributions, then surely the views of a congressman's constituents can also take precedence over those of political action committees. If an incumbent is faced with the choice of either voting for a PAC-backed bill that is very unpopular in his district or forgoing the PAC's money, the odds are that any politician who depends on a majority of votes to remain in office is going to side with his constituency and vote against the PAC's interest. PAC gifts are merely a means to an end: reelection. If accepting money will cause a candidate embarrassment, then even a maximum donation will likely be rejected. The flip side of this proposition makes sense as well: if a PAC's parent organization has many members or a major financial stake in the congressman's home district, he is much more likely to vote the PAC's way—not so much because he receives PAC money but because the group accounts for an important part of his electorate. Does a U.S. senator from a dairy state vote for dairy price supports because he received a significant percentage of his PAC contributions from agriculture, or because the farm population of his state is relatively large and politically active? When congressmen vote the National Rifle Association's preferences is it because of the money the NRA's PAC distributes, or because the NRA, unlike gun-control advocates, has repeatedly demonstrated the ability to produce a sizable number of votes in many legislative districts?

If PACs have appeared more influential than they actually are, it is partly because many people believe legislators are looking for opportunities to exclaim (as one did during the Abscam scandal) "I've got larceny in my blood!" It is certainly disturbing that the National Republican Congressional Committee believed it necessary to warn its PAC-soliciting candidates: "Don't *ever* suggest to the PAC that it is 'buying' your vote, should you get elected."[11] Yet knowledgeable Capitol Hill observers agree that there are few truly corrupt congressmen. Simple correlations notwithstanding, when most legislators vote for a PAC-supported bill, it is because of the *merits* of the case, or the entreaties of their party leaders, peers, or constituents, and not because of PAC money.

When the PAC phenomenon is viewed in the broad perspective of issues, party allegiance, and constituent interests, it is clear that *merit* matters most in the votes most congressmen cast. It is naive to contend that PAC money never influences decisions, but it is unjustifiably cynical to believe that PACs always, or even usually, push the voting buttons in Congress.

PACS IN PERSPECTIVE

As the largely unsubstantiated "vote-buying" controversy suggests, PACs are often misrepresented and unfairly maligned as the embodiment of corrupt special interests. Political action committees are a contemporary manifestation of what James Madison called "factions." In his *Federalist, No. 10,* Madison wrote that through the flourishing of these competing interest groups, or factions, liberty would be preserved.[12]

In any democracy, and particularly in one as pluralistic as the United States, it is essential that groups be relatively unrestricted in advocating their interests and positions. Not only is that the mark of a free society, it also provides a safety valve for the competitive pressures that build on all fronts in a capitalistic democracy. And it provides another means to keep representatives responsive to legitimate needs.

This is not to say that all groups pursue legitimate interests, or that vigorously competing interests ensure that the public good prevails. The press, the public, and valuable watchdog groups such as Common Cause must always be alert to instances in which narrow private interests prevail over the commonweal—occurrences that generally happen when no one is looking.

Besides the press and various public interest organizations, there are two major institutional checks on the potential abuses wrought by factions, associations, and now PACs. The most fundamental of these is regular free elections with general suffrage. As Tocqueville commented:

> Perhaps the most powerful of the causes which tend to mitigate the excesses of political association in the United States is Universal Suffrage. In countries in which universal suffrage exists, the majority is never doubtful, because neither party can pretend to represent the portion of the community which has not voted.
>
> The associations which are formed are aware, as well as the nation at large, that they do not represent the majority: this is, indeed, a condition inseparable from their existence; for if they did represent the prepondering power, they would change the law instead of soliciting its reform.[13]

[Former] Senator Robert Dole (R-Kan.) has said, "There aren't any Poor PACs or Food Stamp PACs or Nutrition PACs or Medicare PACs,"[14] and PAC critics frequently make the point that certain segments of the electorate are underrepresented in the PAC community. Yet without much support from PACs, there are food stamps, poverty and nutrition programs, and Medicare. Why? Because the recipients of governmental assistance constitute a hefty slice of the electorate, and *votes matter more than dollars to politicians.* Furthermore, many citizens *outside* the affected groups have also made known their support of aid to the poor and elderly—making yet a stronger electoral case for these PAC-less programs.

The other major institution that checks PAC influence is the two-party system. While PACs represent particular interests, the political parties build coalitions of groups and attempt to represent a national interest. They arbitrate among competing claims, and they seek to reach a consensus on matters of overriding importance to the nation. The parties are one of the few unifying forces in an exceptionally diverse country. . . .

However limited and checkmated by political realities PACs may be, they are still regarded by a skeptical public as thoroughly unsavory. PACs have become the embodiment of greedy special interest politics, rising campaign costs, and corruption. It does not seem to matter that most experts in the field of campaign finance take considerable exception to the prevailing characterization of political action committees. PACs have become, in the public's mind, a powerful symbol of much that is wrong with America's campaign process, and candidates for public office naturally manipulate this symbol as well as others for their own ends. It is a circumstance as old as the Republic.

PACs, however, have done little to change their image for the better. Other than the business-oriented Public Affairs Council, few groups or committees have moved to correct one-sided press coverage or educate the public on campaign financing's fundamentals. In fact, many PACs fuel the fires of discontent by refusing to defend themselves while not seeming to care about appearances. Giving to both candidates in the same race, for example—an all-too-common practice—may be justifiable in theory, but it strikes most people as unprincipled, rank influence purchasing. Even worse, perhaps, are PACs that "correct their mistakes" soon after an election by sending a donation to the winning, but not originally PAC-supported, candidate. In the seven 1986 U.S. Senate races where a Democratic challenger defeated a Republican incumbent, there were 150 instances in which a PAC gave to the GOP candidate *before* the election and to the victorious Democrat once the votes were counted.[15] These practices PACs themselves should stop. Every PAC should internally ban double giving, and there should be a moratorium on gifts to previously opposed candidates until at least the halfway point of the officeholder's term.

Whether PACs undertake some necessary rehabilitative steps or not, any fair appraisal of their role in American elections must be balanced. PACs are neither political innocents nor selfless civic boosters. But, neither are they cesspools of corruption and greed, nor modern-day versions of Tammany Hall.

PACs will never be popular with idealistic reformers because they represent the rough, cutting edge of a democracy teeming with different peoples and conflicting interests. Indeed, PACs may never be hailed even by natural allies; it was the business-oriented *Wall Street Journal,* after all, that editorially referred to Washington, D.C., as "a place where politicians, PACs, lawyers, and lobbyists for unions, business or you-name-it, shake each other down full time for political money and political support."[16]

Viewed in perspective, the root of the problem in campaign finance is not PACs; it is money. Americans have an enduring mistrust of the mix of money (particularly business money) and politics, as Finley Peter Dunne's Mr. Dooley revealed:

> I niver knew a pollytician to go wrong ontil he'd been contaminated be contact with a business man. . . . It seems to me that th' only thing to do is to keep pollyticians an' business men apart. They seem to have a bad infloonce on each other. Whiniver I see an alderman an' a banker walkin' down th' street together I know th' Recordin' Angel will have to ordher another bottle iv ink.[17]

As a result of the new campaign finance rules of the 1970s, political action committees superseded the "fat cats" of old as the public focus and symbol of the role of money in politics, and PACs inherited the suspicions that go with the territory. Those suspicions are valuable because they keep the spotlight on PACs and guard against undue influence. It may be regrettable that such supervision is required, but human nature—not PACs—demands it.

NOTES

1. Quotations from Common Cause direct-mail package to members, January 1987.
2. *The New Republic,* May 28, 1984, p. 9.
3. For a much more extended discussion of these subjects, see Larry Sabato, *PAC POWER: Inside the World of Political Action Committees,* rev. ed. (New York: Report of the Twentieth Century Fund Task Force on Political Action Committees, 1984).
4. Michael J. Malbin, "The Problem of PAC-Journalism," *Public Opinion,* December/January 1983, pp. 15–16, 59.
5. See Larry Sabato, *The Rise of Political Consultants* (New York: Basic Books, 1981); see also *National Journal,* April 16, 1983, pp. 780–81.
6. See Sabato, PAC POWER, pp. 122–59, 222–28.
7. See, for example, Edwin M. Epstein, "An Irony of Electoral Reform," *Regulation,*

May/June 1979, pp. 35–44; and Christopher Madison, "Federal Subsidy Programs under Attack by Unlikely Marriage of Labor and Right," *National Journal,* December 31, 1983, pp. 2682–84.

8. Elizabeth Drew, "Politics and Money, Part I" *The New Yorker,* December 6, 1982, pp. 38–45.

9. Herbert E. Alexander, *Financing the 1980 Election* (Lexington, Mass.: D.C. Heath, 1983), p. 379.

10. Robert J. Samuelson, "The Campaign Reform Failure," *The New Republic,* September 5, 1983, pp. 32–33.

11. From the NRCC publication "Working with PACs" (1982).

12. See *The Federalist, No. 10,* for a much fuller discussion of the role of factions in a democratic society.

13. Alexis de Tocqueville, *Democracy in America,* vol. 1 (New York: Vintage Books, 1954), p. 224.

14. As quoted in Drew, "Politics and Money," p. 147.

15. Common Cause "If At First You Don't Succeed, Give, Give Again" (Press release, Washington, D.C., March 20, 1987).

16. "Cleaning Up Reform," *The Wall Street Journal,* November 10, 1983, p. 26.

17. Finley Peter Dunne, *The World of Mr. Dooley,* edited with an introduction by Louis Filler (New York: Collier Books, 1962), pp. 155–56.

10

CONGRESS

Representation

The three selections in this section are illustrative of a long-standing debate among political theorists and elected officials alike—namely, whose views should prevail on a given issue, the constituents' or the representatives'? In the first selection, taken from an early debate in the General Assembly of Virginia, the argument is made that legislators are obliged to act as instructed delegates—*that is, that they must vote in accordance with the will of their constituents. In the second selection, former Massachusetts senator and president, John F. Kennedy, writing in 1956, argued that legislators should act as* trustees, *voting according to their own conscience, regardless of whether their choices reflect the sentiments of their constituents. Finally, George Galloway, a former staff assistant in Congress, contends that on some occasions legislators must follow public opinion, while on others they are obliged to vote according to their own conscience. This view, which combines both the delegate and the trustee approach, is characterized as the* politico *role.*

The Legislator as Delegate

General Assembly of Virginia

There can be no doubt that the scheme of a representative republic was derived to our forefathers from the constitution of the English House of Commons; and that that branch of the English government . . . was in its origin, and in theory always has been, purely republican. It is certain, too, that the statesmen of America, in assuming that as the model of our own institutions, designed to adopt it here in its purest form, and with its strictest republican tenets and principles. It becomes, therefore, an inquiry of yet greater utility than curiosity, to ascertain the sound doctrines of the constitution of the English House of Commons in regard to this right of the constituent to instruct the representative. For the position may safely be assumed that the wise and virtuous men who framed our constitutions deigned, that, in the United States, the constituent should have at least as much, if not a great deal more, influence over the representative than was known to have existed from time immemorial in England. Let us then interrogate the history of the British nation; let us consult the opinions of their wise men.

Instances abound in parliamentary history of formal instructions from the constituent to the representative, of which . . . the following may suffice: In 1640, the knights of the shire for Dorset and Kent informed the commons *that they had in charge from their constituents* seven articles of grievances, which they accordingly laid before the House, where they were received and acted on. In the 33rd year of Charles II, the citizens of London instructed their members to insist on the bill for excluding the Duke of York (afterward King James II) from the succession to the throne; and their representative said "that his *duty* to his electors *obliged* him to vote the bill." At a subsequent election, in 1681, in many places, formal instructions were given to the members returned, to insist on the same exclusion bill; we know, from history, how uniformly and faithfully those instructions were obeyed. . . . In 1741, the citizens of London instructed their members to vote against standing armies, excise laws, the septennial bill, and a long train of evil measures, already felt, or anticipated; and expressly affirm their right of instruction—"We think it" (say they) "our *duty,* as it is *our undoubted right,* to acquaint you, with *what we desire and expect from you, in discharge of the great trust we repose in you,* and what we take to be *your duty as our representative,* etc." In the same year, instructions of a similar character were sent from all parts of England. In 1742, the cities of London, Bristol, Edinburgh, York, and many others, instructed their members in parliament to seek redress against certain individuals suspected to have betrayed and deserted the cause of the people. . . .

Instances also are on record of the deliberate formal knowledgement of the right of instruction by the House of Commons itself, especially in old times. Thus the commons hesitated to grant supplies to King Edward III *till they had the consent of their con-*

From Commonwealth of Virginia, General Assembly, Journal of the Senate, *1812, pp. 82–89. In some instances, spelling and punctuation have been altered from the original in order to achieve greater clarity.*

*stituents, a*nd desired that a new parliament might be summoned, which might be *prepared with authority from their constituents*. . . .

"Instructions" (says a member of the House of Commons) "ought to be *followed implicitly,"* after the member has *respectfully* given his constituents *his opinion* of them: *"Far be it from me to oppose my judgment to that of 6000 of my fellow citizens."* "The practice" (says another) "of consulting our constituents was good. I wish it was continued. *We can discharge our duty no better, than in the direction of those who sent us hither. What the people choose is right, because they choose it."* . . .

Without referring to the minor political authors . . . who have maintained these positions (quoted from one of them)—"that the people have a right to instruct their representatives; that no man ought to be chosen that will not receive instructions; that the people understand enough of the interests of the country to give general instructions; that it was the custom formerly to instruct all the members; and the nature of deputation shows that the custom was well grounded"—it is proper to mention that the great constitutional lawyer Coke . . . says, "It is the *custom of parliament,* when any new device is moved for on the king's behalf, for his aid and the like, that the commons may answer, *they dare not agree to it without conference with their counties."* And Sydney . . . maintains "that members derive their power from those that choose them; that those who give power do not give an unreserved power; that many members, in all ages, and sometimes the whole body of the commons have refused to vote until they consulted with those who sent them; that the houses have often adjourned to give them time to do so and if this were done more frequently, or if cities, towns and counties had on some occasions given instructions to their deputies, matters would probably have gone better in parliament than they have done." . . . The celebrated Edmund Burke, a man, it must be admitted, of profound knowledge, deep foresight, and transcendent abilities, disobeyed the instructions of his constituents; yet, by placing his excuse on the ground that the instructions were but the clamour of the day, he seems to admit the authority of instructions soberly and deliberately given; for he agrees, "he ought to look to their opinions" (which he explains to mean their permanent settled opinions) "but not the flash of the day"; and he says elsewhere, that he could not bear to show himself "a representative, whose face did not reflect the face of his constituents—a face that did not joy in their joys and sorrow in their sorrows." It is remarkable that, notwithstanding a most splendid display of warm and touching eloquence, the people of Bristol would not re-elect Mr. Burke, for this very offense of disobeying instructions. . . .

It appears, therefore, that the right of the constituent to instruct the representative, is firmly established in England, on the broad basis of the nature of representation. The existence of that right, there, has been demonstrated by the only practicable evidence, by which the principles of an unwritten constitution can be ascertained—history and precedent.

To view the subject upon principle, the right of the constituent to instruct the representative, seems to result, clearly and conclusively, from the very nature of the representative system. Through means of that noble institution, the largest nation may, almost as conveniently as the smallest, enjoy all the advantages of a government by the people, without any of the evils of democracy—precipitation, confusion, turbulence, distraction from the ordinary and useful pursuits of industry. And it is only to avoid those and the like mischiefs, that representation is substituted for the direct suffrage of the people in the office of legislation. The representative, therefore, must in the nature of things, represent his own particular constituents only. He must, indeed, look to the general good of the nation, but he must look also, and especially to the interests of his particular constituents as concerned in the commonweal; because the general good is but the aggregate of individual happiness. He must legislate for the whole nation; but laws are expressions of the general will; and the general will is only the result of individual wills fairly collected and compared. In order . . . to express the general will . . . it is plain that the representative must express the will and speak the opinions of the constituents that depute him.

It cannot be pretended that a representative is to be the organ of his own will alone; for then, he would be so far despotic. *He must be the organ of others*—of whom? Not of the nation, for the nation deputes him not; but of his constituents, who alone know, alone have trusted, and can alone displace him. And if it be his province and his duty, in general, to express the will of his constituents, to the best of his knowledge, without being particularly informed thereof, it seems impossible to contend that he is not bound to do so when he is so especially informed and instructed.

The right of the constituent to instruct the representative, therefore, is an essential principle of the representative system. It may be remarked that wherever representation has been introduced, however unfavorable the circumstances under which it existed, however short its duration, however unimportant its functions, however dimly understood, the right of instruction has always been regarded as inseparably incidental to it. . . .

A representative has indeed a wide field of discretion left to him; and great is the confidence reposed in his integrity, fidelity, wisdom, zeal; but neither is the field of discretion boundless, nor the extent of confidence infinite; and the very discretion allowed him, and the very confidence he enjoys, is grounded on the supposition that he is charged with the will, acquainted with the opinions, and devoted to the interests of his constituents. . . .

Various objections have been urged to this claim of the constituent, of a right to instruct the representative, on which it may be proper to bestow some attention.

The first objection that comes to be considered . . . is grounded on the supposed impossibility of fairly ascertaining the sense of the constituent body. The *impossibility* is denied. It may often be a matter of great *difficulty;* but then the duty of obedience resolves itself into a question, not of principle, but of fact: whether the right of instruction has been exercised or not. The representative cannot be bound by an instruction that is not given; but that is no objection to the obligation of an instruction *actually given.* . . .

It has been urged that the representatives are not bound to obey the instructions of their constituents because the constituents do not hear the debates, and therefore, cannot be supposed judges of the matter to be voted. If this objection has force enough to defeat the right of instruction, it ought to take away, also, the right of rejecting the representative at the subsequent election. For it might be equally urged on that occasion, as against the right of instruction, that the people heard not the debate that enlightened the representative's mind—the reasons that convinced his judgment and governed his conduct. . . . In other words, the principle that mankind is competent to self-government should be renounced. The truth is, that our institutions suppose that although the representative ought to be, and generally will be, selected for superior virtue and intelligence, yet a greater mass of wisdom and virtue still reside in the constituent body than the utmost portion allotted to any individual. . . .

Finally, it has been objected, that the instructions of the constituent are not obligatory on the representative because the obligation insisted on is fortified with no sanction—the representative cannot be punished for his disobedience, and his vote is valid notwithstanding his disobedience. It is true that there is no mode of legal punishment provided for this . . . default of duty and that the act of disobedience will not invalidate the vote. It is true, too, that a representative may perversely advocate a measure which he knows to be ruinous to his country; and that neither his vote will be invalidated by his depravity, nor can he be punished by law for his crime, heinous as it surely is. But it does not follow that the one representative is *not bound to obey the instructions* of his constituents any more than that the other is not bound to obey the dictates of his conscience. Both duties stand upon the same foundation, with almost all the great political and moral obligations. The noblest duties of man are without any legal sanction: the great mass of social duties . . ., our duties to our parents, to our children, to our wives, to our families, to our neighbor, to our country, our duties to God, are, for the most part, without legal sanction, yet surely not without the strongest obligation. The duty of the *representative* to obey the instructions of the *constituent* body cannot be placed on higher ground.

Such are the opinions of the General Assembly of Virginia, on the subject of this great right of instruction, and such the general reasons on which those opinions are founded. . . .

The Legislator as Trustee

John F. Kennedy

The primary responsibility of a senator, most people assume, is to represent the views of his state. Ours is a federal system—a union of relatively sovereign states whose needs differ greatly—and my constitutional obligations as senator would thus appear to require me to represent the interests of my state. Who will speak for Massachusetts if her own senators do not? Her rights and even her identity become submerged. Her equal representation in Congress is lost. Her aspirations, however much they may from time to time be in the minority, are denied that equal opportunity to be heard to which all minority views are entitled.

Any senator need not look very long to realize that his colleagues are representing *their* local interests. And if such interests are ever to be abandoned in favor of the national good, let the constituents—not the senator—decide when and to what extent. For he is their agent in Washington, the protector of their rights, recognized by the vice president in the Senate Chamber as "the senator from Massachusetts" or "the senator from Texas."

But when all of this is said and admitted, we have not yet told the full story. For in Washington we are "United States senators" and members of the Senate of the United States as well as senators from Massachusetts and Texas. Our oath of office is administered by the vice president, not by the governors of our respective states; and we come to Washington, to paraphrase Edmund Burke, not as hostile ambassadors or special pleaders for our state or section, in opposition to advocates and agents of other areas, but as members of the deliberative assembly of one nation with one interest. Of course, we should not ignore the needs of our area—nor could we easily as products of that area—but none could be found to look out for the national interest if local interests wholly dominated the role of each of us.

There are other obligations in addition to those of state and region—the obligations of the party. . . . Even if I can disregard those pressures, do I not have an obligation to go along with the party that placed me in office? We believe in this country in the principle of party responsibility, and we recognize the necessity of adhering to party platforms—if the party label is to mean anything to the voters. Only in this way can our basically two-party nation avoid the pitfalls of multiple splinter parties, whose purity and rigidity of principle, I might add—if I may suggest a sort of Gresham's Law of politics—increase inversely with the size of their membership.

And yet we cannot permit the pressures of party responsibility to submerge on every issue the call of personal responsibility. For the party which, in its drive for unity, discipline and success, ever decides to exclude new ideas, independent conduct or insurgent members, is in danger. . . .

Of course, both major parties today seek to serve the national interest. They would do so in order to obtain the broadest base of support, if for no nobler reason. But when party and officeholder differ as to how the national interest is to be served, we must place first the responsibility we owe not to our party or even to our constituents but to our individual consciences.

But it is a little easier to dismiss one's obligations to local interests and party ties to face squarely the problem of one's responsibility to the will of his constituents. A senator who avoids this responsibility would appear to be accountable to no one, and the basic safeguards of our democratic system would thus have vanished. He is no longer representative in the true sense, he has violated his public trust, he has betrayed the confidence demonstrated by those who voted for him to carry out their views. "Is the creature," as John Tyler asked the House of Representatives in his maiden speech, "to set himself in opposition to his Creator? Is the servant to disobey the wishes of his master?"

> How can he be regarded as representing the people when he speaks, not their language, but his own? He ceases to be their representative when he does so, and represents himself alone.

In short, according to this school of thought, if I am to be properly responsive to the will of my constituents, it is my duty to place their principles, not mine, above all else. This may not always be easy, but it nevertheless is the essence of democracy, faith in the wisdom of the people and their views. To be sure, the people will make mistakes—they will get no better government than they deserve—but that is far better than the representative of the people arrogating for himself the right to say he knows better than they what is good for them. Is he not chosen, the argument closes, to vote as they would vote were they in his place?

It is difficult to accept such a narrow view of the role of a United States senator— a view that assumes the people of Massachusetts sent me to Washington to serve merely as a seismograph to record shifts in popular opinion. I reject this view not because I lack faith in the "wisdom of the people," but because this concept of democracy actually puts too little faith in the people. Those who would deny the obligation of the representative to be bound by every impulse of the electorate—regardless of the conclusions his own deliberations direct—do trust in the wisdom of the people. They have faith in their ultimate sense of justice, faith in their ability to honor courage and respect judgment, and faith that in the long run they will act unselfishly for the good of the nation. It is that kind of faith on which democracy is based, not simply the often frustrated hope that public opinion will at all times under all circumstances promptly identify itself with the public interest.

The voters selected us, in short, because they had confidence in our judgment and our ability to exercise that judgment from a position where we could determine what were their own best interests, as a part of the nation's interests. This may mean that we must on occasion lead, inform, correct and sometimes even ignore constituent opinion, if we are to exercise fully that judgment for which we were elected. But acting without selfish motive or private bias, those who follow the dictates of an intelligent conscience are not aristocrats, demagogues, eccentrics, or callous politicians insensitive to the feelings of the public. They expect—and not without considerable trepidation—their constituents to be the final judges of the wisdom of their course; but they have faith that those constituents—today, tomorrow, or even in another generation—will at least respect the principles that motivated their independent stand.

If their careers are temporarily or even permanently buried under an avalanche of abusive editorials, poison-pen letters, and opposition votes at the polls—as they sometimes are, for that is the risk they take—they await the future with hope and confidence, aware of the fact that the voting public frequently suffers from what ex-Congressman T. V. Smith called the lag "between our way of thought and our way of life." . . .

Moreover, I question whether any senator, before we vote on a measure, can state with certainty exactly how the majority of his constituents feel on the issue as it is presented to the Senate. All of us in the Senate live in an iron lung—the iron lung of politics, and it is no easy task to emerge from that rarefied atmosphere in order to breathe the same fresh air our constituents breathe. It is difficult, too, to see in person an appreciable number of voters besides those professional hangers-on and vocal elements who gather about the politician on a trip home. In Washington I frequently find myself believing that forty or fifty letters, six visits from professional politicians and lobbyists, and three editorials in Massachusetts newspapers constitute public opinion on a given issue. Yet in truth I rarely know how the great majority of the voters feel, or even how much they know of the issues that seem so burning in Washington.

Today the challenge of political courage looms larger than ever before. For our everyday life is becoming so saturated with the tremendous power of mass communications that any unpopular or unorthodox course arouses a storm of protests. . . . Our political life is becoming so expensive, so mechanized, and so dominated by professional politicians and public relations men that the idealist who dreams of independent statesmanship is rudely awakened by the necessities of election and accomplishment. . . .

And thus, in the days ahead, only the very courageous will be able to take the hard and unpopular decisions necessary for our survival. . . .

The Legislator as Politico

George B. Galloway

One question which the conscientious congressman must often ask himself, especially when conflicts arise between local or regional attitudes and interests and the national welfare, is this: "As a member of Congress, am I merely a delegate from my district or state, restricted to act and vote as the majority which elected me desire, bound by the instructions of my constituents and subservient to their will? Or am I, once elected, a representative of the people of the United States, free to act as I think best for the country generally?

In a country as large as the United States, with such diverse interests and such a heterogeneous population, the economic interests and social prejudices of particular states and regions often clash with those of other sections and with conceptions of the general interest of the whole nation. The perennial demand of the silver-mining and wool interests in certain western states for purchase and protection, the struggle over slavery, and the . . . filibuster of southern senators against the attempt to outlaw racial discrimination in employment are familiar examples of recurring conflicts between local interests and prejudices and the common welfare. These political quarrels are rooted in the varying stages of cultural development attained by the different parts of the country. It is the peculiar task of the politician to compose these differences, to reconcile conflicting national and local attitudes, and to determine when public opinion is ripe for legislative action. Some conflicts will yield in time to political adjustment; others must wait for their legal sanction upon the gradual evolution of the conscience of society. No act of Congress can abolish unemployment or barking dogs or racial prejudices. . . .

TYPES OF PRESSURES ON CONGRESS

One can sympathize with the plight of the conscientious congressman who is the focal point of all these competing pressures. The district or state he represents may need and want certain roads, post offices, courthouses, or schools. Irrigation dams or projects may be needed for the development of the area's resources. If the representative is to prove himself successful in the eyes of the people back home, he must be able to show, at least occasionally, some visible and concrete results of his congressional activity. Or else he must be able to give good reasons why he has not been able to carry out his pledges. The local residence rule for congressmen multiplies the pressures that impinge upon him. Faithful party workers who have helped elect him will expect the

George B. Galloway (1898–1967) formerly was senior specialist in American government with the Legislative Reference Service of the Library of Congress. Selected excerpts from pp. 284–85, 301, 319–22 from Congress at the Crossroads *by George B. Galloway. Copyright 1946 by George B. Galloway. Copyright renewed. Reprinted by permission of HarperCollins Publishers, Inc.*

congressman to pay his political debts by getting them jobs in the federal service. Constituents affected by proposed legislation may send him an avalanche of letters, telegrams, and petitions which must be acknowledged and followed up. The region from which he comes will expect him to protect and advance its interests in Washington. All the various organized groups will press their claims upon him and threaten him if he does not jump when they crack the whip. Party leaders may urge a congressman to support or oppose the administration program or to "trade" votes for the sake of party harmony or various sectional interests. He is also under pressure from his own conscience as to what he should do both to help the people who have elected him and to advance the best interests of the nation. Besieged by all these competing pressures, a congressman is often faced with the choice of compromising between various pressures, of trading votes, of resisting special interests of one sort or another, of staying off the floor when a vote is taken on some measure he prefers not to take a stand on, of getting support here and at the same time running the risk of losing support there. Dealing with pressure blocs is a problem in political psychology which involves a careful calculation of the power of the blocs, the reaction of the voters on election day, and the long-haul interests of the district, state, and nation. . . .

SHOULD CONGRESS LEAD OR FOLLOW
PUBLIC OPINION?

It is axiomatic to say that in a democracy public opinion is the source of law. Unless legislation is sanctioned by the sense of right of the people, it becomes a dead letter on the statute books, like Prohibition and the Hatch Act. But public opinion is a mercurial force; now quiescent, now vociferous, it has various moods and qualities. It reacts to events and is often vague and hard to weigh.

Nor is public opinion infallible. Most people are naturally preoccupied with their personal problems and daily affairs; national problems and legislative decisions seem complex and remote to them, despite press and radio and occasional Capitol tours. Comparatively few adults understand the technicalities of foreign loans or reciprocal trade treaties, although congressional action on these aspects of our foreign economic policy may have far-reaching effects upon our standard of living. . . .

In practice, a congressman both leads and follows public opinion. The desires of his constituents, of his party, and of this or that pressure group all enter into his decisions on matters of major importance. The influence of these factors varies from member to member and measure to measure. Some congressmen consider it their duty to follow closely what they think is the majority opinion of their constituents, especially just before an election. Others feel that they should make their decisions without regard to their constituents' wishes in the first place, and then try to educate and convert them afterward. Some members are strong party men and follow more or less blindly the program of the party leaders. Except when they are very powerful in the home district, the pressure groups are more of a nuisance than a deciding influence on the average member. When a legislator is caught between the conflicting pressures of his constituents and his colleagues, he perforce compromises between them and follows his own judgment.

The average legislator discovers early in his career that certain interests or prejudices of his constituents are dangerous to trifle with. Some of these prejudices may not be of fundamental importance to the welfare of the nation, in which case he is justified in humoring them, even though he may disapprove. The difficult case occurs where the prejudice concerns some fundamental policy affecting the national welfare. A sound sense of values, the ability to discriminate between that which is of fundamental importance and that which is only superficial, is an indispensable qualification of a good legislator.

Senator Fulbright* gives an interesting example of this distinction in his stand on the poll-tax issue and isolationism. "Regardless of how persuasive my colleagues or the national press may be about the evils of the poll tax, I do not see its fundamental importance, and I shall follow the views of the people of my state. Although it may be symbolic of conditions which many deplore, it is exceedingly doubtful that its abolition will cure any of our major problems. On the other hand, regardless of how strongly opposed my constituents may prove to be to the creation of, and participation in, an ever stronger United Nations Organization, I could not follow such a policy in that field unless it becomes clearly hopeless."[1]

A TWO-WAY JOB

As believers in democracy, probably most Americans would agree that it is the duty of congressmen to follow public opinion insofar as it expresses the desires, wants, needs, aspirations, and ideals of the people. Most Americans probably would also consider it essential for their representatives to make as careful an appraisal of these needs and desires as they can, and to consider, in connection with such an appraisal, the ways and means of accomplishing them. Legislators have at hand more information about legal structures, economic problems, productive capacities, manpower possibilities, and the like, than the average citizen they represent. They can draw upon that information to inform and lead the people—by showing the extent to which their desires can be realized.

In other words, a true representative of the people would follow the people's desires and at the same time lead the people in formulating ways of accomplishing those desires. He would lead the people in the sense of calling to their attention the difficulties of achieving those aims and the ways to overcome the difficulties. This means also that, where necessary, he would show special interest groups or even majorities how, according to his own interpretation and his own conscience, their desires need to be tempered in the common interest or for the future good of the nation.

Thus the job of a congressman is a two-way one. He represents his local area and interests in the national capital, and he also informs the people back home of the problems arising at the seat of government and how these problems affect them. It is in the nature of the congressman's job that he should determine, as far as he can, public opinion in his own constituency and in the whole nation, analyze it, measure it in terms of the practicability of turning it into public policy, and consider it in the light of his own

*At the time this article was written, J. William Fulbright was a U.S. senator from Arkansas—*Editors.*

knowledge, conscience, and convictions. Occasionally he may be obliged to go against public opinion, with the consequent task of educating or reeducating the people along lines that seem to him more sound. And finally, since he is a human being eager to succeed at his important job of statesmanship and politics, he is realistic enough to keep his eyes on the voters in terms of the next election. But he understands that a mere weathervane following of majority public opinion is not always the path to reelection. . . .

NOTE

1. In an address on "The Legislator" delivered at the University of Chicago on February 19, 1946. *Vital Speeches,* May 15, 1946, pp. 468–72.

Legislative Process: The Filibuster

The legislative process in Congress requires the building of coalitions among its members over and over again until all legislative hurdles have been overcome. Thus, successful legislators are those who are able to shepherd legislation through various committees in both houses, then to the floors of the House and Senate, then to the conference committees, and back to the floors. If the legislation requires an appropriation, then the whole process is repeated with different committees.

Although there is much that is the same legislatively in the House of Representatives and the Senate, there are some critical differences that, in the end, make the passage of legislation very difficult. One such difference is the filibuster *in the Senate.*

In the House of Representatives, the majority party leadership (i.e., the speaker of the house, the majority leader, and others) control the flow of legislation. In the Senate that control is ultimately in the hands of senators themselves. Typically, if the speaker of the house wants something, he or she can get it. In the Senate, however, a group of senators determined to block action can do so through the filibuster.

The filibuster is a legislative device to prevent action on a bill. It grows out of the necessity, under Senate custom and rules, for the Senate as a whole to determine when debate shall end on a bill. Under the current rule, a three-fifths vote is required to end debate. This "supermajority"—60 senators—is extremely difficult to achieve.

For much of the twentieth century, the filibuster was used sparingly, and usually on the most critical of issues, such as civil rights bills. In recent years, however, the filibuster has been elevated to a new level, with senators from both parties either threatening or carrying out a filibuster almost as a matter of course on any manner of bills. Indeed, there have been more than 30 filibusters a year since 1993.

The central issue surrounding the filibuster is the extent to which a minority of senators should be able to block the will of the majority. Some argue, as does Senator Tom Harkin (D-Iowa) in the first selection below, that whatever validity the filibuster had in history (and he thinks it was very little), it should not be allowed to continue unchanged today. The filibuster, he argues, only leads to gridlock in the legislative process, contributing to even greater cynicism and frustration among the American people.

In the second selection, a former member of the House of Representatives, Bill Frenzel (R-Minn.), makes the case for keeping the filibuster. Frenzel argues that the filibuster fits into the general scheme of limited government fashioned by the framers of the Constitution and should not be cast aside merely because it is viewed today as a major impediment to majority rule. According to Frenzel, if a majority of the people truly want the government to act, the Congress, including the Senate, will act. In the meantime, the filibuster is a useful device to filter out unneeded or unwise legislation.

It's Time to Change the Filibuster

Tom Harkin

Mr. HARKIN. Mr. President, for the benefit of the Senators who are here and watching on the monitors, we now have before us an amendment by myself, Senator LIEBERMAN, Senator PELL, and Senator ROBB that would amend rule XXII, the so-called filibuster rule of the U.S. Senate. . . .

This amendment would change the way this Senate operates more fundamentally than anything that has been proposed thus far this year. It would fundamentally change the way we do business by changing the filibuster rule as it currently stands.

Mr. President, the last Congress showed us the destructive impact filibusters can have on the legislative process, provoking gridlock after gridlock, frustration, anger, and despondency among the American people, wondering whether we can get anything done at all here in Washington. The pattern of filibusters and delays that we saw in the last Congress is part of the rising tide of filibusters that have overwhelmed our legislative process.

While some may gloat and glory in the frustration and anger that the American people felt toward our institution which resulted in the tidal wave of dissatisfaction that struck the majority in Congress, I believe in the long run that it will harm the Senate and our Nation for this pattern to continue. . . . Mr. President, there has . . . been a rising tide in the use of the filibuster. In the last two Congresses, in 1987 to 1990, and 1991 to 1994, there have been twice as many filibusters per year as there were the last time the Republicans controlled the Senate, from 1981 to 1986, and 10 times as many as occurred between 1917 and 1960. Between 1917 and 1960, there were an average of 1.3 per session. However, in the last Congress, there were 10 times that many. This is not healthy for our legislative process and it is not healthy for our country.

I have [also] compare[d] filibusters in the entire 19th century and in the last Congress. We had twice as many filibusters in the 103d Congress as we had in the entire 100 years of the 19th century.

Clearly, this is a process that is out of control. We need to change the rules. We need to change the rules, however, without harming the longstanding Senate tradition of extended debate and deliberation, and slowing things down.

I have here [also] the issues that were subject to filibusters in the last Congress. Some of these were merely delayed by filibusters. Others were killed outright, despite having the majority of both bodies and the President in favor of them. That is right. Some of these measures had a majority of support in the Senate and in the House, and by the President. Yet, they never saw the light of day. Others simply were perfunctory housekeeping types of issues.

Tom Harkin is a Democratic U.S. Senator from the state of Iowa. Excerpted from a speech delivered in the U.S. Senate, Congressional Record, *Proceedings and Debates of the 104th Congress. First Session, Senate, January 4, 1995, vol. 141, No. 1, 530–33 and January 5, 1995, vol. 141, No. 2, 5431.*

For example, one might understand why someone would filibuster the Brady Handgun Act. There were people that felt very strongly opposed to that. I can understand that being slowed down, and having extended debate on it. Can you say that about the J. Larry Lawrence nomination? I happen to be a personal friend of Mr. Lawrence. He is now our Ambassador to Switzerland, an important post. He was nominated to be Ambassador there, and he came through the committee fine. Yet, his nomination was the subject of a filibuster. Or there was the Edward P. Berry, Jr., nomination. There was the Claude Bolton nomination. You get my point.

We had nominations that were filibustered. This was almost unheard of in our past. We filibustered the nomination of a person that actually came through the committee process and was approved by the committee, and it was filibustered here on the Senate floor.

Actually, Senators use these nominations as a lever for power. If one Senator has an issue where he or she wants something done, it is very easy. All a Senator needs to do is filibuster a nomination. Then the majority leader or the minority leader has to come to the Senator and say, "Would you release your hold on that, give up your filibuster on that?"

"OK," the Senator will reply. "What do you want in return?"

Then the deals are struck.

It is used, Mr. President, as blackmail for one Senator to get his or her way on something that they could not rightfully win through the normal processes. I am not accusing any one party of this. It happens on both sides of the aisle.

Mr. President, I believe each Senator needs to give up a little of our pride, a little of our prerogatives, and a little of our power for the good of this Senate and for the good of this country. Let me repeat that: Each Senator, I believe, has to give up a little of our pride, a little of our prerogatives, and a little of our power for the better functioning of this body and for the good of our country.

I think the voters of this country were turned off by the constant bickering, the arguing back and forth that goes on in this Senate Chamber, the gridlock that ensued here, and the pointing of fingers of blame.

Sometimes, in the fog of debate, like the fog of war, it is hard to determine who is responsible for slowing something down. It is like the shifting sand. People hide behind the filibuster. I think it is time to let the voters know that we heard their message in the last election. They did not send us here to bicker and to argue, to point fingers. They want us to get things done to address the concerns facing this country. They want us to reform this place. They want this place to operate a little better, a little more openly, and a little more decisively.

Mr. President, I believe this Senate should embrace the vision of this body that our Founding Fathers had. There is a story—I am not certain whether it is true or not, but it is a nice story—that Thomas Jefferson returned from France, where he had learned that the Constitutional Convention had set up a separate body called the U.S. Senate, with its Members appointed by the legislatures and not subject to a popular vote. Jefferson was quite upset about this. He asked George Washington why this was done. Evidently, they were sitting at a breakfast table. Washington said to him, "Well, why did you pour your coffee in the saucer?" And Jefferson replied, "Why, to cool it, of course."

Washington replied, "Just so: We created the Senate to cool down the legislation that may come from the House."

I think General Washington was very wise. I think our Founding Fathers were very wise to create this body.

They had seen what had happened in Europe—violent changes, rapid changes, mob rule—so they wanted the process to slow things down, to deliberate a little more, and that is why the Senate was set up.

But George Washington did not compare the Senate to throwing the coffee pot out the window. It is just to cool it down, and slow it down.

I think that is what the Founding Fathers envisioned, and I think that is what the American people expect. That is what we ought to and should provide. The Senate should carefully consider legislation, whether it originates here, or whether it streams in like water from a fire hose from the House of Representatives, we must provide ample time for Members to speak on issues. We should not move to the limited debate that characterizes the House of Representatives. I am not suggesting that we do that. But in the end, the people of our country are entitled to know where we stand and how we vote on the merits of a bill or an amendment.

Some argue that any supermajority requirement is unconstitutional, other than those specified in the Constitution itself. I find much in this theory to agree with—and I think we should treat all the rules that would limit the ability of a majority to rule with skepticism. I think that this theory is one that we ought to examine more fully, and that is the idea that the Constitution of the United States sets up certain specified instances in which a supermajority is needed to pass the bill, and in all other cases it is silent. In fact, the Constitution provides that the President of the Senate, the Vice President of the United States, can only vote to break a tie vote—by implication, meaning that the Senate should pass legislation by a majority vote, except in those instances in which the Constitution specifically says that we need a supermajority.

The distinguished constitutional expert, Lloyd Cutler, a distinguished lawyer, has been a leading proponent of this view. I have not made up my mind on this theory, but I do believe it is something we ought to further examine. I find a lot that I agree with in that theory.

But what we are getting at here is a different procedure and process, whereby we can have the Senate as the Founding Fathers envisioned—a place to cool down, slow down, deliberate and discuss, but not as a place where a handful—yes, maybe even one Senator—can totally stop legislation or a nomination.

Over the last couple of years, I have spent a great deal of time reading the history of this cloture process. Two years ago, about this time, I first proposed this to my fellow Democratic colleagues at a retreat we had in Williamsburg, VA. In May of that year, I proposed this to the Joint Committee on Congressional Reform. Some people said to me at that time: Senator HARKIN, of course you are proposing it, you are in the majority, you want to get rid of the filibuster. Well, now I am in the minority and I am still proposing it because I think it is the right thing to do.

Let me take some time to discuss the history of cloture and the limitations on debate in the Senate. Prior to 1917 there was no mechanism to shut off debate in the Senate. There was an early version in 1789 of what was called the "previous question." It was used more like a tabling motion than as a method to close debate.

In the 19th century, Mr. President, elections were held in November and Congress met in December. This Congress was always a lame duck session, which ended in March of the next year. The newly elected members did not take office until the following December, almost 13 months later. During the entire 19th century, there were filibusters. But most of these were aimed at delaying congressional action at the end of the short session that ended March 4. A filibuster during the 19th century was used at the end of a session when the majority would try to ram something through at the end, over the objections of the minority. Extended debate was used to extend debate to March 4, when under the law at that time, it automatically died.

If the majority tried to ram something through in the closing hours, the minority would discuss it and hold it up until March 4, and that was the end of it. That process was changed. Rather than going into an automatic lame-duck session in December, we now convene a new Congress in January with the new Members. I think this is illustrative that the filibuster used in the 19th century was entirely different in concept and in form than what we now experience here in the U.S. Senate.

So those who argue that the filibuster in the U.S. Senate today is a time-honored tradition of the U.S. Senate going clear back to 1789 are mistaken, because the use of the filibuster in the 19th century was entirely different than what it is being used for today, and it was used in a different set of laws and circumstances under which Congress met.

So that brings us up to the 20th century. In 1917, the first cloture rule was introduced in response to a filibuster, again, at the end of a session that triggered a special session. This cloture rule provided for two-thirds of Members present and voting to cut off debate. It was the first time since the first Congress met that the Senate adopted a cloture rule in 1917. However, this cloture rule was found to be ineffective and was rarely used. Why? Because rulings of the chair said that the cloture rule did not apply to procedural matters. So, if someone wanted to engage in a filibuster, they could simply bring up a procedural matter and filibuster that, and the two-thirds vote did not even apply to that. For a number of years, from 1917 until 1949, we had that situation.

In 1949 an attempt was made to make the cloture motion more effective. The 1949 rule applied the cloture rule to procedural matters. It closed that loophole but did not apply to rules changes. It also raised the needed vote from two-thirds present and voting to two-thirds of the whole Senate, which at that time meant 64 votes. That rule existed for 10 years.

In 1959, Lyndon Johnson pushed through a rules change to change the needed vote back to two-thirds of those present and voting, and which also applied cloture to rules changes.

There were many attempts after that to change the filibuster. In 1975, after several years of debate here in the Senate, the current rule was adopted, as a compromise proposed by Senator BYRD of West Virginia. The present cloture rule allows cloture to be invoked by three-fifths of Senators chosen and sworn, or 60 votes, except in the case of rules changes, which still require two-thirds of those present and voting.

This change in the rule reducing the proportion of votes needed for cloture for the first time since 1917, was the culmination of many years of efforts by reformers' numerous proposals between 1959 and 1975.

Two of the proposals that were made in those intervening years I found particularly interesting. One was by Senator Hubert Humphrey in 1963, which provided for majority cloture in two stages. The other proposal I found interesting was one by Senator DOLE in 1971 that moved from the then current two-thirds present and voting down to three-fifths present and voting, reducing the number of votes by one with each successive cloture vote.

We drew upon Senator DOLE's proposal in developing our own proposal. Our proposal would reduce the number of votes needed to invoke cloture gradually, allowing time for debate, allowing us to slow things down, but ultimately allowing the Senate to get to the merits of a vote.

Under our proposal, the amendment now before the Senate, Senators still have to get 16 signatures to offer a cloture motion. The motion would still have to lay over 2 days. The first vote to invoke cloture would require 60 votes. If that vote did not succeed, they could file another cloture motion needing 16 signatures. They would have to wait at least 2 further days. On the next vote, they would need 57 votes to invoke cloture. If you did not get that, well, you would have to get 16 signatures, file another cloture motion, wait another couple days, and then you would have to have 54 votes. Finally, the same procedure could be repeated, and move to a cloture vote of 51. Finally, a simple majority vote could close debate, to get to the merits of the issue.

By allowing this slow ratchet down, the minority would have the opportunity to debate, focus public attention on a bill, and communicate their case to the public. In the end, though, the majority could bring the measure to a final vote, as it generally should in a democracy.

Mr. President, in the 19th century as I mentioned before, filibusters were used to delay action on a measure until the automatic expiration of the session.

Senators would then leave to go back to their States, or Congressmen back to their districts, and tell people about the legislation the majority was trying to ram through. They could get the public aroused about it, to put pressure on Senators not to support that measure or legislation.

Keep in mind that in those days, there was no television, there was no radio, and scant few newspapers. Many people could not read or write and the best means of communication was when a Senator went out and spoke directly with his constituents. So it was necessary to have several months where a Senator could alert the public as to what the majority was trying to do, to protect the rights and interests of the minority.

That is not the case today. Every word we say here is instantaneously beamed out on C-SPAN, watched all over the United States, and picked up on news broadcasts. We have the print media sitting up in the gallery. So the public is well aware and well informed of what is happening here in the Senate on a daily basis. We do have a need to slow the process down, but we do not need the several months that was needed in the 19th century.

So as a Member of the new minority here in the Senate, I come to this issue as a clear matter of good public policy. I am pleased to say that it is a change that enjoys overwhelming support among the American people.

A recent poll conducted by Action Not Gridlock . . . found that 80 percent of Independents, 84 percent of Democrats, and 79 percent of Republicans believe that once all Senators have been able to express their views, the Senate should be permitted to vote for or against a bill. . . .

. . . [S]laying the filibuster dinosaur—and that is what I call it, a dinosaur, a relic of the ancient past—slaying the filibuster dinosaur has also been endorsed by papers around the country, including the *New York Times, USA Today,* and the *Washington Post. . . .*

* * *

But I will close my opening remarks, with this quote:

> It is one thing to provide protection against majoritarian absolutism; it is another thing again to enable a vexatious or unreasoning minority to paralyze the Senate and America's legislative process along with it.

I could not have said it better, and it was said by Senator ROBERT DOLE, February 10, 1971.

If Senator DOLE thought the filibuster was bad in 1971, certainly when we are down here, the filibuster has increased at least threefold on an annual basis since then. So it is time to get rid of this dinosaur. It is time to move ahead with the people's business in a productive manner.

Defending the Dinosaur
The Case for Not Fixing the Filibuster

Bill Frenzel

Defending the filibuster may not be quite as nasty as taking candy from a baby, but neither is it a good route to popular acclaim. Few kind words are ever spoken in defense of filibusters. Conventional wisdom and political correctness have pronounced them to be pernicious. The very word is pejorative, evoking ugly images of antidemocratic activities.

During the last biennium, filibusters became so unlovable that a group, including former senators, formed "Action, Not Gridlock!" to try to stamp them out. The public, which had tested both gridlock and action, seemed to prefer the former. The organization disappeared.

As that public reaction suggests, political correctness is a sometime thing and conventional wisdom oft goes astray. The American public may not be rushing to embrace the filibuster, but neither has it shown any inclination to root it out. The Senate's overwhelming vote . . . against changing the filibuster means that the practice won't go away soon, so it is worth examining. Despite its bad press, the story of the modern filibuster is not one-sided.

FILIBUSTERS, THE CONSTITUTION, AND THE FRAMERS

Filibuster haters claim they are contrary to the spirit of the Constitution because they require extraordinary majorities. The rationale is that the Framers, who created a majority system and rejected supermajorities, would be horrified by filibusters. Perhaps, but don't be too sure. Remember that no one has dug up a Framer lately to testify to the accuracy of this theory.

The Framers created our system based on their profound distrust of government. They loaded the system with checks and balances to make it work very slowly and with great difficulty. Their intention was to prevent swift enactment of laws and to avoid satisfying the popular whimsy of each willful majority. Maybe they would trade popular election for a filibuster rule.

Without any live Framers, we can only speculate about their feelings. However, it is hard to believe that, having designed an extremely balky system, they would want to speed it up today. More likely, they would merely remind us that for more than 200 years major American policymaking has been based on "concurrent majorities" anyway.

Bill Frenzel is a former Republican U.S. Representative from the State of Minnesota (1971–1991). From Bill Frenzel, "Defending the Dinosaur: The Case for Not Fixing the Filibuster," The Brookings Review, *Summer, 1995, pp. 47–49.*

PARLIAMENTARY COMPARISONS

Most of the parliaments of the world are copies, or variants, of Westminster [England]. With only one strong house and no separated executive branch, they can usually deliver laws swiftly. But when their actions affront public opinion, there is a political price to be paid, often very quickly. The government that offends the people soon becomes the opposition.

In our regional system, our majorities, assisted by a wide range of taxpayer-paid perks, do not usually pay any price. Our members of Congress are unbeatable (even in the earthquake of 1994, more than 90 percent of them who sought reelection were re-elected). Our majorities are not eternal, but they are long-lived, unlike the Westminster forms.

It might make sense to consider trading the filibuster for congressional mortality (perhaps through term limits), but it is probably unwise to accept the blockbuster majority power of the Westminster system without accepting its balance of political turnover in return.

Actually, filibusters are not unique to the United States. Other parliaments are finding new opportunities for dilatory practices. The Japanese upper house recently presented its "ox-step," and an appointed majority in the Canadian Senate frustrated the intentions of the prime minister and his government on the ratification of the U.S.–Canada Free Trade Agreement. The strokes are different for different folks, but we are not alone. Delay is a time-honored political exercise that transcends political boundaries.

THE FILIBUSTER AND THE POPULAR WILL

The filibuster has been often indicted for denying the popular will, but over recent history, that point is hard to demonstrate. In the first place, it is not easy to get, and hold, 41 votes in the Senate under any circumstances. It is practically impossible to do so against a popular proposal. Filibusters simply do not succeed *unless* they have popular support or unless there is a lack of enthusiasm for the proposal being filibustered.

In 1993 Senator Bob Dole (R-KS) led a filibuster against the Clinton Emergency Spending Bill. It succeeded because the public liked the filibuster better than the spending. In the Bush years, Senator George Mitchell (D-ME) stopped a capital gains proposal by threat of filibuster. Senator Mitchell succeeded because the people saw no urgency in the proposal. In both cases, political reality prevailed.

If the public wants a vote, it tells its representatives. In 1994 Senate Republicans tried to filibuster the Crime Bill. Based on hot flashes from home, more than 60 senators perceived that the bill was popular, so the filibuster was broken quickly. The same thing happened to the Motor Voter Bill, the National Service Bill, and five out of six presidential appointments. If any proposal has substantial public support, a couple of cloture votes will kill the filibuster. The political reality is: frivolous filibusters do not succeed. The modern filibuster can gridlock ideas that are not popular, but it has not gridlocked the people.

THE BICAMERAL SYSTEM

In our unique system, the two houses of Congress have developed similar, but not identical, personalities and processes. The House of Representatives, with 440 orators, is harder to manage and has therefore created a set of rules to limit debate. In recent years, its majority has handled bills under rules that permitted few, if any, amendments and only an hour or two of debate.

The Senate, with only 100 orators, has stayed with free debate and an open amendment system. That is not a bad division of process. One house has been too closed, the other too open. The House operates with the relentlessness of Westminster majority, and the Senate has more time to examine, to delay, to amend, and, if necessary, to kill. All are vital functions of any legislature. . . .

There is still a relatively open pipeline for bills flowing from the House. . . . Following the Framers' wisdom, it is prudent to have a sieve in the Senate to compete with that open pipe in the House. At least some of the worst legislative lumps may be smoothed out in the finer mesh. . . .

KEY TO COMPROMISE

Many filibusters are not filibusters at all, but merely threats. Most are undertaken to notify the managers of the proposal that problems exist. They are a signal from a minority to a majority that negotiations are in order. Sometimes the majority tries a cloture vote or two before negotiating. Sometimes it negotiates. Sometimes it does not.

Most of these procedures end in a modified bill, not a dead bill. The Crime Bill noted above passed. The Dole filibuster of emergency spending did not prevent passage of many of its bits of pork in regular appropriations bills. . . .

The filibuster surely gives a minority a little more clout, but it does not prevent a majority from passing reasonably popular proposals. It gives a minority the opportunity to negotiate what it believes is an intolerable proposal into one it can live with. That compromise may serve the needs of the majority tolerably well too.

NO NEED FOR A HEAVY HAND

One political reality test for the filibuster is the congressional ingenuity in finding ways to avoid it when necessary. Trade and Reconciliation bills are considered under laws that obviate filibusters. When there is a good reason to finesse the filibuster, the Senate always seems to get the job done.

Many other Senate rules, only dimly understood by common folks, reduce the legislative pace. I do not mean to bless multiple efforts to filibuster the same proposal. Once on the bill and once on the conference report is enough. Unlimited amendment after cloture is also too much opportunity for mischief.

Former Senate Majority Leader Mitchell has left constructive proposals to speed the work of the Senate without damaging the filibuster. They ought to be considered.

The minority needs rights for protection. The majority needs the ability to move its program. Both needs can be well served by the modern 60-vote cloture rule. It should not be changed.

KEEP THE FILIBUSTER

The test of the filibuster ought to be whether it is fair, appropriate, and constructive. It may have been a killer in the old days, when it slew civil rights bills, but under the new 60-vote system, it is difficult to recall a filibustered proposition that stayed dead if it was popular.

Most antifilibuster noise comes from advocates of ideas that were going to fail anyway. It is not essential for every idea that comes bouncing up or down Pennsylvania Avenue to become law. The filibuster is a useful legislative tool, consistent with the goals of the Framers, that keeps whimsical, immature, and ultimately unpopular bills out of the statute books. . . .

11

THE PRESIDENCY

In 1973, the noted historian Arthur Schlesinger wrote a book titled The Imperial Pres-idency, *in which he argued that the powers and prerogatives of the office had grown so extensive that our cherished principle of balanced government was being seriously threatened.*

The resignation of President Richard Nixon, along with the travails of those pres-idents who followed him, have caused many political observers to conclude that warn-ings of an imperial presidency are no longer applicable. In the first selection that fol-lows, however, Michael Lind argues quite the contrary. He insists that on the crucial questions of foreign policy presidents can still do pretty much as they please; and, thanks to actions taken by Carter, Reagan, and Bush, future presidents will find their powers considerably greater in the domestic sphere as well. Meanwhile, according to Lind, the imperial character of the office continues to be reinforced by two other dis-turbing developments that have actually been in place for some time. One is the view of the presidency as the "tribune of the people"—a view first articulated by Andrew Jack-son, later embellished by Woodrow Wilson, and now routinely embraced by our presi-dents; and the second, a White House bureaucracy that has been steadily expanding since the end of the Second World War. According to Lind, we urgently need to cut the presidency down to size, and he proposes a number of changes designed to do so.

R. Gordon Hoxie, the author of the second selection, rejects any notion of an im-perial presidency, suggesting instead that "imperiled" would be a more apt description of the office. Where Lind sees power grabs by our recent presidents, Hoxie sees presi-dents conscientiously exercising their responsibilities under the Constitution; or mak-ing use of options and resources granted to the president by Congress; or bolstering the institutional presidency so that it can more effectively compete against both an over-reaching Congress and hostile bureaucratic interests within the Executive branch.

As Hoxie sees it, presidents, operating as they must in a separation-of-powers sys-tem, nearly always have to struggle for what they get. This constitutional fact of life, moreover, has become even more burdensome for presidents in light of the diminished importance of political parties in the American political process.

The Out-of-Control Presidency

Michael Lind

I.

The president is shrinking. The institution of the presidency, magnified by half a century of world war and cold war, is rapidly diminishing in terms of both power and respect. . . . Meanwhile, Congress has become bloated and arrogant, swelling the ranks of its own staff while encroaching on the constitutional prerogatives of the White House. Congressional supremacy would be a disaster, particularly in foreign affairs. We cannot have 535 commanders in chief.

This tale of the decline of the presidency and the rise of Congress is the emerging conventional wisdom in Washington. It is familiar, widely believed—and wrong. . . .

[The president elected in 2000] will be handed the Nixonian imperial presidency, with most of its powers intact and with a few new prerogatives added.

In foreign policy, the [newly elected] president [will] discover that, like every president since Truman, he can wage war at will, without consulting Congress. Though he might consent to a congressional vote as a matter of public relations (as Bush did before the Gulf war), he is more likely to invoke his supposed "inherent" authority as commander-in-chief. If necessary, his aides will concoct legalistic rationalizations, citing dangers to U.S. citizens (Grenada, Panama), authorization by the United Nations (Somalia, Haiti), NATO treaty obligations (Libya). Whether a liberal or a conservative, the [new] president will dismiss the War Powers Resolution as unconstitutional.

Nor is de facto presidential supremacy in foreign affairs limited to war-making, the [new] president will discover. Bush and Clinton will have bequeathed an important technique for ramming economic treaties through Congress with little debate: fast-track legislation, which limits the time allowed for debate and forbids amendments. The Senate, which the Founders wanted to have weigh treaty commitments deliberately, was granted a mere 20 hours to consider the treaty that committed the United States to the jurisdiction of the World Trade Organization (WTO). Perhaps the [new] president can insist that it be limited even further—to, say, half an hour or 15 minutes.

In the domestic arena, the [new] president will find even greater enhancements of his prerogatives. Thanks to Jimmy Carter, who reformed the Senior Executive Service to give the White House more control over career bureaucrats, and Ronald Reagan, who politicized the upper levels of the executive branch to an unprecedented degree, the [new] president will find it easy to stack government with his spoilsmen or reward partisan bureaucrats. And he can thank George Bush for a technique that enhances presi-

Michael Lind is a staff writer for New Yorker *magazine and formerly assistant to the director of the Center for the Study of Foreign Affairs, the Foreign Service Institute, U.S. Department of State. From Michael Lind, "The Out-of-Control Presidency," the* New Republic, *August 14, 1995, pp. 18–23. Reprinted by permission of the New Republic. ©* *1995, The New Republic, Inc.*

dential prerogative even further—signing laws while announcing he will not obey them.

Bush engaged in the greatest institutional power grab of any president since Nixon. In 1991 Bush, delivering a commencement address at Princeton, said: "[O]n many occasions during my presidency, I have stated that statutory provisions that violate the Constitution have no binding legal force." As Charles Tiefer points out in the *Semi-Sovereign Presidency,* Bush used "signing statements"—statements accompanying his signing of a bill, during which he announced he would not enforce this or that provision—to exercise an unconstitutional line-item veto (White House counsel C. Boyden Gray concocted the idea). In one such instance, when Congress amended the Clean Air Act in 1990 to permit lawsuits by citizen groups against companies that had violated the act, Bush used a signing statement to declare, on supposed "constitutional grounds," that the executive branch would continue to act as though such citizen lawsuits were prohibited—nullifying the intent of Congress. Ironically, the "take care" clause of the Constitution was intended to compel the president to enforce laws he disapproved of (often, Colonial governors had refused to enforce parts of legislation passed by Colonial legislatures). As Tiefer points out, Bush was asserting a sovereign power to ignore statutes that had been denied the English king in the Seven Bishops case of 1688.

Yet another new instrument of arbitrary presidential power is the "czar." The institution of presidential commissars with vague, sweeping charges that overlap with or supersede the powers of department heads is utterly alien to the American constitutional tradition. Most famous is the celebrated position of "drug czar," which William Bennett held under Bush, and General Barry McCaffrey now occupies, which arrogates duties that were previously handled perfectly adequately by agencies of Justice and other departments. Similarly, Vice President Dan Quayle acted as a "czar" as the head of Bush's Council on Competitiveness, designed to circumvent Cabinet heads and Congress in regulatory matters.

The White House staff that has ballooned since World War II seems close to becoming an extra-constitutional "fourth branch" of government. For obvious reasons, presidents have preferred to govern through their staffers, most of whom need not be confirmed by the Senate and many of whom are young and pliant, rather than deal with the heads of Cabinet departments and independent agencies, experienced people who are less likely to be mere tools of the president's will. Nor is it any accident that the major presidential scandals of the past generation—Watergate and Iran-contra—have involved attempts by shadowy and scheming courtiers of law-breaking presidents to circumvent or suborn the older, established executive departments. Every time the high-handed actions of White House courtiers drag a president into scandal, Congress, the press and the public denounce the courtiers—Nixon's plumbers, Ollie North—or the president and then, under a new president, sigh with relief: the system worked. That future presidents will almost certainly be tempted to use their White House staffers as Nixon and Reagan did is ignored.

The imperial presidency, then, is intact, merely waiting to be powered up and taken out of the hangar. If today's Congress has its way, the presidency will become even more imperial. Having captured Congress after half a century, the Republicans are hastening to give away the powers of the branch they control.

Some of these powers are formal, such as the line-item veto. States whose governors have the line-item veto don't balance their budgets any better than states without it. A line-item veto simply shifts the power to protect pork from a legislature to an executive. Giving the president the line-item veto would not balance the budget; it would merely permit the president to zero out the bounties of his enemies while keeping bounties for his allies. It would also wreck the constitutional design, which intended the branch closest to the people to have the last word on spending the people's money.

Other reforms backed by Republicans in Congress would weaken their institution indirectly. Term limits would reduce the expertise of representatives and senators—and boost their reliance on executive-branch experts, as well as on K Street lobbyists and think-tank flacks. Abolishing such independent congressional fact-finding agencies as the Office of Technology Assessment would hardly make a dent in the deficit but would make it easier for Congress to be hoodwinked by the executive branch it is supposed to oversee. A balanced budget amendment would shift the final arena of budgetary policy from the Capitol to federal courts, civil servants or White House staffers. . . .

II.

Madison and other Founders did not conceive of the president as a "representative" with a popular constituency at all. The president was to be a nonpartisan chief magistrate. The Founders designed the Electoral College with the expectation that presidents would frequently be chosen by the House, voting by states, from lists of candidates nominated by special state electors. The idea of the chief executive as chief representative is French, not American. As Louis Napoleon observed, his uncle Napoleon I "earnestly claimed the title of first Representative of the People, a title which seemed about to be given exclusively to members of the Legislative Body."

Andrew Jackson was the first president to claim, like the two Napoleons, to be a tribune of the masses: "The president is the direct representative of the American people." His attempt to act as a democratic monarch produced a backlash against such claims until the 20th century. Lincoln justified his sweeping war powers using legal arguments, not the claim that he was the sole legitimate representative of the nation; indeed, this former Whig opponent of "King Andrew" Jackson was hesitant about suggesting legislation to Congress, for fear of arousing suspicions of executive supremacy. "My political education," he declared, "strongly inclines me against a very free use of any of these means [recommending legislation and using the veto], by the Executive, to control the legislation of the country. As a rule, I think it better that Congress should originate, as well as perfect its measures, without external bias."

The modern conception of the president as an all-powerful tribune of the people comes from Woodrow Wilson. . . .Wilson argued for a different, Rousseauian conception of democracy, in which the president is the nation personified: "The nation as a whole has chosen him, and is conscious that it has no other political spokesman." Wilson was the first president since Washington to address Congress in person. He argued that the

American constitutional tradition should never obstruct an activist president: "If he rightly interpret the national thought and boldly insist upon it, he is irresistible; and the country never feels the zest of action so much as when its president is of such insight and caliber. Its instinct is for unified action, and it craves a single leader."

The Great Leader is to lead not only the United States but the world: "Our president must always, henceforth, be one of the great powers of the world, whether he act wisely or not." Not the United States, but the presidency itself, is to be a great power! Wilson called for the president to ignore the prerogatives of the House and the Senate in foreign policy and to present the legislature with treaties as faits accomplis. "He need disclose no step of negotiation until it is complete." This strategy backfired when Wilson tried to impose the League of Nations treaty on the Senate, but later presidents have used it effectively. Bush's military buildup in the Gulf more or less forced Congress to ratify his planned war against Iraq, while the Clinton administration followed its Republican predecessors in ramming through GATT and NAFTA by means of fast-track legislation.

The plebiscitary theory of the presidency, the theory that the president, like Napoleon I, is First Representative of the Nation, is shared by all presidents today, Republican or Democratic. Though most presidents are elected with a plurality, not a majority—meaning most voters wanted someone else—every president today claims a "mandate" from the "majority" of "the people," considered as an undifferentiated mass with one General Will. The nomination of today's presidential candidates by primaries, rather than by congressional caucuses (the first system) or brokered party conventions (the system from the 1830s to the 1960s), has reinforced the illusion that the president represents the popular will, unmediated by either government structures or party organizations. The plebiscitary president is free to run against Washington, and even against political parties, in the manner of Ross Perot.

Running against Washington means running against Congress and "the bureaucracy," which are treated as villains in a morality play. The virtuous heroes are the president, and (for conservatives) state governments and an idealized free market. Presidentialists build up the legitimacy of the presidency by grossly exaggerating the faults of Congress and the parts of the executive branch that the White House does not directly control, such as the civil service and the independent agencies.

Consider the myth that the budgets and staffs of Congress and federal agencies have been escalating out of control. The money spent on the entire legislative branch is minuscule compared to that which goes to the executive. As James Glassman has pointed out, "You can eliminate all of Congress . . . just get rid of the whole darn thing, you'd save exactly as much as you would save if you cut the defense budget by less than 1 percent." What's more, during the 1980s, appropriations for Congress actually fell, in real terms. U.S. representatives are paid much less than their counterparts in many other democracies, such as Japan, and their salaries compare unfavorably with those of professionals and corporate executives, many of whom have less onerous responsibilities. Congressional staff, though it has grown along with government in general, actually declined in the 1980s, while the number of employees in the executive and judicial branches expanded. . . .

Nor has the other half of the hated "Washington establishment," the federal bureaucracy, been growing out of control. Most Americans would be surprised to learn that in
terms of manpower—about 2 million—the federal government has hardly grown at all
since World War II. State bureaucracies have grown faster, local bureaucracies even
faster still. Federal funds, to be sure, have paid for much of the expansion of state and
local bureaucracies, but conservatives have been concentrating their attacks not on federal funds, but on federal employees.

But, unlike Congress and the federal civil service, one federal institution does resemble the caricature of an ever-expanding, arrogant, corrupt bureaucracy. Since World
War II, the White House staff and the Executive Office of the President have metasta-
sized. Dwight Eisenhower made do with 29 key assistants as his White House staff in
1960; Bush needed 81 in 1992. The Executive Office of the President, created in 1939,
has grown to include thousands of bureaucrats functioning in a presidential court, a
miniature executive branch superimposed on the traditional departmental executive envisioned by the Constitution.

Meanwhile, the number of presidential appointees and senior executives has ballooned an astonishing 430 percent between 1960 and 1992, from 451 to 2,393. Most of
this growth has not been in jobs for the hated career civil servants, but in positions for
upper-middle-class political activists who donated money to, or worked in, presidential
campaigns, or roomed with somebody in college, or whatever.

Presidents have consistently sought to expand the number of these political appointees. Mostly from elite law, lobbying, business, banking or academic backgrounds,
these courtiers have ever more elaborate titles: principal deputy assistant secretary, assistant associate office director. As the titles grow, the average tenure shrinks (down to
18 months from three years during the Johnson years). The in-and-outers, once in, can't
wait to get out and cash in their fancy titles for higher lobbyist fees or an endowed pro-
fessorship of government. If conservatives are serious about cutting back government,
why not abolish most of the post-'60s presidential branch? Where is the outcry against
the expansion of the presidential bureaucracy? Why is a congressional barbershop a
greater enormity than four White House staffers devoted to dealing with flowers? . . .

Ideologues of all persuasions have an interest in promoting presidential prerogative. Why battle over years to build a congressional majority, when you can persuade a
president to enact your favored reform—gays in the military or gays out of the
military—with a stroke of a pen? This accounts for the spitting fury with which op-ed
pundits, think tankers and spin doctors pounce on any president who does not use "the
power of his office" to enact their pet projects by ukase, preferably in the next few days
or weeks.

Our press also helps the presidentialists of right and left by its obsessive focus on
the person of the president at the expense of other executive branch officials, to say
nothing of members of Congress and the judiciary. It makes for an easier story, of
course, but laziness is no excuse for distorted coverage. Would the country crumble into
anarchy if the major networks ignored the president for a week and followed the
speaker, or the Senate majority leader, or the chief justice of the Supreme Court? Newspaper editors are just as bad. Several times, when I have written op-eds concerning gov-

ernment policy, I have been told by an editor, "You need to conclude by saying what the president should do."

Robert Nisbet has it right: "It is nearly instinctual in the political clerisy . . . to portray the president as one elected representative of the entire people . . . with congressmen portrayed as like mayors and city councilmen, mere representatives of wards, sections and districts." When appeals to plebiscitary legitimacy are insufficient, presidentialists can turn to the "court party" of legal and constitutional scholars, who are always ready with a defense of this or that supposed presidential prerogative. Judge Robert Bork, for example, has argued "that the office of the president of the United States has been significantly weakened in recent years and that Congress is largely, but not entirely, responsible." If one were comparing Reagan, Bush or Clinton to FDR at the height of his power, this might seem plausible. In a 200-year perspective it is absurd. . . .

III.

Presidential democracy is not democracy. In theory a single politician could be answerable to a constituency of hundreds of millions—but only in theory. In practice, the more presidential the U.S. government becomes, the less responsive it is to most Americans. Stunts like Jimmy Carter's "Phone the President" notwithstanding, any president will necessarily be remote from most citizens and accessible chiefly to concentric tiers of CEOs, big-money contributors, big-labor leaders, network anchors and movie stars. Any reader who doubts this should try to get appointments with both his or her representative and the president.

Under the Constitution of 1787, representative democracy in the United States means congressional democracy. Restoring congressional democracy must begin with discrediting in the public mind the plebiscitary theory of democracy. Americans must conclude that democracy does not mean voting for this or that elective monarch every four years and then leaving government to the monarch's courtiers. Democracy means continuous negotiation among powerful and relatively autonomous legislators who represent diverse interests in society.

This battle on the level of theory should be accompanied by a campaign at the level of symbolism. Congress, as an institution, is slighted by our public iconography. "We celebrate Presidents' Day," Thomas Langston notes in his new book about the presidency, *With Reverence and Contempt.* "Why not celebrate Speakers' Day? How about a Speakers' Memorial in Washington, D.C., . . . [or] proposing that famous speakers of the House, or senators, also ennoble our currency[?]" The royalism symbolized by pharaonic presidential libraries should be combated by a law requiring that all presidential papers hereafter be deposited permanently in a single, modest presidential library in Washington.

Changes in government organization would need to accompany changes in perceptions of congressional legitimacy. An electoral reform such as proportional representation for the House might actually strengthen the separation of powers; it would encourage a multiparty system, but the same multiparty coalition would not likely hold the House, Senate and White House at once. In a multiparty system, the president might also be forced to appoint coalition Cabinets, as in parliamentary regimes. He would have less influence over a Cabinet secretary of another party than over some servile functionary from his own.

As for the executive branch, the slow seeping of authority from Cabinet secretaries to courtiers needs to be halted and reversed. Congress could drastically cut the White House staff—if representatives aren't intimidated by the divinity that hedges our elected king. The depths of the reverence surrounding the presidential court became clear on Thursday, June 25, 1995 when a House Appropriations subcommittee released a plan to abolish the Council of Economic Advisers. "Democrats," the *New York Times* reported, "said they were startled at the lack of respect for a separate and equal branch of government displayed by the gesture, and even the subcommittee chairman, [Republican] Representative Jim Ross Lightfoot of Iowa, said he recognized that they could be accused of 'micromanagement' and lack of proper respect for the office of the president." It is as though the British parliament had threatened to cancel the changing of the guard at Buckingham Palace. The irony is particularly delicious since the Council of Economic Advisers was imposed on the presidency as part of the Employment Act of 1946 by conservatives in Congress hoping to check a free-spending White House.

The evolution of the council is typical of the process by which every agumentation of the executive branch in the interest of "efficiency" soon serves to enhance the power and prestige of the presidency. An even better example is the Office of Management and Budget, which was created after World War I as an independent agency (the Bureau of the Budget), drifted under presidential control during the administration of FDR and under Reagan became one of the White House's chief instruments of partisan control of executive agencies. Like a black hole, the presidency grows by absorbing ever more power and light.

Unlike a black hole, however, the presidency can be shrunk. Congress can not only scale back the White House to bring it in line with the staffs of prime ministers, but it can also make the heads of executive departments more independent of the president. The Founders expected department heads to carry out their duties more or less on their own (the Constitution gives the president the modest power to request reports in writing from department heads). The idea that department heads should be mere creatures of particular presidents is a modern misconception. Their duty is to use their own judgment to implement the laws passed by Congress, not to promote an imaginary "mandate" given the president by 40 or 45 percent of the voters. The Constitution permits Congress to vest the appointment of "inferior officers" in the heads of departments. Why not give it a try? It would strengthen their ties to their department head—and make it more likely that they would hang up when a White House staffer phoned to intervene, for the short-run political benefit of his boss, in the department's operations.

Reducing the president from a Latin American-style caudillo to something like a 19th- or 18th-century U.S. chief magistrate can be done, then, without revising the

Constitution, merely by passing a few laws. It is hard to see how else the U.S. can avoid the completion of its slow evolution from a congressional republic into a full-fledged presidential state. The real trend in the world at the end of the 20th century, it can be argued, is not so much from "dictatorship" to "democracy" as from unelected dictatorship to elective dictatorship—from Gorbachev to Yeltsin. The executive rulers have to face election, but rule by decree still tends to supplant rule by laws passed by representative legislatures. It could happen here—as the Founding Fathers feared it would. Ben Franklin, among others, predicted, "The Executive will always be increasing here, as elsewhere, till it ends in a monarchy." The new Republican majority in Congress should ponder that warning, as it sets about the further dismantling of the popular branch of government.

The Not-So-Imperial Presidency

R. Gordon Hoxie

In a recent essay entitled "The Out-of-Control Presidency," Michael Lind contends that recent portrayals "of the decline of the presidency and the rise of Congress" are "wrong." He concludes, "The imperial presidency . . . is intact, merely waiting to be powered up and taken out of the hanger."

This perception predated Lind's essay, or even Arthur Schlesinger's 1973 volume, *The Imperial Presidency.* At least one early and strong president, Andrew Jackson (1829–1837) was even termed "King Andrew I" by his political enemies. Many presidents since have enjoyed presidential pomp. However, the American constitutional system, together with the media and public opinion have generally held in check any tendencies toward presidential excesses. Each of the four 20th-century presidents who won the biggest victories, and thereafter engaged in excesses, were slapped down by a combination of Congress, the courts, the media, and public opinion: Franklin Roosevelt in 1937 with his scheme to pack the Supreme Court with additional judges; Lyndon Johnson after 1965 with his escalation of the Vietnam War; Richard Nixon in 1973 with his Watergate cover-up; and Ronald Reagan in 1985 with the Iran-Contra affair.

Michael Lind portrays the president as an all-powerful chief executive. To the contrary, among the leading industrial nations the American president is one of the weakest political leaders. The French president and the British prime minister have the fewest constraints on their power. In the *New York Times,* May 1, 1997, political scientist and pollster Stanley B. Greenberg, comparing British prime minister Tony Blair to the American president, asserted that the difference "could not be more stark. Mr. Clinton was unable to move his party in a new direction. Mr. Blair, however, was able to change his party before his campaign began." Despite our common language and political heritage, the British system of government, with its clear lines of accountability, could not be more different from the American system, with its system of checks and balances, which defies clear lines of accountability and imperialistic aspirations.

Far from being imperial and out of control, presidents are frustrated and unable to carry out the principal programs on their agenda. This frustration comes primarily from two sources: the framers of the Constitution, who distrusted centralization of powers and therefore created a separation-of-powers system; and the contemporary decline of the American political party system, which, in the past has been the engine of presidential strength.

I.

With respect to the decline of political parties, it is not unreasonable to suggest that, except for Washington, whose presidency preceded parties, our strongest presidents—

R. Gordon Hoxie is founder and Chair Emeritus of the Center for the Study of the Presidency, Washington, D.C. This article was written especially for Points of View *in 1997.*

Jefferson, Jackson, Polk, Lincoln, Wilson, and the two Roosevelts—all led through effective *party support.* In the case of Wilson, that support was lost in his last two years in office when Republicans gained control of Congress.

Today party no longer strengthens the presidency. This can be seen in the decline of voting turnout, which, in part, is a reflection of the diminished importance that voters attach to parties; and secondly, the decline of elections of the same party in Congress and the presidency. These factors have weakened the presidency and caused it to seek the means of support that Lind criticizes.

The sharp decline in voting for candidates for the presidency means there is no strong popular mandate for the programs of the candidate who is elected president. By contrast, a high voter turnout coupled with a wide margin of victory sends a strong signal to Congress to support the winning presidential candidate's programs. This was clearly indicated in the record number of voters for the presidency and the landslide victories of Franklin Roosevelt in the 1932 and 1936 presidential elections and in the record number of voters for the presidency in 1964 and Lyndon Johnson's formidable margin of victory. In these instances, Congress responded with overwhelming support for the Roosevelt and Johnson programs, changing the social structure of the nation. By contrast, the low voter turnout in the 1996 election—a mere 49 percent and the lowest since 1924—is reflected in few presidential program initiatives pending or enacted by the current Congress.

In the election of 1900, only 3.4 percent of congressional districts recorded split results (ie., voting for one party for Congress and another for presidential candidates) for presidential and congressional candidates. Partisanship binding the Congress and the presidency was alive and well. By 1948, however, 21.3 percent of congressional districts recorded split voting. In 1996, split results occurred in 25 percent of congressional districts. In brief, the "coattail" effect of presidential candidates influencing the election of congressional candidates of their own party has diminished considerably, thereby increasing the incidence of divided government in which one party controls the presidency and the other one or both houses of Congress.

II.

While party support may serve to mute the struggle between the legislative and executive branches, it cannot eliminate it altogether, for the separation-of-power systems builds competition into the relationship. From the presidency of George Washington to the present there has been a struggle between the Congress and the president, a struggle that has manifested itself in both foreign and domestic arenas. In foreign policy, the framers of the Constitution made the president both the chief diplomat and the commander-in-chief. Although Jefferson was highly critical of the conduct of foreign policy by President Washington, and proposed roles for Congress in foreign policy, when he became president, he insisted that the conduct of foreign affairs is "executive altogether." The War Powers Resolution of 1973, an attempt to curb presidential war making, and forced upon a weakened President Nixon, has, as Lind acknowledges, been viewed as unconstitutional by Nixon and subsequent presidents. But Lind fails to note that the act gives Congress the authority to contravene the orders of the president as commander-in-chief by forcing the withdrawal of troops from combat at the end of 60 to 90 days. Nixon's successor, Gerald Ford, referring to the 535 members of Congress, where he had been a member, asserted, "Our forefathers knew you could not have 535 commanders-in-chief and secretaries of state."

As for the Gulf War, the congressional vote authorizing the use of force in this military engagement in spring 1991 was not "a matter of public relations," as Lind charges. Indeed, any assertion to that effect wholly misreads the seriousness of the entire war and the historic debate that transpired on the floors of Congress as it considered whether or not to authorize military action. The fact is President Bush sought, and by a narrow voting margin, got congressional support. Other presidents as early as John Adams and Jefferson engaged in undeclared wars *without* congressional authorization: In the case of Adams there was a naval war with France and in the case of Jefferson a punitive expedition led by the United States Navy and Marines against the Barbary pirates in the Tripolitan War. Adams and Jefferson acted in their capacity as commander-in-chief as many presidents have since. By contrast, Bush did earnestly seek congressional support, even while necessarily readying a force to repel Iraqi aggression.

There are, of course, times of grave emergency when the very security of the nation is so threatened that a president must in his position as commander-in-chief assume authority, even before turning to Congress for legislative authorization. Indeed, such was the action taken by President Lincoln in the Civil War and by President Roosevelt in aiding Great Britain in the desperate 1940–41 period before the United States, by congressional declaration, entered World War II.

In another area related to the separation-of-powers issue, Lind charges Bush with "the greatest institutional power grab of any president since Nixon." He portrays Bush's White House counsel, C. Boyden Gray, as having "concocted" the idea of using the "signing statements" that accompany the signing of a bill to declare invalid provisions of a law with which the president disagreed. President Bush's signing statement policy of ignoring what he views as unconstitutional provisions is nothing more than a reflection of his oath to see that the laws are faithfully executed, pursuant to which the Constitution always supersedes a statute—for all three branches of government. Prudentially, of course, the president has to have a high degree of certainty about constitutionality, higher than the other two branches, but this factor does not negate his oath to uphold the Constitution. And even in this context, the president can rarely act unilaterally in any event. Every president, while enforcing the law, has the right to inquire as to the wisdom of any legislation and seek revision or repeal of legislation deemed unwise. However, as for example, the War Powers Resolution, which presidents have deemed unconstitutional, it remains on the statute books and presidents go through the motions of seeking to comply.

In the domestic arena, Lind charges that President Bush created "a new instrument of arbitrary presidential power" called the "czar," and calls this action "entirely alien to the American constitutional system." He also chastises Bush for making his vice-president, Dan Quayle, a czar in the Council on Competitiveness. It is perhaps a compliment that any vice-president—the occupant of the weakest political office in the American political system—could be considered a "czar" of anything.

Actually, the term "czar" was coined to emphasize the urgent need to combat the drug problem. Moreover, the drug czar is a statutory office *set up by Congress itself* to compensate for its own hopeless fragmentation of responsibility among 50 or more committees and subcommittees.

Lind charges that the Republican's newly won control of Congress is contributing to a new imperial presidency. He asserts that "having captured Congress [in 1994] after a half century, the Republicans are hastening to give away the powers of the branch they control." He cites their advocacy of the line-item veto and term limits. These are not advocacies only of Republicans, however. True, the line-item veto was a favorite of Reagan, but it has also been advocated by Democrats, as has congressional term limits.

Mr. Lind laments the large executive branch staffs in the American system. These staffs, however, grow out of weakness rather than strength, as the president seeks to respond to the pressures of both the Congress and the courts as they relate to presidential proposals and programs. It is Congress that often creates executive agencies as it did the National Security Council, Council of Economic Advisers, and Bureau of the Budget, the latter restructured as the Office of Management and Budget. Nor should it be forgotten that the strength of the judicial system in our three-part government causes the executive departments as well as the president and vice-president to appoint large numbers of government counsels to see how far they can go in testing the limits of our checks-and-balances system. Finally, the enormous growth of entitlements since the beginning of the Social Security system in 1935, and the social sensitivity that is aroused whenever there are proposals for reductions, indicates that it is the public, not the presidents, which has demanded the growth in government. In this connection, let us not forget that President and Mrs. Clinton's efforts to revise the health care system were completely defeated when it became known that the public opposed the plan.

Lind laments, in particular, the growth of the White House staff, but much of that growth, it should be noted, was a reaction to the growth of the congressional staff. By creating its own budget office, the Congress challenged the White House Office of Management and Budget to further growth in order to address the questions posed to it by the Congressional Budget Office. Further, ever since the Senate Watergate Hearings in 1973–74, the Congress has continued to increase its oversight activity. In 1961, only 8.2 percent of congressional committee hearings and meetings related to oversight of the executive branch. Between 1961 and 1983, however, oversight activity rose 207.3 percent. Currently, there is a record amount of congressional oversight in all areas of public policy. Congressional efforts to micromanage both foreign and domestic policy causes increase in all executive branch staffs as they constantly seek to respond to questions and defend executive positions.

III.

Lind concludes that "like a black hole, the presidency grows by absorbing ever more power and light." What this comparison overlooks, however, is that the policy-making machinery in our government has for a long time been characterized by "iron triangles" or, if you will, subgovernments consisting of three key actors that together comprise a powerful policy-making machine. One part of the triangle are the special interest lobbyists, the second are the members of Congress located in the congressional sub-committees, and the third are the federal bureaucrats working within the myriad administrative agencies in the executive branch of government. Whether it is in agriculture, defense policy, education, labor, veterans affairs, or whatever, as Hedrick Smith has written, "The object of the Iron Triangle is a closed power game," and they are often arrayed against the president. Lind denies this, asserting that "Presidentialists build up the legitimacy of the presidency by grossly exaggerating the faults of Congress and the parts of the executive branch that the White House does not directly control, such as the civil service and the independent agencies." In point of fact, Lind makes no reference to the reality of these "iron triangles."

Lind perceives in any presidential reforms a scheme to grab power. He does so even with President Carter's proposal to enhance the civil service by the addition at the top of the Executive Service Corps. Lind finds in this a scheme to tie the civil service more closely to the presidency. Given the influence of the iron triangles, any president is to be applauded for his efforts to more effectively relate the civil service to the presidency.

In the final analysis, there is a need for a strong and vigorous presidency. This was so very well set forth by Alexander Hamilton on March 15, 1788, during the period when the ratification of the Constitution was being debated. In *Federalist 70* he wrote, "Energy in the executive is a leading character in the definition of good government. It is essential to the protection of the community against foreign attacks. It is not less essential to the steady administration of the laws. . . ." Hamilton concluded, "The ingredients, which constitute energy in the executive, are first unity, secondly duration, thirdly an adequate provision for this support, fourthly competent powers." In *Federalist 69,* in 1788, Hamilton made clear that there is nothing imperial in the presidency as created by the Constitution and in 70 he points to the fallacy that vigor in the executive "is inconsistent with the genius of republican government." To the contrary, Hamilton states "a feeble executive" is a source of "bad government." In *Federalist 71,* Hamilton goes further and warns of "the tendency of the legislative authority to absorb every other." He adds, "The representatives of the people, in a popular assembly seem sometimes to fancy that they are the people themselves." That is what Lind would invite with his call for congressional democracy.

True, strong presidents, including Jackson and the two Roosevelts, have viewed themselves as the tribune of the people—a formulation denounced by Lind as a "plebiscitary presidency" (i.e., representing the will of the whole people). But that is precisely what the two Roosevelts stated they were doing: Theodore representing the people against the powerful moneyed interests, the railroads, monopolies, the trusts; and Franklin in combating unemployment, lack of social security, and in defense of the nation. Quite unfairly, Lind describes presidents as elective monarchs, and presidential libraries as symbols of royalism. Quite the contrary, it is not a question of monarchy, but a matter of leadership. In a dangerous world, bold leadership is required, and that leadership, thrust upon the United States more than a half-century ago, must, of necessity, be exercised by the president. As for presidential libraries, they are not symbols of royalism, but rather valuable depositories of our historical heritage.

So far as the separation of powers is concerned, we would do well to recall Madison in *Federalist 47*. Therein he contended that the Constitution set forth not so much a *separation* as it did a *sharing* of powers, asserting that "the legislative, executive, judiciary departments are by no means totally separate and distinct from each other." He perceived not so much a struggle as, by necessity, a working together of Congress and the presidency. Former Senator Nancy Landon Kassebaum (R-Kansas) likened it to two people in a three-legged race: "If one balks the other trips." What is needed is more coming together of the Congress and the presidency, not a shutdown of government as the Congress caused in 1996 over the budget. Bipartisan consensus with the president peaked at nearly 70 percent during the two terms of Eisenhower, and unfortunately, steadily went down thereafter, reaching a low point in 1995–96. Far from Lind's contention that we have been moving into "a full-fledged presidential state," we have been moving into a congressional state. What we have seen from the Nixon presidency to the present is a constantly more constrained and impeded presidency. Contrary to Lind's view we are *not* witnessing an imperial presidency. Rather we are witnessing a presidency more and more in a state of siege, and a Congress more and more unwilling to work with the president. A balance must be restored. One can only hope that the budget agreement that, as of this writing (spring 1997), appears to have been reached between Congress and the Clinton administration, signals an effort to restore that balance.

Lind concludes with a quote from Benjamin Franklin about our executive becoming a monarch. There is another quote, however, that Lind might have recalled. When asked after the Constitutional Convention what kind of government had been created, Franklin replied, "a Republic if you can keep it." We have kept it, and will continue to do so.

12

THE PRESIDENT
AND CONGRESS

If the critical problems facing our nation are to be addressed in a timely and effective way, cooperation between the president and the Congress is essential. For this reason, the relationship between these two branches is arguably the most important in our government.

The Founding Fathers, of course, fully expected that the division of power in our national government would create conflict between the executive and legislative branches. Indeed, they welcomed it, believing that interbranch rivalry would prevent the government from becoming too powerful. But with a divided government (in which one party controls the presidency and the other controls one or both houses of Congress), has this relationship grown too confrontational? And if it has, has this affected the government's ability to act? Each of the following articles offers a decidedly different answer to this much-discussed question.

In the first, political scientist David Mayhew maintains that, contrary to what one might expect, a careful review of the legislative output of Congress over a 44-year period finds little evidence to support the claim that divided government leads to stalemated government. James Sundquist, on the other hand, insists that the constitutional tension that normally exists between the two branches has in fact been greatly compounded by the partisanship *that accompanies divided government. As Sundquist sees it, this state of affairs not only has diminished the government's ability to act and administer the laws, but also has impeded the public's ability to hold its government accountable. As for the evidence presented by Mayhew in the first selection, Sundquist finds it unconvincing.*

Divided Party Control
Does It Make a Difference?

David R. Mayhew

Since World War II, party control of the U.S. national government has been formally divided for 26 years and unified for 18. (That is the span between the elections of 1946 and 1990.) Truman, Eisenhower, Nixon, Ford, Reagan, and Bush have had to coexist—for at least a two-year stretch in each case—with opposite-party majorities in the Senate or House or both. Truman, Eisenhower, Kennedy, Johnson, and Carter have had—again, for at least a two-year stretch—House and Senate majorities of their own party.

In other respects bearing on relations between the president and Congress, this postwar era shows a high degree of continuity or commonality stemming from events or precedents of the 1930s and 1940s. The New Deal and the war ratcheted the government to new levels of activity, and Franklin Roosevelt permanently strengthened the presidency. The La Follette-Monroney Act of 1946 streamlined the congressional committee system. Soon after the war the government took on new commitments in defense, foreign policy, and macroeconomic management that are with us still. Truman developed the custom of presenting "the president's program" to Congress each year. Televising of major congressional investigations began in 1948 with HUAC's [House Un-American Activities Committee's] probe of Alger Hiss.

The postwar era presents, then, a checkered pattern of unified-versus-divided party control set against a background of commonalities. That makes 1946–90 a good span of experience to look into if one wants to track the consequences of unified party control against divided party control, with at least one congressional house organized by the party not holding the White House. How well any generalizations based on 1946–90 would hold for previous eras in American history is not clear, though they might well hold for the near future.

. . . I have tried to find out how well two pieces of conventional wisdom about party control stand up against the experience of 1946–90.[1] The first conventional view is: *Congressional committees, acting as oversight bodies, will give more trouble to administrations run by the opposite party than to those of their own party.*[2] The second view, which comes close to being an axiom of political science, is: *Major laws will pass more frequently under unified party control than under divided control.*[3] A party that controls the House, the Senate, and the presidency, the logic goes, can put through a program. Absent such party control, legislative "deadlock" or "stalemate" will set in. In Woodrow Wilson's words, "You cannot compound a successful government out of antagonisms."[4]

David R. Mayhew is Alfred Cowles Professor of Government at Yale University. From David R. Mayhew, "Divided Party Control: Does It Make a Difference?" P.S.: Political Science and Politics 24 (December 1991), pp. 637–40. Reprinted by permission of the American Political Science Association. The author's references have been adjusted to conform to endnote style of presentation.

My conclusion is that both assertions are false—or at least largely or probably false. (I hedge because I use evidence that requires many individual judgments that can be disputed.) On balance, neither the "beat up on the other party's administration" effect nor the "divided control causes deadlock" effect makes a significant showing in the political record of 1946–90.

HIGH-PUBLICITY INVESTIGATIONS

The evidence on oversight is for a particular variety of that activity—congressional investigations that deal with alleged executive misbehavior and draw media attention. Included are such amply reported enterprises as HUAC's Hiss-Chambers probe of 1948, Senator McCarran's investigation of China policy in 1951–52, Senator McCarthy's Army and State Department hearings of 1953–54, the House probe of corruption in the regulatory agencies in 1958, Senator Fulbright's hearings on the Indochina war during 1966–70, the Senate and House Watergate inquiries of 1973–74, and the Iran-Contra investigations of 1987.

"Misbehavior" here means anything from treason or usurpation through corruption to simply making mistakes. The charges could be true, partly true, or fantasy. The target could be any present or past executive official or agency. An investigation made it onto a final list if it inspired front-page stories in the *New York Times* on at least 20 days. For any day, the test for content was whether anyone connected with a congressional committee made a charge against the executive branch, or someone in the executive branch answered such a charge.

Thirty-one investigations between 1946 and 1990 made the list. First prize went to the McCarthy hearings of 1953–54, which generated front-page stories on 203 days. The Senate and House Watergate inquiries ranked second and third. The results do not sort in any remarkable way according to divided versus unified party control. Probes of corruption split about equally between times of unified and divided control; it is a good bet that the ones conducted by Democratic Congresses against the Truman administration caused the most damage politically.[5] The Watergate inquiries, which occurred under divided control, may deserve a status all their own. Still, for overall significance it is hard to surpass the loyalty investigations of 1948 through 1954, and notwithstanding the 1948 Hiss probe, those occurred mostly under unified control. . . .

For 1946–90, at least, there is not a convincing case that Congress increases its high-publicity probes of the executive branch during times of divided party loyalty.

IMPORTANT LAWS

The evidence here is a list of 267 major statutes enacted between 1947 and 1990—ranging from the Taft-Hartley Labor-Management Relations Act and Marshall Plan of 1947–48 through the Clean Air Act and Americans with Disabilities Act of 1990. The 267 items are the product of two sweeps through the 44-year history. Sweep One picked up enactments that observers of the Washington scene judged (according to my coding) to be particularly important at the times the laws passed. Those observers were journalists who wrote "wrapup stories" at the close of each congressional session, or other witnesses whose appraisals have been relayed or embodied in secondary works. Sweep Two picked up enactments that policy specialists, writing recently in 43 policy areas, have indicated to be particularly important in discussing the postwar histories of their areas. "Important" in these contexts means both innovative and consequential—or at least expected at the time of passage to be consequential.

As expected, Johnson's Great Society Congress of 1965–66 emerges in first place (or at least in a tie for it) with 22 major laws—Medicare, the Voting Rights Act (VRA), the Elementary and Secondary Education Act (ESEA) and many others. Eisenhower's last Democratic Congress of 1959–60, which ended in classic deadlock, finishes in last place with five enactments. Taken alone, these reports ratify the triumph-of-party-government story that Sundquist wrote concerning the mid-1950s through the mid-1960s.[6]

But precious little else during these decades follows that "party government" script. On average, about as many major laws passed per Congress under divided control as under unified control. In several policy areas where specialists' judgments come through clearly—for example, foreign aid, foreign trade, immigration, agriculture, and tax reform—sets of key enactments became law in time patterns unrelated to conditions of party control. For example, the three post-1950 "major expansions" of Social Security occurred with disability insurance in 1956 (divided control), Medicare in 1965 (unified), and a "quantum increase" in cash benefits in 1969–72 (divided).[7] Otherwise, several notable statutes emerged from Congress and won out over presidential vetoes—for example (besides the Taft-Hartley Act), the McCarran Internal Security Act of 1950, the McCarran-Walter Immigration Act of 1952, the Water Pollution Control Act of 1972, the War Powers Act of 1973, and South Africa sanctions in 1986. The "do-nothing"-ness of Truman's Republican Congress of 1947–48 was largely Democratic propaganda; policy specialists point back, for example, to the precedent-setting Federal Insecticide, Fungicide, and Rodenticide Act (FIFRA) of 1947 and the Water Pollution Control Act of 1948. Under Reagan and Bush, the last few years . . . featured, for example, the Tax Reform Act of 1986, Speaker Jim Wright's considerable program of 1987–88, and Bush's controversial $500 billion budget-reduction package of 1990.

At the level of ambitious presidential programs, Johnson succeeded memorably in 1964 through 1966 with a Congress of his own party, but so did Reagan in 1981 despite having to deal with a House of the opposite party. Truman's Fair Deal and Kennedy's New Frontier largely failed as legislative enterprises, despite the availability of Congresses of the same party. Carter's years proved a washout for his party's lawmaking aspirations, despite sizable Democratic House and Senate majorities of 292–143 and 62–38 during 1977–78. On the only occasion since 1840 when a party took over the House, Senate, and presidency all at once—in 1952 when the Republicans did—that party turned out not to have much of a program to enact. As a result, virtually no laws of importance passed in the seemingly favorable circumstances of 1953, though Eisenhower won some victories later.

The real story of these decades is the prominent, continuous lawmaking surge that lasted from late 1963 through 1975 or 1976. That was under Johnson, Nixon, and Ford.

Whether one looks at legislative workload in general[8] or major laws passed,[9] it was during that span of years—or roughly that span; assessments of boundaries differ a bit—that the postwar legislative mill operated at full steam. Everyone knows that happened under Johnson, but the Vietnam war, wrangling over "social issues," and Watergate have clouded our picture of legislating under Nixon and Ford. In fact, the state-enhancing thrust of the 1960s toward greater expenditure and regulation continued with great force in the 1970s. Budget growth owed to Johnson's Great Society programs, but also to post-1968 legislative initiatives in the areas of, for example, food stamps, Supplementary Security Income (SSI), CETA [Comprehensive Employment and Training Act] jobs, unemployment compensation, housing block grants, mass transit, and water pollution, as well as Social Security benefits.[10] The "new social regulation," to use Vogel's term,[11] came to pass largely by statute under Nixon.[12] That featured, to cite some highlights, the National Environmental Policy Act (NEPA) of 1969, the Occupational Safety and Health Act (OSHA) of 1970, the Clean Air Act of 1970, the Equal Employment Opportunity Act of 1972, and the Consumer Product Safety Act of 1972. Campaign finance and private pensions came under comprehensive regulation for the first time through laws enacted in 1974. Statutory regulation of state governments reached new heights under Nixon.[13] The Equal Rights Amendment (ERA) cleared Congress in 1972, though the states would not buy it.[14] These and many other items from the Nixon-Ford years are probably familiar to readers, but I do not think we have appreciated their volume or sifted them through our doctrines about party control and legislative action. In terms of volume and also ideological direction of lawmaking, there arguably existed an era of Johnson-Nixon (or Johnson-Nixon-Ford), and it overlapped different circumstances of party control.

Since World War II, to sum up, neither high-publicity investigations nor major laws have accumulated on a schedule that the rules of party control would predict. Why not? That is too complicated a question to tackle here. The material cited above makes it obvious that no simple arithmetic theory involving Democratic presidents and sizes of cross-party "conservative coalitions" on Capitol Hill can work very well. If that were the key factor, why all the lawmaking under Nixon? Why the slump under Carter? Evidently, speculation about causes needs to center on features of the modern U.S. regime that dominate, override, or blot out parties to a greater degree than we may have supposed. Some good candidates for that role seem to be Capitol Hill electoral incentives that foster lawmaking and investigating, presidential leadership qualities that operate more or less independently of party, the practical need for non-narrow roll-call majorities to pass laws regardless of conditions of party control, forcing public events, public opinion cleavages that crosscut parties, and "public moods" like that of 1963–76 that seem capable of overriding everything else.[15]

NOTES

1. David R. Mayhew, *Divided We Govern: Party Control, Lawmaking, and Investigations, 1946–1990* (New Haven, CT: Yale University Press, 1991).

2. Morris S. Ogul, *Congress Oversees the Bureaucracy: Studies in Legislative Supervision* (Pittsburgh: University of Pittsburgh Press, 1976), p. 18; Seymour Scher, "Conditions for Legislative Control," *Journal of Politics* 25 (1963), 526–51.

3. James L. Sundquist, "Needed: A Political Theory for the New Era of Coalition Government in the United States," *Political Science Quarterly* 103 (1988–89), 616–24; V. O. Key, Jr., *Politics, Parties, and Pressure Groups,* 5th ed. (New York: Crowell, 1964), pp. 656, 687–88; Randall B. Ripley, *Congress: Process and Policy* (New York: W. W. Norton, 1983), pp. 347–56; Lloyd N. Cutler, "Some Reflections About Divided Government," *Presidential Studies Quarterly* 18 (1988), 485–92.

4. Quoted in James L. Sundquist, "Needed: A Political Theory for the New Era of Coalition Government in the United States," p. 618.

5. Andrew J. Dunar, *The Truman Scandals and the Politics of Morality* (Columbia: University of Missouri Press, 1984).

6. James L. Sundquist, *Politics and Policy: The Eisenhower, Kennedy and Johnson Years* (Washington, DC: Brookings, 1968).

7. Martha Derthick, *Policymaking for Social Security* (Washington, DC: Brookings, 1979), p. 296.

8. Roger H. Davidson, "The New Centralization on Capitol Hill," *Review of Politics* 50 (1988), 345–64.

9. David R. Mayhew, *Divided We Govern: Party Control, Lawmaking, and Investigations, 1946–1990,* ch. 4.

10. Robert J. Lampman, *Social Welfare Spending: Accounting for Changes from 1950 to 1978* (New York: Academic Press, 1984), pp. 8–9; Timothy Conlan, *New Federalism: Intergovernmental Reform from Nixon to Reagan* (Washington, DC: Brookings, 1985), p. 81; Robert X. Browning, *Politics and Social Welfare Policy in the United States* (Knoxville: University of Tennessee Press, 1986), pp. 79–83; David R. Mayhew, *Divided We Govern: Party Control, Lawmaking, and Investigations, 1946–1990,* ch. 4.

11. David Vogel, "The 'New' Social Regulation in Historical and Comparative Perspective," in Thomas K. McCraw (ed.), *Regulation in Perspective: Historical Essays* (Cambridge, MA: Harvard University Press, 1981).

12. See also Murray L. Weidenbaum, *Business, Government, and the Public* (Englewood Cliffs, NJ: Prentice-Hall, 1977), pp. 5–10; *Robert Higgs, Crisis and Leviathan: Critical Episodes in the Growth of American Government* (New York: Oxford University Press, 1987), pp. 246–54.

13. Timothy Conlan, *New Federalism: Intergovernmental Reform from Nixon to Reagan,* pp. 84–89.

14. Jo Freeman, *The Politics of Women's Liberation* (New York: David McKay, 1975), ch. 6.

15. David R. Mayhew, *Divided We Govern: Party Control, Lawmaking, and Investigations, 1946–1990,* chs. 5, 6.

A Government Divided Against Itself

James L. Sundquist

In November 1956, when the voters reelected Republican President Dwight D. Eisenhower by an overwhelming margin but at the same time confirmed control of both houses of the Congress by the opposition Democratic party, they began what has become a transformation of the American political system. No such division of the government between opposing parties had resulted from any of the preceding seventeen presidential contests, not since Grover Cleveland's victory in 1884. But since Eisenhower and especially after 1968, the government has been divided almost all the time.

No Republican president of the past half century has ever been given a Congress of his own party to support him, except for Eisenhower in his first two years. After that, Eisenhower had to contend with an opposition-controlled Congress for his remaining six years, Richard Nixon and Gerald Ford for all of their eight, Ronald Reagan for all of his eight (in six, he did have a Republican Senate majority), and George Bush for all of his four. Under Democratic Presidents John Kennedy, Lyndon Johnson, and Jimmy Carter, the government was unified, but with Bill Clinton even that was changed. After only a two-year honeymoon between Clinton and a Congress of the same party came the Newt Gingrich revolution in 1994 and division was restored as the normal state of affairs, with a reversal of party roles. In sum, in the last 46 years of the century, the government was divided 70 percent of the time; in the last 32 years 81 percent.

Is this new American political system—which can be called a form of coalition government—better or worse than the structure of party government it replaced, or does the transformation simply make no difference? The scholars who found the discipline of political science, and those who wrote about the American governmental system before its current transfiguration, would surely have termed it undesirable, had they had occasion to comment at all. But for the most part they ignored the question, because the transformation had not happened yet. True, the government had sometimes been divided in the last half of the president's term when the voters reacted against the ruling party in the mid-term election—as in 1918 or 1940 or 1946—but that aberration had always been corrected at the next presidential election and unified government restored.

In the political theory that evolved, unity was seen not only as normal but as the way things ought to be. And the instrument indispensable to producing that unity was, of course, the institution not mentioned in the Constitution—and openly distrusted and even feared by the Founders—the political party. In their zeal to forestall tyranny, the Founders had scattered the powers of government, separating the executive and legislative branches and splitting the latter between two independent houses. Yet as soon as they began to operate the new government, their very generation saw that to make things happen, power had to be reassembled; to pass laws, three of those separated in-

James L. Sundquist is senior fellow emeritus at The Brookings Institution, a government and public policy research organization in Washington, D.C. From James L. Sundquist, "A Government Divided Against Itself," the Chronical of Higher Education, *June 24, 1992, B1-2. Reprinted with permission of the author.*

stitutions had to be brought into harmony—the House, the Senate, and the presidency. In this process, the party role was central. Political scientists came to describe political parties with a variety of metaphors: the tie, the web, the cement, the glue that binds the competing centers of power; the bridge across the chasms that divide them.

A corollary to the doctrine of party government was that of presidential leadership. No government could be dynamic without a leader. And, logically, that leader had to be the president, who as head of the government party could set the course of the legislative branch as well as direct the executive.

Does *divided* government violate this model? Obviously, and absolutely. The political party cannot be the tie, the web, that unites the branches of government unless it controls them both. The president cannot lead the entire government when his political enemies control one or both houses of the legislature.

The question is, is the traditional theory obsolete, and does divided government work well enough, or can it be made to work? Or does the partisan division of the government, as its critics contend, stalemate the legislative process? Does it lead to incoherence and breakdown in the administration of the laws? Does it intensify the partisan conflict and rancor that destroy public confidence in politicians and in government itself? Does it vitiate the accountability of policy-makers to voters that is essential for popular rule in a democracy? Not all political scientists who write on these issues agree, but to me the answers to all four questions are affirmative, and together they constitute a powerful indictment of divided government as an acceptable model for our third century of national life.

How does divided government affect the legislative process? People organize opposing parties because they disagree in fundamental ways about what government should do, for whom, and how. The clash of conflicting philosophies and program ideas in political campaigns, with the electorate as the arbiter, is what gives democracy its spirit and its meaning. But when the election is over, if the government is divided, the normal and healthful campaign debate is carried over into partisan warfare between the branches of government themselves, with each trying to discredit and undermine the other. The president vetoes congressional proposals; the Congress labels his recommendations "dead on arrival." If compromises emerge, they are often watered down and truly satisfactory to neither side. The whole process is "stymied by relentless . . . maneuvering for short-term political advantage," as Democratic Senator Timothy E. Wirth of Colorado put it when in "anger and frustration" he announced his retirement a few years ago.

How does divided government affect administration? When government is unified, the congressional majorities are more willing to delegate to administrators in the executive branch the flexibility and discretion they require to execute the laws, because the power goes to like-minded officials supervised by the leader of their own party, namely, the president. But in divided government, any delegated authority flows to administrators dedicated to leading their agencies in a different, even an opposite, direction from the president. So legislators inevitably try to tighten their control of policy by withholding discretion, writing detailed and sometimes unworkable prescriptions into law, earmarking appropriations, proliferating congressional staff for purposes of "micromanaging" executive agencies, and befuddling lines of authority and responsibility within the executive branch.

What does divided government do to public confidence? When the partisan debate becomes a power struggle between the branches, not only does Washington appear impotent to solve the nation's problems but its affairs are conducted in tones of rancor and recrimination. The president and Congress condemn each other as incompetent, irresponsible, and tainted with corruption. In time, the evidence suggests, the people come to believe both sides; they damn all politicians as a class, grasp at panaceas such as term limits, and either stay away from the polls in growing numbers or chase after some chimerical source of salvation like Ross Perot.

Lastly, *what does divided government do to accountability?* Clearly, it opens the way to passing the buck and avoiding blame. In the days of unified government, the ruling party was accountable. If it satisfied the country, it was returned to office. If it failed, it was cast out. But now, if the government fails, who can be held responsible—when, in fact, neither party had the power to decide policy, and then to act?

Some of those who defend divided government do so by invoking democratic principles. Division of government, is, after all, the consequence of free elections, they remind us, and the voters' sovereign will must be respected. But is that consequence truly an expression of the popular will or simply the accidental product of an electoral system that—virtually unique in the world—allows voters to split their tickets in choosing presidents and legislators? The evidence suggests the latter. In every quadrennial election, an overwhelming majority of those who vote Republican for president express their desire for unified government—under G.O.P. auspices—by supporting that party's candidates for Congress. And likewise among the Democrats. The ticket-splitters who cause the divided government are always a minority, and often a small one, be they Reagan Democrats or Clinton Republicans. Their choice is based primarily on personalities, not on any conscious preference for divided government as such.

Some find benefits in divided government that offset, or even outweigh, its disadvantages. This view may have ideological roots. For those who believe steadfastly that "that government is best which governs least," any circumstance that inactivates the government is welcome. Some credit the government's division with restraining an "imperial presidency" intent on military ventures—or, conversely, thwarting a Congress committed to dismantling popular domestic programs. Divided government sometimes appears to hasten rather than retard popular/progressive measures, by stimulating the parties to compete for plaudits (environmental legislation comes to mind). And in the last Clinton years, ironically, governmental deadlock was being hailed as a serendipitous boon to economic management, for it blocked either excessive Republican tax cuts or exorbitant Democratic spending, leaving the surplus nowhere to go but to reduce the national debt, thereby bringing joy to those who thought that's where it should have gone all along.

David Mayhew presents empirical data suggesting that, over nearly half a century, divided governments have not been significantly less capable than unified ones in producing important legislation. But I find his data, summarized in his own contribution in this volume, less than conclusive in ending the debate.

First of all, any comparison of legislative output by the two forms of government in the period covered by his study (1947–90) needs to recognize that during most of that time the nominal unity of what appeared as unified government was a myth. The governing party in such times was Democratic (except in 1953–54), and it was so internally divided between liberal presidents and northern legislators, on the one hand, and conservative southern lawmakers, on the other, that the ruling party on Capitol Hill much of the time was in fact a conservative bipartisan coalition that resisted presidential leadership as fiercely as any strictly Republican majority would have done. Data from these years essentially compare one form of divided government with another, shedding little light on the contrast between divided and unified government as they manifest themselves now—when realignment in the South has made both national parties more nearly homogeneous—and will in the future.

Second, Mayhew's study is limited to examining the timing of important legislation that *was* enacted—that is, instances of success—whereas the criticism of divided government has centered on instances of failure, of nonperformance. Whether the government should have legislated when it did not, or should have acted sooner, or passed laws adequate to the need when it finally did respond, are all questions that rest heavily on the analyst's subjective judgment and hence defy a rigorous empirical examination. But they cannot be disregarded in weighing the consequences of divided government.

Third, Mayhew's list of important measures enacted by unified Democratic governments includes a not insignificant number that were opposed by a majority of Republican legislators and would presumably have been blocked had the government been divided. Thus, for example, were the study extended to the Clinton years, the president's economic program of 1993, passed over solid Republican opposition would join the list.

Discussion of this subject should not end without at least a mention of another, little-noticed transformation of the American governmental system. Even when the government is nominally unified, as in the first two Clinton years, the essential attribute of a divided government remains always present, because the Senate by its internal rules has made bipartisan agreement essential for almost any piece of legislation. That body's hallowed tradition of the filibuster—in former times, by gentlemen's agreement, invoked only on rare occasions—has now been extended to virtually every measure that is controversial between the parties. Sixty of the one hundred senators must vote to close off debate, and the majority party rarely numbers that many. So coalition government is in force all the time, and the whole debate over the issue as defined in these pages may have been rendered moot.

But probably not. Skillful presidents and able congressional majority leaders, in unified governments, have resources to attract votes from the Senate minority and overcome at least some filibuster threats. So, those who are persuaded that, on the whole, unified governments are more harmonious, more cohesive, more effective, as well as more accountable, than divided ones, should still exhort the voters: Don't split your tickets. If you like the record of the Republican congressional majorities, reelect them but give them a president of their own party who will sign their bills. Or, if you want to see another Democrat installed in the White House, give him congressional majorities of his party to work as teammates with him.

13
BUREAUCRACY

From the days of President Franklin Roosevelt's New Deal, beginning in the 1930s, until the late 1970s, the prevailing view in this country was that the federal government had a large and important role to play in the development of the nation. The range of that role included providing social security for senior citizens, maintaining a stable economy, and regulating private industry so as to provide a healthy workplace and a clean environment. As a result of these and other activities, the federal government over the years grew bigger and bigger, and often more cumbersome, to the point that in the presidential campaign of 1980, the Republican nominee, Ronald Reagan, declared that "Government is not the solution to our problems; government is the problem." Some 16 years later, in 1996, Democratic President Bill Clinton declared in his State of the Union Address, "The era of big government is over."

Such bipartisan agreement on an issue is rare in politics and reflects the extent to which Americans have concluded that government needs to be reformed. Underlying that reform is the belief that the federal government should be downsized and made more efficient and responsive to citizen needs.

The Clinton administration, in response to this public demand, launched in its first term a program to do just that. Labeled "Reinventing Government," this program was an ambitious attempt to streamline government, thereby making it not only more cost efficient but also better able to respond to the needs of the people. Vice President Al Gore was placed in charge of this effort, and portions of his report appear as the first selection of this chapter. As suggested by the title of the Gore report, The Best Kept Secrets in Government, *the vice president is attempting to trumpet the accomplishments of the Reinventing Government program. Indeed, Gore's "best kept secret" is an impressive list of reforms accomplished across a wide range of government activities.*

Not all of what the vice president views as accomplishments, however, is seen as such by his critics, who argue that the reforms are more apparent than real. Washington Monthly *writer Robert Worth maintains that if real reform is to take place, it must start with rooting out employees who are "deadwood" and replacing them with workers committed to getting the job done. Worth also contends that reform should not only be about making government more efficient, but should include as well examining the government's general mission and performance in various areas—eliminating what it should no longer do and ensuring that what it does, it does well.*

195

The Best Kept Secrets in Government

Al Gore

"The era of big government is over."
—Bill Clinton, 1996 State of the Union Address

When President Clinton said the era of big government is over, he wasn't just making a promise, he was reporting on his progress. The Clinton-Gore Administration has made the federal government smaller by nearly a quarter of a million jobs.[1] This is the largest, swiftest government-wide cut in the history of the United States. It's not just a post-Cold War defense reduction; every department except Justice has become smaller. . . .

The federal government workforce is now the smallest it has been in more than 30 years, going all the way back to the Kennedy Administration. The cuts were long overdue. People had long since grown tired of new government programs initiated each year, with none ever ending. They were tired of stories about senseless sounding government jobs, like the Official Tea-Taster, tired of larger and larger bureaucracies in Washington interfering more and more with their lives. For years, presidential candidates have been promising to make government smaller. But until Bill Clinton, none delivered.

The workforce cuts are saving lots of money. For fiscal year 1996, the average government worker costs more than $44,000 a year, not including office space and supplies.[2] Cutting a quarter million jobs, therefore, can save well over $10 billion annually. But that's not the half of it. The savings from all the common-sense reforms we have put in place total $118 billion. . . .

Even though big cuts in government were long overdue, and even though they are a crucial step in getting the country out of the red, there is a right way and a wrong way to cut government. The right way is to show some consideration for the workers. It is wrong just to hand out the pink slips and let government employees fend for themselves—workers who have devoted their careers to public service and who have families to support.

We've made the cuts the right way, with layoffs as a last resort. First, we slowed down hiring. The government used to hire well over 100,000 people each year just to replace those who retired or quit. We brought hiring down to fewer than 50,000 a year.[3] We did not stop hiring altogether because many government jobs, such as air traffic controllers, simply must be filled.

Next, we encouraged our current employees to retire or quit by offering them buyout payments. The offers ranged from a few thousand dollars up to $25,000, depending on the workers' salaries and how long they had worked. It was a good deal for the employees and for the taxpayers. Even at $25,000, a buyout costs less than the

Al Gore is Vice President of the United States and the Democratic candidate for President in 2000. From Al Gore, The Best Kept Secrets in Government *(New York: Random House, 1996), ix–xvi, 11–31, 122–25.*

paperwork and severance pay that goes with a layoff.[4] Nearly 115,000 workers took buyouts.[5]

By slowing down hiring and speeding up retirements, we've managed to limit layoffs to a small proportion of the workforce that left federal service.[6] We are helping those who have been laid off to find jobs with private companies. It's tough, but we're trying. It's all part of making cuts the right way.

Another part of cutting government the right way is to be selective and cut out just the parts we don't need anymore—not the parts we do need. It's wrong to cut activities and services that most people depend on, things like ensuring that our food and water are safe, that our neighborhoods are free from drugs and crime, that tax refunds and social security payments arrive on time. Our plan is ultimately to eliminate jobs we no longer need: jobs in bloated headquarters, excess layers of management, and offices that churn out arcane rules, like the rules that have made government procurement so costly and ridiculous. So far, the personnel reductions have occurred pretty much across the board, because we were trying to avoid layoffs. We'll have to retrain and reassign some people to get them into the right jobs.

A lot of the credit for cutting goes to the very federal workers whose jobs were at stake. For example, it was a procurement specialist, Michellee Edwards, who suggested that we change the law to make small purchases so simple that we no longer need a procurement specialist. Those small purchases used to generate 70 percent of the work in a typical procurement office.[7] Michellee says, "I don't think any government employees would cling to senseless work just to protect their jobs. I certainly wouldn't. For me, it's more important to keep in mind the bigger picture and promote change where it makes sense. We're all taxpayers too, you know."

This might be surprising, but lots of government workers think like Michellee. Why else would teams of personnel specialists have worked so hard to scrap the 10,000 page Federal Personnel Manual and have then gone on to cut out much of a typical personnel office's day-to-day workload by letting employees use self-serve computer kiosks? Why else would U.S. Customs Service employees have come up with the plan that eliminated an entire layer of regional Customs headquarters that was full of high-paying jobs? Even Washington's regulation writers are tossing out 16,000 pages of their own creations and removing the bureaucratic jargon from another 31,000 pages.[8] Behind virtually every bit of our successful downsizing and streamlining are the ideas and the enthusiasm of federal workers. More than anyone, they have the know-how and the desire to make government cost less. Our hats are off to them.

A cheaper, smaller government was only half our goal. President Clinton and I were determined to make government *work better,* too. You probably haven't read or heard much about this part of reinvention—although we never intended it to be a secret—but we've made real progress. The government is beginning to produce more results and less red tape. I'll be the first to say that there is still plenty of room for improvement, but Americans are beginning to see the results in the form of fast, courteous service. Business owners and local government leaders are noticing the change, too, as the federal government becomes more of a partner and less of an adversary. President Clinton and I think it's time everyone knows about these changes—it's time for these secrets to get out. . . .

PROCUREMENT REFORM

Most Americans have known for years that government procurement is a mess. But to get a full appreciation, it helps to work here. Before the reinventing government reforms launched in 1993, the typical federal worker was not trusted to buy so much as a $4 stapler for the office. Only trained procurement specialists were allowed to buy things—only a trained specialist could understand the rules—and they would make the buy only if a worker came to them with the forms properly filled out and signed by several bosses up the line and even then, only if they thought you deserved whatever was requested.

Buying anything associated with a computer was even worse. Federal workers told us about having to get a dozen signatures, and then waiting a year or more to get a simple PC. When it arrived, it was already obsolete, and it cost more than the new, higher-powered models at Circuit City. To cap off their frustration, federal employees would read in the papers, along with the rest of America, that "the procurement system," which did not trust them to buy anything, had gone out and paid $400 for a hammer.

The government's procurement system was enough of a challenge that we decided to double-team it. We got long-time critic of procurement and former Harvard professor of management Steve Kelman to lead some government-wide changes, and brought Colleen Preston in from a Congressional staff to lead reform at the Defense Department. Rather than try to explain all the ins and outs of the regulatory changes backed by the National Performance Review—changes that the Administration has made on its own authority, and changes we have persuaded Congress to enact into law—let's look at some results.

First, results that benefit the entire government and, of course, the taxpayers who foot the bill:

- Last May, we signed a contract with FedEx for overnight package delivery. A three pound package, at retail—$27. For the government, and the taxpayers—$3.62.
- Long-distance telephone calls: Someone who shops around can make peak-hour long-distance calls for as low as 16¢ per minute. Starting in October, government calls to anyone anywhere in the country will cost about 5¢ per minute. Calls between government agencies are even less, about 2¢ per minute.
- The government used to do over $50 worth of paper work for every small purchase—even for something like a $4 office stapler—and there are millions of small purchases each year. Now, we have gotten rid of the paperwork and we use special Visa cards. What's special? The average American pays from 12 to 18 percent interest, and a yearly fee of up to $50. The government pays no interest, no annual fee, and we earn cash rebates for paying on time.[9]
- Earlier this year, President Clinton signed a new law and an executive order that fixes one of procurement's biggest nightmares: buying computers and other information technology.[10] Under the President's order, agencies will invest in information technology only when there is a clear payback, and they won't be locked into cumbersome contracts that can't keep up with rapidly changing technology. The idea is to buy a little, test a little, fix a little, and do it quick.

Now for the Defense Department, which accounts for about three-fourths of the federal government's purchases:

- Remember the $400 hammer? How about a $500 telephone—one especially designed for an aircraft carrier. What was so special? It worked even after the ship had sunk. Following changes in the communications system and by challenging every requirement, the Navy determined it could use commercial phones that cost 30 bucks.[11]
- Let's look at socks and underwear (it reminds us of the old days for Customs inspectors). If you were ever a soldier, your GI socks probably fell down because there was no elastic at the top, and they made everything in the washing machine with them turn olive drab. The reinvented Army now issues ordinary, color-fast socks with elastic. The sad-sack socks cost $1.99 a pair—the nice, new ones cost $1.49.
- Concerning underwear, we think this letter speaks for itself.[12]

June 7, 1996

For many years, Jockey International, Inc. declined to bid on government business. We took this position because the solicitations asked us to manufacture a T-shirt to unique government specifications. The solicitations also asked us to provide sensitive pricing data so the government could determine a fair price. . . .

When we saw the latest solicitation for T-shirts we were excited. The government was asking for our standard product, style 9711, without all the headaches of a custom design. Moreover, our current catalog price was the basis to negotiate a fair price. It is with great pleasure that we were able to accept the T-shirt award. . . .

The T-shirt will be made in the USA. The production is at our Belzoni, Mississippi plant, an economically depressed area. This plant was closed in 1993, but reopened in 1995 on a temporary basis. With a pick up in business and the award of this military contract we now have 175 employees at this facility.

Peter J. Hannes
President, Special Markets Division
Jockey International, Inc.

Of course, the savings are not all just from socks and undershirts—the biggest savings come from changes in buying big-ticket items. When the Pentagon and Congress agreed to a multi-year purchase and the elimination of detailed military specifications, manufacturers could use more standard commercial parts. As a result, the price tag on the contract for their new C-17 cargo plane went down by more than $2.7 billion. Similarly, they saved $2.9 billion on smart munitions, and over $100 million on the Fire Support Combat Arms Tactical Trainer.[13] NASA is doing the same kind of thing and making the same kind of savings on space gear.

In addition to some very important legislative changes, the procurement system only needed a little trust (that workers . . . won't steal us blind), some common sense (that Jockey can make decent T-shirts without government instructions), and some shrewd bargaining (just try to find long distance rates as low as 2¢ a minute). That is the heart of the procurement reforms that the National Performance Review recommended in 1993 and that became the basis for three major legislative changes that have been signed by the President: the Federal Acquisition Streamlining Act of 1994, the Federal Acquisition Reform Act of 1996, and the Information Technology Management Reform Act of 1996. President Clinton has gone even further by issuing a variety of directives that enhance and speed the legislative reforms.[14]

Trust, common sense, and shrewd bargaining might not sound like a revolutionary formula to fix government procurement. But added all together, our procurement reforms are expected to save $12.3 billion over five years. Pretty good, huh?

By the way, we are not just buying smarter, we are selling smarter, too. The government actually used to give away the incredibly valuable rights to broadcast on certain frequencies. This included radio, TV, cell phones—you get the picture. Now, the Federal Communications Commission auctions them to the highest bidder. So far, we have taken in $20.3 billion.[15]

MANAGEMENT SYSTEMS AND STRUCTURE

. . . Back in 1991, when we began reinventing government, we discovered that one out of every three government employees was part of a network of micromanagement and overcontrol. They were headquarters staff, personnel, budget, procurement, audit, finance, or supervisors. One-third of our employees had been assigned to keep the other two-thirds from ever doing anything wrong. They were writing and promulgating internal rules, administering internal rules, and auditing compliance with internal rules. That occupied almost 700,000 workers, who cost tax payers around $35 billion a year, plus office space and lots of paper.[16] But at least nothing ever went wrong. Right? Wrong!

Big headquarters and big rule books never have kept the government from making big mistakes. In fact, they often kept front-line workers from doing things right. So we asked agencies to cut layers of supervisors, headquarters staff, and other management control jobs by 50 percent. . . .

Because we started offering buyouts and putting the brakes on hiring, the reductions have not been concentrated in management control positions to the extent the National Performance Review recommended. But 11 of the 27 largest agencies are at least halfway to the goal on supervisors, and eight have cut headquarters staff by 25 percent or more. In addition, certain bureaus and agencies within selected departments are also making big progress that is not reflected in their departments' overall figures. Overall, it is fair progress, but we still have a long way to go.

Numbers are not everything. Many bosses are changing the way they do their jobs—encouraging innovation and customer service instead of just making workers toe the line. Many national and regional management organizations are taking on a new role whose primary job is support. Ultimately, we have to bring down the number of people in management jobs and headquarters, but the shift in attitude is every bit as important.

REINVENTION LABS

The first thing we did to encourage a change of attitude at headquarters and to move more authority and accountability to the front lines was to create "reinvention laboratories," where front-line workers and managers could try out *their* ideas for a change. Now there are about 250 reinvention labs leading the reinvention revolution. They have been called "islands of innovation in a sea of bureaucracy."[17] . . . Here are some . . . examples:

- The General Services Administration established the first electronic shopping mall for Federal customers, which cut the cost of real estate sales by 50 percent while generating revenue of $73 million.
- The Air Force medical organization prototyped an automated system for maintaining patients' records. The system will save millions of dollars and improve care as it spreads throughout the Defense Department.
- A joint effort between the Defense Contract Audit Agency and the Defense Logistics Agency cut the government's and contractors' overhead expenses by substituting international quality control standards for the government standard. Quality rose, and government costs have fallen by over $150 million so far.
- The Department of Justice's SENTRI project in southwest California uses state-of-the-art technology to reduce the average waiting time to cross the border from 45 minutes to just three minutes for registered travelers. Inspectors now can focus on non-registered, higher-risk travelers.
- A reinvention lab in Anchorage is combining seven separate libraries into a single one-stop shop for information about natural resources. The Department of the Interior is joining forces with state agencies and the University of Alaska to create a single natural resources library that will eliminate duplication, save money, require less staff, and provide better service to customers.

PERSONNEL REFORM

In 1883, two years before the first gasoline powered automobile and six years before the White House had electric lights, the U.S. Civil Service laws were written.[18] Not only is the civil service system old, our first report called it "elaborate, complex, and over-regulated, preventing agencies and their managers, employees, and unions from designing effective and mission supporting human resource management programs." No one argued with us about that.

We have done what we could to fix it. We have done quite a bit.

Common-Sense Job Applications

We scrapped the Standard Form 171, the ridiculously long job application that said, in so many words, "Welcome to the fun house." Now applicants can send in a regular resume, like regular people do for regular jobs.[19] Even better, the Office of Personnel Management has a toll-free phone service and a World Wide Web site that lets people find out what is available and even apply by phone or fax for many jobs.[20]

Less Red Tape

We junked all but a few parts of the 10,000 page Federal Personnel Manual that specified everything down to the color of personnel folders. We actually hauled it out to a dumpster in a wheel barrow. The death of the manual gave agencies more freedom to tailor things to fit their own operations.

Labor-Management Partnerships

CEOs who had reinvented big corporations told us we could not succeed without a true partnership between management and labor. The President signed an executive order in 1993 establishing the National Partnership Council.[21] Now there are more than 650 partnership councils, and labor-management relations are improving all across government. One of the most successful councils is at the U.S. Mint in Denver, led by Greg Wikberg, president of the local union, and Jack DeBrockert, the manager of the Mint. Since the partnership started, disputes have nearly vanished, litigation costs have dropped by $10 million and, in 1995, they set an all-time record by producing 10.3 billion coins.[22] . . .

Family-Friendly Workplaces

Government workers should have lives, too. Moms and dads need time with the kids, with their own parents, and with each other. So, the Clinton-Gore Administration is encouraging job sharing, part-time work, alternative work schedules, telecommuting from home and from satellite locations, leave banks, and child-and-elder-care services.[23] Top business leaders agree that this approach increases productivity and morale, and reduces lost time.

Performance Appraisals

Every year, everyone who works for the government is to be formally and individually judged by his or her boss. The process can cause tension and is widely viewed as ineffective. Most government work depends on team, not individual, effort. And often, a worker's teammates and customers are better able than the boss to judge that employee's effectiveness. Several agencies are experimenting with different evaluation methods that enhance teamwork and give more influence to the customers. The Department of Education is using a 360-degree appraisal, an evaluation from all directions—the boss, subordinates, colleagues, customers, and suppliers. The other new kind of evaluation is not of the individual, but of the team. It is based on measurable results, and everybody who contributes to the results gets the same grade. Workers are being judged and rewarded in terms of how well their teams achieve measurable results. Several variations of the new systems are being tried, and all have pluses and minuses; the hope is to find better, more productive means of gauging worker performance.

New Civil Service Legislation

Right now, we cannot be as flexible or innovative as we would like to be because the personnel system applies a single set of rules to all federal employees, from patent attorneys to park rangers. No corporation would operate this way. General Electric makes light bulbs, buys and sells mortgage loans, and leases cars. GE does not try to squeeze such a diverse cadre of workers into a single set of personnel rules, and neither should the federal government.

Legislation now moving through Congress will grant agencies more flexibility in administering personnel systems that support their missions, while preserving basic common values like veterans preference and merit. It will allow each agency to set up its own method of rewarding good performance and dealing with poor performance.

Reinforcing Success: The Hammer Award

From the start, Vice President Gore has spotlighted the people and teams that were showing the way to reinvention by giving them a "Hammer Award"—a $6 hammer wrapped in ribbon and mounted with an aluminum frame. It symbolizes the dramatic change from the days when government paid a bit more for hammers. The awards are highly prized, and teams are eager to publicize initiatives that they once would have kept under wraps due to fear of criticism. Nearly 500 Hammer Awards have gone to such teams as:

- the Interior Department team that converted its rules and regulations into "plain English";
- the Transportation team that, along with their California teammates, figured out how to get the Santa Monica Freeway back into operation in record time after the Northridge earthquake; and
- the team from the National Park Service that reduced the review time for construction of park visitor centers and other major projects by over 50 percent.

Several agencies followed the Vice President's lead and encouraged reinvention with special awards. For example, the Deputy Secretary of Veterans Affairs gives the "Scissors Award" to VA employees who have cut red tape.

FRANCHISE FUNDS

Our government has long opposed private monopolies while creating public ones. A federal manager needing some administrative service—like help from personnel, legal, procurement, financial, or computer specialists—had to go to the departmental monopoly in charge of that service. This approach was thought to offer economies of scale.

Today almost everybody understands that monopolies provide poor services at high costs. So the original National Performance Review report recommended introducing competition by lifting the requirement that agencies buy supplies from the General Services Administration. GSA's Federal Supply Service gave up its monopoly on office supplies in 1994 and has been competing successfully for government business ever since. Their new motto is "Better, faster, cheaper, or not at all."

The National Performance Review also encouraged agencies to promote competition by establishing "franchise funds."[24] These funds allow selected agencies to offer their common administrative services to other agencies. Congressional approval was obtained in May 1996 for franchise funds in Interior, Treasury, Veterans Affairs, the Environmental Protection Agency, and Commerce. The funds will allow these agencies to

sell to other agencies such services as mainframe computing, records storage, personnel and accounting systems, background checks, and travel management.

OUR SECRET WEAPON

Telepathology equipment at the Veterans Hospital in Milwaukee rivals the sick bay on
Star Trek's *Enterprise*. But, the real reason the vets get world-class care there is Dr. Bruce
Dunn. Dr. Dunn thinks we owe veterans a debt that can never quite be repaid. His research
to get vets the best pathology on the planet sets the scales a bit closer to balance.

Helen Wassick went to work part-time in the Morgantown office of the Forest
Service in a program that employs seniors at minimum wage. Her office sends out publications all over the country on tree management. Helen prides herself on not giving
up on a request until she gets an answer. She says, "I treat people the way I want to be
treated." And when the Forest Service started giving comment cards to customers,
Helen wrote her own name on the cards. Hundreds of customers told the Forest Service
that Helen is the greatest. So now Helen's on the payroll full-time serving customers.

George Hawkins works for EPA in Boston. He used to practice law at Ropes and
Gray for more money, and he had a lot less fun. George is the champion in EPA's
Boston office for EPA efforts to build partnerships with companies and communities
that want to protect the environment. George thinks that this is the future of environmental protection and that building that future is worth doing. He'll tell anyone who
will listen. In fact, he wrote 1,000 letters to businesses and towns offering to come and
explain the partnership programs. He got a lot of takers. True to his pledge he has made
150 visits so far this year.

Bruce, Helen, and George all have something in common. A big part of why these
people work for government is that they want to make a contribution, to add value, to
serve. They brag about it too, over a back fence or at a soccer game. Federal employees haven't done much of that for years. But, in offices where reinvention has begun,
the employee teams are inspired by the idea of finding ways to change the system so it
serves Americans again.

This motivation is a potent force, a kind of pure energy source for change that has
been bottled up. Reinvention turns it loose. The government is filled with good people
like Bruce, Helen, and George. . . . The problem is that for years we have kept these
good people trapped in bad systems. We are changing the systems so all our people can
devote more of their time, intelligence, and energy to what they signed up for in the first
place serving the people of America.

NOTES

1. The Postal Service is not included. It has grown because it has more mail to deliver, but it is financed primarily from the sale of stamps, not from taxes.
2. Unpublished calculation prepared by the Office of Management and Budget, based
   on civilian pay and benefits budgeted for fiscal year 1996.

3. Office of Personnel Management, Office of Workforce Information, Central Personnel Data File (unpublished data).

4. General Accounting Office, *Federal Downsizing: The Costs and Savings of Buyouts versus Reductions-In-Force* (Washington, D.C.: Government Printing Office), GAO/GGD-96-63, May 14, 1996.

5. Office of Personnel Management, Office of Workforce Information, Central Personnel Data File (unpublished data). This figure (114,856 buyouts) includes all civilian defense and non-defense personnel who took buyouts between January 1993 and January 1996.

6. Office of Personnel Management, Office of Workforce Information, Central Personnel Data File (unpublished data). Between January 1993 and January 1996, 239,286 personnel left federal employment. Of these, 21,125 were separated involuntarily.

7. Stephen Barr, "A Simple Suggestion Worth Millions: Civil Servant's Idea Expected to Mean Big Savings in Procurements," *Washington Post,* October 13, 1994.

8. Vice President Al Gore, *Common Sense Government: Works Better and Costs Less* (New York: Random House, 1995), p. 26.

9. General Accounting Office, *Acquisition: Purchase Card Use Cuts Procurement Costs, Improves Efficiency* (Washington, D.C.: Government Printing Office), GAO/NSIAD, 96–138, August 6, 1996.

10. Public Law 104-106, *National Defense Authorization Act for FY 1996,* February 10, 1996; Executive Order 13011, *Federal Information Technology,* July 17, 1996.

11. Unpublished data from the Office of Management and Budget.

12. Letter from Peter J. Hannes, President, Special Markets Division, Jockey International, Inc. to Mr. Dennis Dudek, Department of Defense, June 7, 1996.

13. Department of Defense, Office of Assistant Secretary (Public Affairs), "Defense Acquisition Pilot Programs Forecast Cost/Schedule Savings of Up to 50 Percent From Acquisition Reform," News Release No. 138-96, March 14, 1996; and unpublished data provided by the Department of Defense.

14. See Presidential Memorandum, *Streamlining Procurement Through Electronic Commerce,* October 26, 1993; Executive Order 12931, *Federal Procurement Reform,* October 13, 1994; Executive Order 12979, *Agency Procurement Protests.* October 25, 1995; and Executive Order 13011, *Federal Information Technology,* July 17, 1996.

15. Unpublished data from the Federal Communications Commission.

16. Al Gore, *Creating a Government That Works Better & Costs Less* (Washington, D.C.: Government Printing Office, September 7, 1993), pp. 13–14.

17. James Thompson, "The Reinvention Revolution," *Government Executive,* Vol. 28, No. 5, May 1996, pp. 39–41. See also, General Accounting Office, *Management Reform: Status of Agency Reinvention Lab Efforts* (Washington, D.C.: Government Printing Office) GAO-GGD-96-69, March 20, 1996.

18. President and Mrs. Harrison were afraid to touch the light switches, so a civil servant was assigned to switch the lights on in the evening, let them burn all night, and return in the morning to switch them off. James Trager, *The People's Chronology* (New York: Henry Holt and Company, Inc., 1996), pp. 561, 572, 587.

19. Congressional Testimony by James King, Director, Office of Personnel Management, before the House Committee on Government Reform and Oversight, October 12, 1995.

20. Each agency now has the authority to do its own hiring (Public Law 104-52), but many agencies choose to hire through the Office of Personnel Management's phone-in center.

21. Executive Order 12871, *Labor-Management Partnerships,* October 1, 1993.

22. U.S. Mint, "Denver Mint Receives National Partnership Award for Improved Labor-Management Relations," Press Release, February 14, 1996.

23. Presidential Memorandum, *Expanding Family-Friendly Work Arrangements in the Executive Branch,* July 11, 1994; Presidential Memorandum, *Supporting the Role of Fathers in Families,* June 16, 1995; and Presidential Memorandum, *Implementing Family-Friendly Work Arrangements,* June 21, 1996.

24. Michael Serlin, "The Competitors," *Government Executive,* Vol. 28, No. 6, June 1996, pp. 29–33.

Reinvention Lite
Why Al Gore Still Has a Long Way to Go

Robert Worth

On April 30, 1998, a woman named Maureen O'Dwyer testified before the Senate Finance Committee along with six other current and former Internal Revenue Service employees. The press, weary after months of blockbuster hearings on abused taxpayers, didn't pay much attention. After all, the House and Senate were already writing legislation to make the IRS more user-friendly. But Maureen's story wasn't the usual tale of rude or threatening auditors. Instead, she told how her manager had ignored one company's $24 million tax debt because he wanted to close the case quickly so as to collect a $2,000 productivity bonus. Other witnesses told similar stories of IRS auditors who "zeroed out" multimillion-dollar tax bills because they didn't want to spend the time, or to curry favor with corporations that might offer them jobs. In short, the hearings showed that the IRS wasn't just suffering from rudeness. It had lost track of its most basic mission as an agency, it had failed to monitor the performance of its agents, and it was retaining plenty of people who should have been fired long before.

The IRS wasn't alone. In July, the Clinton administration declared confidently that our nation's nursing homes were in fine shape; only 1 percent suffered any serious health or safety problems. Then the General Accounting Office released the results of an investigation charging that one in three nursing homes in California—a state with a better enforcement reputation than most—suffered from "serious or life-threatening problems." The GAO described hallways that reek of urine and feces, and aging patients lying neglected on their beds, half dead from hunger and thirst, their bedsores festering until they become gaping, infected wounds. One woman described how her mother was both beaten and neglected for years, and that she "always seemed to be begging for food or water" in the three nursing homes where she stayed until she died suspiciously earlier this year.

What have Al Gore and his team of "reinventing government" experts done about problems like these? "We have expanded and improved service hours and phone support" at the IRS, declared Gore proudly in late July, along with a few other measures "focused on improving customer service." Magnify those comments across the federal government and you'll see far too much of what Gore has achieved since Clinton handed him the task of reinvention in early 1993. To be sure, making government a little nicer and more accessible to the average citizen is a desirable reform. And there's no doubt that some of Gore's other changes will save time and money. He's updated the government's information technology, improved its procurement policies, and trimmed some unnecessary regulations. He's also taken a thick slice out of the federal workforce—351,000 at last count since he started in 1993.

Robert Worth is a managing editor of Washington Monthly *magazine. From Robert Worth, "Reinvention Lite: Why Al Gore Still Has a Long Way to Go,"* Washington Monthly, *September, 1998, pp. 28–33.*

What Gore doesn't seem to understand is that these changes, while laudable, don't get to the root of America's shrunken faith in government. Serious reform starts with taking a fresh look at what government agencies should be doing in the first place, then asking how well they're doing it and whom they need for the job. The IRS reform bill, which Clinton recently signed, is a step in the right direction. But improving "customer service"—the heart of the bill—won't change the fact that the agency is still failing at its central duty: An estimated $195 billion in taxes go uncollected every year. Nor has Gore addressed the fact that many of the problems at the IRS—and throughout the federal bureaucracy—stem from its inability to fire corrupt and incompetent employees. Tackling this personnel problem should be at the heart of reinvention, but so far Gore's team has been content to simply let the government get smaller by offering workers a chunk of cash to leave early, regardless of whether they're truants or geniuses. As a result, according to the government observers and federal managers I spoke with, too many of the best people left, and too many bench-warmers stuck around. The government got smaller without getting any smarter. Finally, the nursing-home scandals point to a third major area for reform: performance. Reinvention won't get very far until the government starts not only re-examining its mission, but paying more attention to how it's being carried out—in this case, by keeping closer tabs on the federal and state regulators who enforce its laws.

Overhauling the government's mission, performance, and personnel is no easy task. But if you don't want to see your parents starving to death in a nursing home or lose your life savings to a corrupt IRS auditor, you should give a damn about the fact that Gore doesn't seem to be taking it on.

MISSION IMPROBABLE

Reinvention is not for the fainthearted. Anyone who wants to take a fresh look at the mission of any particular agency has to be willing to dead-lift the federal bureaucracy and the unions that support it, as well as a staggering array of special interest groups that profit from keeping the system in its present state, and the congressmen who depend on those groups for money and political support.

Let's start with the bureaucracy. Remember the Rural Electrification Administration? As you may recall from high school, the REA was one of the nobler examples of government's power to help people back in the 1930s, when FDR charged it with providing electricity (and later, phone service) to rural Americans. Five decades later, that worthy goal had been achieved, but the program lumbered on, subsidizing companies that provided power to resorts like Hilton Head, Aspen, and Vail, and making loans to enormous telephone holding companies. Why? Because the REA's bureaucracy had become a self-justifying enterprise, and no one stopped to think about its original mission. The REA may be a particularly flagrant case of unnecessary bureaucracy, but the same tendency plagues agencies that do—or rather, should—have an important mission to carry out. For decades, Forest Service officials who want to put a higher priority on maintaining forest health have found themselves under attack from within the agency, because blindly cutting more timber meant bigger budgets and more jobs.

Reformers at these agencies also found themselves under attack from the outside. As the REA drifted into corporate welfare, the power and phone companies it subsidized saw what a good gig they had, and began lobbying their congressmen and donating PAC money to make sure they didn't lose their windfall from Uncle Sam. The congressmen, grateful and eager to keep the campaign cash flowing, mastered the REA's arcane regulations and became its expert defenders. The same thing happens at the Forest Service: Congressmen who are dependent on the timber industry for PAC money and political support put pressure on the agency to keep cutting timber, no matter how much that may conflict with the higher public good of maintaining healthy forests.

Of course, not all civil servants want to go along with this corrupt cycle, even if they stand to benefit. But those who don't, recognizing that congressional and bureaucratic inertia, the unions, and public ignorance are all working against them, don't usually bother to raise a stir. Instead, they stay quiet, hoping that no one will notice the small improvements they've made. Their only other option, after all, is to turn to the press, in the hopes of igniting some public outrage. And that seldom works, because far too often editors prefer to devote their political coverage to juicier and higher-profile stories. . . .

If the press would peer into the darkness of the executive branch and dramatize its unsung heroes on a regular basis, reform might not be so rare. If you doubt that such heroes exist, consider the amazing story of one federal agency that turned itself around in record time, without any help from Al Gore. Just over five years ago the Federal Emergency Management Agency (FEMA), which is responsible for organizing and assisting in relief efforts to victims of earthquakes, fires, floods, and other natural or unnatural disasters, was widely considered the worst of all federal agencies. Sen. Ernest Hollings dubbed it "the sorriest bunch of jackasses I've ever seen in my life" when it bungled relief efforts after Hurricane Hugo in 1989. When the California earthquake hit later that year, FEMA's medical coordinator left for vacation the next day—because he had bought nonrefundable tickets. The agency's incompetence was legendary, and its effects on helpless disaster victims could not have been clearer. By the time James Lee Witt became the agency's new director in 1993, many disaster specialists considered it beyond hope, and Rep. Pete Stark of California had introduced a bill to abolish it.

Five years later, nearly all of FEMA's former critics hail it as a first-rate agency. In 16 recent surveys of disaster victims, more than 80 percent of respondents approved of the way the agency was doing its job. "Simply put, there is a tremendous difference in FEMA today," said Florida's director of emergency management last year. What happened?

John Kamensky, the deputy director of Gore's reinvention team, says it was James Lee Witt's leadership that did the trick. That's certainly part of it; choosing the right people to run an agency is the first step to making it work. Amazing as it sounds, James Lee Witt was the first FEMA director with real experience in disaster management—he had served as Arkansas' state emergency management director. Clinton hasn't always made his appointments so well. . . . If Gore is smart, he'll recognize that competence is what matters when you're delegating authority, not loyalty to friends and campaign donors or filling ethnic and gender quotas.

But Witt's personal leadership isn't the whole story. Here's how Witt describes what he did: "It is absolutely critical that you look at your role and mission, and redefine that role and mission to what you feel is important for that agency to be responsible for." Specifically, Witt saw that the agency's ability to respond to natural disasters like Hurricane Andrew was hampered by its prior commitment to spending half its budget on preparations for a massive nuclear attack. When it did get around to disasters, the agency's priorities were still seriously misguided. It was set up to provide federal loans and grants to disaster areas, and it could not deliver or even prepare emergency aid until a state governor requested it.

Once Witt clarified the agency's goals by moving it out of the nuclear war business and into natural disasters, he conducted a top-to-bottom review of the agency's personnel and resources. Here Witt benefited from FEMA's relatively high proportion of political appointees, which allowed him to replace a lot of the incompetents with experienced professionals. He wrote a strategic plan to bring the agency into line with its mission, and he was careful to include his managers: "It made them feel part of the reorganization, rather than like someone cramming it down their throats." He did the same thing in Congress, meeting with all the chairs of the 20 congressional committees that had an interest in the agency.

LAB TESTS

What have Gore and his team done to encourage other agencies to follow FEMA's example? Essentially, they've done what idealistic government workers have so often done in the past: kept their heads down and hoped that no one would notice their good deeds. Instead of challenging the system out in the open, Gore's team has tried to encourage individual programs and offices scattered throughout the government to do so by designating them "reinvention labs," and inviting them to find less burdensome and more effective ways of doing their work. The lab strategy, which grew out of a 1980s Defense Department experiment, "has been consciously structured to avoid hierarchy," says Elaine Kamarck, who directed Gore's reinvention effort from its inception until last year. The idea is to wage guerilla warfare out in the rice paddies, with the hope that a thousand small victories against the bureaucracy will eventually bring it crashing to the ground. And it must be said, there are some fascinating and inspiring stories coming out of the labs. "It's really the front line of reinvention," says Don Kettl, the director of the Brookings Institution's Center for Public Management and the dean of reinvention scholars.

Consider, for instance, the New York office of the Veterans Benefits Administration (VBA), which was the first reinvention lab to win one of Gore's "Hammer" awards for success at reinvention in March 1994, and has since won two more. When Joe Thompson became director of the New York regional office in 1990 he was already determined to reform the way benefits and pensions were handled. It's not hard to see why. When a veteran called to ask about his claim, he spoke to a counselor in the Veterans Services Division. But claims were handled by the Adjudication Division, which, in the New York office, was three floors above. So the counselor would have to walk up, get the file, and then struggle to make sense of it, since he or she generally hadn't seen it before. When the veteran called again, he would often get a different counselor, who would go through the process all over again. The office employed 18 full-time "searchers" whose sole job was looking for lost folders. When the claim was finally processed, it passed from one examiner to the next, each of them performing just one of 26 separate steps. (Claims letters would go from a mail clerk to a correspondence clerk to a development clerk and finally to a claims examiner before any real work was even started on it.) This mindless slow-dance, which was standard practice in all of the VBA's 60 regional offices, "frequently infuriated our customers and sucked the life out of our employees," says Thompson.

So he decided to change it. Like James Lee Witt, Thompson started by rethinking the mission of his organization. "He always had one thing in mind," one manager told me, "what's best for the veteran. No one else had focused in like that." He conducted surveys of veterans, and their answers helped to point the way. Starting in 1992, Thompson merged the jobs of counselor and adjudicator into a single job, case manager. Each veteran's claim was now handled from start to finish by one person. He also radically reorganized the office hierarchy and made a variety of administrative changes. The results are clear: The claims process now works faster and much more efficiently. Five years ago veterans who showed up in person might have to wait hours; now no one waits more than a few minutes. The phone system, which was virtually impenetrable just a few years ago, is now a model of efficiency. Surveys show that veterans are much happier with the new system on all counts, and every employee I spoke with seemed proud to have been part of it. Like FEMA, the New York VBA office is a case study in successful reinvention: They had the right man, they rethought their mission, and they focused on improving their performance.

But the higher-ups at VA headquarters in D.C. didn't like Thompson's reforms at all, and he told me he had to fight "many battles" to preserve them. This has been true elsewhere, too: In its one major report on the labs, published in March 1996, the General Accounting Office quoted lab managers who had met with "staggering resistance" and even "payback" from managers who felt their authority was being usurped. The only real weapon the labs possess against bureaucratic inertia is the regulatory waiver, which frees them (temporarily) from agency rules so that they can try to find more efficient ways of doing business. The GAO found that 60 percent of the labs had not even sought waivers from regulations, and that 50 percent of those who tried reported trouble getting them. A report to Congress on the Veterans Administration last year declared that "many key officials do not believe they have the power to achieve change. One aspect of this is fear of offending powerful political interests."

These interests exist in every agency, because upper-level bureaucrats know that real change could mean the end of their job. At last year's IRS hearings, one agent described how she had been rewarded for challenging her office's corrupt business practices: She was sent on armed raids in Tennessee, even though she was 60 years old, and she was the only one not issued a flak jacket. Another agent voiced her concerns about harassment in her office to her congressman, and when her IRS superiors found out about it they went to the congressman themselves—not to reassure him but because they hoped to find information that would help them fire her.

Fighting back against this kind of deeply rooted resistance requires strong support from the top, and thus far Gore has not supplied it. . . . Even where the labs have had their greatest successes, change has been slow and piecemeal. Although Joe Thompson has been promoted to permanent undersecretary for benefits at the Veterans Administration national headquarters in Washington, and he is trying to implement his reforms in the rest of the Veterans Benefits Administration's 60 regional offices, he hasn't yet succeeded. Nationally, the VBA is still using the same assembly-line system Thompson worked so hard to dismantle. "The organizational structure has remained basically unchanged since the end of World War II," said an internal agency report issued last year.

In fact, Gore often appears to have descended on the labs with a "Hammer" award—his token of a successful reinvention—and forgotten all about them. Consider, for instance, the fate of just one exemplary reform at the Department of Agriculture, where a group of claims officers focused on what happens when a truck owned by the USDA backs up and crushes somebody's new Nissan like a bug. It may sound like an outlandish question if you live in Manhattan, but the claims officers say it happens all the time. What would you do if it were your car? Well, you'd file what's called a "tort claim." The local claims officers would review the case, and then send it on to the regional general counsel's office, which would conduct its own separate review. If the general counsel concurred with the regional office's judgment, the claim would then proceed to the regional treasury office, which would conduct its own review. Finally, you'd receive a check, if you hadn't already been arrested for taking violent revenge on government property. Debbie Redpath, a claims officer at the USDA's Minnesota Animal and Plant Health Inspection Service (APHIS) office, told me that it often used to take eight months for claims to go through. "These were often people who were living hand to mouth," she adds, "and the process put them out of pocket for repairs."

So Debbie and her fellow claims officers decided to change things. They pointed out that the general counsel and Treasury agreed with their own initial judgments on the claims 98 to 99 percent of the time. So they applied for authority to adjudicate claims of $2,500 or less (which constituted 76 percent of their caseload last year) by themselves. "Now we can get a claim in the morning and put a check in the mail by afternoon." In short, Debbie and her fellow claims officers are proof that the government can't do its job without smart, imaginative workers at the front lines as well as at the top.

But what about the follow-up? Shouldn't Gore's reinventors be spreading the word and working hard to make sure that the APHIS reforms get applied throughout the government? "You would think they would," Debbie Redpath told me, "but I don't know if we've received any inquiries." She thought about it a minute, and said yes—someone from the Forest Service claims division had called. She gave me the name. I called the Forest Service officer, who told me she had read about Debbie and APHIS in a magazine (not one of Gore's publications). She said the Forest Service claims adjudication procedure is even more complex than the old one at APHIS. She'd like to change it, she said, especially because she works in a reinvention lab too. But she has not gotten anywhere so far.

Like the rest of the government, workers such as Debbie Redpath are swimming against the current of a bureaucratic culture that strongly discourages innovation. Until that changes, the "guerilla warfare" principle behind the labs isn't likely to succeed. In its 1996 report on the reinvention labs, the General Accounting Office concluded that their value "will only be realized when lab efforts proven to be effective spread beyond the lab sites." So far, there's little evidence that this is happening.

THE PERSONNEL TOUCH

And it isn't likely to happen until Gore starts finding ways to bring gifted people into all levels of government—people like James Lee Witt at the top of the agency, Joe Thompson in the regional offices, and Debbie Redpath on the front lines. As Sen. John Glenn put it during a hearing on reinvention efforts in 1992, "We can give them some organizational tools, and we can give them all the studies and pilot projects you want, but until we get some really good people in here, we aren't going to solve this problem."

What's really tragic about Gore's failure to make any headway on this front is that the need for better workers has never been greater, and the press—bored with Gore's jargon-rich presentations and hung up on Monicagate—has utterly ignored it. Think about it: There are now more people on the verge of retirement in the government than ever before, and the quality of new hires is still going downhill. "When we asked supervisors to tell us to what extent the quality of applicants had worsened or improved in the past three years," concluded a 1998 study by the Merit Systems Protection Board, "we found that their assessment of applicant quality had fallen for just about every type of job category." As Seth Grossman points out in this issue, some agencies can't even answer phone calls from prospective applicants. And the failings of the current workforce have become legendary. One Defense Department official failed to show up for work for seven straight months, and successfully challenged an effort to fire him on the grounds that his boss made him nervous and gave him a "stress disorder." Another federal worker, fired for truancy, kept his case bouncing from one appeal to another for over 12 years. As one VA official told me, his union is "a refuge where you can go if you don't want to do any work. It's a black hole." For the most part, supervisors don't even try to fire incompetent or lazy employees. Under these circumstances, having a lot of political appointees who can be replaced at will, as James Lee Witt did at FEMA, is a distinct advantage.

But incompetence and stubborn unions aren't the only problems. One former government official told me he used to work alongside three men who spent two-thirds of their time communicating with each other. "What seemed to make sense was to combine their work into one job," he added. Clearly, Gore needs to start doing what Joe Thompson did at the New York VBA office: looking at the work that needs to be done and consolidating jobs. So far, however, Gore's cutbacks in the federal workforce have not taken such inefficiencies into account. "Some of my best people have left," one manager at Joe Thompson's former office in New York told me. Meanwhile, his claims division is seriously overworked. And he still can't fire his problem employees.

One way to tackle what the government tactfully calls its "poor performer" problem would be to hire a substantial number, perhaps half, of all new people on a limited term basis—say two-and-a-half or five years. These contracts could be renewed at the end of the term, but they could also be dropped painlessly without the current interminable appeals process. That would limber up the workforce and get rid of some of the deadwood. Retaining tenure for some employees would prevent the government from becoming so transient that it had no institutional memory. In a way, it's odd that this solution (which this magazine has long advocated) shouldn't have occurred to Gore before, since his sister Nancy worked in the one government office that has used limited-term appointments: the Peace Corps. It's been successful there, and it's also been a central part of the wholesale public sector reforms in New Zealand, which are widely acknowledged to have improved government performance, and which were part of the basis for Gore's reforms in 1993. The Defense Department is about to launch an experimental program along the same lines, hiring a substantial number of new employees under one- and five-year contracts instead of labeling them "permanent" from the start. If Gore wants reinvention to last, he'll encourage other agencies to follow suit.

Embracing reforms like these isn't easy, and it would take a big bite out of the union campaign donations Gore is counting on in the 2000 election. But the benefits could mean a lot more to the rest of us than anything he's done so far. Cutting costs and trimming regulations are fine things, but the difference between good government workers and inept ones is the difference between life and death. This past July an air traffic controller who had twice tested positive for drugs was reinstated by the Federal Labor Relations Authority, and she wasn't even told to go into rehab. Think about that the next time you fasten your seat belt, and ask yourself whether reinventing government is really so dull after all.

14

COURTS

The Supreme Court and Judicial Review

While few would question the Supreme Court's authority to interpret the Constitution, there has long been disagreement over how the nine justices should approach this awesome responsibility. This debate grew in intensity during the Reagan era as the president and his attorney general inveighed against the Supreme Court, charging that justices had all too often substituted their own values and principles for those contained in the Constitution.

In the first selection, Edwin Meese, U.S. attorney general during part of the Reagan administration, calls upon judges to interpret the Constitution in accordance with the intent of those who wrote and ratified it. Insisting that the Founding Fathers expected as much from the members of the Supreme Court, Meese goes on to suggest how the justices should approach this task. He remains convinced that the application of original intent—undistorted by the personal values of well-meaning judges—will best preserve the principles of democratic government.

The second selection offers a markedly different perspective from someone who has had the responsibility of interpreting our Constitution. Irving Kaufman, chief judge of the United States Court of Appeals for the Second Circuit, maintains that ascertaining the original intent of the Founding Fathers is decidedly more difficult than Edwin Meese would lead us to believe. Nor, for that matter, is the strict application of original intent necessarily desirable in every instance. This is not to say that judges are at liberty to read whatever they choose into the wording of our Constitution. On the contrary, Kaufman points to several factors that serve to restrain judges from doing so.

A Jurisprudence of Original Intention

Edwin Meese III

. . . Today I would like to discuss further the meaning of constitutional fidelity. In particular, I would like to describe in more detail this administration's approach.

Before doing so, I would like to make a few commonplace observations about the original document itself. . . .

The period surrounding the creation of the Constitution is not a dark and mythical realm. The young America of the 1780s and '90s was a vibrant place, alive with pamphlets, newspapers and books chronicling and commenting upon the great issues of the day. We know how the Founding Fathers lived, and much of what they read, thought, and believed. The disputes and compromises of the Constitutional Convention were carefully recorded. The minutes of the convention are a matter of public record. Several of the most important participants—including James Madison, the "father" of the Constitution—wrote comprehensive accounts of the convention. Others, Federalists and Anti-Federalists alike, committed their arguments for and against ratification, as well as their understandings of the Constitution, to paper, so that their ideas and conclusions could be widely circulated, read, and understood.

In short, the Constitution is not buried in the mists of time. We know a tremendous amount of the history of its genesis. . . .

With these thoughts in mind, I would like to discuss the administration's approach to constitutional interpretation. . . .

Our approach . . . begins with the document itself. The plain fact is, it exists. It is something that has been written down. Walter Berns of the American Enterprise Institute has noted that the central object of American constitutionalism was "the effort" of the Founders "to express fundamental governmental arrangements in a legal document—to 'get it in writing.'"

Indeed, judicial review has been grounded in the fact that the Constitution is a written, as opposed to an unwritten, document. In *Marbury v. Madison* John Marshall rested his rationale for judicial review on the fact that we have a written constitution with meaning that is binding upon judges. "[I]t is apparent," he wrote, "that the framers of the Constitution contemplated that instrument as a rule for the government of *courts,* as well as of the legislature. Why otherwise does it direct the judges to take an oath to support it?"

The presumption of a written document is that it conveys meaning. As Thomas Grey of the Stanford Law School has said, it makes "relatively definite and explicit what otherwise would be relatively indefinite and tacit."

We know that those who framed the Constitution chose their words carefully. They debated at great length the most minute points. The language they chose meant some-

Edwin Meese III served as U.S. Attorney General under President Ronald Reagan. Excerpted from a speech by Attorney General Meese before the Washington, D.C., chapter of the Federal Society, Lawyers Division, November 15, 1985, pp. 2–14.

thing. They proposed, they substituted, they edited, and they carefully revised. Their words were studied with equal care by state ratifying conventions.

This is not to suggest that there was unanimity among the framers and ratifiers on all points. The Constitution and the Bill of Rights, and some of the subsequent amendments, emerged after protracted debate. Nobody got everything they wanted. What's more, the framers were not clairvoyants—they could not foresee every issue that would be submitted for judicial review. Nor could they predict how all foreseeable disputes would be resolved under the Constitution. But the point is, the meaning of the Constitution can be known.

What does this written Constitution mean? In places it is exactingly specific. Where it says that Presidents of the United States must be at least 35 years of age it means exactly that. (I have not heard of any claim that 35 means 30 or 25 or 20.) Where it specifies how the House and Senate are to be organized, it means what it says.

The Constitution also expresses particular principles. One is the right to be free of an unreasonable search or seizure. Another concerns religious liberty. Another is the right to equal protection of the laws.

Those who framed these principles meant something by them. And the meanings can be found. The Constitution itself is also an expression of certain general principles. These principles reflect the deepest purpose of the Constitution—that of establishing a political system through which Americans can best govern themselves consistent with the goal of securing liberty.

The text and structure of the Constitution is instructive. It contains very little in the way of specific political solutions. It speaks volumes on how problems should be approached, and by *whom*. For example, the first three articles set out clearly the scope and limits of three distinct branches of national government. The powers of each being carefully and specifically enumerated. In this scheme it is no accident to find the legislative branch described first, as the framers had fought and sacrificed to secure the right of democratic self-governance. Naturally, this faith in republicanism was not unbounded, as the next two articles make clear.

Yet the Constitution remains a document of powers and principles. And its undergirding premise remains that democratic self government is subject only to the limits of certain constitutional principles. This respect for the political process was made explicit early on. When John Marshall upheld the act of Congress chartering a national bank in *McCulloch v. Maryland* he wrote: "The Constitution [was] intended to endure for ages to come, and, consequently, to be adapted to the various crises of human affairs." But to use McCulloch, as some have tried, as support for the idea that the Constitution is a protean, changeable thing is to stand history on its head. Marshall was keeping faith with the original intention that Congress be free to elaborate and apply constitutional powers and principles. He was not saying that the Court must invent some new constitutional value in order to keep pace with the times. In Walter Berns's words: "Marshall's meaning is not that the Constitution may be adapted to the 'various crises of human affairs,' but that the legislative powers granted by the Constitution are adaptable to meet these crises."

The approach this administration advocates is rooted in the text of the Constitution as illuminated by those who drafted, proposed, and ratified it. In his famous Commentary on the Constitution of the United States Justice Joseph Story explained that:

The first and fundamental rule in the interpretation of all instruments is, to construe
them according to the sense of the terms, and the intention of the parties.

Our approach understands the significance of a written document and seeks to discern the particular and general principles it expresses. It recognizes that there may be
debate at times over the application of these principles. But it does not mean these principles cannot be identified.

Constitutional adjudication is obviously not a mechanical process. It requires an
appeal to reason and discretion. The text and intention of the Constitution must be understood to constitute the banks within which constitutional interpretation must flow. As
James Madison said, if "the sense in which the Constitution was accepted and ratified
by the nation . . . be not the guide in expounding it, there can be no security for a consistent and stable, more than for a faithful exercise of its powers."

Thomas Jefferson, so often cited incorrectly as a framer of the Constitution, in fact
shared Madison's view: "Our peculiar security is in the possession of a written Constitution. Let us not make it a blank paper by construction."

Jefferson was even more explicit in his personal correspondence:

On every question of construction [we should] carry ourselves back to the time, when
the constitution was adopted; recollect the spirit manifested in the debates; and instead
of trying [to find], what meaning may be squeezed out of the text, or invented against
it, conform to the probable one, in which it was passed.

In the main a jurisprudence that seeks to be faithful to our Constitution—a jurisprudence of original intention, as I have called it—is not difficult to describe. Where
the language of the Constitution is specific, it must be obeyed. Where there is a demonstrable consensus among the framers and ratifiers as to a principle stated or implied by
the Constitution, it should be followed. Where there is ambiguity as to the precise
meaning or reach of a constitutional provision, it should be interpreted and applied in a
manner so as to at least not contradict the text of the Constitution itself.

Sadly, while almost everyone participating in the current constitutional debate
would give assent to these propositions, the techniques and conclusions of some of
the debaters do violence to them. What is the source of this violence? In large part I believe that it is the misuse of history stemming from the neglect of the idea of a written
constitution.

There is a frank proclamation by some judges and commentators that what matters
most about the Constitution is not its words but its so-called "spirit." These individuals
focus less on the language of specific provisions than on what they describe as the "vision" or "concepts of human dignity" they find embodied in the Constitution. This approach to jurisprudence has led to some remarkable and tragic conclusions.

In the 1850s, the Supreme Court under Chief Justice Roger B. Taney read blacks
out of the Constitution in order to invalidate Congress's attempt to limit the spread of
slavery. The *Dred Scott* decision, famously described as a judicial "self-inflicted
wound," helped bring on civil war.

There is a lesson in this history. There is danger in seeing the Constitution as an
empty vessel into which each generation may pour its passion and prejudice.

Our own time has its own fashions and passions. In recent decades many have come to view the Constitution—more accurately, part of the Constitution, provisions of the Bill of Rights and the Fourteenth Amendment—as a charter for judicial activism on behalf of various constituencies. Those who hold this view often have lacked demonstrable textual or historical support for their conclusions. Instead they have "grounded" their rulings in appeals to social theories, to moral philosophies or personal notions of human dignity, or to "penumbras," somehow emanating ghostlike from various provisions—identified and not identified—in the Bill of Rights. The problem with this approach, as John Hart Ely, Dean of the Stanford Law School, has observed with respect to one such decision, is not that it is bad constitutional law, but that it is not constitutional law in any meaningful sense, at all.

Despite this fact, the perceived popularity of some results in particular cases has encouraged some observers to believe that any critique of the methodology of those decisions is an attack on the results. This perception is sufficiently widespread that it deserves an answer. My answer is to look at history.

When the Supreme Court, in *Brown v. Board of Education,* sounded the death knell for official segregation in the country, it earned all the plaudits it received. But the Supreme Court in that case was not giving new life to old words, or adapting a "living," "flexible" Constitution to new reality. It was restoring the original principle of the Constitution to constitutional law. The *Brown* Court was correcting the damage done 50 years earlier, when in *Plessy v. Ferguson* an earlier Supreme Court had disregarded the clear intent of the framers of the Civil War amendments to eliminate the legal degradation of blacks, and had contrived a theory of the Constitution to support the charade of "separate but equal" discrimination.

Similarly, the decisions of the New Deal and beyond that freed Congress to regulate commerce and enact a plethora of social legislation were not judicial adaptations of the Constitution to new realities. They were in fact removals of encrustations of earlier courts that had strayed from the original intent of the framers regarding the power of the legislature to make policy.

It is amazing how so much of what passes for social and political progress is really the undoing of old judicial mistakes.

Mistakes occur when the principles of specific constitutional provisions—such as those contained in the Bill of Rights—are taken by some as invitations to read into the Constitution values that contradict the clear language of other provisions.

Acceptances to this illusory invitation have proliferated in recent decades. One Supreme Court justice identified the proper judicial standard as asking "what's best for this country." Another said it is important to "keep the Court out in front" of the general society. Various academic commentators have poured rhetorical grease on this judicial fire, suggesting that constitutional interpretation appropriately be guided by such standards as whether a public policy "personifies justice" or "comports with the notion of moral evolution" or confers "an identity" upon our society or was consistent with "natural ethical law" or was consistent with some "right of equal citizenship."

Unfortunately, as I've noted, navigation by such lodestars has in the past given us questionable economics, governmental disorder, and racism—all in the guise of constitutional law. Recently one of the distinguished judges of one of our federal appeals courts got it about right when he wrote: "The truth is that the judge who looks outside the Constitution always looks inside himself and nowhere else." Or, as we recently put it before the Supreme Court in an important brief: "The further afield interpretation travels from its point of departure in the text, the greater the danger that constitutional adjudication will be like a picnic to which the framers bring the words and the judges the meaning."

In the *Osborne v. Bank of United States* decision 21 years after *Marbury,* Chief Justice Marshall further elaborated his view of the relationship between the judge and the law, be it statutory or constitutional:

> Judicial power, as contradistinguished from the power of the laws, has no existence. Courts are the mere instruments of the law, and can will nothing. When they are said to exercise a discretion, it is a mere legal discretion, a discretion to be exercised in discerning the course prescribed by law; and, when that is discerned, it is the duty of the Court to follow it.

Any true approach to constitutional interpretation must respect the document in all its parts and be faithful to the Constitution in its entirety.

What must be remembered in the current debate is that interpretation does not imply results. The framers were not trying to anticipate every answer. They were trying to create a tripartite national government, within a federal system, that would have the flexibility to adapt to face new exigencies—as it did, for example, in chartering a national bank. Their great interest was in the distribution of power and responsibility in order to secure the great goal of liberty for all.

A jurisprudence that seeks fidelity to the Constitution—a jurisprudence of original intention—is not a jurisprudence of political results. It is very much concerned with process, and it is a jurisprudence that in our day seeks to depoliticize the law. The great genius of the constitutional blueprint is found in its creation and respect for spheres of authority and the limits it places on governmental power. In this scheme the framers did not see the courts as the exclusive custodians of the Constitution. Indeed, because the document posits so few conclusions it leaves to the more political branches the matter of adapting and vivifying its principles in each generation. It also leaves to the people of the states, in the Tenth Amendment, those responsibilities and rights not committed to federal care. The power to declare acts of Congress and laws of the states null and void is truly awesome. This power must be used when the Constitution clearly speaks. It should not be used when the Constitution does not.

In *Marbury v. Madison,* at the same time he vindicated the concept of judicial review, Marshall wrote that the "principles" of the Constitution "are deemed fundamental and permanent," and except for formal amendment, "unchangeable." If we want a change in our Constitution or in our laws we must seek it through the formal mechanisms presented in that organizing document of our government.

In summary, I would emphasize that what is at issue here is not an agenda of issues or a menu of results. At issue is a way of government. A jurisprudence based on first principles is neither conservative nor liberal, neither right nor left. It is a jurisprudence that cares about committing and limiting to each organ of government the proper ambit of its responsibilities. It is a jurisprudence faithful to our Constitution.

By the same token, an activist jurisprudence, one which anchors the Constitution only in the consciences of jurists, is a chameleon jurisprudence, changing color and form in each era. The same activism hailed today may threaten the capacity for decision through democratic consensus tomorrow, as it has in many yesterdays. Ultimately, as the early democrats wrote into the Massachusetts state constitution, the best defense of our liberties is a government of laws and not men.

On this point it is helpful to recall the words of the late Justice Frankfurter. As he wrote:

> [T]here is not under our Constitution a judicial remedy for every political mischief, for every undesirable exercise of legislative power. The framers carefully and with deliberate forethought refused so to enthrone the judiciary. In this situation, as in others of like nature, appeal for relief does not belong here. Appeal must be to an informed, civically militant electorate. . . .

What Did the Founding Fathers Intend?

Irving R. Kaufman

. . . In the ongoing debate over original intent, almost all federal judges hold to the no-tion that judicial decisions should be based on the text of the Constitution or the struc-ture it creates. Yet, in requiring judges to be guided solely by the expressed views of the framers, current advocates of original intent seem to call for a narrower concept. Jurists who disregard this interpretation, the argument runs, act lawlessly because they are im-posing their own moral standards and political preferences on the community.

As a federal judge, I have found it often difficult to ascertain the "intent of the framers," and even more problematic to try to dispose of a constitutional question by giving great weight to the intent argument. Indeed, even if it were possible to decide hard cases on the basis of a strict interpretation of original intent, or originalism, that methodology would conflict with a judge's duty to apply the Constitution's underlying principles to changing circumstances. Furthermore, by attempting to erode the base for judicial affirmation of the freedoms guaranteed by the Bill of Rights and the 14th Amendment (no state shall "deprive any person of life, liberty, or property without due process of law; nor deny to any person . . . the equal protection of the laws"), the intent theory threatens some of the greatest achievements of the Federal judiciary.

Ultimately, the debate centers on the nature of judicial review, or the power of courts to act as the ultimate arbiters of constitutional meaning. This responsibility has been acknowledged ever since the celebrated 1803 case of *Marbury v. Madison,* in which Chief Justice John Marshall struck down a congressional grant of jurisdiction to the Supreme Court not authorized by Article III of the Constitution. But here again, originalists would accept judicial review only if it adhered to the allegedly neutral prin-ciples embalmed in historical intent.

In the course of 36 years on the federal bench, I have had to make many difficult constitutional interpretations. I have had to determine whether a teacher could wear a black armband as a protest against the Vietnam War; whether newspapers have a non-actionable right to report accusatory statements; and whether a school system might be guilty of de facto segregation. Unfortunately, the framers' intentions are not made suf-ficiently clear to provide easy answers. A judge must first determine what the intent was (or would have been)—a notoriously formidable task.

An initial problem is the paucity of materials. Both the official minutes of the Philadelphia Convention of 1787 and James Madison's famous notes of the proceed-ings, published in 1840, tend toward the terse and cursory, especially in relation to the judiciary. The congressional debates over the proposed Bill of Rights, which became ef-fective in 1791, are scarcely better. Even Justice William Rehnquist, one of the most ar-

Irving R. Kaufman is a judge of the 2d U.S. Circuit Court of Appeals. From Irving R. Kaufman, "What Did the Founding Fathers Intend?" New York Times Magazine, Feb-ruary 23, 1986, pp. 59–69. Copyright © 1986 by The New York Times Company. Reprinted by permission.

ticulate spokesmen for original intent, admitted in a recent dissent in a case concerning school prayer that the legislative history behind the provision against the establishment of an official religion "does not seem particularly illuminating."

One source deserves special mention. *The Federalist Papers*—the series of essays written by Alexander Hamilton, James Madison and John Jay in 1787 and 1788—have long been esteemed as the earliest constitutional commentary. In 1825, for example, Thomas Jefferson noted that *The Federalist* was regularly appealed to "as evidence of the general opinion of those who framed and of those who accepted the Constitution of the United States."

The Federalist, however, did not discuss the Bill of Rights or the Civil War amendments, which were yet to be written. Moreover, the essays were part of a political campaign—the authors wrote them in support of New York's ratification of the Constitution. The essays, therefore, tended to enunciate general democratic theory or rebut anti-Federalist arguments, neither of which offers much help to modern jurists. (In light of the following passage from *The Federalist,* No. 14, I believe Madison would be surprised to find his words of 200 years ago deciding today's cases: "Is it not the glory of the people of America that . . . they have not suffered a blind veneration for antiquity . . . to overrule the suggestions of their own good sense . . . ?")

Another problem with original intent is this: Who were the framers? Generally, they are taken to be the delegates to the Philadelphia Convention and the congressional sponsors of subsequent amendments. All constitutional provisions, however, have been ratified by state conventions or legislatures on behalf of the people they represented. Is the relevant intention, then, that of the drafters, the ratifiers or the general populace?

The elusiveness of the framers' intent leads to another, more telling problem. Originalist doctrine presumes that intent can be discovered by historical sleuthing or psychological rumination. In fact, this is not possible. Judges are constantly required to resolve questions that 18th-century statesmen, no matter how prescient, simply could not or did not foresee and resolve. On most issues, to look for a collective intention held by either drafters or ratifiers is to hunt for a chimera.

A reading of the Constitution highlights this problem. The principles of our great charter are cast in grand, yet cryptic, phrases. Accordingly, judges usually confront what Justice Robert Jackson in the 1940s termed the "majestic generalities" of the Bill of Rights, or the terse commands of "due process of law," or "equal protection" contained in the 14th Amendment. The use of such open-ended provisions would indicate that the framers did not want the Constitution to become a straitjacket on all events for all times. In contrast, when the framers held a clear intention, they did not mince words. Article II, for example, specifies a minimum Presidential age of 35 years instead of merely requiring "maturity" or "adequate age."

The First Amendment is a good example of a vaguer provision. In guaranteeing freedom of the press, some of our forefathers perhaps had specific thoughts on what publications fell within its purview. Some historians believe, in light of Colonial debates, that the main concern of the framers was to prevent governmental licensing of newspapers. If that were all the First Amendment meant today, then many important decisions protecting the press would have to be overruled. One of them would be the landmark *New York Times v. Sullivan* ruling of 1964, giving the press added protection in libel cases brought by public figures. Another would be *Near v. Minnesota,* a case involving Jay Near, a newspaper publisher who had run afoul of a Minnesota statute outlawing "malicious, scandalous and defamatory" publications. The Supreme Court struck down the statute in 1931, forbidding governmental prior restraints on publication; this ruling was the precursor of the 1971 Pentagon Papers decision.

The Founding Fathers focused not on particularities but on principles, such as the need in a democracy for people to engage in free and robust discourse. James Madison considered a popular government without popular information a "Prologue to a Farce or a Tragedy." Judges, then, must focus on underlying principles when going about their delicate duty of applying the First Amendment's precepts to today's world.

In fact, our nation's first debate over constitutional interpretation centered on grand principles. Angered at John Adams's Federalist Administration, advocates of states' rights in the late 18th century argued that original intent meant that the Constitution, like the Articles of Confederation, should be construed narrowly—as a compact among separate sovereigns. The 1798 Virginia and Kentucky Resolutions, which sought to reserve to the states the power of ultimate constitutional interpretation, were the most extreme expressions of this view. In rejecting this outlook, a nationalistic Supreme Court construed the Constitution more broadly.

The important point here is that neither side of this debate looked to the stated views of the framers to resolve the issue. Because of his leading role at the Philadelphia Convention, Madison's position is especially illuminating. "Whatever veneration might be entertained for the body of men who formed our Constitution," he declaimed on the floor of Congress in 1796, "the sense of that body could never be regarded as the oracular guide in expounding the Constitution."

Yet, I doubt if strict proponents of original intent will be deterred by such considerations. Their goal is not to venerate dead framers but to restrain living judges from imposing their own values. This restraint is most troublesome when it threatens the protection of individual rights against governmental encroachment.

According to current constitutional doctrine, the due process clause of the 14th Amendment incorporates key provisions of the Bill of Rights, which keeps in check only the Federal Government. Unless the due process clause is construed to include the most important parts of the first eight amendments in the Bill of Rights, then the states would be free, in theory, to establish an official church or inflict cruel and unusual punishments. This doctrine is called incorporation.

Aside from the late Justice Hugo Black, few have believed that history alone is a sufficient basis for applying the Bill of Rights to the states. In his Georgetown University address, Justice Brennan noted that the crucial liberties embodied in the Bill of Rights are so central to our national identity that we cannot imagine any definition of "liberty" without them.

In fact, a cramped reading of the Bill of Rights jeopardizes what I regard as the true original intent—the rationale for having a written Constitution at all. The principal reason for a charter was to restrain government. In 1787, the idea of a fundamental law set down in black and white was revolutionary. Hanoverian England in the 18th century did not have a fully written, unified constitution, having long believed in a partially written one, based on ancient custom and grants from the Crown like the Magna Carta. To this day, the British have kept their democracy alive without one. In theory, the "King-in-Parliament" was and is unlimited in sovereign might, and leading political theorists, such as Thomas Hobbes and John Locke, agreed that governments, once established by a social contract, could not then be fettered.

Although not a Bill of Rights, the Magna Carta—King John's concessions to his barons in 1215—was symbolic of the notion that even the Crown was not all-powerful. Moreover, certain judges believed that Parliament, like the king, had to respect the traditions of the common law. This staunch belief in perpetual rights, in turn, was an important spark for the Revolutionary conflagration of 1776.

In gaining independence, Americans formed the bold concept that sovereignty continually resided with the people, who cede power to governments only to achieve certain specific ends. This view dominated the Philadelphia Convention. Instead of merely improving on the Articles of Confederation, as they had been directed to do, the framers devised a government where certain powers—defined and thereby limited—flowed from the people to the Congress, the President and the Federal judiciary.

Alexander Hamilton recognized that the basic tenets of this scheme mandated judicial review. Individual rights, he observed in *The Federalist,* No. 78, "can be preserved in practice no other way than through the medium of courts of justice, whose duty it must be to declare all acts contrary to the manifest tenor of the Constitution void." Through a written constitution and judicial enforcement, the framers intended to preserve the inchoate rights they had lost as Englishmen.

The narrow interpretation of original intent is especially unfortunate because I doubt that many of its proponents are in favor of freeing the states from the constraints of the Bill of Rights. In fact, I believe the concern of many modern "intentionalists" is quite specific: outrage over the right-of-privacy cases, especially *Roe v. Wade,* the 1973 Supreme Court decision recognizing a woman's right to an abortion. (The right of privacy, of course, is not mentioned in the Constitution.) Whether one agrees with this controversial decision or not, I would submit that concern over the outcome of one difficult case is not sufficient cause to embrace a theory that calls for so many changes in existing law. . . .

. . . [I]f original intent is an uncertain guide, does some other, more functional approach to interpreting the Constitution exist?

One suggestion is to emphasize the importance of democratic "process." As John Hart Ely, dean of the Stanford Law School forcefully advocates, this approach would direct the courts to make a distinction between "process" (the rules of the game, so to speak) and "substance" (the results of the game). Laws dealing with process include those affecting voting rights or participation in society; the Supreme Court correctly prohibited segregation, for example, because it imposed on blacks the continuing stigma of slavery. Judges, however, would not have the power to review the substantive decisions of elected officials, such as the distribution of welfare benefits.

Basically, such an approach makes courts the guardians of democracy, but a focus on process affords little help when judges decide between difficult and competing values. Judicial formulation of a democratic vision, for example, requires substantive decision-making. The dignities of human liberty enshrined in the Bill of Rights are not merely a means to an end, even so noble an end as democratic governance. For example, we cherish freedom of speech not only because it is necessary for meaningful elections, but also for its own sake.

The truth is that no litmus test exists by which judges can confidently and consistently measure the constitutionality of their decisions. Notwithstanding the clear need for judicial restraint, judges do not constitute what Prof. Raoul Berger, a retired Harvard Law School fellow, has termed an "imperial judiciary." I would argue that the judicial process itself limits the reach of a jurist's arm.

First, judges do not and cannot deliberately contravene specific constitutional rules or clear indications of original intent. No one would seriously argue or expect, for instance, that the Supreme Court could or would twist the Presidential minimum-age provision into a call for "sufficient maturity," so as to forbid the seating of a 36-year-old.

I doubt, in any event, that federal judges would ever hear such a question. The Constitution limits our power to traditional "cases" and "controversies" capable of judicial resolution. In cases like the hypothetical one regarding the presidential age, the High Court employs doctrines of standing (proving injury) and "political question" to keep citizens from suing merely out of a desire to have the government run a certain way.

Moreover, the issues properly before a judge are not presented on a tabula rasa. Even the vaguest constitutional provisions have received the judicial gloss of prior decisions. Precedent alone, of course, should not preserve clearly erroneous decisions; the abhorrent "separate but equal" doctrine survived for more than 50 years before the Warren Court struck it down in 1954.

The conventions of our judicial system also limit a jurist's ability to impose his or her own will. One important restraint, often overlooked, is the tradition that appellate judges issue written opinions. That is, we must support our decisions with reasons instead of whims and indicate how our constitutional rulings relate to the document. A written statement is open to the dissent of colleagues, possible review by a higher court and the judgment, sometimes scathing, of legal scholars.

In addition, the facts of a given case play a pivotal role. Facts delineate the reach of a legal decision and remind us of the "cases and controversies" requirement. Our respect for such ground rules reassures the public that, even in the most controversial case, the outcome is not just a political ruling.

Judges are also mindful that the ultimate justification for their power is public acceptance—acceptance not of every decision, but of the role they play. Without popular support, the power of judicial review would have been eviscerated by political forces long ago.

Lacking the power of the purse or the sword, the courts must rely on the elected branches to enforce their decisions. The school desegregation cases would have been a dead letter unless President Eisenhower had been willing to order out the National Guard—in support of a decision authored by a Chief Justice, Earl Warren, whose appointment the President had called "the biggest damned-fool mistake I ever made."

Instead of achieving the purple of philosopher-kings, an unprincipled judiciary would risk becoming modern King Canutes, with the cold tide of political reality and popular opprobrium lapping at their robes.

My revered predecessor on the Court of Appeals, Judge Learned Hand, remarked in a lecture at Harvard in the late 1950s that he would not want to be ruled by "a bevy of Platonic Guardians." The Constitution balances the danger of judicial abuse against the threat of a temporary majority trampling individual rights. The current debate is a continuation of an age-old, and perhaps endless, struggle to reach a balance between our commitments to democracy and to the rule of law. . . .

Crime and the Courts

Courts have a special role to play in our society. Unlike the two political branches of our government—Congress and the Executive—which are most sensitive to majority public opinion, courts must protect and defend minorities. Indeed, courts most often are called upon to ensure that the government acts in a fair and reasonable manner and to make certain that individual rights are protected.

Courts have a particularly important role to play in the protection of criminal rights, for in this area they must see that no injustice is done to the person accused of a crime.

In the last 30 years, the U.S. Supreme Court has taken great care in enforcing the constitutional rights of persons accused of a crime. These include such protections as the right to remain silent and the right to counsel. Some of these criminal procedural safeguards have evoked considerable controversy among law-enforcement officials, political leaders, commentators, and the general public. Typically, critics of the criminal justice system point to its failures—failures that either put criminals back on the streets or penalize innocent and unsuspecting people.

In the two articles that follow, the role of the courts in the criminal justice system is examined. In the first article, journalist Bernard Gavzer reports on the views of New York State judge, Harold Rothwax, an outspoken critic of today's criminal justice system and author of Guilty: The Collapse of Criminal Justice. *According to Judge Rothwax, the criminal justice system, with all its procedural guarantees, is tilted too much in favor of criminal suspects, so much so that he believes "We're in the fight of our lives" to preserve a law-abiding society.*

In the second article John Kilwein, a professor of political science at West Virginia University, challenges the views of Judge Rothwax. While conceding that crime continues to be a major problem in the United States, Professor Kilwein argues that it would be unwise to adopt Judge Rothwax's "reforms" of the criminal justice system. Kilwein contends that the real issue in the criminal justice system is whether all citizens are fully protected from the possible abuses and excesses of law-enforcement officials. The many procedural guarantees of the Constitution and the courts, he argues, are merely the means to assure a "fair fight" between a criminal defendant and a criminal justice system that is stacked heavily in favor of the government. Without these guarantees, he contends, there exists the very real possibility that innocent persons might be accused, tried, convicted, and punished without adequate protection of the law.

"We're in the Fight of Our Lives"

Bernard Gavzer

At 2 A.M. on November 20, 1990, Leonardo Turriago was pulled over for speeding by two state troopers. They asked if they could look into his van, and Turriago said they could. Inside, the troopers saw a trunk and asked Turriago about it. He sprang open its lock, then ran away. Opening the trunk, the troopers found the body of a man shot five times.

Turriago was quickly caught. In his apartment, police found 11 pounds of cocaine and guns. The suspect told them where to look for the murder weapon, and it was recovered. Turriago was convicted of second-degree murder and sentenced to 45 years to life.

The defense appealed, saying the troopers had no right to search the van. On June 6, 1996, Turriago's conviction was overturned. A New York appellate court ruled that the police search was not justified and had been coerced.

"Criminal justice in America is in a state of collapse," says Judge Harold J. Rothwax, who has spent 25 years presiding over criminal cases in New York City. "We have formalism and technicalities but little common sense. It's about time America wakes up to the fact that we're in the fight of our lives."

Rothwax believes cases such as Turriago's illustrate that the procedural dotting of every "i" and crossing of every "t" has become more important than the crime's substance. "The bottom line is that criminals are going free," he says. "There is no respect for the truth, and without truth, there can be no justice."

While the search for truth should be the guiding principle of our courts, instead, the judge says, "our system is a carefully crafted maze, constructed of elaborate and impenetrable barriers to the truth.". . .

Practices we have taken for granted—such as the *Miranda* warning, the right to counsel, even unanimous jury verdicts—need to be reconsidered, says the judge. "You know." Rothwax confides, "more than 80 percent of the people who appear before me are probably guilty of some crime."

Rothwax insists there is a fundamental difference between the investigative and the trial stages of a case. The investigative stage is marked by the notion of probable guilt, he asserts, not the presumption of innocence. "Until a defendant goes on trial, he is probably guilty," the judge says, noting that by the time a person reaches trial he has been deemed "probably guilty" several times. "When a person is arrested, indicted by a grand jury, held in detention or released on bail, it is all based on probable guilt." Rothwax adds. "Once *on trial,* he is presumed innocent.". . .

Bernard Gavzer is a contributing editor for Parade *magazine. From Bernard Gavzer,* "We're in the Fight of Our Lives," Parade, *July 28, 1996, pp. 4–6. Reprinted with permission from* Parade, *Copyright © 1996.*

The positions the judge has staked out in what he regards as his crusade to bring sense to the criminal justice system have shocked those who long associated him with strong liberal causes. A lifelong Democrat, Rothwax was a senior defense trial attorney for the Legal Aid Society in New York and a stalwart of the New York Civil Liberties Union early in his career.

"I represented Lenny Bruce and Abbie Hoffman, the Black Panthers and the Vietnam war protesters," he says, "I am today as much a civil libertarian as ever. But that does not mean I must close my eyes to the devastation that has occurred in criminal justice. We have the crime, but where is the justice? It is all tilted in favor of the criminal, and it is time to bring this into balance."

The interests of the victim weigh solidly in Rothwax's courtroom in the Criminal Court Building in Manhattan. However, he is troubled by some decisions of the U.S. Supreme Court, saying: "Its rulings over the last 35 years have made the criminal justice system incomprehensible and unworkable."

Although neither the Supreme Court nor the Courts of Appeals decide the guilt or innocence of a defendant, they do make rulings on the constitutionality of acts by the police and lower courts and thus have a significant impact on our justice system. Key practices of our current system—which have come about as a result of Supreme Court rulings in recent decades—need to be changed, Rothwax believes. Among them are:

The Miranda Warning   In New York, Alfio Ferro was arrested in 1975 in connection with a fur robbery that turned into a murder. In the lockup, a detective—without saying a word—dropped some of the stolen furs in front of Ferro's cell. Ferro then made incriminating statements that led to his conviction for second-degree murder.

In 1984, an appellate court overturned the conviction, saying that the detective's action amounted to interrogation and violated Ferro's *Miranda* rights. The *Miranda* warning requires that the suspect be told he has a right to remain silent, that any statement he makes might be used against him and that he has the right to have a lawyer present.

"*Miranda* came about because of abuses such as prolonged custodial interrogation, beatings and starving in order to get a confession," says Rothwax. "I think those abuses have been largely dealt with. Now the police officer is put in the position of telling a suspect in a murder or rape, 'Look, you don't have to tell us anything, and that may be the best thing for you.' And it produces a situation in which a proper confession is thrown out because of the way in which it was read or that it wasn't read at the right time."

Rothwax believes *Miranda* can be replaced by the recording of an arrest and interrogation through videotapes, tape recorders and other technology. This would probably show whether a confession or statement was coerced.

The Exclusionary Rule   [In the winter of 1996] Federal Judge Harold Baer Jr. refused to admit as evidence 80 pounds of cocaine and heroin obtained in the arrest of a drug courier in the Washington Heights neighborhood of New York City. The evidence was excluded because, said Baer, the police had violated the Fourth Amendment protection against unreasonable search and seizure when they searched the car in which the drugs were found.

The police said their search was proper in view of the fact that they saw men hastily loading bags into an out-of-state car in a high drug area in the middle of the night, and the men ran away when the police approached. Judge Baer, however, said just because the men ran off was no reason to suspect them of a crime. In Washington Heights, the judge said, it was not unusual for even innocent people to flee, because police there were regarded as "corrupt, violent and abusive."

Under a growing chorus of criticism. Judge Baer first reversed himself and then asked that the case be assigned to another judge. It was. Rothwax says this is the sort of muddled episode which arises from the exclusionary rule, producing "truth and justice denied on a technicality."

"The Supreme Court has consistently ruled that evidence seized in violation of the Fourth Amendment *should* be excluded from a criminal trial. But if you read the Fourth Amendment, nowhere does it say that *illegally* obtained evidence *must* be excluded," says Rothwax. "In my view, when you exclude or suppress evidence, you suppress the truth."

Judge Rothwax has a remedy: "Make the exclusionary rule *discretionary* instead of mandatory. If it was at the discretion of the judge, there could be a test of reasonableness. A judge could consider factors such as whether a police officer acted with objective reasonableness and subjective good faith. As it is now, the exclusionary rule is irrational, arbitrary and lacks proportion. No wonder that in 90 percent of exclusionary cases, the police don't know what the law is."

The Right to Counsel   In 1982, Kenneth West of New York, an alleged drug dealer, was suspected of being involved in killing a man who had taken his parking place. His lawyer, at a police lineup, told the police not to question West in his absence. Nothing came of the case for three years. Then police arrested a former cohort of West who said West had been one of the shooters. The informer secretly taped West talking about the killing. West was convicted, but in 1993 the New York Court of Appeals reversed the conviction, saying the secret taping amounted to questioning him without the presence of counsel.

The right to counsel is provided by the Sixth Amendment. "It is essential there be a right to counsel," Judge Rothwax says. "But the amendment doesn't say it has to be during police questioning and investigation. As a result of technicalities over this issue of counsel, I have seen murderers go free. Make it clear that the right to a lawyer shouldn't be a factor in the *investigative* stage but only in pre-trial and trial stages."

Instructions to the Jury   After closing arguments in the O. J. Simpson murder trial, Judge Ito took great care in telling jurors that Simpson's failure to take the stand in his own defense should in no way be taken to mean anything negative or to draw any other adverse conclusion.

This instruction to the jury occurs in all cases in which the defense asks for it, because of a Supreme Court ruling in 1981 that said not to do so amounted to a violation of the Fifth Amendment. [The Fifth Amendment states that no person shall be forced to testify against himself.] "The Fifth Amendment does *not* say that one might not draw reasonable inferences from the silence of a defendant," Judge Rothwax says. "I think we must find a way to return to the standard that existed before, that the judge could tell the jury that the failure to explain could amount to an inability to explain."

The judge would like to see other changes made to the jury system. Among them:

1. *Unanimous jury verdicts should no longer be required.* Why? Rothwax cites a murder case he presided over. "It was an overwhelming case of clear guilt. Yet there was a hung jury. One juror was convinced the defendant was not guilty. How did she know? Well, as she explained it, 'Someone that good-looking could not commit such a crime.' We had to retry the case, and the man was quickly found guilty."

   By allowing verdicts to be decided by a vote of 11–1 or 10–2, Rothwax says, there could be a reduced risk that a single juror could cause a retrial or force a compromise in the face of overwhelming evidence of guilt.

2. *Preemptory challenges to prospective jurors should be strictly limited or abolished.* Peremptory challenges allow lawyers to knock someone off the jury without giving any reason. "As we saw in the Simpson case," Rothwax says, "it makes it possible to stack a jury so that the most educated juror is excused, and you end up with a jury that can be manipulated to accept innuendo as evidence."

Judge Rothwax regards the entire conduct of the Simpson trial as an unspeakable insult to the American people, one that left them "feeling wounded and deeply distrustful of the system." He adds: "There was an opportunity to show a vast audience the potential vitality of justice at work. Instead we are assaulted by an obscene circus. We saw proof that the American courtroom is dangerously out of order.". . .

To sit with Rothwax in court, as this writer did, is to get a sense of his urgency for reform. In three hours, there was a procession of men and women charged with felonies from murder to drug dealing. Rothwax was all business, and he was tough with everyone. After 47 cases had been considered and dealt with, the judge turned to me and asked, with irony, about the defendants we had seen: "Did you notice the huge display of remorse?" There hadn't been any. "That's why" he said, "we are in the fight of our lives."

"Just Make It a Fair Fight"

John C. Kilwein

Crime is a significant problem in this country. Almost 25,000 persons are the victims of homicides each year. Property loss and medical expenses related to crime exceed $17 billion per year. Responding to these and other troubling statistics, President Clinton has promised 100,000 new police officers on the streets in American cities and towns. Congress has "federalized" dozens of crimes that were formerly only state offenses, and state legislatures have passed mandatory minimum sentence laws that require convicted criminals to spend more time in prison. The U.S. Bureau of Justice Statistics reports that as a result of these changes the number of people incarcerated in federal and state prisons more than tripled, increasing from 319,600 in 1980 to 999,800 in 1994. In addition, Congress has made it much more difficult for prisoners to use the federal courts, the Constitution, and writs of *habeas corpus* to appeal their convictions. All of this is evidence of a concerted national effort, some might argue excessive effort, to deal with the crime problem.

But efforts such as these are not enough for New York Judge Harold Rothwax. He wants to shock us into taking action in the criminal courts, and in so doing he uses arguments that are based on fear.[1] Judge Rothwax warns Americans, as they read their Sunday papers, of the ominous threats of such dark predators as Leonardo Turriago, who cart murder victims around in the trunks of their automobiles and who walk the streets thanks to legal "technicalities." But as Judge Rothwax spins his frightening yarn, he fails to tell the reader that the crime rate is actually dropping, in spite of the alleged flaws of the criminal justice system. Violent crime, for example, dropped 12.4 percent in 1995, the largest drop since 1973.[2] Why the paradox: A reduction in crime, while Judge Rothwax thinks we are in "the fight of our lives."?

Judge Rothwax offers us a new system of criminal justice that assumes that all police officers and prosecutors do their jobs in a fair and objective manner, free of any systematic bias against groups or individuals in society. The Rothwax system assumes that prosecutors will base their prosecutorial decisions strictly on legal grounds, ignoring other factors such as political gain or racial animus. Judge Rothwax believes that as a society we have largely solved the problem of police brutality; that American law-enforcement officials no longer use uncomfortable detention, physical violence, or psychological coercion to secure convictions. The Rothwax system assumes that criminal defendants in the United States have more legal representation than they deserve, and that the system would benefit by reducing the formal rules that lawyers bring to the pretrial process. Unfortunately, the real world of American criminal justice is far more complex than the "good vs. evil" morality play suggested by Judge Rothwax.

John C. Kilwein is a professor of political science at West Virginia University. This article was written especially for Points of View *in 1997 and revised by Dr. Kilwein in 2000.*

THE GOVERNMENT VS. THE CRIMINAL DEFENDANT:
A FAIR FIGHT?

The legal system in the United States is based on the belief that the best way for a court to discover the truth in a legal dispute is to allow the parties to battle it out in the courtroom before a jury or judge. The judge acts as an independent and objective arbiter or referee who makes sure that the disputants battle fairly by following the rules of law. The disputants are responsible for developing the case they will bring into the courtroom and will understandably have a strong incentive to seek out any evidence or witnesses that might assist them. The disputants also have the right to challenge the veracity of their opponent's presentation. The confrontation in court between these two competing sides, each presenting a very different version of a contested dispute, will, in theory, maximize the likelihood that the truth will come out.[3] Of course, the difficult job for the judge or the jury is sifting through the two accounts to arrive at a sense of what actually took place and what justice should be.

When applied to disputes involving a crime, the disputants in the adversarial system are the defendant, or the person charged with committing the crime, and the state. The state, rather than the victim, is the litigant in criminal cases because by definition crimes not only harm victims, they also harm and threaten society as a whole. In a criminal case, therefore, the battle to be played out in the courtroom is between a person charged with a crime and a prosecutor who represents the interests of society—a battle that strains the notion of a fair fight. The government clearly has a lot more advantages than the criminal defendant. The extent of this mismatch is underscored by the fact that prosecutors have available to them the machinery of government, including the vast investigative powers of law enforcement, whereas defendants must do it on their own.

The American justice system takes into account this disparity, however, by providing the defendant with certain procedural rights and advantages that are intended to equalize the courtroom battle in criminal cases. This system assumes that when a powerful litigant, the state, faces a weaker litigant, the defendant, there is a high probability of a wrongful conviction of an innocent person unless the state follows procedures designed to make it a fair fight. And in our criminal legal tradition, there is no greater miscarriage of justice than sending innocent individuals to prison or to their death. Modern-day criminal procedure protections seek to prevent such an outcome.

Among the equalizers built into the American legal system are: the presumption of innocence; the beyond-a-reasonable-doubt standard of proof; the prohibitions against unreasonable search and seizure, forced self-incrimination, excessive bail, excessive fines, double jeopardy, and cruel and unusual punishment; the right to counsel, a trial by jury, a public and speedy trial, to speak at trial, to confront and cross-examine hostile witnesses, to present favorable witnesses, and guaranteed access to the writ of *habeas corpus.* Some of these "equalizers" have been incorporated into our system as part of formal documents, or constitutions, that act as the blueprints for our American governments, while others were added as our criminal justice system evolved and became part of our legal tradition.

For Judge Rothwax the balance between the state and the criminally accused is fundamentally flawed. Criminal defendants are not the "weak sisters" in a criminal trial;

the state is. For Judge Rothwax, a "liberal" judiciary led by the U.S. Supreme Court has conspired to create new and extreme rights for the defendant. These extravagant rights, moreover, make it extremely difficult for the prosecutor and the police to do their jobs. Seemingly guilty defendants are released from custody because their defense lawyers exploited some constitutional technicality. The murder trial of O. J. Simpson is seen as a case in point. Overworked, underpaid, and inept prosecutors fumbled before a group of highly paid "dream team" defense lawyers, who exploited every procedural technicality to achieve a verdict of innocence.

Judge Rothwax offers up an alternative system of criminal justice that tips the balance in the courtroom battle toward the side of the prosecution by limiting a defendant's right to counsel, altering the presumption of innocence, increasing the power of police to search for proof of criminality and to interrogate defendants, allowing more evidence favoring the prosecution's case to be admitted in court, and altering the nature of jury deliberations in criminal trials. In short, the Rothwax system makes it easier for the prosecution to prove to a jury that a criminal defendant is guilty as charged, and deserving of punishment.

THE "SUSPECT RIGHTS" OF SUSPECTS

The Presumption of Innocence

Our legal system recognizes that a criminal dispute is more serious than a civil dispute. In criminal law, society has the capacity to publicly punish the convicted criminal, using several forms of punishment. First, the defendant faces the shame and consequences associated with being declared a convicted criminal, including the loss of certain freedoms and rights, as for example, access to a variety of licenses, or the freedom to perform certain jobs. Second, criminal conviction can bring with it the possibility of substantial monetary fines, often in the thousands of dollars. Third, criminal conviction can result in a complete loss of freedom through incarceration, with all the unintended consequences of life behind bars, a violent world often filled with physical assault, rape, and other indignities. Finally, in 38 states and at the federal level, defendants charged with capital crimes face the ultimate punishment of being put to death by the state.

Given the seriousness of being charged with a crime, the American legal system confers on the defendant an important protection: the presumption of innocence. The primary purpose of this rule is to prevent a wrongful conviction that sends an innocent person to prison or to death. There is a simple yet profound logic behind this rule. When a criminal victimizes an individual, society intervenes to find, try, and punish the criminal. The harm suffered by the victim can never be undone, but some solace comes from the fact that the state takes a direct interest in resolving the criminal dispute. On the other hand, when the state wrongfully punishes an innocent defendant, the victimization is absolute. There is no solace available to the innocent person, since the perpetrator is the state. This perspective gives rise to the old saw that it is better to let ten guilty persons go free than to send one innocent individual to prison or death. For Judge Rothwax, however, that old saw is apparently a bit rusty and should be replaced by a new motto: The criminal justice system almost never convicts the wrong person; and those guilty individuals who are set free are threatening us all.

Judge Rothwax makes a distinction between the investigative (pretrial) and trial stages of the criminal process. Rothwax argues that during the investigative stage, defendants are assumed to be guilty by the police and the prosecutor or they would not have been arrested and indicted in the first place. He concludes that when defendants appear before his bench, they are probably guilty of the charges or their cases would never have reached his court. In short, Judge Rothwax gives the state the benefit of the doubt that it only prosecutes clearly guilty people. This perspective is troubling because it ignores the basic idea behind adversarial justice: Legal conflicts are not prejudged but decided through the courtroom battle.

While it is true that the great majority of police officers and prosecutors are honest people who play by the rules and who have no desire to harm innocent people, Rothwax's position ignores a number of very real problems. The most obvious problem of the proposed system is that it fails to take into account that justice officials can and do make mistakes, and the importance of the trial process in detecting these honest errors. Second, Judge Rothwax ignores the fact that a minority of justice officials, however small, are lazy, dishonest, corrupt, racist, or some combination of these. Examples of these troubling behaviors abound in our criminal justice system. In 2000, the Republican governor of Illinois, George Ryan, established a temporary moratorium on executions is his state. Governor Ryan cited a "shameful record of convicting innocent people and putting them on death row."[4] While a complete investigation of the circumstances that led to innocent men being sentenced to death in Illinois remains to be completed, it seems clear that either incompetence or criminality on the part of police investigators and prosecutors played a significant role. And a year earlier in Los Angeles, police officers admitted to systematically committing crimes to convict innocent individuals.[5] By March 1, 2000, the Los Angeles District Attorney's Office had taken the unprecedented action of seeking the reversal of forty felony convictions, because it had clear evidence that those convictions were based on the false testimony of the errant officers.

In 1997, an internal U.S. Department of Justice investigation revealed that agents of the highly respected FBI crime laboratory altered evidence and skewed testimony to assist prosecutors.[6] In Texas and West Virginia false testimony given by an incompetent and dishonest medical examiner sent at least six innocent men to prison.[7] To avoid the embarrassment and political fallout of being unable to convict the perpetrators of an arson fire with multiple deaths in New York[8] and the killing of a police officer in Houston,[9] prosecutors in both cities tenaciously pursued capital murder charges against apparently innocent individuals, while ignoring or concealing exculpatory evidence in the prosecution's possession. And evidence that some police officers and prosecutors target young black and Hispanic men for questionable arrest and prosection comes to light with alarming frequency, as in the case of Carlton Brown.[10]

The case of Carlton Brown is particularly enlightening. Mr. Brown, who is black, is paralyzed from the chest down following injuries he sustained while under arrest in New York City's 63rd Precinct. Charged with driving with a suspended license, Mr. Brown contended that the arresting officers, after becoming irritated with his demands for information on his arrest, smashed his head while he was handcuffed into a bullet-proof, double-plate glass window and severely injured his spine. The two police officers involved with his arrest countered that Mr. Brown had hurt himself falling down in the police station. The police officers were charged, tried before a judge, and acquitted. In a subsequent civil proceeding, however, the city of New York agreed to pay Mr. Brown $4.5 million in civil damages, a record-setting pretrial settlement. Needless to say, such a settlement calls into question Judge Rothwax's confidence in the criminal justice system's ability to function in an unbiased manner. Our system of justice assumes that people, including law-enforcement officials, are not angels[11] or saints; nor are they infallible; and it builds in protections, like the presumption of innocence, accordingly. The Rothwax system depends on an angelic conversion among these officials, an unlikely occurrence now or ever.

Miranda and the Right to Remain Silent and the Right to Counsel

Judge Rothwax reserves some of his harshest criticism for the U.S. Supreme Court's 1966 decision in *Miranda v. Arizona*.[12] In that decision the Court ruled that a confession made by Ernest Miranda, who was charged with kidnapping and raping an 18-year-old woman, was unconstitutionally obtained by police interrogators.[13] Extending its ruling beyond the immediate circumstances of the arrest and interrogation of Miranda, the Court required that henceforth all police officers and prosecutors must inform defendants of their rights to remain silent and to have counsel.[14] Commenting on state law-enforcement officials, the Court observed:

> The use of physical brutality and violence is not, unfortunately, relegated to the past or to any part of the country. Only recently in Kings County [Brooklyn Borough], New York the police brutally beat, kicked and placed lighted cigarette butts on the back of a potential witness under interrogation for the purpose of securing a statement incriminating a third party.[15]

The Court added that while not using physical violence, other police interrogators use psychological abuse and lies to trick defendants into confessing to crimes.

Seen as an indictment against all police officers and prosecutors, the decision in *Miranda* was, and, as highlighted by Judge Rothwax, still is, very unpopular within the law-enforcement community. This is unfortunate because, as Chief Justice Warren argued in the opinion, the *Miranda* requirements do not prevent good law-enforcement officers from doing their job. Indeed, as pointed out by Warren, agents of the FBI had already been using the warnings and were still able to investigate and assist in the conviction of federal defendants. What the warnings were designed to do was prevent an innocent defendant from confessing in order to bring an end to an abusive interrogation. The fact of the matter is that police officers who do not abuse defendants have nothing to fear from the *Miranda* requirements.

The *Miranda* decision also sought to make effective two important equalizers in the Bill of Rights: the prohibition against self-incrimination and the right to counsel. The right against self-incrimination or the right to remain silent is based on an old common law principle that the state cannot force defendants to testify against themselves. Rather, the state makes the charges and must prove its case. Although the right to counsel came later in the Anglo-American legal tradition, it is based on the belief that it is unreasonable to expect ordinary persons to understand the legal implications of statements they might make or actions they might take in the pretrial stage, actions that might again lead to their wrongful conviction. The *Miranda* requirement was based on the reasonable assumption that illiterate or uniformed defendants probably are not aware of these protections and therefore the state has a responsibility to inform them.

Judge Rothwax argues against this necessity, contending that, because defense attorneys step in and convince their clients to do otherwise, *Miranda* prevents the police from securing confessions from cooperative defendants. Apparently Judge Rothwax is opposed to the general principle of informed consent, that is, that defendants should know what they are doing before they say anything or confess. Judge Rothwax also seems to believe that the abuse of defendants while in police custody, cited by Chief Justice Warren in *Miranda,* is no longer a problem. Unfortunately, evidence suggests that in his zeal to get tougher on crime and criminals, Judge Rothwax is ignoring the fact that abuses continue in the interrogation stage of the pretrial process. An example from Rothwax's own hometown underscores this conclusion.[16] Police officers in New York's 24th Precinct arrested a 17-year-old white male for a misdemeanor. He refused to confess. The defendant was held in a jail cell for two nights. At one point, he was placed in a van and chained in the sweltering heat. At another point a police officer waved his gun in front of the defendant and threatened to "shoot his dick off." One wonders if the cameras in the precinct, called for by Judge Rothwax to protect against such abuse, would have captured this particular "Kodak moment"! The evidence suggests that this incident is not a random occurrence, in New York or nationally. Amnesty International has cited 90 cases of police brutality allegedly perpetrated by officers of the New York Police Department alone. Similar charges by other watchdog groups have been leveled at other departments around the country.[17]

Sometimes law enforcement officers use less violent forms of coercion in the interrogation room. For example, in 1999, FBI agents lied to Wen Ho Lee, a Department of Energy employee suspected of spying for China, by informing him that he had failed a lie detector test, when, in fact, he had registered a score indicating he was telling the truth.[18] Building on this lie, the agents then told Mr. Lee that if he did not provide them with a confession, he would likely die in the electric chair.

For most first-time defendants the pretrial process can be a very frightening experience. Defendants, innocent or guilty, who cannot post bail are held in jail until their trial. The pace of some criminal justice systems can be glacial, taking up to two years for a case to make it to trial. This delay, moreover, can be used to entice or coerce a defendant into making a confession, even a false one. For example, a prosecutor can offer defendants awaiting trial a plea bargain that gives them credit for time served while awaiting trial in exchange for a guilty plea. Given this offer, an innocent defendant might make a false confession, assuming that the conviction is a small price to pay for immediate release from prison.[19] The deal may be especially appealing if the defendant considers that a guilty verdict by jury at trial could yield an even stiffer sentence. Interrogations are also daunting for a defendant unfamiliar with the law. And although the great majority of questionings are conducted by professional officers observing all relevant constitutional requirements, the fact remains that police officers have substantially more experience in the process than do defendants, thereby increasing the probability that defendants will unwittingly damage their own case. In these and every other pretrial situation defendants would be at a severe disadvantage without legal representation.

In the end, the Rothwax system would punish the ignorant, the weak, and the poor. Wealthy or more highly educated defendants, who have a basic understanding of the legal system, are more likely to know they have the right to remain silent and to make informed choices about its use. Likewise, sophisticated defendants who are not intimidated by pretrial detention and rough treatment are also more likely to refuse to assist the police in developing the state's case against them. Moreover, defendants with long-standing criminal records are also likely to be especially cognizant of their right to remain silent. In addition, multiple offenders who have experienced the daily violence of the corrections system are probably less likely to be frightened into confessing as the result of a difficult interrogation.

The most troubling aspect of Rothwax's system, however, from the point of view of equal justice for all, is that it rewards wealthier criminal defendants. Individuals who can afford to hire a lawyer and post bail are able to avoid the various forms of pretrial pressure since they can await trial in the comfort of their own homes; and, with the advice of counsel, they are more likely to remain silent, thereby putting the government to its full task of convicting them without their assistance. It is quite possible, therefore, that the system proposed by Judge Rothwax will have the unintended consequence of convicting more innocent, first-time criminal defendants, while releasing those defendants with experience and/or money. These potential biases do not seem to concern Judge Rothwax. Like some American generals in Vietnam, Judge Rothwax seems to be singularly concerned only with body counts: So what if these new convictions are gained at the expense of fairness; they're convictions; and that's what counts! A justice system that operates in this manner has abandoned any pretense of being blind to a defendant's wealth or social status. It is a justice system more likely to convict an innocent defendant whose real crime is that he or she lives in the South Bronx rather than on Long Island.

The Exclusionary Rule

The exclusionary rule is an American invention, created by the U.S. Supreme Court in 1914.[20] It was designed to resolve the question of what should be done when a police officer or prosecutor violates the constitutional protections of defendants who have been the targets of illegal searches or interrogations. By making this ruling, the Supreme Court, using a classic American "free-market" approach, has ruled that such evidence is tainted and must therefore be excluded from trial. The exclusionary rule, the Court has argued, removes any incentive for law-enforcement officials to engage in unconstitutional and illegal activities, since ill-gotten gains cannot be used in court.

Since the Bill of Rights make no mention of this rule in the Fourth Amendment's prohibition against unreasonable searches and seizures, Judge Rothwax contends that the rule is an illegitimate hindrance to the criminal justice system's operation. He argues that excluded evidence prevents the court from getting the total truth surrounding a case. To accept this logic, however, one must, again, accept, as Rothwax clearly does, that in the rule's absence, police officers or prosecutors are unlikely to violate the Fourth or Fifth Amendments in their search for evidence or confessions. Given the examples of illegal police conduct cited above, it is difficult to share Justice Rothwax's views of the motives and actions of the police.

Judge Rothwax is also upset because the exclusionary rule has, in his view, been used by judges in an overly technical and picky manner, with good cases being thrown out because investigating officers forgot to "dot the i's and cross the t's." He blames the "liberal" U.S. Supreme Court for decisions that favor criminal defendants. What Judge Rothwax disingenously ignores, however, is that the Supreme Court of 1997 is, in fact, a quite conservative one, particularly in its decisions dealing with the rights of criminal defendants. Since the mid-1970s, the U.S. Supreme Court has consistently shifted the constitutional advantage in criminal matters away from criminal defendants toward the police and prosecution. Specifically, in terms of the exclusionary rule, the Court has ruled in ways that enable prosecutors to use more questionable evidence and confessions against criminal defendants. Two examples highlight this shift. In *U.S. v. Havens,*[21] the Court allowed illegally obtained evidence to be used in trial to discredit testimony during cross examination. And in *Nix v. Williams,*[22] the Court ruled that tainted evidence can be used against the defendant if the trial court judge concludes that evidence would inevitably have been discovered. Finally, in 2000, the Supreme Court agreed to review *Dickerson v. United States,* a case decided by the U.S. Fourth Circuit Court of Appeals. In the *Dickerson* case, the Court decided, over the objections of the U.S. Department of Justice, that a 1968 congressional statute had eliminated the need for law enforcement officers to follow the guidelines set out in *Miranda.* The Fourth Circuit ruled that instead courts must determine whether confessions were voluntarily given, regardless of whether defendants know their rights. Supreme Court watchers now anxiously await the Court's decision in the *Dickerson* appeal.

Peremptory Challenges and Unanimous Jury Verdicts

Judge Rothwax's remaining indictments of the present criminal justice system deal with criminal juries. Responding to the controversy surrounding the O. J. Simpson murder trial, he criticizes the defense team's use of peremptory challenges to eliminate prospective jurors.[23] He argues that the Simpson defense team used such challenges to seat a jury that could be easily fooled by courtroom pyrotechnics. Whether this is true or not is a matter of conjecture, but it should be noted that Judge Rothwax ignores the fact that the prosecution had the same opportunity to affect the makeup of the jury. In reality, peremptory challenges help both sides in the courtroom battle, and thus we can assume that their removal would potentially hurt both sides as well. Rothwax, however, clearly presumes that these challenges only help the defendant; in fact, this presumption is not warranted. In 1997, for example, a videotape surfaced that was used as a training device for assistant prosecutors in Philadelphia.[24] The tape shows a senior prosecutor counseling his trainees to exclude black citizens from serving on criminal juries because they are distrustful of the police, and therefore less likely to convict. The tape tells the trainees they should especially avoid placing young black women on their juries, because they are very bad for the prosecution's case. Although this episode remains to be investigated, and the attorney featured in the video vehemently denies having done anything illegal or morally wrong, the advice presented on this tape would appear to violate a Supreme Court ruling prohibiting race from being used as a factor in selecting jurors. More fundamentally, this example calls into question Judge Rothwax's contention that the justice system has solved the problem of systemic racism.

Judge Rothwax also opposes the requirement that a criminal jury reach a verdict of guilt unanimously, suggesting instead that we should allow a jury to convict a defendant with a substantial majority, for example, a vote of 11–1 or 10–2. In fact, the practice of jury unanimity[25] is merely a legal custom and not an explicit constitutional right, and the U.S. Supreme Court has established that if states choose, they can allow juries to reach their decision with a clear, nonunanimous verdict.[26] Given the Supreme Court's view on this issue, Judge Rothwax's gripe, then, is with the legal system of the state of New York, which apparently has decided to continue the practice of jury unanimity, and not with the rulings of the so-called liberal U.S. Supreme Court in Washington.

WE FACE THE CHOICE OF OUR LIVES

The late Senator Sam Ervin once said: "In a free society you have to take some risks. If you lock everybody up, or even if you lock up everybody you think might commit a crime, you'll be pretty safe, but you won't be free."[27] To this one might add, and you might end up getting locked up yourself!

This country was shaped in part by a healthy concern for the potential abuses of governments. The U.S. Bill of Rights and the civil liberty protections of the state constitutions were created to ensure certain fundamental protections to all citizens. These guarantees were designed to withstand the shifting winds created by agitated majorities. Judge Rothwax is not the first American, nor will he likely be the last, to tell his fellow citizens that we live in a particularly dangerous time and that to survive we must forego the "luxury" of our civil liberties.

Judge Rothwax is wrong. The guarantees created by James Madison and the Constitution are not luxuries. Rather, they make up a very battered constitutional firewall that barely protects us from the police state that he, cynical politicians, and a very conservative U.S. Supreme Court seem to be inching towards. These civil liberties are not excessive; if anything, they provide too little protection for the realities of daily life in an increasingly urban, multicultural society facing the 21st century.

Of course, many Americans share Judge Rothwax's concern over criminal predators, like Leonardo Turriago, who prey on their fellow citizens. These violent criminals should be punished severely. But the same level of concern ought to be expressed in regard to how today's criminal justice system treats black, Hispanic, American Indian, poor, and uneducated Americans. Americans ought to be concerned about the rights of innocent, hardworking Americans who are harassed, injured, maimed, or killed every day by abusive police officers for being in the "wrong" neighborhood or driving too "nice" a car. Judge Rothwax's system will not win the war against the Leonardo Turriagos of the world; it will likely create more Carlton Browns.

NOTES

1. Bernard Gavzer, "We're in the Fight of Our Lives," *Parade,* July 28, 1996, 4–6.
2. Haya El Nasser, "Historic Crime Drop," *USA Today,* April 14, 1997, 1A.
3. In other countries, for example, most of the nations of continental Europe, an inquisitorial system of justice is used. In this system, it is the judge who determines the direction of the trial by calling witnesses, examining evidence, and drawing final conclusions of fact. When compared to an adversarial justice system, inquisitorial disputants and, more importantly, their lawyers play a much less active role in affecting the composition of the case. Instead of a courtroom battle, the inquisitorial trial might be likened to a trip to the principal's office to determine who did what to whom and what should be done about it.
4. Dirk Johnson, "Illinois, Citing Verdict Errors, Bars Executions," *New York Times,* February 1, 2000, A1.
5. James Sterngold, "Los Angeles Police's Report Cites Vast Command Lapses," *New York Times,* March 2, 2000, A14.
6. David Johnston, "Report Criticizes Scientific Testing at FBI Crime Lab," *New York Times,* April 16, 1997, A1.
7. Mark S. Warnick, "A Matter of Conviction," *Pittsburgh Post-Gazette,* September 24, 1995, A1.
8. Bob Herbert, "Brooklyn's Obsessive Pursuit," *New York Times,* August 21, 1994, E15.
9. "Mexican Once Nearly Executed Wins Freedom in Texas," *New York Times,* April 17, 1997, A8.
10. Bob Herbert, "Savagery Beyond Sense," *New York Times,* October 18, 1996, A12.
11. James Madison, the leading figure in the development of the U.S. Constitution and Bill of Rights, commented on the need for checks on human behavior associated with the affairs of the state in *Federalist* No. 51: "If men were angels, no government would be necessary. If angels were to govern men, neither external nor internal controls on government would be necessary."
12. 384 U.S. 436.
13. Both sides conceded that during the interrogation, the police did not use any force, threats, or promises of leniency if Miranda would confess. Both sides also conceded that at no point did the police inform Miranda that he had a constitutional right to refuse to talk to the police and that he could have counsel if he so desired.
14. Thus yielding the famous *Miranda* warnings:

    You have the right to remain silent.

    Anything you say can and will be used against you in a court of law.

    You have a right to a lawyer.

    If you can't afford a lawyer one will be provided to you.

    If you say at any point that you do not want to talk to the police the interrogation must cease.

15. 384 U.S. 446.

16. *Economist,* July 13, 1996, 29.

17. *Ibid.*

18. David Ignatius, "Tricks, Lies and Criminal Confessions," *The Washington Post National Weekly Edition,* January 24, 2000, 26.

19. It is important to note that only about 10 percent of criminal cases are resolved through the formal trial process. Most criminal convictions in this country are the result of plea bargaining between the defendant and the prosecutor.

20. *Weeks v. U.S.,* 232 U.S. 383 (1914).

21. 446 U.S. 620 (1980).

22. 467 U.S. 431 (1984).

23. When a jury is used as the fact finder in a criminal case the defense and prosecution have a significant role in determining who will sit on the jury. In the jury selection process both sides can challenge a prospective juror in two ways. A challenge for cause is used when an attorney can show the court that there are tangible characteristics of the prospective jurors that make them biased and warrant their removal from consideration; lawyers have an unlimited ability to challenge for cause. A peremptory challenge allows a lawyer to remove a potential juror without giving a reason; each lawyer in a case gets a limited number of these. But peremptory challenges are not as peremptory as their name implies. The Supreme Court has ruled that lawyers cannot use them to systematically exclude all blacks or women from consideration for jury service.

24. Michael Janofsky, "Under Siege, Philadelphia's Criminal Justice System Suffers Another Blow," *New York Times,* April 10, 1997, A9.

25. Jury unanimity is another balancer, and is based on the notion that the prosecutor should be required to present a case that convinces all jurors that the defendant is guilty beyond a reasonable doubt.

26. *Johnson v. Louisiana,* 406 U.S. 356 (1972), and *Apodaco v. Oregon,* 406 U.S. 404 (1972).

27. Quoted in Richard Harris, *Justice* (New York: Avon 1969), p. 162.

15

CIVIL LIBERTIES

Free Speech

*F*reedom of speech is one of the most important freedoms accorded citizens of the United States. Nowhere is that freedom more highly prized than in its universities, whose central mission—the generation and transmission of knowledge—is predicated upon the free expression of ideas. Thus, it should occasion no surprise that considerable debate erupts on campuses from time to time over the extent to which universities are fostering an environment conducive to free expression.

The most recent debate on this question centers around the matter of student fees—a practice whereby the university imposes mandatory fees imposed on students by the university for the purpose of supporting various student organizations and activities on campus. More specifically, five students at the University of Wisconsin took strong exception to the fact that their student fees were going to support certain campus organizations whose views and purposes they did not share. Indeed, they were so offended by it that they decided to challenge this practice in court. In the first selection are portions of an amicus curiae *brief submitted to the U.S. Supreme Court by the American Council on Education on behalf of the University of Wisconsin. It insists that universities have a responsibility to create an environment which fosters a free market place of ideas. One of the ways to do so is to support with student fees a host of different campus organizations. Such support, in the view of the American Council on Education, in no way diminishes the free speech of students paying those fees.*

The second selection also contains portions of an amicus curiae *brief submitted to the U.S. Supreme Court—this one by the Pacific Legal Foundation on behalf of the five students. It argues that by requiring students to support, through their fees, organizations with which they disagree, the University of Wisconsin is in fact abridging their right to freedom of speech.*

Mandatory Student Fees Do Not Abridge Freedom of Speech

American Council on Education

I. A UNIVERSITY'S USE OF COMPULSORY FEES TO CREATE A STUDENT ACTIVITY FUND SHOULD BE ANALYZED AS THE CREATION OF A FORUM, RATHER THAN AS COMPELLED SPEECH AND ASSOCIATION

A. A University, as a Marketplace of Ideas, Has a Compelling Interest in Promoting the Presence of a Diversity of Viewpoints

" 'It is the business of a university to provide that atmosphere which is most conducive to speculation, experiment and creation.' "[1] A university can provide this atmosphere only by offering an environment in which a rich diversity of ideas, values, and perspectives is championed and challenged. In this sense, "[t]he college classroom with its surrounding environs is peculiarly the 'marketplace of ideas.' "[2]

This marketplace trains future citizens and leaders by providing "wide exposure to that robust exchange of ideas which discovers truth 'out of a multitude of tongues.' "[3] If a university is to provide such training, some members of the academic community will inevitably encounter speech that they find unfamiliar, even abhorrent. Furthermore, learning to tolerate and respond to such speech is an important part of the educational process. "To endure the speech of false ideas or offensive content and then to counter it is part of learning how to live in a pluralistic society, a society which insists upon open discourse towards the end of a tolerant citizenry."[4]

The marketplace extends beyond the classroom to extracurricular activities, which are "a critical aspect of campus life."[5] Education involves more than tests, textbooks, lectures, and libraries. Fundamentally, it is about the development of character.[6] Consequently, education does not end at the classroom door, but permeates campus and university life. As this Court recognizes, a "great deal of learning occurs informally."[7] Indeed, since the nineteenth century, extracurricular activities have played an increasingly significant role in advancing the core mission of universities:

> Over time . . . extracurricular programs have come to be seen not merely as useful services but as an integral part of the educational process itself. Educators point to the dangers of a college that stresses only learning and cognitive skills while ignoring opportunities for students to engage in cooperative activities in which each relies on the efforts of others and is relied upon by others in return. . . . More and more, [extracurricular activities] are regarded not only as a source of enjoyment but as ideal experiences for learning to cooperate and take responsibility for the welfare of one's peers.

From the amicus curiae *brief filed by the American Council on Education in support of the University of Wisconsin in the U.S. Supreme Court case of* Board of Regents, University of Wisconsin v. Scott Southworth *(1999), 5–21.*

. . . The contemporary college or university does not concentrate only on formal education; it assumes the larger responsibility of promoting human development in all its forms.[8]

. . . In sum, colleges and universities hold a unique position in our society and pursue a correspondingly unique mission. Their business is to provide "that atmosphere which is most conducive to speculation, experiment and creation."[9] This mission can be achieved only by fostering a marketplace of ideas on campus and by ensuring that the resultant diversity of thoughts and perspectives informs the full range of experiences—from course selections to lecture series to student organizations. If a university is barred from this essential business, it cannot prepare its students "to live in a pluralistic society, a society which insists upon open discourse towards the end of a tolerant citizenry."[10]

B. Consistent with the First Amendment, a University Can Use Mandatory Fees to Fund a Neutral Forum that Helps Support a Diverse Variety of Organizations

. . . [T]he University of Wisconsin (and many other colleges and universities) pay fees not to particular groups but to the student government, which then uses the money to fund a wide array of organizations in a viewpoint-neutral manner.[11] "The speech of the offending groups can hardly be attributed to the student government, which funds groups of radically different views."[12] . . .

The University of Wisconsin simply requires its students to support a neutral forum, just as if it "built a large auditorium and held it open for everyone."[13] The fact that this case concerns a fund, rather than a physical space like an auditorium or an amphitheater, does not mean that forum analysis does not apply. . . .

Application of these principles makes clear that a critical difference exists between (a) supporting a forum and (b) supporting the speakers that ultimately use that forum. Thus, in *Widmar v. Vincent*,[14] this Court rejected a university's argument that if it were to allow religious groups to use its buildings it would create an impression that it endorsed religion in violation of the Establishment Clause: "[B]y creating a forum the University does not thereby endorse or promote any of the particular ideas aired there."[15] A student compelled to pay a restoration fee for a university amphitheater can hardly complain that her First Amendment rights are violated because she disagrees with some of the speakers who appear there. She has no greater constitutional cause to complain of a content-neutral student activity fund because she disagrees with some of the organizations it ultimately supports.

If a forum supports organizations in a truly neutral fashion, as is stipulated here, . . . and thereby funds groups that take radically differing positions on the same issues, it cannot be said to endorse or promote any particular group or any specific position.[16] . . .

II. EVEN IF A UNIVERSITY'S USE OF MANDATORY FEES TO FUND STUDENT GOVERNMENT AND ORGANIZATIONS IS ANALYZED UNDER ABOOD-KELLER AS COMPELLED SPEECH AND ASSOCIATION, RATHER THAN AS THE CREATION OF A NEUTRAL FORUM, SUCH A USE OF FEES DOES NOT VIOLATE THE FIRST AMENDMENT

A. The Challenged Use of Mandatory Fees Is Germane to a University's Broad Educational Mission, Including Its Interests in Promoting Diverse Expression and in Providing a Marketplace of Ideas

Abood and *Keller* involve contexts very different from colleges and universities. *Keller* holds that compulsory state bar dues cannot be used to finance ideological activities unrelated to the purposes of the compelled association—regulation of the legal profession and improvement of legal services. Similarly, *Abood* holds that a union may not use a dissenting individual's dues to fund ideological activities not germane to collective bargaining. The purposes of the State Bar in *Keller,* to supervise attorney conduct, and of the union shop in *Abood,* to negotiate contracts, are relatively narrow and definable. The educational mission of a university is substantially broader.[17] ("The goals of the university are much broader than the goals of a labor union or a state bar, and they are inextricably connected with the underlying policies of the First Amendment.")[18]

It is the business of a university to create a marketplace of ideas, exposing its students to a broad range of viewpoints on many issues, including the political and the ideological. This happens in classrooms—in courses in history, literature, political science, sociology, philosophy, and many other disciplines. It happens in auditoriums—when guest lecturers speak on ethics, contemporary problems, civil rights, and the like. And it happens in extracurricular activities—in connection with student government, student newspapers, and student organizations identical to those at issue here. Neither state bars nor unions—nor perhaps any institutions other than American colleges and universities—have this broad mission and mandate.

As a result, numerous courts recognize that a university's mission unquestionably reaches the funding of student organizations. Thus, the Second Circuit holds that a university may allocate student activity fees to a group with whose speech some students disagree.[19] *Carroll* recognizes three distinct university interests served by the compulsory fee: "the promotion of extracurricular life, the transmission of skills and civic duty, and the stimulation of energetic campus debate."[20] . . .

B. Courts Should Afford Universities Wide Latitude to Determine Whether the Use of Student Fees Is Germane to Their Educational Mission

Amici respectfully submit that the court below failed to give proper deference to the University of Wisconsin's decision that the use of mandatory fees advances its educational mission. Universities have interests in academic freedom that are a special concern of the First Amendment. This freedom is lost if courts do not afford universities discretion to define the contours of their educational mission and to determine the most effective means of achieving it. Judicial intervention in academic decision-making affects not only the academic freedom of the university, but it results as well in a loss of the freedom of the students, faculty, and other members of the academic community, all of whom participate in and help to create the marketplace of ideas.

For these reasons, this Court has recognized that government intervention in the intellectual life of a university is to be avoided.[21] Universities are "characterized by the spirit of free inquiry," and academic freedom gives the university the ability "to determine for itself on academic grounds who may teach, what may be taught, how it shall be taught, and who may be admitted to study."[22] . . .

In this case, the University of Wisconsin—a campus with a rich history of the "robust exchange of ideas"[23]—made a judgment that funding a forum that supports a wide variety of student groups, including some engaged in political and ideological activities, plays an important role in its educational mission. This decision deserves respect, "breathing room," and some significant measure of deference. . . .

III. FORCING THE UNIVERSITY TO DISTINGUISH BETWEEN "EDUCATIONAL" ORGANIZATIONS AND "POLITICAL" OR "IDEOLOGICAL" ORGANIZATIONS RISKS VIOLATING STUDENTS' FIRST AMENDMENT RIGHTS

The court below effectively requires universities to distinguish political from non-political, and ideological from non-ideological organizations, and then to grant or withhold funding based upon these distinctions. Such distinctions may be constitutionally workable in the context of the activities of a union or a state bar, where the government has a narrower interest and where that interest does not include exposure to a diverse marketplace of ideas. Such distinctions emphatically do not work in the context of a university, however, where the government has a broad interest, and where that interest includes exposure to various political and ideological perspectives. Further, in the context of a university campus activities, such distinctions not only fail to work, but they actually create significant constitutional mischief.

Consider a student debate club that sponsors a public forum on presidential impeachment; or a student economic society that hosts a series of speakers on tax reform; or a student group that distributes leaflets asserting that a university discriminates because it hires too few minority professors; or a film society that sponsors a film concerning the events at Tiananmen Square; or an environmental organization that presents a series of lectures on the impact of logging; or a literary studies club that funds a panel discussion of alternative theories of literary criticism, including Marxist, feminist, deconstructionist, and Freudian approaches. At some point it simply becomes impossible to separate the ideological and political from the educational and informative.[24]

Furthermore, a university that attempts to make such distinctions, and then to make funding decisions based upon them, may run afoul of First Amendment prohibitions against content- and viewpoint-based discrimination. In other words, forcing universities to draw these lines does not avoid constitutional difficulties; it compounds them. The University of Wisconsin uses the mandatory activity fee to create a public forum that distributes fees on a content-neutral basis. . . . By supporting groups without regard to the content or viewpoint of their speech, the forum detaches funding decisions from endorsement or condemnation of the political or ideological positions of the different organizations. In contrast, the holding of the *Southworth I* court, which would require the University to refuse funding for groups that are too ideological or political, violates the rule against content and viewpoint discrimination in a public forum. . . .

Faced with a project that calls upon them to do the impossible, with the knowledge that in the effort they might also do the unconstitutional, many universities will respond by funding no student organizations at all or only those that seem to pose no risk whatsoever.[25] As the dissenting judges in *Southworth II* cautioned, such a requirement may "spell the end, as a practical matter, to the long tradition of student-managed activities on these campuses."[26] As funding fails, and as organizations disband, some voices—including, in all likelihood, the most provocative and stimulating, if also the least popular voices—will no longer be heard at our universities. The marketplace of ideas on our campuses will suffer immeasurably.

NOTES

1. *Sweezy v. New Hampshire,* 354 U.S. 234, 263 (1957) (Frankfurter, J., concurring).
2. *Healy v. James,* 408 U.S. 169, 180 (1972) (quoting *Keyishian v. Board of Regents of Univ. of N.Y.,* 385 U.S. 589, 603 (1967)).
3. *Keyishian,* 385 U.S. at 603 (quoting *United States v. Associated Press,* 52 F. Supp. 362, 372 (D.N.Y., 1943)).
4. *Lee v. Weisman,* 505 U.S. 577, 590 (1992).
5. *Widmar v. Vincent,* 454 U.S. 263, 279 n. 2 (1981) (Stevens, J., concurring).
6. See Higher Education Amendments of 1998, Pub. L. No. 105-244, §863, 112 Stat. 1581, 1826 (Congress recognizes that "the development of virtue and moral character, those habits of mind, heart, and spirit that help young people to know, desire, and do what is right, has historically been a primary mission of colleges and universities. . . .").
7. *Regents of the Univ. of Cal. v. Bakke,* 438 U.S. 265, 313 n. 48 (1978) (opinion of Powell, J.) (quoting William J. Bowen, "Admissions and the Relevance of Race," *Princeton Alumni Weekly* 7, 9 (Sept. 26, 1977)).
8. Derek C. Bok, *Higher Learning* 51–52 (1986). . . .
9. *Sweezy,* 354 U.S. at 263 (Frankfurter, J., concurring).
10. *Lee,* 505 U.S. at 590.
11. The only exception to this procedure may be Wisconsin PIRG, for which funding is authorized by direct student referendum. This brief does not address the separate and different issue raised by this direct funding, although the "germaneness" analysis discussed below would apply to this funding as well.
12. *Southworth II,* 157 F. 3d at 1125.
13. Id. at 1129 (Wood, J., dissenting).
14. 454 U.S. 263 (1981).
15. See also Carolyn Wiggin, Note, *A Funny Thing Happens When You Pay for a Forum: Mandatory Student Fees to Support Political Speech at Public Universities,* 103 Yale L.J. 2009, 2017 (1994) ("[T]he lack of content-based standards . . . enables the system to support a legitimate campus forum, and this in turn creates a distance between those who fund the forum and any particular view expressed within it, thus avoiding unconstitutional forced speech").
16. See Robert M. O'Neil, "Student Fees and Student Rights: Evolving Constitutional Principles," 15 J.C. & U.L. 569, 574 (1999). . . .
17. See *Rounds,* 166 F. 3d at 1039.
18. See also William Walsh, Comment, *Smith v. Regents of the University of Califor-*

nia: The Marketplace Is Closed, 21 J.C. & U.L. 405, 423 (1994) ("[T]he organizations' purposes in *Keller* and *Abood* were much narrower than the university's purpose. It is much easier to see something as 'political or ideological,' and therefore ineligible for funding, because it is unrelated to collective bargaining that it is to distinguish the same from and 'educational mission'").

19. See *Carroll v. Blinken,* 957 F. 2d 991, 992 (2d Cir. 1992).
20. Id. at 1001. . . .
21. See, e.g., *Sweezy,* 354 U.S. at 262 (Frankfurter, J. concurring).
22. Id. at 262–63.
23. *Keyishian,* 385 U.S. at 603.
24. See Smith, 844 P. 2d at 524–25 (Arabian, J., dissenting).
25. An "opt-out refund" procedure might address certain constitutional concerns, see O'Neil, supra, 575, 578, and use of such a procedure certainly should not be foreclosed by this Court. For the reasons set forth in this brief, however, such a procedure should not be required to save the constitutionality of mandatory fees.
26. 157 F. 3d at 1127 (Wood, J., dissenting).

Mandatory Student Fees Violate Students' Right to Free Speech

Pacific Legal Foundation

THE UNIVERSITY HAS NO CONSTITUTIONAL JUSTIFICATION TO COMPEL PAYMENT OF FEES TO PROMOTE STUDENT EXPRESSIVE ACTIVITIES

A. The University Has No Compelling Interest in Coercing Students to Subsidize Voluntary Organizations' Political and Ideological Activities

While a university may well have a compelling interest in *exposing* students to various conflicting viewpoints, it does not have a compelling interest in coercing *support* for those viewpoints.

> [T]he freedom to keep silent as well as to speak is grounded in something broader than a national fear of the state. It is equally the product of our view of personhood, which encompasses what the Supreme Court later referred to as "freedom of thought," "freedom of mind" and a "sphere of intellect and spirit." Were there no state at all, or were it inalterably benign, our conception of what it means to be human would still lead us to respect the individual autonomy of intellect and will enshrined in the First Amendment.[1]

By coercing support for political groups, the university sends a troubling message to students: If students want to advance a political position for which they cannot find support, the government will give them money to propagate their unpopular views. This is an illegitimate lesson for a public university to teach its students. The defendants in *Abood* and *Keller* understood that mandating support for an organization smothers, rather than stokes, contrary speech.[2] Moreover, the university, let alone the political groups themselves, does not create a free marketplace or forum for the expression of ideas. Rather it requires students to be the financial sponsors of someone else's speech. Indeed, the notion that a free marketplace of ideas can be created and encouraged by involuntary contributions is an oxymoron. The strength of an idea (*i.e.,* its acceptance in the marketplace) is best measured by how many people will volunteer to spread the idea or to help finance its propagation.

The university's position also implies that the First Amendment has only limited application within the confines of a public university campus. As the court below noted,

> far from *serving* the school's interest in education, forcing objecting students to fund objectionable organizations undermines that interest. In some courses students are likely taught the values of individualism and dissent. Yet despite the objecting students' dissent they must fund organizations promoting opposing views or they don't graduate.[3]

From the amicus curiae *brief filed by the Pacific Legal Foundation in support of the plaintiff, Scott Southworth, in the U.S. Supreme Court case of* Board of Regents, University of Wisconsin v. Scott Southworth *(1999), 24–27.*

If the university really wants students to learn practical civics lessons, it should encourage politically active groups to learn the art of fund-raising. In real political campaigns, opponents of the message do not give money to the cause.

B. A State University May Permit Voluntary Funding of Student Groups as a Less Intrusive Method of Promoting Such Groups on Campus

Universities are free to adopt any system of funding student activities that avoids constitutional defects. The best system, however, is the "positive check-off" voluntary system. Such a check-off could be designed in a number of ways. For example, it could list each recognized student group eligible for funding and permit students to choose which particular groups they wish to subsidize. Alternatively, it could simply provide a single box which, if checked, would mean that the student assents to funding all eligible student groups. By requiring students to designate affirmatively that they wish to fund particular groups, either individually or as a whole, the university advances several compelling goals. First, it requires thought on the part of the student, rather than mindless contributions to groups the student may not even be able to identify. Second, it encourages student groups to organize and articulate their messages clearly so as to attract as much financial support as possible.[4] Third, and most importantly, it sends a strong message to the entire student body that the university respects the constitutional rights of *all* students and has taken the strongest measures possible to protect those rights.[5]

Supporters of compelled funding have derided such a method, complaining that

> funding will soon devolve into a political *popularity* contest. Thus, in a setting where provocative ideas should receive the most support and encouragement, precisely the opposite will occur; student groups will be subject to an ideological referendum, and the most marginal groups will receive the least financial assistance. This is truly Orwellian.[6]

Justice Arabian's reasoning is backwards. What is Orwellian is a situation in which marginal groups are presented to the community as having support where there is none and presented as mainstream rather than extreme. Giving these ideas the cover of legitimacy and acceptability because of coerced subsidization from students who oppose the message perpetrates a great disservice. Students who wish to attract adherents to unconventional ideas must do so by convincing others of the soundness of their theories. Giving these unconventional thinkers the unwilling financial support of their dissenters grants them the means to speak more loudly than their actual support would permit.

CONCLUSION

The students in *West Virginia State Board of Education v. Barnette,* by being forced to salute the flag, were more than exposed to patriotism; they were forced to support it with a raised hand. Like them, the students at UW-Madison were not simply exposed to divergent views, they were forced to reach into their pockets to finance their opponents views. Ideas that could not win adherence through persuasion and reason were thus kept alive by the state by imposing fees on those who do not support the idea in question. The First Amendment was designed to prevent just such an exercise of state power.

Attempts by the government, whether through a public agency, a legislature, or a court, to force individuals to financially support political and ideological activities with which they disagree have been rejected from the time of Thomas Jefferson to the present. This Court has on numerous occasions protected the rights of teachers, attorneys, and nonunion agency shop fee payers to refrain from supporting speech which they oppose. Students are entitled to no less protection.

NOTES

1. *Carroll v. Blinken,* 957 F. 2d 991, 996 (2d Cir.) cert. denied, 506 U.S. 906 (1992).
2. Two previous cases in which the Supreme Court ruled that non-union teachers and members of a bar association did not have to support the political activities of their groups—*Editors. Abood v. Detroit Board of Education* 431 U.S. 209 (1977) and *Keller v. State Bar of California* 496 U.S. 1 (1990).
3. Southworth v. Grebe 151 F. 3d 728 (1998).
4. The groups benefit in another way: if they suffer a funding shortfall when their opponents are no longer forced to subsidize their activities, the groups will likely turn to their own members to make up the difference. A person who pays a membership fee to belong to one of these groups will have a more personal stake in the group's successful attainment of its objectives. Bevilacqua, *Public Universities, Mandatory Student Activity Fees, and the First Amendment,* 24 J.L. & Educ. 1, 29–30 (1995).
5. La Fetra, "Recent Developments in Mandatory Student Fee Cases," 10 J.L. & Pol. 579, 612–13 (1994).
6. *Smith v. Regents of the University of California,* 4 Cal. 4th 843, 881 (1993) (Arabian, J., dissenting).

Pornography

The two previous selections highlighted the difference of opinion over what we should be free to say. Similar disagreement exists over what we should be free to see, read, and hear, when the subject matter in question is "obscene" or "pornographic" in character.

In the first of the following essays, Ernest van den Haag is concerned with two basic questions: First, is pornographic material clearly definable so that it can be distinguished from other kinds of expression we would not want to suppress? Second, even if we can define it, is there any public interest to be served by prohibiting our citizens from having access to it? Van den Haag answers both questions in the affirmative.

Geoffrey Stone does not object to laws against child pornography nor to age and zoning restrictions limiting access to pornography in general. In contrast to van den Haag, however, he wholly opposes any attempt to limit the distribution of obscene material to consenting adults. In his judgment, a careful weighing of the costs and benefits associated with censorship clearly reveals that the individual incurs very great costs, while the society derives very little benefit.

Pornography and Censorship

Ernest van den Haag

Ultramoralists want to prohibit any display of nudity while ultralibertarians feel that even the most scabrously prurient display must be tolerated. However, most people are not that extreme. They are uneasy about obscene incitements to lechery; but uncertain about what to do about them. They wonder whether distaste, even when shared by a majority, is reason enough to prohibit what a minority evidently wants. Beyond distaste, is there enough actual harm in pornography? Where will suppression end, and how harmful might it be? Can we legally distinguish the valuable from the pornographic, the erotic from the obscene? Would courts have to act as art critics? Not least, we wonder about our own disapproval of obscenity. We are aware, however dimly, of some part of us which is attracted to it. We disapprove of our own attraction—but also worry whether we may be afraid or hypocritical when we suppress what attracts us as well as many others.

Still, most people want something done about pornography. As so often in our public life, we turn to the Constitution for a rule. "Congress" it tells us "shall make no law . . . abridging the freedom of speech or of the press." Although addressed to the federal government only, the First Amendment has been echoed in many state constitutions and applied to all states by the courts. Further, its scope has been broadened, perhaps unduly so, by court decisions which hold that all expressions rather than just words are protected by the First Amendment. Yet speech—words, spoken, or printed, or otherwise reproduced—is a narrow subclass of expression and the only one protected by the First Amendment. Music, painting, dance, uniforms, or flags—expressions but not words—are not.[1] The framers wanted to protect political and intellectual discourse—they thought free verbal interchange of ideas indispensable to consensual government. But obscenity hardly qualifies as an interchange of ideas, and is no more protected than music is. Whatever their merits, neither addresses the intellect, nor is indispensable to free government. For that matter words without cognitive content, words not used as vehicles for ideas—e.g., "dirty words" or expletives—may not be constitutionally protected. And even the constitutional right to unfettered verbal communication of ideas is limited by other rights and by the rights of others. Else there could be no libel or copyright laws and no restrictions on incitements to illicit or harmful action.

The Constitution, then, gives us the right to outlaw pornography. Should we exercise it? Is there a sufficient social interest in suppression? And how can we separate pornography from things we constitutionally cannot or do not want to suppress?

Some people feel that there can be no objective standard of obscenity: "Beauty is in the eye of the beholder—and so is obscenity," they argue. This notion is popular

Ernest van den Haag was John M. Olin Professor of Jurisprudence and Public Policy at Fordham University before joining the Heritage Foundation as distinguished scholar in 1981. From Ernest van den Haag, "Pornography and Censorship," Policy Review, *13 (Summer 1980), pp. 73–81. Reprinted with permission of* Policy Review. *Published by the Heritage Foundation.*

among pseudo-sophisticates; but it seems wildly exaggerated. Is the difference between your mother-in-law and the current Miss America merely in the eye of the beholder (yours)? How come everyone sees the difference you see? Is the distinction between pictures which focus on exposed human genitals or on sexual intercourse, and other pictures only in the eye of the beholder? To be sure, judgments of beauty, or of obscenity, do have subjective components—as most judgments do. But they are not altogether subjective. Why else do even my best friends not rate me a competitor to Apollo? For that matter judgments of art are not altogether subjective either. Museums persistently prefer Rembrandt's paintings to mine. Do they all have a subjective bias against me?

Pornography seems a reasonably objective matter which can be separated from other things. Laws, if drawn sensibly, might effectively prohibit its display or sale. An in-between zone between the obscene and the nonobscene may well remain, just as there is such a twilight zone between brightly lit and dark areas. But we still can tell which is which; and where necessary we can draw an arbitrary, but consistent (i.e., non-capricious), line. The law often draws such a line: to enable the courts to deal with them the law treats as discontinuous things that in nature may be continuous. The law quite often leaves things to the judgment of the courts: just how much spanking is cruelty to children? Just when does behavior become reckless?—courts always have to decide cases near the dividing line. But courts would have to decide only the few cases near the line which divides obscene from nonobscene matters. Most of the obscene stuff now displayed is not even near that line. With sensible laws it will no longer be displayed or offered for sale. The doubtful cases will be decided by juries applying prevailing standards. Such standards vary greatly over time and space, but at any given time, in any place, they are fairly definite and knowable. Lawyers who argue otherwise never appear in court, or for that matter in public places, without pants (or skirts, as the case may be). They seem to know what is contrary to the standards prevailing in the community in which they practice—however much they pretend otherwise.

A word on the current legal situation may not be amiss. The courts have not covered themselves with glory in clarifying the notion of obscenity. At present they regard the portrayal of sex acts, or of genitalia, or of excretion, as obscene if (a) patently offensive by contemporary community standards and if (b) taken as a whole[2] it appeals dominantly to a prurient (morbid or shameful) interest in sex and if (c) it lacks serious scientific, literary or artistic merit. The courts imply that not all appeals to sexual interest are wrong—only prurient ones are. They have not said directly which appeals are prurient. The courts might have been more explicit but they are not unintelligible.

An appeal to sexual interest need not be obscene per se; only attempts to arouse sexual interest by patently offensive, morbid, shameful means are. By contemporary standards a nude is not obscene. But an appeal to sexual interest is, when carried out by focusing on exposed genitalia, or on the explicit, detailed portrayal of sex acts. Detailed portrayals of excretion may be patently offensive too, but since they scarcely appeal to the sexual interest of most people they may pass under present law unless specifically listed as unlawful; so may portrayals of sexual relations with animals for the same reason—if the jury is as confused as the law is. The courts never quite made up their minds on the relative weight to be given to "offensive," to "prurient," and to "sexual." Thus intercourse with animals may be offensive to most people and prurient, i.e., morbid and shameful, but not necessarily sexual in its appeal to the average person. Therefore some exhibitors of such spectacles have been let off. But should the fact that some sexual acts are so disgusting to the majority as to extinguish any sexual appeal they might otherwise have legitimize these acts? Offensiveness, since in effect it is also a criterion for the prurience of a sexual appeal, is a decisive element of obscenity; yet the other two elements must be present.

If more clearly drawn laws would leave few doubtful cases for juries to decide, why do many literary, sociological, or psychological experts find it so hard to determine what is obscene? Why do they deny that such laws can be fashioned? Most people who protest that they cannot draw the line dividing the pornographic from the nonpornographic are deliberately unhelpful. "None so blind as they that won't see." They don't want to see because they oppose any pornography laws. They certainly have a right to oppose them. But this right does not entitle anyone to pretend that he cannot see what he does see. Critics who testify in court that they cannot distinguish pornography from literature, or that merely pornographic stuff has great literary or educational merit, usually know better. If they didn't they would have no business being critics or experts. To oppose pornography laws is one thing. It is quite another thing to attempt to sabotage them by testifying that hardcore stuff cannot be separated from literature or art, pornographic from aesthetic experience. Such testimony is either muddleheaded beyond belief or dishonest.

Once we have decided that the obscene is not inseparable from the nonobscene, we can address the real issue: are there compelling grounds for legally restraining public obscenity?

Some argue that pornography has no actual influence. This seems unpersuasive. Even before print had been invented Francesca blamed a book for her sin: "Galeotto fu il libro" (the book was the panderer) she told Dante in the *Divine Comedy*. Did she imagine the book's influence? Literature—from the Bible to Karl Marx or to Hitler's *Mein Kampf*—does influence people's attitudes and actions, as do all communications, words or pictures. That is why people write, or, for that matter, advertise. The influence of communications varies, depending on their own character, the character of the person exposed to them, and on many other circumstances. Some persons are much influenced by the Bible—or by pornography—others not. Nor is the direction of the influence, and the action to which it may lead altogether predictable in each case. But there is little doubt that for the average person the Bible fosters a religious disposition in some degree and pornography a lecherous one.

Granted that it has some influence, does pornography harm nonconsenting persons? Does it lead to crime? Almost anything—beer, books, poverty, wealth, or existentialism—can "lead" to crime in some cases. So can pornography. We cannot remove all possible causes of crime—even though we might remove those that can be removed without much difficulty or loss. But crime scarcely seems the major issue. We legally prohibit many things that do not lead to crime, such as polygamy, cocaine, or dueling. Many of these things can easily be avoided by those who do not wish to participate; others cannot be shown to be actually harmful to anyone. We prohibit whatever is *perceived* as socially harmful, even if merely contrary to our customs, as polygamy is.

When we prohibit cartels, or the sale of marijuana, when we impose specific taxes, or prohibit unlicensed taxis from taking fares, we believe our laws to be useful, or to prevent harm. That belief may be wrong. Perhaps the tax is actually harmful or unjust, perhaps we would all be better off without licensing any taxis, perhaps cartels are economically useful, perhaps marijuana smoking is harmless or beneficial. All that is needed to justify legislation is a rational social interest in accomplishing the goals of the legislation. Thus, an activity (such as marijuana smoking) can be prohibited because it is *perceived* to be socially harmful, or even merely distasteful. Pornography is. The harm it actually may do cannot be shown the way a man can be shown to be guilty of a crime. But such a demonstration of harm or guilt is not required for making laws—it is required only if someone is to be convicted of breaking them.

Still, unless we are convinced that pornography is harmful the whole exercise makes little sense. Wherein then is pornography harmful? The basic aim of pornographic communication is to arouse impersonal lust, by, in the words of Susan Sontag (incidentally a defender of pornography), driving "a wedge between one's existence as a full human being and one's sexual being . . . a healthy person prevents such a gap from opening up. . . ." A healthy society too must help "prevent such gaps from opening up," for, to be healthy, a society needs "full human beings," "healthy persons" who integrate their libidinal impulses with the rest of their personality, with love and with personal relationships.

We all have had pre-adolescent fantasies which ignore the burdens of reality, of commitment, concern, conflict, thought, consideration and love as they become heavier. In these fantasies others are mere objects, puppets for our pleasure, means to our gratification, not ends in themselves. The Marquis de Sade explored such fantasies most radically; but all pornographers cater to them: they invite us to treat others merely as means to our gratification. Sometimes they suggest that these others enjoy being so treated; sometimes they suggest, as the Marquis de Sade did, that pleasure lies in compelling unwilling others to suffer. Either way pornography invites us to reduce fellow humans to mere means. The cravings pornography appeals to—the craving for contextless, impersonal, anonymous, totally deindividualized, as it were abstract, sex—are not easy to control and are, therefore, felt as threats by many persons, threats to their own impulse-control and integration. The fear is real and enough sex crimes certainly occur . . . to give plausibility to it. People wish to suppress pornography, as they suppress within themselves impulses that they feel threaten them. Suppression may not be an ideal solution to the problem of anxiety arousing stimuli, external or internal. Ideally we should get rid of anxiety, and of unwelcome stimuli, by confrontation and sublimation. But we are not ideal and we do not live in an ideal world. Real as distinguished from ideal persons must avoid what threatens and upsets them. And real as distinguished from utopian societies must help them to do so.

However, there are stronger grounds for suppressing pornography. Unlike the 18th-century rationalists from whom the ultralibertarians descend, I do not believe that society is but an aggregation of individuals banded together for their mutual convenience. Although society does have utilitarian functions, it is held together by emotional bonds, prior to any rational calculations. Societies survive by feelings of identification and solidarity among the members, which lead them to make sacrifices for one another, to be considerate and to observe rules, even when they individually would gain by not doing so. In animal societies (e.g., among social insects) the members identify one another instinctively, for example, by smell. The identification leads them not to attack or eat one another and it makes possible many manifestations of solidarity. It makes the insect society possible. Human societies, too, would be impossible without such identification and solidarity among the members. Else we would treat one another as we now treat insects or chickens—or as the Nazis treated Jews. It is to preserve and strengthen traditional emotional bonds, and the symbols that stand for them, that the government of Israel prohibits the raising of pigs, that of India the slaughtering of cows.

Solidarity is as indispensable to the United States as it is to Israel. It is cultivated by institutions which help each of us to think of others not merely as means to his own gratification, but as ends in themselves. These institutions cultivate shared customs, expectations, traditions, values, ideals and symbols. The values we cultivate differ from those of an aboriginal tribe; and the range left to individual choice is broader. Social solidarity is less stringent than it is in most primitive tribes. But neither our society nor an aboriginal tribe could survive without shared values which make it possible for us to identify with one another.

One of our shared values is the linkage of sexual to individual affectional relations—to love and stability. As our society has developed, the affectional bonds associated with sexual love have become one of its main values. Indeed with the weakening of religious institutions these bonds have acquired steadily more importance. Love is worshiped in numerous forms. There is, to be sure, a gap between the reality and the ideal, just as there is a gap between the reality of patriotism—or nationalism—and the ideal. But it would be silly to deny that patriotism plays an important role in our society—or that love, affection, and compassion do.

Pornography tends to erode these bonds, indeed, all bonds. By inviting us to reduce others and ourselves to purely physical beings, by inviting each of us to regard the other only as a means to physical gratification, with sensations, but without emotions, with contacts but without relations, pornography not only degrades us (and incidentally reduces sex to a valueless mechanical exercise),[3] but also erodes all human solidarity and tends to destroy all affectional bonds. This is a good enough reason to outlaw it.

There are additional reasons. One is very simply that the majority has a right to protect its tradition. The minority is entitled to argue for change. But not to impose it. Our tradition has been that sexual acts, sexual organs, and excretion are private rather than public. The majority is entitled to preserve this tradition by law where necessary just as the majority in India, offended by the slaughtering of cows which is contrary to Hindu tradition, can (and does) prohibit it.

Nobody is forced to see the dirty movie or to buy the pornographic magazine. Why then should the minority not be allowed to have them? But a public matter—anything for sale—can never be a wholly private matter. And once it is around legally one cannot really avoid the impact of pornography. One cannot avoid the display and the advertising which affect and pollute the atmosphere even if one does not enter or buy. Nor is it enough to prohibit the movie marquee or the display of the magazine. Anything legally for sale is the more profitable the more customers it attracts. Hence the purveyors of pornography have a strong interest in advertising and in spreading it, in persuading and in tempting the public. Prohibitions of advertising will be circumvented as long as the sale of pornography is lawful. Moreover, if the viewer of the pornographic movie is not warned by the marquee that he is about to see a dirty movie, he might very likely complain that he has been trapped into something that upsets him without being warned.

I should not prohibit anyone from reading or seeing whatever he wishes in his own home. He may be ill advised. But interfering with his home habits surely would be more ill advised. Of course if the stuff is not legally available the pornography fan will have difficulty getting it. But society has no obligation to make it easy. On the contrary, we can and should prohibit the marketing, the public sale of what we perceive as harmful to society even if we do not wish to invade homes to punish those who consume it.

NOTES

1. The First Amendment right to peacefully assemble may protect whatever is part of, or required for, peaceful assembly. It is hard to see that either nudity or swastikas are needed for that purpose.
2. Thus a prurient passage does not make a magazine or a book offensive unless, taken as a whole, the magazine or book dominantly appeals to the prurient interest.
3. As feminists have pointed out, pornography often degrades females more directly than males. But, in reducing themselves to a mere craving for physical gratification males degrade themselves as well.

Repeating Past Mistakes
The Commission on Obscenity and Pornography

Geoffrey R. Stone

[In 1986] the Attorney General's Commission on Pornography had a unique opportunity to redirect society's regulation of obscene expression. The current state of the law is marred by overly broad, ineffective, and wasteful regulation. This was an appropriate opportunity to take a fresh look at the problem and to strike a new balance—a balance that more precisely accommodates society's interests in regulation with the individual's often competing interests in privacy, autonomy, and free expression. The commission squandered this opportunity. Instead of taking a fresh look, it blindly performed its appointed task of renewing and reaffirming past mistakes.

The United States Supreme Court has held that federal, state, and local government officials have the power, consonant with the First Amendment, to prohibit all distribution of obscene expression. The mere existence of power, however, does not mean that its exercise is sound. The commission should have recommended that government officials exercise restraint. Specifically, the commission should have recommended the repeal of laws that criminalize the distribution of obscene expression to consenting adults.

The Supreme Court itself is sharply divided over the constitutional power of government officials to prohibit the distribution of obscene expression to consenting adults. In its 1973 decisions in *Miller v. California* and *Paris Adult Theatre v. Slaton,* the Court divided five-to-four on this issue. Justices Douglas, Brennan, Stewart, and Marshall concluded that the First Amendment strips government officials of any power to deny consenting adults the right to obtain obscene expression.

Even apart from the division of opinion in these cases, the Court's analysis of obscene expression is anomalous in terms of its overall First Amendment jurisprudence. At one time, obscene expression was merely one of several categories of expression held by the Supreme Court to be "of such slight social value as a step to truth that any benefit that may be derived from them is clearly outweighed by the social interest in order and morality." In the past quarter-century, the Court has increasingly recognized that such previously unprotected categories of expression as profanity, commercial advertising, incitement, and libel can no longer be regarded as wholly unprotected by the First Amendment. The Court has held that, although such categories of expression have only a "subordinate position in the scale of First Amendment values," they can nonetheless be restricted only if government has at least a substantial justification for the restriction. The Court has thus recognized that even low-value expression may have some First Amendment value, that government efforts to restrict low-value expression will often chill more valuable expression, and that the constitutional and institutional risks of restricting low-value expression are worth taking only if the restriction furthers at least a substantial governmental interest.

Obscene expression now stands alone. No other category of expression is currently regarded as wholly outside the protection of the First Amendment. No other category of expression may be suppressed merely because it has only "slight social value." No other category of expression may be censored without a showing that the restriction serves at least a substantial governmental interest. The current analysis of obscene expression is thus the sole remaining artifact of a now discarded jurisprudence.

The current analysis of obscenity is not necessarily wrong as a matter of constitutional law. Nevertheless, the constitutional authority to act in this context hangs by the slender thread of a single vote and is very much in doubt as a matter of constitutional principle. In such circumstances, government must exercise special care in deciding whether and how to exercise its power. We should not simply assume that because it is constitutional to act it is wise to do so. The very closeness of the constitutional question is itself a compelling reason for caution.

In deciding on the appropriate regulation of obscene expression, we must consider both the costs and benefits of regulation. Laws prohibiting the distribution of obscene expression to consenting adults impose at least three types of costs. First, although the Court has held that such expression has only low First Amendment value, it may nonetheless serve a useful function both for society and the individual. That the demand for sexually explicit expression is as great as it is, suggests that such expression serves an important psychological or emotional function for many individuals. It may satisfy a need for fantasy, escape, entertainment, stimulation, or whatever. Thus, whether or not obscene expression has significant First Amendment value, it may have important value to the individual. Laws prohibiting its distribution to consenting adults may frustrate significant interests in individual privacy, dignity, autonomy, and self-fulfillment.

The suppression of obscene expression may also have a severe chilling effect on more valuable expression. The legal concept of obscenity is vague in the extreme. As a consequence, individuals who wish to purchase or distribute sexually explicit expression will invariably censor themselves in order to avoid being ensnared in the ill-defined net of our obscenity laws. Laws prohibiting the distribution of obscene expression spill over and significantly limit the distribution of constitutionally protected expression as well.

Any serious effort to enforce laws prohibiting the distribution of obscene expression to consenting adults necessarily draws valuable police and prosecutorial resources away from other areas of law enforcement. In a world of limited resources, we must recognize that the decision to criminalize one form of behavior renders more difficult and less effective the enforcement of laws directed at other forms of behavior. It is necessary to set priorities, for the failure to enforce our laws vigorously can serve only to generate disrespect for law enforcement and bring the legal system into disrepute.

Two interests are most commonly asserted in support of laws prohibiting the distribution of obscene expression to consenting adults. First, it is said that government must suppress the distribution of such expression to consenting adults in order to prevent the erosion of moral standards. The moral fabric of a society undoubtedly affects the tone and quality of life. It is thus a legitimate subject of government concern; but as

Justice Brennan recognized in his opinion in *Paris Adult Theatre,* "the State's interest in regulating morality by suppressing obscenity, while often asserted, remains essentially ill-focused and ill-defined." It rests ultimately on "unprovable . . . assumptions about human behavior, morality, sex, and religion." Perhaps more importantly, the notion that government may censor expression because it may alter accepted moral standards flies in the face of the guarantee of free expression. A democratic society must be free to determine its own moral standards through robust and wide-open debate and expression. Although government may legitimately inculcate moral values through education and related activities, it may not suppress expression that reflects or encourages an opposing morality. Such paternalism is incompatible with the most basic premises of the First Amendment.

Second, it is said that government must suppress the distribution of obscene expression to consenting adults because exposure to such expression may "cause" individuals to engage in unlawful conduct. The prevention of unlawful conduct is a legitimate governmental interest, but the correlation between exposure to obscene expression and unlawful conduct is doubtful, at best. As the President's Commission on Obscenity and Pornography found in 1970, there is "no evidence to date that exposure to explicit sexual materials plays a significant role in the causation of delinquent or criminal behavior." The Attorney General's Commission's contrary conclusion in 1986 is based more on preconception than on evidence. An issue that has long divided social scientists and other experts in the field can hardly be definitively resolved by a commission of nonexperts, most of whom were appointed because of their preexisting commitment to the suppression of obscene expression. In any event, even those who claim a connection between exposure to obscene expression and unlawful conduct claim no more than an indirect and attenuated "bad tendency." Thus, although some individuals may on some occasions commit some unlawful acts "because of" their exposure to obscene expression, the connection is indirect, speculative, and unpredictable. It is not even remotely comparable to the much more direct harm caused by such products as firearms, alcohol, and automobiles. The suppression of obscene expression is also a stunningly inefficient and overly broad way to deal with this problem, for even a modest change in law enforcement or sentencing practices would have a much more direct and substantial impact on the rate of unlawful conduct than the legalization or criminalization of obscene expression.

Laws prohibiting the distribution of obscene expression to consenting adults impose significant costs on society and frustrate potentially important privacy and autonomy interests of the individual for only marginal benefits. It is time to bring our regulation of such expression into line with our constitutional traditions, our law enforcement priorities, and our own self-interest and common sense.

The course I propose, and which the commission emphatically rejected, would leave government free to direct its enforcement energies at the more important concerns generated by obscene expression. These fall into three related categories: the protection of juveniles, the protection of captive viewers, and the regulation of the secondary effects of obscene expression. The Court has long recognized government's interest in sheltering children from exposure to obscene expression. What I propose does not undermine this interest. Nor does it interfere with society's substantial interest in restricting child pornography, which poses significantly different issues. My proposal would not in any way prevent government from protecting individuals against the shock effect of unwanted exposure to obscene expression. Government would remain free to prohibit children from viewing movies or buying books found "obscene," and it would remain free to prohibit or otherwise regulate the exhibition of obscene expression over the airwaves. Sensible accommodations can also be devised for other media, such as cable television. Also, my proposal would not prevent government from using zoning and other regulatory devices to control the distribution of obscene expression in order to prevent the decay of neighborhoods or other secondary effects associated with the availability of obscene expression.

By leaving consenting adults free to obtain obscene expression at their discretion, and by protecting our important interests through narrowly defined regulations, we can strike a sensible balance, protecting important societal interests while at the same time preserving our traditional respect for free expression and for the privacy and autonomy of the individual.

The commission has opted to do otherwise and repeat past mistakes—with a vengeance. It has recommended, among other things, significant changes in state and federal legislation to enable more vigorous enforcement of antiobscenity laws; creation of a special Obscenity Task Force in the office of the attorney general to coordinate the prosecution of obscenity cases at the national level; allocation of additional resources at the federal, state, and local levels for the prosecution of obscenity cases; "aggressive" Internal Revenue Service investigation of the "producers and distributors of obscene materials"; and imposition of "substantial periods of incarceration" for violators of antiobscenity laws. This draconian approach is wasteful, misguided, and inconsistent with the real concerns of most of our citizens.

16

CIVIL RIGHTS

Affirmative Action

*F*or more than three decades, the federal government and many state governments have pursued a policy of "affirmative action," which requires government agencies and many public and private groups to take positive steps to guarantee nondiscrimination and a fair share of jobs, contracts, and college admissions for racial minorities and women. The underlying assumption of these requirements has been that because racial minorities, particularly African Americans, have been historically discriminated against, special efforts must be made to correct past discriminatory policies and practices and to assure greater opportunities in the future.

In recent years, "affirmative action" has become a "hot-button" issue, often generating heated debate between proponents and opponents. The debate revolves around these fundamental questions: Should minorities and women, because of past discrimination, be given special consideration in employment, admission to colleges and universities, government contracts, and the like; or should race and gender be totally ignored, even if the result leads to a lack of diversity and opportunity in many fields?

The two selections in this chapter speak to these and other questions in the affirmative action debate. In the first article, Terry Eastland presents the case for ending affirmative action, arguing that government should never use race either "to confer or deny a benefit" in society. To do otherwise is to act at odds with the "best principles" of our nation, including the principle of equal protection of the law without regard to race, color, or gender. The response to Eastland is provided by Barbara R. Bergmann, who argues that the abandonment of affirmative action is neither warranted by present-day conditions nor contrary to historic principles, including principles of racial and cultural diversity and a fair and just society.

Ending Affirmative Action
The Case for Colorblind Justice

Terry Eastland

BY ANY OTHER NAME

When he joined the police department in Memphis, Tennessee, in 1975, Danny
O'Connor wanted someday to make sergeant. In 1988, he took a shot at it. Like the
other 209 officers competing for 75 promotions, O'Connor completed the written exam
and sat for his interview. When his scores on both parts were added to points awarded
for seniority and on-the-job performance over the past year, he placed fifty-sixth on the
Composite Scores List. The department had indicated that the 75 top-ranked officers on
this list would be the ones promoted. O'Connor knew his ranking and thought he had
realized his dream. But then affirmative action struck.

When the candidates took the written exam, they were required on the answer
sheets to indicate their race and sex. On the basis of this information, the department
created a second set of rankings—the Promotional Eligibility List. This new list, created to satisfy the department's affirmative action plan, modified the Composite Scores
List by bumping blacks up into every third position. Necessarily, whoever had been
there originally was bumped down. Some 26 blacks were on the eligibility list; 7 had
been on the composite list. So 19 blacks (originally ranked between 76 and 132) had
been bumped up the list—in some cases way up—and were promoted. Whites were
bumped down, and those who had been ranked in the lower regions of the composite
list were bumped below the 75th spot—and thus out of a promotion, Danny O'Connor,
who is white, was one of these.

Undaunted, O'Connor tried again the next year. The department proceeded much as
it had in 1988, using the same four-part process (though it changed the basis for award-
ing seniority points). Of 177 candidates, 94 would be promoted. They received their composite scores and on the basis of those scores were ranked. Affirmative action stepped in
again, however, as the department used race to rerank the candidates. Where 15 blacks
had made the top 94 on the composite list, 33 blacks were among the top 94 on the new
list. Eighteen blacks had been bumped up into the top 94 and 18 whites previously in the
top 94 had been bumped down. One of these was O'Connor, 75th on the original list.

Over the two years, while Danny O'Connor remained a patrol officer, 43 candidates with lower composite scores were bumped ahead of him and promoted to sergeant
in the name of affirmative action.

*Terry Eastland is former Director of Public Affairs in the U.S. Department of Justice
(1985–88) and currently publisher and president of* The American Spectator *magazine.
Excerpted from Terry Eastland,* Ending Affirmative Action: The Case of Colorblind Justice *(New York: Basic Books, 1997), pp. 1–20, 219–220. Notes have been renumbered
to correspond to edited text.*

Affirmative action was begun in the late 1960s to benefit blacks and over time has come to embrace certain other minority groups, as well as women (in the areas of employment and public contracting). There are, of course, forms of affirmative action that do not bump people out of an opportunity on account of race or sex. In employment, these forms of affirmative action can include outreach, recruitment, and training programs that are open to all, regardless of race or sex. But the affirmative action Danny O'Connor experienced is the kind that for years has been unsettling America. While it takes different guises and has different justifications, this type of affirmative action makes a virtue of race, ethnicity, and sex in order to determine who gets an opportunity and who does not. To call it by its proper name, it is discrimination.

Cheryl Hopwood had an experience like Danny O'Connor's. In 1992 she applied for admission to the University of Texas School of Law. She had earned a degree in accounting from California State University in 1988, achieving a 3.8 grade point average and scoring 39 (the highest score being 48) on the Law School Admissions Test (LSAT). She was, in addition, a certified public accountant. In the four years since finishing at Cal State, Hopwood had married and moved close to San Antonio, where her husband, an air force captain, was stationed. A Texas resident, she had just given birth to her first child when she applied for admission to the prestigious University of Texas law school.

Hopwood thought her credentials were excellent, but the law school turned her down. "The only thing I could think of," she says of her initial response to the news, "was that the class the school admitted must have been very, very good." Wanting to find out just how good, she discovered instead that because she is white she had not been able to compete with all other applicants for admission. Under the school's affirmative action plan, 15 percent of the approximately 500 seats in the class had been set aside for blacks and Mexican-Americans, who were admitted under academic standards different from—in fact, lower than—those for all other students. Hopwood's admissions score—a composite number based on her undergraduate grade point average and her LSAT score—was 199. Eleven resident Mexican-American applicants had scores this high or higher, and only one resident black had a score of 199. The school admitted all 12 of these applicants but not Hopwood, and then, in pursuit of its 15 percent affirmative action goal, admitted 84 additional resident Mexican-American and black applicants. Their scores were lower—in some cases substantially lower—than Hopwood's. Indeed, the school admitted every resident black with a score of 185 or higher. If Hopwood were black or Mexican American, she would have been admitted.

Hopwood's experience differs from O'Connor's only in terms of the opportunity she sought, an educational one. Like O'Connor, she was bumped down and out by affirmative action that bumped others below her up and in. "I can't change my race," she says.

Neither can Randy Pech. The owner of Adarand Constructors, Inc., in Colorado Springs, Colorado, Pech, who is white, submitted the low bid for the guardrail portion on a federal highway construction project. But the business went to Gonzales Construction Company, which submitted a higher bid but is Hispanic-owned. That happens to be a virtue in the eyes of the U.S. Department of Transportation, which enforces a law that "sets aside" a portion of federal construction funds for businesses owned by minorities and women. Pech says he competes with four other companies in Colorado that build guardrails. Two are owned by Hispanics. Two are owned by women. Set-aside laws, he says, work solely against him. "If I weren't here, they'd have no impact.". . .

Danny O'Connor, Cheryl Hopwood, [and] Randy Pech, decided to challenge in court the discrimination that goes by the name of affirmative action.[1] They are gallant foot soldiers in the fight against a policy that by allocating opportunity on the basis of race and sex is dividing and damaging the nation. The time has come for us to end it.

A BARGAIN WITH THE DEVIL

. . . The original purpose of affirmative action was to remedy the ill effects of past dis-crimination against blacks. "To get beyond racism," as Justice Harry Blackmun fa-mously put it in his opinion in the 1978 case *Regents of the University of California v. Bakke,* "we must first take account of race.[2] "Taking account of race" meant distin-guishing on the basis of race and treating blacks differently. In the old days, this would have looked like racial discrimination. But the first advocates of affirmative action as-sured us that affirmative action was well intentioned. Race could be regulated to good effect, we were told, and affirmative action would end soon enough, with the nation the better for it. As one of the early architects of affirmative action put it, "We are in con-trol of our own history."[3]

By the early 1970s, affirmative action was extended to cover additional minority groups and in some contexts women, and over the years its backers have offered addi-tional justifications, such as overcoming "underrepresentation" and achieving "diver-sity." But the nation has paid a steep price for departing from colorblind principle, for affirmative action has turned out to be a bargain with the devil. Not only has the policy worked discrimination against those it does not favor—a Danny O'Connor or a Cheryl Hopwood, for example—but it also has guaranteed the salience of race and ethnicity in the life of the nation, thus making it harder to overcome the very tendency the civil rights movement once condemned; that of regarding and judging people in terms of their racial and ethnic groups. . . .

By formally drawing racial and ethnic lines, affirmative action invites judgments about the abilities and achievements of those who are members of the targeted groups. One persistent judgment is that those who received a benefit through affirmative action could not have secured it on their own. In many cases, this happens to be true. Indeed, the whole point of many affirmative action programs is to help those who otherwise could not have landed the opportunity in open competition. The program Cheryl Hop-wood encountered at the Texas law school lowered the school's academic standards in order to admit blacks and Mexican Americans. The school also segregated the applica-tions of blacks and Mexican Americans, assigning them to a separate admissions com-mittee while a different committee reviewed the merits of the "white and other" appli-cants. Thus treated differently, the members of the two minority groups competed only among themselves. Had they competed among all applicants under the same standards, many fewer blacks and Mexican Americans would have gained admission to the Texas law school.

This is not, however, the whole story. The black and Mexican-American applicants admitted under affirmative action were not *un*qualified to study law; their academic qualifications were good enough to win admission under nonaffirmative action standards at fully two-thirds of the nation's law schools.[4] Affirmative action thus stigmatizes beneficiaries who could succeed—and be seen to succeed—without it. At the same time, it stigmatizes those eligible for it who are not its beneficiaries. At the Texas law school, one Hispanic student who had a composite score good enough to warrant admission under the standards applicable to "whites and others" said that he felt he needed a shirt indicating he got in on his own, just to let people know the genuine nature of his accomplishment.[5] It is sadly ironic that affirmative action can put a non–affirmative action minority student in this situation, but the student's response is hardly irrational. He knows that the mere existence of the law school's program invites people to think, in his case: "You're Hispanic, so you got in through affirmative action."

An abiding truth about much affirmative action is that those who are its ostensible beneficiaries are burdened with the task of overcoming it—if, that is, they wish to be treated as individuals, without regard to race. It is possible, of course, for someone extended an opportunity through affirmative action to overcome it by doing extraordinarily well, meeting the highest standards. But some minorities have concluded that the best way to escape the public implications of affirmative action is to say "no" when they know it is being offered. In 1983, Freddie Hernandez, a Hispanic who serves in the Miami fire department, rejected an affirmative action promotion to lieutenant. Instead, he waited three years until he had the necessary seniority and had scored high enough to qualify for the promotion under procedures that applied to nonminorities. This decision cost Hernandez $4,500 a year in extra pay and forced him to study 900 additional hours to attain the required test results. But, as he proudly told the *Wall Street Journal,* "I knew I could make it on my own."[6]

Hernandez rejected the affirmative action bargain. He wanted to be judged as an individual, on his own merits, without regard to his ethnic background—just the way the old civil rights pioneers said he had a right to be judged.

THE LANGUAGE OF AFFIRMATIVE ACTION

Affirmative action has taken a toll on public discourse. Through the years its supporters have said, for example, that they do not support quotas. But . . . there was a reason police officer Danny O'Connor was bumped down and out of a promotion. There was a reason black officers were bumped up into every third position. The Memphis police department was trying to fill a quota that reserved one-third of the promotions for blacks. Bumping blacks up into every third position on the list of 75 may have been a crude way of making the quota, but it got the job done. Faced with evidence of a quota, supporters of affirmative action backtrack, saying that they are against "hard and fast" or "rigid" quotas and for "flexible" goals. The distinction in practice may mean that a slightly lesser number of the preferred minority group or women is hired or admitted. This happened at the University of Texas School of Law, which in 1992 fell a bit short of its 15 percent goal for black and Mexican-American admittees. But whatever term is used to describe what the law school was doing, race was determining the bulk of these admissions decisions.

Affirmative action supporters may concede that race is the determining factor but insist that the practice benefits only qualified people. Yet what matters to those competing for a limited number of openings or opportunities is not whether they are qualified in the abstract, but whether they are *more* qualified than the others seeking that position. The rankings Danny O'Connor earned showed that he was more qualified than officers bumped above him and promoted to sergeant on account of race. And Cheryl Hopwood's composite score showed she was more qualified than many of those with lower scores who were admitted under the Texas law school's affirmative action plan. Some supporters of affirmative action respond by claiming that differences in qualifications—above a certain minimum—are negligible. They will not say, however, that differences in qualifications are unimportant in the case of those who are *not* eligible for affirmative action. And judgments about who is better are routinely made by all of us when we seek the services of, say, a doctor or lawyer. Not surprisingly, though most unfortunately, some affirmative action programs have dispensed with even minimal qualifications. In 1993, in an effort to increase the "diversity" of its workforce, the U.S. Forest Service's Pacific Southwest Region established "upward mobility positions" that it set aside for applicants who do not meet the service's usual employment requirements. The dictionary of affirmative action does not appear to include words like "excellence" and "outstanding" and "best.". . .

THE MYTH OF "TEMPORARY" AFFIRMATIVE ACTION

In the late 1960s and during the 1970s, advocates of affirmative action often said that it was only a temporary measure whose success would render it unnecessary in the future. But these temporary measures often seem to go on and on and on—well beyond the point at which they were supposed to end.

Let us return to Danny O'Connor's story. It actually began back in 1974, when the Justice Department sued the city of Memphis under Title VII of the Civil Rights Act of 1964, alleging that it had engaged in unlawful employment discrimination against blacks and women. Quickly, the city and the federal government settled the suit through a consent decree that won federal court approval. Other lawsuits followed: black police officers sued the city in 1975, charging racially discriminatory promotion practices, and a black firefighter filed a similar suit in 1977. Judicially approved consent decrees also concluded these cases. And then, in 1981, the city and the federal government amended their 1974 agreement. Though the city never admitted to past discrimination, it did agree to hire and promote blacks and females in proportions, as the 1981 decree put it, "approximating their respective proportions in the relevant Shelby County civilian labor force."

Now, we may regard the lawsuits of the 1970s as necessary in forcing change upon an Old South city. And for the sake of argument, let us concede that proportional hiring and promoting were needed to effect change in the 1970s and early 1980s. But having achieved proportional representation in the fire and police workforces by the mid-

1980s, the city did not end its attachment to proportionalism, as Danny O'Connor's case shows. City officials claim that the 1981 decree tied their hands, but it did not *require* race-based employment decisions. In fact, the decree provided that the city was not ob-ligated to hire or promote a less-qualified person over a better-qualified person. The in-convenient truth appears to be that proportional hiring and promoting proved adminis-tratively a lot easier for the city than trying to treat applicants and employees fairly without regard to race. In 1994, a federal appeals court rejected the city's motion to dis-miss the complaint brought by Danny O'Connor and other white employees. In its opin-ion the court expressed concern that the city "has made no effort to limit the duration of the [race-based promotional] remedies."[7]

The federal executive branch has made no effort in this regard, either. The 1981 consent decree governing the city of Memphis could have been dissolved by agreement of the parties as early as March 1984, but the Justice Department under Ronald Reagan did not ask the city to end its hiring and promotional remedies. Nor, for that matter, did the Justice Department under George Bush. And when the city found itself in 1994 in the court of appeals trying to fend off Danny O'Connor's lawsuit, the Justice Depart-ment under Bill Clinton filed a brief in support of the city's never-ending affirmative action. . . .

THE CHOICE

Failing to make good on its promise to be only temporary, affirmative action has en-trenched itself more deeply in our institutions, attracting political constituencies that de-mand its retention. Surveys of public opinion show, however, that preferences have never enjoyed the majority support of the American people. Moreover, the substantial immigration the nation has experienced since, coincidentally, the advent of affirmative action is rendering the policy increasingly incoherent.

Roughly three-quarters of those who come to the United States each year are of a race or ethnic background that makes them eligible for affirmative action, and most af-firmative action programs are indifferent as to whether their beneficiaries are U.S. citi-zens or not, or whether, if they are U.S. citizens, they recently arrived here or not. We thus have a policy originally designed to remedy the ill effects of past discrimination that is open to immigrants with no past in the United States during which they could have experienced discrimination. . . .

. . . [I]mmigration since the late 1960s has swollen the ranks of Hispanics and Asians, making them, combined, more numerous than blacks. As a result, we now face the prospect (especially in our largest cities, where the Hispanic and Asian populations are most concentrated) of increasing conflict among affirmative action groups.

Los Angeles, a city being dramatically reshaped by Hispanic immigration, is a case in point. In 1988 the Los Angeles County Office of Affirmative Action Compliance is-sued a report showing that while Hispanics made up 27.6 percent of the county popu-lation and held 18.3 percent of county jobs, blacks constituted 12.6 percent of the pop-ulation and 30 percent of the workforce. The county board of supervisors accepted the affirmative action office's recommendation to hire minorities in accordance with a scheme of "population parity."[8] This meant members of the "underrepresented" group, that is, Hispanics—would be preferred over those belonging to the "overrepresented" group—blacks. Black county employees quickly protested, declaring their opposition to preferential treatment based on race and ethnicity. Over the years the struggle has continued, and now the county is thinking about dropping population parity in favor of an affirmative action approach that would result in fewer preferences for Hispanics, whose portion of the county population has risen to 38 percent. To prevent this change, Hispanic county employees have filed a lawsuit.[9]

The impact of immigration is another reason to reevaluate affirmative action. We can choose to stick with the status quo, perhaps mending it a bit here and there, or we can end affirmative action once and for all. The choice was clarified politically in the months following the 1994 midterm elections in which the Republicans, for the first time in 40 years, captured both houses of Congress. Though the campaign was not explicitly about affirmative action, the election results necessarily altered the nation's political agenda, pushing it in a more conservative direction. . . . [T]he new Congress voted to terminate a 17-year-old program under which corporations selling their broadcast outlets at a discounted price to minorities may defer sales taxes indefinitely. President Clinton, sensing the shift in political sentiment, signed the bill into law. Senator Robert Dole, preparing to draft legislation on affirmative action, asked the Congressional Research Service (CRS) to supply him with a list of programs containing preferences for minorities or women, whereupon President Clinton ordered his own review of government programs. Both branches of government had a lot to digest—the CRS reported to Dole more than 160 federal programs that might be construed as requiring or authorizing or encouraging preferences.

And then on June 12, 1995, the Supreme Court handed down its decision in the case involving Randy Pech. In *Adarand Constructors v. Pena,* the Court held that federal affirmative action programs must be held to a standard of "strict scrutiny," the most demanding level of justification, whose application routinely has led to the invalidation of governmental measures that classify on the basis of race and ethnicity.[10] Sending Randy Pech's case back to the lower courts for review under the tougher standard, the Court signaled that preferential treatment deserves not only strict judicial scrutiny but also strict political scrutiny, since the very idea that government should distinguish on the basis of race to confer or deny a benefit is at odds with our best principles as a nation. No fewer than four times did Justice Sandra Day O'Connor, who wrote the Court's opinion, refer to the luminous passage in the 1943 *Hirabayashi* decision: "Distinctions between citizens solely because of their ancestry are by their very nature odious to a free people whose institutions are founded upon the doctrine of equality." O'Connor emphasized that the Constitution protects *"persons,* not *groups,"* and that "all governmental action based on race" is a *"group* classification" that should be examined to make sure that "personal" rights have been protected.

Affirmative action broke with the colorblind tradition, one acknowledged in the Japanese Relocation Cases. Indeed, this tradition stretches back to the American founding. In making the choice before us about the future of affirmative action, it is imperative that we as a nation return to the place from which we began, and understand afresh the compelling and true case for colorblind justice.

NOTES

Note: Quotes besides those cited in the text itself or in the following endnotes are from interviews with the author.

1. In December 1995, all . . . cases were still in litigation.
2. 438 U.S. 265 (1978).
3. Alfred W. Blumrosen, *Black Employment and the Law* (New Brunswick, N.J.: Rutgers University Press, 1971), p. viii.
4. Lino A. Graglia, "*Hopwood v. Texas:* Racial Preferences in Higher Education Upheld and Endorsed," *Journal of Legal Education* 45, no. 1 (March 1995): 82.
5. "Suit Against U. of Texas Challenges Law School's Affirmative-Action Effort." *Chronicle of Higher Education,* February 9, 1994. Hopwood and three other applicants rejected by the law school filed the lawsuit. . . .
6. Sonia L. Nazario, "Many Minorities Feel Torn by Experience of Affirmative Action," *Wall Street Journal,* June 27, 1989.
7. *Aiken v. City of Memphis,* 37 F. 3d. 1155 (6th Cir. 1994).
8. Peter Skerry, "Borders and Quotas: Immigration and the Affirmative-Action State," *The Public Interest,* no. 96 (summer 1989): 93.
9. Jonathan Tilove, "Affirmative Action Has Drawbacks for Blacks," *Cleveland Plain Dealer;* July 20, 1995.
10. 115 S. Ct. 2097 (1995). . . .

In Defense of Affirmative Action

Barbara R. Bergmann

IS DISCRIMINATION A THING OF THE PAST?

Pollsters surveying people about their attitudes toward affirmative action frequently ask, "Do you think blacks or women should receive preference in hiring and promotion to make up for past discrimination?" This wording encourages respondents to assume that discrimination has ended and is no longer an important problem. Respondents to one such poll, when asked to comment on their answers, spoke of discrimination that had occurred "100 years ago" and said that such ancient history did not justify "preferences" in the present.[1]

As we shall see . . . there are good reasons to believe that discrimination by race and sex is not a thing of the past. Those under the impression that discrimination ended a long time ago are simply mistaken. However, they are right about one thing: our need for affirmative action depends not on what happened 100 years ago but on the situation in the labor market today. . . .

THE EVIDENCE ON WAGES

In judging the conflicting claims about the state of the labor market, it is useful to start by looking at how much change has actually occurred. Chart 1 shows the weekly wages of those who worked full-time in the years 1967–95, corrected to eliminate the effect of inflation.[2] The inflation-corrected wages of white men have been on a downtrend since the mid-1970s. However, white men have not lost their superior position in the labor market: a substantial gap remains between their wages and those of white women and black men and women. Given the slowness of change in the labor market, as shown in Chart 1, that gap will not close anytime soon.

Modest reductions have been made in that gap since 1967. Black men's wages were 69 percent of white men's in 1967. By 1976 their wages had risen to 79 percent of white men's. Since then, they have been losing rather than gaining ground on white men. The loss of manufacturing jobs, some of them unionized and thus relatively well-paying, has hit both white and black men, but the latter have been particularly hard hit.[3] White women gained no ground on white men until the early 1980s; they have been gaining in the years since. In 1995 their wages were 73 percent of white men's, compared with 61 percent in 1967. Black women have made gains throughout the

Barbara R. Bergmann is Distinguished Professor of Economics, American University, Washington, D.C. Excerpted from Barbara R. Bergmann, In Defense of Affirmative Action *(New York: Basic Books, 1996), pp. 32–33, 36–38, 48–52, 78–81, 84–85, 94–96, 102–105, 126–130, 183–184, 186–187, 190–191. Notes have been renumbered to correspond to edited text.*

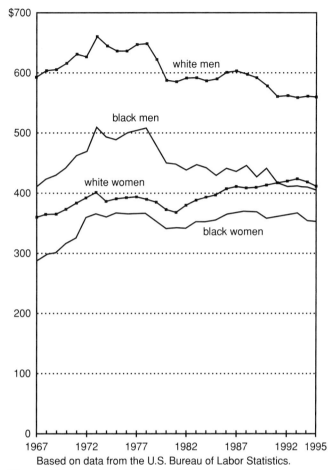

Based on data from the U.S. Bureau of Labor Statistics.

Chart 1 Weekly Wages by Sex and Race in 1995 Dollars

period, but recently their gains have not matched those of white women. In 1995, black women's wages were 63 percent of white men's.

The fall in black men's wages relative to white men's over the last twenty years suggests that whatever help they have received from affirmative action has been modest at best, and has not been enough to counterbalance the effects of their buffeting from market forces. The globalization of the labor market has reduced the demand by U.S. employers for the labor of the less skilled—both black and white—and black men have suffered disproportionately. While affirmative action has allowed some college-educated black men to enter the middle class, the deterioration of the labor market for non-college-educated black men has been disastrous. It has made their lives increasingly precarious; their decreased chances for decently paid work have contributed to the fall in the black marriage rate, the increase in single parenthood, and the recruitment of black men into crime and the drug trade in the inner city. . . .

THE EVIDENCE FROM LAWSUITS

Lucky Stores, Inc., a West Coast grocery chain, agreed in 1993 to pay nearly $75 million in damages to women who had been denied promotion opportunities and another $20 million to set up and run affirmative action programs.[4] The women had been denied full-time slots, and the relatively small group of women in management jobs had been segregated into certain departments (bakery and delicatessen) marked off as dead end. The managers of these departments received lower pay than other managers. One of the women whose complaint sparked the suit had worked at the cash register for 21 years. When her teenage son came to Lucky and worked beside her, he was offered training opportunities that had been denied to her. Suits alleging similar employment practices have been filed against Safeway Stores and several other grocery chains.

The facts of the Lucky Stores case were strikingly similar to the facts in a 1972 suit against Giant Foods, a Washington, D.C.-area grocery chain. That suit was settled, with the company under order until the late 1980s to remedy the problems. However, a 1994 telephone survey to ascertain the sex of managers by department revealed that in the 20 years since the suit, very little integration of managerial positions had been accomplished.[5] Meat cutting, a skilled trade requiring apprenticeship, had been maintained as an all-male specialty. Bakery managers, still overwhelmingly female, continued to receive lower salaries than other department managers, almost all male. The cost of remedying the bakery managers' relatively low pay would have amounted to a few dollars an hour per store; the fact that their pay had not been increased raises questions about the symbolic significance of low pay to those in control. Giant's history illustrates the stubbornness of discrimination problems and the difficulty of fixing them when management is indifferent or opposed to change. A successful lawsuit may give the particular complainants some recompense but leave the underlying situation unchanged. The supermarket cases also show the complicity of some unions in maintaining segregation by sex and women's lower pay.

A recent claim of racial discrimination against the Shoney restaurant chain listed 211 Shoney officials against whom there was direct evidence of discriminatory behavior. Employment applications were color-coded by race, Blacks were tracked to kitchen jobs so that all employees in the dining area would be white. The case began when two white managers complained that they had been pressured by their supervisors to limit the number of black employees, and that they had been terminated when they resisted the pressure. The case was settled out of court for $65 million. Kerry Scanlon, an attorney for the black plaintiffs, said, "This was going on while the Bush Administration and others were telling the country that in the area of civil rights, the major problem was quotas and unfair protection for blacks. The quota that African Americans are most familiar with in employment is zero.[6]

EVIDENCE BASED ON "TESTING" THE JOB MARKET

So far, in reviewing the labor market situation for women and blacks, we have been looking at their treatment on the job, that is, where they are placed and what they are paid. We need also to look at their ability to land jobs. An important aspect of the labor market disadvantage suffered by African Americans is their high unemployment rate. People are counted as "unemployed" in government statistics only if they are actively looking for work. In good times and bad, unemployment rates for African Americans are twice as high as those for whites. The problem is particularly acute for 18- to 19-year-old black people, who suffer unemployment rates above 30 percent.[7] When they leave school, it is very hard for them to find jobs, and when they lose a job, they are typically in for a long spell of unemployment before landing the next one.

The results of a recent research project reveal the extent of discrimination against young black men in hiring and give an insight into the connection between that discrimination and their high rate of unemployment.[8] The Urban Institute assembled pairs of young men to serve as "testers." In each pair, one tester was black, the other white. Entry-level job openings were chosen at random from the newspaper, and a pair of testers was assigned to apply for each opening.

The researchers made the pairs of testers as similar as possible, except with regard to race. Testers were matched in physical size and in the education and experience they claimed to have. An attempt was also made to match each pair in openness, energy level, and articulateness. The testers were actually college students, but most of them posed as recent high school graduates and were supplied with fictional biographies that gave them similar job experience. They were put through mock interviews and coached to act like the person they were paired with to the greatest possible extent. The testers were then sent to apply for low-skill, entry-level jobs usually filled by young high-school graduates in manufacturing, hotels, restaurants, retail sales, and office work. The job titles ranged from general laborer to management trainee. The testers were instructed to refuse any job offered them so that the other member of the pair could have a chance at it.

The black testers posing as job seekers were carefully coached to present qualifications apparently equal to those of their white counterparts. In reality they were all, black and white, excellently qualified for the jobs they applied for. The Urban Institute researchers found that the young white men were offered jobs 45 percent more than the young black men. This result clearly reveals that some employers were not treating male minority job seekers equally with white males of similar qualifications.

The same researchers paired white Anglo testers and Hispanic testers who were fluent in English.[9] Again, the pairs of young men were matched to minimize the differences between them; the only apparent differences were the slight accents, somewhat darker complexions, and Spanish names of the Hispanic testers. The Anglos received 52 percent more job offers than the Hispanics.

THE DIFFICULTY OF CHANGING HIRING HABITS

Patterns of occupational segregation by race and sex tend to persist in part because people have good reason to be cautious in making hiring and promotion decisions. These decisions are the most crucial to any organization's success. A bad mistake in hiring or promotion can result in large monetary losses and a lot of misery. When an unsuitable person has been chosen for a job, there may be painful weeks or months during which work is botched, tempers flare, feelings are bruised, and customers are alienated. Employers have an understandable tendency to move cautiously and to continue doing what has worked well previously. Hiring candidates of a different race or sex is likely to be seen as risky, as asking for trouble. . . .

If the people involved in the selection process want to do nothing more than select the candidate who will perform the best, regardless of sex, race, or ethnicity, they are not likely to select a candidate of a nontraditional race or gender, even if very promising candidates of this kind are available. People use minimal clues of manner and appearance and way of talking to make snap judgments about candidates of a familiar type. A white person who has little experience with the performance of blacks on the job may not feel capable of making good judgments about their abilities based on such clues, and he or she may find it safer to stick with candidates of a familiar kind.

One way employers stick with the kinds of workers they are used to is by filling their vacancies with people recommended by those already working there in the kind of job they are filling. There is a considerable incentive for employers to fill jobs this way, and the practice is apparently widespread.[10] It saves recruiting expenses and may make for congenial work groups. A worker who recommends someone vouches for that person as someone likely to do well. Unfortunately, this seemingly innocent recruiting practice makes it particularly hard for African Americans to improve their status. Relying on employee recommendations effectively excludes from good jobs those who do not have relatives and friends with good jobs.

Women candidates may be particularly disadvantaged by sexual conventions. A woman who wears a standard amount of makeup and jewelry may be judged to be unbusinesslike, since the standard businessperson—a man—wears none. On the other hand, a woman who wears less than the standard amount of makeup and jewelry risks being considered not feminine enough to be a normal woman and is therefore judged to be peculiar. People making hiring decisions tend to shy away from people who seem peculiar.

PROBLEMS OF ACCEPTANCE BY COWORKERS

Production on the job has its social aspects. Each worker has to learn from and teach others, engage in cooperative endeavors, transmit and receive information, help provide a friendly environment, cover occasionally for another's mistakes, and at least appear to be amused by the jokes that go around. The people doing the hiring customarily consider not only a candidate's technical abilities and general pleasantness but also the chances of the candidate being accepted by coworkers so that they will interact well. . . .

Some of the hostility to the worker of untraditional race or sex may be motivated by self-defense. Men know that jobs in which white males predominate tend to be compensated with high status and pay; feeling those benefits threatened, they may not welcome a coworker who dilutes the maleness or whiteness of their job. They may fear that future vacancies will be filled with lower-status people or that they will have to leave the occupation or risk being trapped in a devalued job. As a result of such worries, there may be difficulties in convincing the old hands to introduce the newcomer of untraditional race or gender to the tricks of the trade.

Donald Tomaskovic-Devey reports an instance of this problem:

> A pilot told me a story about the first woman pilot at the busy corporate airport where he worked. The other pilots knew from the start that she would not be able to cut it. To give her a "fair" chance to prove herself, they had decided not to show her the ropes, to allow her to figure out on her own the controls on planes she had not flown before, and not to introduce her to the control tower and maintenance staffs, although this information was routinely shared with new male pilots. After all, they knew from the start that a woman could not be a pilot. Of course, what they knew did not matter; it was what they did that was decisive. By refusing to share their knowledge, they insured her failure. . . .[11]

GOALS AS ENERGIZING DEVICES

When critics of affirmative action say that goals are the same as quotas, and that quotas are bad, they presumably are saying, "Get rid of discrimination if there is any; give everyone a fair chance. But make sure you don't measure success or failure in numbers. If you do, you may be tempted to do some unfair and stupid things to make the numbers look good." The problem is that the directive "Be fair from now on" is far less energizing, and far more easily evaded, than "There are some good black people out there. Have one of them aboard by a month from next Thursday, or at least show that you've tried." Recruitment methods are highly resistant to change. And as our review of labor market realities has shown, there are many workplaces where these methods need changing if we are to make significant progress toward fairness.

The use of numerical goals to spur managers into action and to direct their behavior has been useful in all aspects of modern management; indeed, its use in affirmative action follows from its success in other areas. Modern businesses use numerical goals to manage production, productivity, sales, investments, and costs. The announcement of goals helps to specify explicit standards for performance of managers. In the absence of numerical goals and timetables for meeting them, it is difficult to determine whether managers have done a good job or to hold anyone responsible for failures. When people know they will not be held responsible, they are less likely to make significant efforts. . . .

If we were to establish goals for both sexes and for each of the ethnic groups represented in the United States, the labor market would become a balkanized nightmare: each slot would be earmarked for a person of a particular extraction and gender. Moreover, an expansion of the share of the population for whom goals are set might have an adverse impact on groups for which no goals are set, groups that contain relatively large numbers of high achievers—Jews and Asians, for example. A severe shrinking of the proportion of the population not included in affirmative action goals might reduce tolerance of the high success rates of such groups. In short, there are good reasons to have fewer goals rather than more. Establishing goals for a particular group should not be done without substantial reason. There is no sign that we are tending in the direction of an overproliferation of groups covered by affirmative action goals.

Common sense suggests that employment goals should be set for a group only if all of the following conditions are met:

1. The group is seriously underrepresented in an occupation or at a hierarchical level in the workplace.
2. The underrepresentation continues because of present discrimination, or because of current employer practices or habits that effectively exclude members of the group.
3. The pattern of exclusion is unlikely to change in the absence of special efforts.

For jobs in which discriminated-against groups are overrepresented, goals should be set for integrating whites and males into them. This effort will fail if the salaries for such jobs are significantly lower than what white males with the required skills can earn in other jobs. Nor will it be possible to recruit white males into jobs that have obviously been set up as dead ends, jobs whose duties are overly repetitive, or jobs over which the supervision is more rigid than white males of that skill level are used to. Integrating the all-female jobs with males, or the all-black jobs with whites, will force employers to re-think wage levels and working conditions—to the benefit of those members of disadvantaged groups who stay in traditionally sex- or race-specific occupations.

Different areas of the country, occupations, industries, and hierarchical levels call for different sets of goals. The evidence suggests that goals are needed almost everywhere for black men and women and white women, and in many places for Hispanics of both sexes. The Civil Rights Act would forbid discrimination against people of Hungarian extraction on account of their origin. However, if there is no reason to think that Hungarians are being excluded, we should not have goals for them.

Consider, however, the situation of a New England law firm that employs 40 lawyers and has no partners or associates of Irish or Jewish extraction. There are many people of Irish extraction in New England, and a considerable number of Jews as well. In the past these groups were commonly denied access to jobs reserved for upper-crust males of British extraction. Many lawyers of Irish and Jewish extraction now have elite legal credentials, and if a firm of that size has no such lawyers on its staff, it is likely that some aspects of the recruitment process are keeping them from being hired. Our guidelines suggest that having a goal for hiring lawyers of Irish and Jewish ancestry would be desirable for this firm. On the other hand, in other parts of the country, and in some occupations in which being of Irish or Jewish ancestry has not recently been a substantial disadvantage, goals for such people, even when they are underrepresented, would be unnecessary and undesirable. . . .

THE FUZZINESS OF MERIT

We frequently think and act as though there were only one correct way to define merit, one right and infallibly accurate way to measure it, and one right way to use measurements of merit in making hiring or school admission decisions. We also tend to assume that these obviously right ways are everywhere in current use. They are not, of course.

The rankings of candidates as to merit will depend on which of the candidates' characteristics are taken into consideration, how much weight is given to each characteristic, and how the judging is done—formally, objectively, and consistently for all candidates, or informally and inconsistently. Faye Crosby's research . . . shows that people do unconsciously give more weight to the good points of the person they consider appropriate for the job (for instance, a white man for a management job) and tend to ignore the good points of a person they think is less appropriate.

In thinking about affirmative action erroneous assumptions are frequently made:

1. That for each job opening there is one person who is unambiguously the best among the candidates.
2. That the identity of that candidate is unerringly revealed by the employer's selection process.
3. That the evaluation process is uninfluenced by the sex, race, ethnicity, age, or disability status of the candidates.
4. That the "best" candidate is head and shoulders above all the others, so that the substitution of the one judged third- or fourth-best instead of the one judged best would make a great difference to productivity.

These assumptions are unrealistic in many, even most cases. The American Society for Personnel Administration, in a brief supporting affirmative action in a case before the Supreme Court, said:

> It is a standard tenet of personnel administration that there is rarely a single, "best qualified" person for a job. An effective personnel system will bring before the selecting official several fully-qualified candidates who each may possess different attributes which recommend them for selection. Especially where the job is an unexceptional, middle-level craft position, without the need for unique work experience or educational attainment and for which several well-qualified candidates are available, final determinations as to which candidate is "best qualified" are at best subjective.[12] . . .

Measurements of merit for a job or for school admission, then, are dependent on the methods used and subject to error and subversion; moreover, they may not differentiate among candidates with any great accuracy. A process of assessing merit that cuts out all but white males may mask purposeful discrimination or set up hurdles that female and black candidates, for no job-related reason, have particular difficulty in getting over. An interviewer whose method of measuring congeniality is to chat with candidates about golf is not going to be giving very many black or female candidates high grades for that quality. . . .

THE ILLUSION THAT BLACKS ALWAYS WIN

In their talk of fairness, the foes of affirmative action focus on two individuals—a black person and a white person—competing for a job. The black person in their story is poorly qualified for the job. The white person is highly qualified, has worked very hard to get himself qualified, and is innocent of any wrongdoing toward this black person or any other. Most likely, the white person is from a poor family and the black person grew up in comfortable circumstances. Affirmative action, its foes would have you believe, has turned the labor market into a succession of contests between pairs of individuals like these. In each contest, the undeserving black person is declared the winner and gets 100 percent of the prize, while the deserving white person is left with nothing. With this perennial outcome, the situation has become pretty hopeless if you are a white man. With white males depicted as losing in each of these matchups, one may get the impression that the white male group has suffered severely from affirmative action.

The evidence of how the labor market "contests" actually come out—who is getting seats on the "good jobs bus"—shows, of course, a quite different picture. There has been some desegregation since the 1960s, but as we have seen, many jobs in many workplaces remain segregated. In the wages they earn, black people and white women are still far behind white males of similar education and experience. Members of the white male group continue to win almost all of the contests for the best jobs in each of the major occupational groups in most workplaces.

Affirmative action's removal of white men's privilege of exclusive access to high-paying jobs does inflict losses on white men. The foes of affirmative action fixate on those losses and ignore the reasons they are necessary, desirable, and fair. Foes pay no attention to the losses of those individuals who, in the absence of affirmative action, have been excluded because they are black or female.

The press has spotlighted the loss of privilege of certain white men and rendered invisible those black individuals who are cut out when white privilege is allowed to persist. One suburban county adopted an affirmative action program to desegregate its fire department, which had a history of total segregation by race. Some of the rejected white applicants organized a demonstration and invited the press. The local newspaper ran a photograph of the group of rejected white candidates across the street from the headquarters of the fire department, gazing at it mournfully and reproachfully. No pictures ever appeared in that newspaper showing the far larger group of blacks who for years had been rejected from firefighter jobs by a selection system rigged to exclude them. Able blacks had been excluded in favor of less qualified or equally qualified whites. The invisibility of the blacks who have been excluded by discrimination promotes the topsy-turvy view that whites are victims and blacks are in a privileged position in our society—that blacks have been "given too much."

IS AFFIRMATIVE ACTION A ZERO-SUM GAME?

Would every gain for blacks and other minorities under affirmative action spell an equal loss for whites? Will men lose to the extent that women gain? If there were a rigidly fixed number of "good" jobs and "bad" jobs, then every time a "good" job was assigned through affirmative action to a black or a woman, a white man would be forced into a "bad" job. . . .

. . . Affirmative action, which breaks up the labor market monopolies that have been held by favored groups and makes blacks and women eligible for a greater variety of jobs, should have the effect of reducing the gap in pay and conditions between jobs that whites and blacks with a given education typically get. If affirmative action is successful, some whites will find themselves applying for jobs that hitherto only blacks have applied for, and some men will be applying for jobs that only women have previously held. But these jobs are likely to be better jobs than they would have been in the absence of affirmative action.

Finally, if we can reduce discrimination and segregation in the labor market, there will be gains outside of the labor market as well. All of us will benefit from revitalized central cities, lower crime rates, and fewer panhandlers, fewer homeless. It will be easier, more pleasurable, less guilt-inducing, and safer to live in a more just society.

NOTES

1. Richard Morin and Sharon Warden, "Americans Vent Anger at Affirmative Action," *Washington Post,* March 24, 1995, pp. 1, 4.
2. Weekly wages of full-time workers by race and sex are published by the U.S. Bureau of Labor Statistics in the periodical *Employment and Earnings.*
3. See Francine D. Blau and Lawrence M. Kahn, "Gender and Pay Differentials," in *Research Frontiers in Industrial Relations and Human Resources,* ed. David Lewin, Olivia S. Mitchell, and Peter D. Sherer (Madison, Wisc.: IRRA, 1992), p. 389.
4. Jane Gross, "Big Grocery Chain Reaches Landmark Sex-Bias Accord," *New York Times,* December 17, 1993, pp. A1, B10.
5. Unpublished papers by Akiko Naono (1993) and Jacqueline Chu (1994), Economics Department, American University, Washington, D.C.
6. Lynne Duke, "Shoney's Bias Settlement Sends $105 Million Signal," *Washington Post,* February 5, 1993, pp. A1, A20.
7. *Employment and Earnings* (January 1995): table A-13.
8. Michael Fix and Raymond J. Struyk, eds., *Clear and Convincing Evidence: Measurement of Discrimination in America* (Washington, D.C.: Urban Institute Press, 1993).
9. Ibid.
10. Arthur Stinchcombe, *Information and Organizations* (Berkeley: University of California Press, 1990), pp. 243–44.
11. Donald Tomaskovic-Devey, *Gender and Racial Inequality at Work: The Sources and Consequences of Job Segregation* (Ithaca, N.Y.: ILR Press, 1993), pp. 161–62.
12. American Society for Personnel Administration, amicus curiae brief submitted to the Supreme Court, quoted in Justice William J. Brennan's majority opinion in *Johnson v. Transportation Agency of Santa Clara County, Calif.,* 107 Sup. Ct. 1442 (1987), p. 1457.

Abortion

Probably no domestic issue has polarized the nation more during the last 30 years than abortion. It has proved to be a hotly contested subject in state and national elections and has been the occasion for repeated mass demonstrations in our nation's capital. That abortion has aroused such strong feelings is not surprising, for some see the right to privacy at stake even as others insist that the real issue is the taking of human life.

In the first selection, Susan Estrich and Kathleen Sullivan argue that if the decision on abortion is taken out of the hands of the mother, then she will necessarily be forced to surrender autonomy over both her body and family decisions. Government intrusion into these spheres would constitute an intolerable infringement on the fundamental right to privacy—a view shared by the Supreme Court when it upheld a woman's right to an abortion in Roe v. Wade *(1973).*

In the second essay James Bopp and Richard Coleson contend that the Roe v. Wade *decision was a glaring example of judicial power gone wild, with the justices manufacturing a right to privacy in the Constitution where it was nowhere to be found. In doing so, the Court not only violated its own stated criteria for determining what qualifies as a fundamental right, but also arrogated to itself a power which the people alone may exercise. Bopp and Coleson further argue that the right to abortion should be rejected on moral as well as legal grounds, and they also challenge pro-choice claims that the outlawing of abortions would have harmful social consequences for women.*

Abortion Politics
The Case for the Right to Privacy
Susan R. Estrich and Kathleen M. Sullivan

I. THE EXISTENCE OF A LIBERTY INTEREST

A. Reproductive Choice Is Essential to a Woman's Control of Her Destiny and Family Life

Notwithstanding the abortion controversy, the Supreme Court has long acknowledged an unenumerated right to privacy as a species of "liberty" that the due process clauses protect.[1] The principle is as ancient as *Meyer v. Nebraska*[2] and *Pierce v. Society of Sisters,*[3] which protected parents' freedom to educate their children free of the state's controlling hand. In its modern elaboration, this right continues to protect child rearing and family life from the overly intrusive reach of government.[4] The modern privacy cases have also plainly established that decisions whether to bear children are no less fundamental than decisions about how to raise them. The Court has consistently held since *Griswold v. Connecticut*[5] that the Constitution accords special protection to "matters so fundamentally affecting a person as the decision whether to bear or beget a child," and has therefore strictly scrutinized laws restricting contraception.[6] *Roe* held that these principles extend no less to abortion than to contraception.

The privacy cases rest, as Justice Stevens recognized in *Thornburgh,* centrally on " 'the moral fact that a person belongs to himself [or herself] and not others nor to society as a whole.' "[7] Extending this principle to the abortion decision follows from the fact that "[f]ew decisions are . . . more basic to individual dignity and autonomy" or more appropriate to the "private sphere of individual liberty" than the uniquely personal, intimate, and self-defining decision whether or not to continue a pregnancy.[8]

In two senses, abortion restrictions keep a woman from "belonging to herself." First and most obviously, they deprive her of bodily self-possession. As Chief Justice Rehnquist observed in another context, pregnancy entails "profound physical, emotional, and psychological consequences."[9] To name a few, pregnancy increases a woman's uterine size 500–1,000 times, her pulse rate by 10 to 15 beats a minute, and her body weight by 25 pounds or more.[10] Even the healthiest pregnancy can entail nausea, vomiting, more frequent urination, fatigue, back pain, labored breathing, or water

Susan R. Estrich is Robert Kingsley Professor of Law at the University of Southern California, and Kathleen M. Sullivan is professor of law and dean of Stanford University Law School. This selection is from Susan R. Estrich and Kathleen M. Sullivan, "Abortion Politics: Writing for an Audience of One," University of Pennsylvania Law Review, *138:125–32, pp. 150–55 (1989). Copyright © 1989 by the University of Pennsylvania. Reprinted by permission. Notes have been renumbered to correspond with edited text.*

retention.[11] There are also numerous medical risks involved in carrying pregnancy to term: of every 10 women who experience pregnancy and childbirth, 6 need treatment for some medical complication, and 3 need treatment for major complications.[12] In addition, labor and delivery impose extraordinary physical demands, whether over the 6-to-12 hour or longer course of vaginal delivery, or during the highly invasive surgery involved in a cesarean section, which accounts for one out of four deliveries.[13]

By compelling pregnancy to term and delivery even where they are unwanted, abortion restrictions thus exert far more profound intrusions into bodily integrity than the stomach-pumping the Court invalidated in *Rochin v. California*,[14] or the surgical removal of a bullet from a shoulder that the Court invalidated in *Winston v. Lee*.[15] "The integrity of an individual's person is a cherished value of our society"[16] because it is so essential to identity: as former Solicitor General Charles Fried, who argued for the United States in *Webster*, recognized in another context: "[to say] that my body can be used is [to say] that I can be used."[17]

These points would be too obvious to require restatement if the state attempted to compel abortions rather than to restrict them. Indeed, in colloquy with Justice O'Connor during the *Webster* oral argument, former Solicitor General Fried conceded that in such a case, liberty principles, although unenumerated, would compel the strictest view. To be sure, as Mr. Fried suggested, restrictive abortion laws do not literally involve "laying hands on a woman."[18] But this distinction should make no difference: the state would plainly infringe its citizens' bodily integrity whether its agents inflicted knife wounds or its laws forbade surgery or restricted blood transfusions in cases of private knifings.[19]

Apart from this impact on bodily integrity, abortion restrictions infringe a woman's autonomy in a second sense as well; they invade the autonomy in family affairs that the Supreme Court has long deemed central to the right of privacy. Liberty requires independence in making the most important decisions in life.[20] "The decision whether or not to beget or bear a child" lies at "the very heart of this cluster of constitutionally protected choices,"[21] because few decisions can more importantly alter the course of one's life than the decision to bring a child into the world. Bearing a child dramatically affects " 'what a person is, what [s]he wants, the determination of [her] life plan, of [her] concept of the good' " and every other aspect of the " 'self-determination . . . [that] give[s] substance to the concept of liberty.' "[22] Becoming a parent dramatically alters a woman's educational prospects,[23] employment opportunities,[24] and sense of self.[25] In light of these elemental facts, it is no surprise that the freedom to choose one's own family formation is "deeply rooted in this Nation's history and tradition."[26]

Today, virtually no one disputes that these principles require heightened scrutiny of laws restricting access to contraception.[27] But critics of *Roe* sometimes argue that abortion is "different in kind from the decision not to conceive in the first place."[28] Justice White, for example, has asserted that, while the liberty interest is fundamental in the contraception context,[29] that interest falls to minimal after conception.[30]

Such a distinction cannot stand, however, because no bright line can be drawn between contraception and abortion in light of modern scientific and medical advances. Contraception and abortion are points on a continuum. Even "conception" itself is a complex process of which fertilization is simply the first stage. According to contemporary medical authorities, conception begins not with fertilization, but rather six to seven days later when the fertilized egg becomes implanted in the uterine wall, itself a complex process.[31] Many medically accepted contraceptives operate after fertilization. For example, both oral contraceptives and the intra-uterine device (IUD) not only prevent fertilization but in some instances prevent implantation.[32] Moreover, the most significant new developments in contraceptive technology, such as RU486, act by foiling implantation.[33] All such contraceptives blur the line between contraception and abortion.

In the absence of a bright physiological line, there can be no bright constitutional line between the moments before and after conception. A woman's fundamental liberty does not simply evaporate when sperm meets ovum. Indeed, as Justice Stevens has recognized, "if one decision is more 'fundamental' to the individual's freedom than the other, surely it is the postconception decision that is the more serious."[34] Saying this much does not deny that profound evolutionary changes occur between fertilization and birth. Clearly, there is some difference between "the freshly fertilized egg and . . . the 9-month-gestated . . . fetus on the eve of birth."[35] But as *Roe v. Wade* fully recognized, such differences go at most to the weight of the state's justification for interfering with a pregnancy; they do not extinguish the underlying fundamental liberty.

Thus *Roe* is not a mere "thread" that the Court could pull without "unravel[ing]" the now elaborately woven "fabric" of the privacy decisions.[36] Rather, *Roe* is integral to the principle that childbearing decisions come to "th[e] Court with a momentum for respect that is lacking when appeal is made to liberties which derive merely from shifting economic arrangements."[37] The decision to become a mother is too fundamental to be equated with the decision to buy a car, choose optometry over ophthalmology, take early retirement, or any other merely economic decision that the government may regulate by showing only a minimally rational basis.

B. Keeping Reproductive Choice in Private Hands Is Essential to a Free Society

Even if there were any disagreement about the degree of bodily or decisional autonomy that is essential to personhood, there is a separate, alternative rationale for the privacy cases: keeping the state out of the business of reproductive decision-making. Regimentation of reproduction is a hallmark of the totalitarian state, from Plato's Republic to Hitler's Germany, from Huxley's *Brave New World* to Atwood's *Handmaid's Tale.* Whether the state compels reproduction or prevents it, "totalitarian limitation of family size . . . is at complete variance with our constitutional concepts."[38] The state's monopoly of force cautions against *any* official reproductive orthodoxy.

For these reasons, the Supreme Court has long recognized that the privacy right protects not only the individual but also our society. As early as *Meyer*[39] and *Pierce,*[40] the Court acknowledged that "[t]he fundamental theory of liberty" on which a free society rests "excludes any general power of the State to standardize" its citizens.[41] As Justice Powell likewise recognized for the *Moore* plurality, "a free society" is one that avoids the homogenization of family life.[42]

The right of privacy, like freedoms of speech and religion, protects conscience and spirit from the encroachment of overbearing government. "Struggles to coerce uniformity of sentiment," Justice Jackson recognized in *West Virginia State Board of Education v. Barnett*,[43] are the inevitably futile province of "our totalitarian enemies."[44] Preserving a private sphere for childbearing and childrearing decisions not only liberates the individual; it desirably constrains the state.[45]

Those who would relegate all control over abortion to the state legislatures ignore these fundamental, systematic values. It is a red herring to focus on the question of judicial versus legislative control of reproductive decisions, as so many of *Roe*'s critics do. The real distinction is that between private and public control of the decision: the private control that the courts protect through *Griswold* and *Roe,* and the public control that the popular branches could well usurp in a world without those decisions.

Precisely because of the importance of a private sphere for family, spirit, and conscience, the framers never intended to commit all moral disagreements to the political arena. Quite the contrary:

> The very purpose of a Bill of Rights was to withdraw certain subjects from the vicissitudes of political controversy, to place them beyond the reach of majorities and officials and to establish them as legal principles to be applied by the courts. One's right to life, liberty, and property, to free speech, a free press, freedom of worship and assembly, and other fundamental rights may not be submitted to vote; they depend on the outcome of no elections.[46]

Such "withdrawal" of fundamental liberties from the political arena is basic to constitutional democracy as opposed to rank majoritarianism, and nowhere is such "withdrawal" more important than in controversies where moral convictions and passions run deepest. The inclusion of the free exercise clause attests to this point.[47]

The framers also never intended that toleration on matters of family, conscience, and spirit would vary from state to state. The value of the states and localities as "laborator[ies for] . . . social and economic experiments"[48] has never extended to " 'experiments at the expense of the dignity and personality of the individual.' "[49] Rather as Madison once warned, " ' it is proper to take alarm at the first experiment on our liberties. We hold this prudent jealousy to be the first duty of citizens, and one of [the] noblest characteristics of the late Revolution.' "[50]

Roe v. Wade thus properly withdrew the abortion decision, like other decisions on matters of conscience, "from the vicissitudes of political controversy." It did not withdraw that decision from the vicissitudes of moral argument or social suasion by persuasive rather than coercive means.[51] In withdrawing the abortion decision from the hot lights of politics, *Roe* protected not only persons but the processes of constitutional democracy. . . .

II. THE POLITICAL PROCESS: NOT TO BE TRUSTED

On October 13, 1989, the *New York Times* declared that the tide had turned in the political process on abortion.[52] The Florida legislature, in special session, rejected a series of proposals to restrict abortion, and Congress voted to expand abortion funding for poor women to cases of rape and incest. And most stunningly of all, the Attorney General of Illinois on November 2, 1989, settled a pending challenge to Illinois' abortion clinic regulation rather than risk winning his case in the United States Supreme Court. These events have triggered the assessment that the post-*Webster* pro-choice mobilization has succeeded. Which raises the question: why not leave these matters to the political process?

The short answer, of course, is that we don't leave freedom of speech or religion or association to the political process, even on good days when the polls suggest they might stand a chance, at least in some states. The very essence of a fundamental right is that it "depend[s] on the outcome of no elections."[53]

The long answer is, as always, that fundamental liberties are not occasions for the experimentation that federalism invites. The right to abortion should not depend on where you live and how much money you have for travel.[54] And, regardless of our recent, at long-last successes, the reality remains that the political process is to be trusted the least where, as here, it imposes burdens unequally.

The direct impact of abortion restrictions falls exclusively on a class of people that consists entirely of women. Only women get pregnant. Only women have abortions. Only women will endure unwanted pregnancies and adverse health consequences if states restrict abortions. Only women will suffer dangerous, illegal abortions where legal ones are unavailable. And only women will bear children if they cannot obtain abortions.[55] Yet every restrictive abortion law has been passed by a legislature in which men constitute a numerical majority. And every restrictive abortion law, by definition, contains an unwritten clause exempting all men from its strictures.

As Justice Jackson wrote, legislators threaten liberty when they pass laws that exempt themselves or people like them: "The framers of the Constitution knew, and we should not forget today, that there is no more effective practical guaranty against arbitrary and unreasonable government than to require that the principles of law which officials would impose upon a minority must be imposed generally."[56] The Supreme Court has long interpreted the equal protection clause to require even-handedness in legislation, lest the powerful few too casually trade away for others key liberties that they are careful to reserve for themselves.

For example, in striking down a law permitting castration of recidivist chicken thieves but sparing white collar embezzlers the knife, the Court implied that, put to an all-or-nothing choice, legislators would rather sterilize no one than jeopardize a politically potent class.[57] In the words of Justice Jackson: "There are limits to the extent to which a legislatively represented majority may conduct biological experiments at the expense of the dignity and personality and natural powers of a minority—even those who are guilty of what the majority defines as crimes."[58]

At least there should be. Relying on state legislatures, as Chief Justice Rehnquist would, to protect women against "abortion regulation reminiscent of the dark ages,"[59] ignores the fact that the overwhelming majority of "those who serve in such bodies"[60] are biologically exempt from the penalties they are imposing.

The danger is greater still when the subject is abortion. The lessons of history are disquieting. Abortion restrictions, like the most classic restrictions on women seeking to participate in the worlds of work and ideas, have historically rested on archaic stereotypes portraying women as persons whose "paramount destiny and mission . . . [is] to fulfill the noble and benign office of wife and mother."[61] Legislation prohibiting abortion, largely a product of the years between 1860 and 1880, reflected *precisely* the same ideas about women's natural and proper roles as other legislation from the same period, long since discredited, that prohibited women from serving on juries or participating in the professions, including the practice of law.[62] And modern studies have found that support for laws banning abortion continues to be an outgrowth of the same stereotypical notions that women's only appropriate roles are those of mother and housewife. In many cases, abortion laws are a direct reaction to the increasing number of women who work outside of the home.[63] Those involved in anti-abortion activities tend to echo the well-known views of Justice Bradley in *Bradwell:*

> Men and women, as a result of . . . intrinsic differences, have different roles to play. Men are best suited to the public world of work, whereas women are best suited to rearing children, managing homes, and loving and caring for husbands. . . . Mothering, in their view, is itself a full-time job, and any woman who cannot commit herself fully to mothering should eschew it entirely.[64]

But the lessons of history are not limited to the powers of enduring stereotypes. History also makes clear that a world without *Roe* will not be a world without abortion but a world in which abortion is accessible according to one's constitutional case. While affluent women will travel to jurisdictions where safe and legal abortions are available, paying whatever is necessary, restrictive abortion laws and with them, the life-threatening prospect of back-alley abortion, will disproportionately descend upon "those without . . . adequate resources" to avoid them.[65] Those for whom the burdens of an unwanted pregnancy may be the most crushing—the young, the poor, women whose color already renders them victims of discrimination—will be the ones least able to secure a safe abortion.

In the years before *Roe,* "[p]oor and minority women were virtually precluded from obtaining safe, legal procedures, the overwhelming majority of which were obtained by white women in the private hospital services on psychiatric indications."[66] Women without access to safe and legal abortions often had dangerous and illegal ones. According to one study, mishandled criminal abortions were the leading cause of maternal deaths in the 1960s,[67] and mortality rates for African-American women were as much as nine times the rate for white women.[68] To trust the political process to protect these women is to ignore the lessons of history and the realities of power and powerlessness in America today.

In the face of such lessons, those who would have us put our faith in the political process might first want to look a little more closely at the victories which are said to support such a choice. The Florida legislature's rejection of proposed abortion restrictions came days *after* the state's highest court held that the State Constitution protects the right to choose abortion, rendering the entire session, by the press's verdict before it began, symbolic at best. The session was still a triumph, but hardly one in which the courts were beside the point. And while extending funding to cases of rape and incest would have been a step forward, the narrowness of the victory and the veto of the resulting legislation should give pause, at least.[69]

We believe that energizing and mobilizing pro-choice voters, and women in particular, is vitally important on its own terms. We hope, frankly, that with apportionment approaching in 2000, that mobilization will affect issues well beyond abortion. We hope more women will find themselves running for office and winning. We hope pro-choice voters and the legislators they elect will attack a range of issues of particular importance to women, including the attention that children receive after they are born.

But we have no illusions. We will lose some along the way. Young and poor and minority women will pay most dearly when we do. That's the way it is in politics. That's why politics should not dictate constitutional rights. . . .

NOTES

1. The right of privacy is only one among many instances in which the Court has recognized rights that are not expressly named in the Constitution's text. To name just a few other examples, the Court has recognized unenumerated rights to freedom of association, see *National Association for the Advancement of Colored People v. Alabama,* 357 U.S. 449, 466 (1958); to equal protection under the Fifth Amendment due process clause, see *Bolling v. Sharpe,* 347 U.S. 497, 500 (1954); to travel between the states, see *Shapiro v. Thompson,* 394 U.S. 618, 638 (1966); to vote, see *Harper v. Virginia Bd. of Elections,* 383 U.S. 663, 665–66 (1966); *Reynolds v. Sims,* 377 U.S. 533, 554 (1964); and to attend criminal trials, see *Richmond Newspapers Inc. v. Virginia,* 448 U.S. 555, 579–80 (1980).
2. 262 U.S. 390 (1923).
3. 268 U.S. 510 (1925).
4. See, e.g., *Moore v. City of East Cleveland,* 431 U.S. 494, 503–06 (1977) (plurality opinion) (noting a constitutional right to live with one's grandchildren); *Loving v. Virginia,* 388 U.S. 1, 12 (1967) (affirming a right to interracial marriage).
5. 381 U.S. 479 (1965).
6. *Eisenstadt v. Baird,* 405 U.S. 438, 453 (1972).
7. *Thornburgh v. American College of Obstetricians & Gynecologists,* 476 U.S. 747, 777 n.5 (1985) (Stevens, J., concurring) (quoting former Solicitor General Fried, "Correspondence," 6 *Phil. & Pub. Aff.* 288–89 (1977)).
8. *Thornburgh,* 476 U.S. at 772.
9. *Michael M. v. Sonoma County Superior Court,* 480 U.S. 464, 471 (1981).
10. See J. Pritchard, P. McDonald & N. Gant, *Williams Obstetrics,* 181–210, 260–63 (17th ed. 1985) [hereinafter *Williams Obstetrics*].
11. See *Id.*
12. See R. Gold, A. Kenney & S. Singh, *Blessed Events and the Bottom Line: Financing Maternity Care in the United States,* 10 (1987).
13. See D. Danforth, M. Hughey & A. Wagner, *The Complete Guide to Pregnancy,* 228–31 (1983); S. Romney, M. J. Gray, A. B. Little, J. Merrill, E. J. Quilligan & R. Stander, *Gynecology and Obstetrics: The Health Care of Women,* 626–37 (2d ed. 1981).
14. 342 U.S. 165 (1952).
15. 470 U.S. 753 (1985).

16. *Id.* at 760.
17. C. Fried, *Right and Wrong,* 121 n.* (1978).
18. "Transcript of Oral Argument in Abortion Case," *N.Y. Times,* Apr. 27, 1989, at B12, col. 5.
19. Likewise, a state would surely infringe reproductive freedom by compelling abortions even if it became technologically possible to do so without "laying hands on a woman."
20. See *Whalen v. Roe,* 429 U.S. 589, 599–600 (1977).
21. *Carey v. Population Serv. Int'l,* 431 U.S. 678, 685 (1977).
22. *Thornburgh v. American College of Obstetricians & Gynecologists,* 476 U.S. 747, 777 n.5 (1985) (Stevens, J., concurring) (quoting C. Fried, *Right and Wrong,* 146–47 (1978)).
23. Teenage mothers have high dropout rates: 8 out of 10 who become mothers at age 17 or younger do not finish high school. See Fielding, *Adolescent Pregnancy Revisited,* 299 Mass. Dep't Pub. Health, 893, 894 (1978).
24. Control over the rate of childbirth is a key factor in explaining recent gains in women's wages relative to men's. See Fuchs, "Women's Quest for Economic Equality," 3 *J. Econ. Persp.* 25, 33–37 (1989).
25. This fact is evident even if the biological mother does not raise her child. Relinquishing a child for adoption may alleviate material hardship, but it is psychologically traumatic. See Winkler & VanKeppel, *Relinquishing Mothers in Adoption: Their Long-Term Adjustment,* Monograph No. 3, Institute of Family Studies (1984).
26. *Moore v. City of East Cleveland,* 431 U.S. 494, 503 (1977) (plurality opinion).
27. The United States has conceded before the Supreme Court that the *Griswold* line of cases was correctly decided. See *Brief for the United States as Amicus Curiae Supporting Appellants,* 11–13; *Webster v. Reproductive Health Serv.,* 1109 S.Ct. 3040 (1989) (No. 88-605); "Transcript of Oral Argument in Abortion Case," *N.Y. Times,* Apr. 27, 1989, at B13, col. 1 (Argument of former Solicitor General Fried on behalf of the United States).
28. *Thornburgh,* 476 U.S. at 792 n.2 (White, J., dissenting).
29. See *Eisenstadt v. Baird,* 405 U.S. 438, 463–64 (1972) (White, J., concurring in result); *Griswold v. Connecticut,* 381 U.S. 479, 502–03 (1965) (White, J., concurring in judgment).
30. See *Thornburgh,* 476 U.S. at 792 n.2 (White, J., dissenting) (arguing that the fetus's presence after conception changes not merely the state justification but "the characterization of the liberty interest itself").
31. See *Williams Obstetrics,* supra note 10, at 88-91; Milby, "The New Biology and the Question of Personhood: Implications for Abortion," 9 *Am. J.L. & Med.* 31, 39–41 (1983). Indeed, the American College of Obstetricians & Gynecologists, the preeminent authority on such matters, has adopted the following official definition of conception: conception consists of "the implantation of the blastocyst [fertilized ovum]" in the uterus, and thus is "not synonymous with fertilization." *Obstetric-Gynecologic Terminology* 229, 327 (E. Hughes ed. 1972). Such a definition is not

surprising in view of the fact that less than half of fertilized ova ever successfully become implanted. See "Post-Coital Contraception," 1 *The Lancet* 855, 856 (1983).

32. See R. Hatcher, E. Guest, F. Stewart, G. Stewart, J. Trussell, S. Bowen & W. Gates, *Contraceptive Technology,* 252–53, 377 (14th rev. ed. 1988) [hereinafter *Contraceptive Technology*]; *United States Department of Health and Human Services, IUDs: Guidelines for Informed Decision-Making and Use* (1987).

33. See *Contraceptive Technology,* supra note 32, at 378; Nieman, Choate, Chrousas, Healy, Morin, Renquist, Merriam, Spitz, Bardin, Balieu & Loriaux, "The Progesterone Antagonist RU486: A Potential New Contraceptive Agent," 316 *N. Eng. J. Med.* 187 (1987). RU486 is approved for use in France but not in the United States.

34. *Thornburgh,* 476 U.S. at 776 (Stevens, J., concurring).

35. *Id.* at 779.

36. "Transcript of Oral Argument in Abortion Case," *N.Y. Times,* April 27, 1989, at B12, col. 5 (former Solicitor General Fried, arguing on behalf of the United States). Counsel for Appellees gave the following complete reply: "It has always been my personal experience that when I pull a thread, my sleeve falls off." *Id.* at B13, col. 1 (argument of Mr. Susman).

37. *Thornburgh,* 476 U.S. at 775 (Stevens, J., concurring) (citing *Griswold v. Connecticut,* 381 U.S. 479, 502–03 (1965) (White, J., dissenting)).

38. *Griswold,* 381 U.S. at 497 (Goldberg, J., concurring).

39. *Meyer v. Nebraska,* 262 U.S. 390 (1923).

40. *Pierce v. Society of Sisters,* 268 U.S. 510 (1925).

41. *Id.* at 535.

42. See *Moore v. City of East Cleveland,* 431 U.S. 494, 503 n.11 (1977) (quoting from a discussion of *Griswold* in Pollak, "Thomas I. Emerson, Lawyer and Scholar: *Ipse Custodiet Custodes,"* 84 Yale L.J. 638, 653 (1975)).

43. 319 U.S. 624 (1943).

44. *Id.* at 640–41.

45. See generally Rubenfeld, "The Right of Privacy," 102 *Harv. L. Rev.* 737, 804–07 (1989) (arguing that the constitutional right of privacy protects individuals from being turned into instrumentalities of the regimenting state, or being forced into a state-chosen identity).

46. *Barnette,* 319 U.S. at 638.

47. Justice Douglas wrote:

> The Fathers of the Constitution were not unaware of the varied and extreme views of religious sects, of the violence of disagreement among them, and of the lack of any one religious creed on which all men would agree. They fashioned a charter of government which envisaged the widest possible toleration of conflicting views.

> *United States v. Ballard,* 322 U.S. 78, 87 (1944). See also *Webster,* 109 S. Ct. at 3085 & n.16 (Stevens, J., concurring in part and dissenting in part) (noting that "the intensely divisive character of much of the national debate over the abortion issue reflects the deeply held religious convictions of many participants in the debate").

48. *New State Ice Co. v. Liebmann,* 285 U.S. 262, 311 (1932) (Brandeis, J., dissenting).

49. *Poe v. Ullman,* 367 U.S. 497, 555 (1961) (Harlan, J., dissenting) (quoting *Skinner v. Oklahoma,* 316 U.S. 535, 546 (1942) (Jackson, J., concurring)).

50. *Everson v. Board of Educ.,* 330 U.S. 1, 65 (1947) (Appendix, Rutledge, J., dissenting) (quoting Madison, *Memorial and Remonstrance Against Religious Assessments*).

51. Nor, of course, did it bar political efforts to reduce the abortion rate through noncoercive means, such as funding sex education and contraception, or providing economic security to indigent mothers.

52. See Apple, "An Altered Political Climate Suddenly Surrounds Abortion," *N.Y. Times,* Oct. 13, 1989, at A1, col. 4; see also Berke, "The Abortion-Rights Movement Has Its Day," *N.Y. Times,* Oct. 15, 1989, § 4 at 1, col. 1.

53. *West Virginia Bd. of Educ. v. Barnette,* 319 U.S. 624, 638 (1943).

54. Even if only 10 or 11 states were to preclude abortion within their borders, many women would be held hostage there by the combination of geography, poverty, and youth. This situation would be no more tolerable than the enforcement of racial segregation in a "mere" ten or eleven states in the 1950s.

55. See *Michael M. v. Sonoma County Superior Court,* 450 U.S. 464, 473 (1981) ("[V]irtually all of the significant harmful and inescapably identifiable consequences of teenage pregnancy fall on the young female").

56. *Railway Express Agency v. New York,* 336 U.S. 106, 112 (1949) (Jackson, J., concurring).

57. See *Skinner v. Oklahoma,* 316 U.S. 535 (1942). Cf. Epstein, "The Supreme Court, 1987 Term: Foreword: Unconstitutional Conditions, State Power, and the Limits of Consent," 102 *Harv. L. Rev.* 4 (1988) (arguing that enforcement of unconstitutional conditions doctrine similarly functions to put legislatures to an all-or-nothing choice).

58. *Skinner,* 316 U.S. at 546 (Jackson, J., concurring).

59. *Webster,* 109 S. Ct. at 3045.

60. *Id.*

61. *Bradwell v. Illinois,* 83 U.S. (16 Wall.) 130, 142 (1873) (Bradley, J., concurring).

62. See J. Mohr, *Abortion in America: The Origins and Evolution of National Policy. 1800–1900,* at 168–72 (1978). To many of the doctors who were largely responsible for abortion restrictions, "the chief purpose of women was to produce children; anything that interfered with that purpose, or allowed women to 'indulge' themselves in less important activities, threatened . . . the future of society itself." *Id.* at 169. The view of one such 19th-century doctor drew the parallel even more explicitly: he complained that "the tendency to force women into men's places" was creating the insidious new idea that a woman's "ministrations . . . as a mother should be abandoned for the sterner rights of voting and law making." *Id.* at 105; see also L. Gordon, *Woman's Body, Woman's Right: A Social History of Birth Control in America* (1976) (chronicling the social and political history of reproductive rights in the United States).

63. See generally K. Luker, *Abortion and the Politics of Motherhood,* 192–215 (1984) (describing how the abortion debate, among women, represents a "war" between

the feminist vision of women in society and the homemaker's world view); Luker, "Abortion and the Meaning of Life," in *Abortion: Understanding Differences* 25, 31–33 (S. Callahan & D. Callahan eds. 1984) (concluding that "[b]ecause many prolife people see sex as literally sacred, *and because, for women, procreative sex is a fundamental part of their "career* . . . abortion is, from their [the prolife] point of view, to turn the world upside down").

64. Luker, *supra* note 63, at 31. It is, of course, precisely such stereotypes, as they are reflected in legislation, which have over and over again been the focus of this Court's modern equal protection cases. See, e.g., *Califano v. Goldfarb,* 430 U.S. 199, 206–07 (1977) ("Gender-based differentiation . . . is forbidden by the Constitution, at least when supported by no more substantial justification than 'archaic and overbroad' generalizations."); *Weinberger v. Wiesenfeld,* 420 U.S. 636, 645 (1975) ("Gender-based generalizations" that men are more likely than women to support their families "cannot suffice to justify the denigration of the effects of women who do work. . . ."): *Stanton v. Stanton,* 421 U.S. 7, 14 (1975) ("A child, male or female, is still a child. No longer is the female destined solely for the home and the rearing of the family, and only the male for the marketplace and the world of ideas."); *Frontiero v. Richardson,* 441 U.S. 677, 684 (1973) ("[O]ur Nation has had a long and unfortunate history of sex discrimination . . . which in practical effect put women, not on a pedestal, but in a cage.").

65. *Griswold v. Connecticut,* 318 U.S. 479, 503 (1965) (White, J., concurring).

66. *Polgar & Fried,* "The Bad Old Days: Clandestine Abortions Among the Poor in New York City Before Liberalization of the Abortion Law," 8 *Fam. Plan. Persp.* 125 (1976); see also Gold, "Therapeutic Abortions in New York: A 20-Year Review," 55 *Am J. Pub. Health* 964, 66 (1965) (noting that the ratio of legal hospital abortions per live birth was 5 times more for white women than for women of color, and 26 times more for white women than for Puerto Rican women in New York City from 1951–62); Pilpel, "The Abortion Crisis," in *The Case for Legalized Abortion Now* 97, 101 (Guttmacher ed. 1967) (noting that 93% of in-hospital abortions in New York State were performed on white women who were able to afford private rooms).

67. See Niswander, "Medical Abortion Practice in the United States," in *Abortion and the Law,* 37, 37 (D. Smith ed. 1967).

68. See Gold, *supra* note 66, at 964–65.

69. Requiring prompt reporting of cases of rape and incest to criminal authorities, measured in terms of days if not hours, as the White House has suggested, is to ignore study after study that has found precisely such cases among the least often reported to the police. Yet late reporting, which should be encouraged, becomes grounds to deny funding, and excludes altogether those who fear, often with reasons, to report at all. The pain and suffering of brutal victimization and of an unwanted pregnancy are in no way affected by the speed of the initial criminal report. A small victory, indeed.

  President Bush vetoed the legislation on October 21, 1989. The House vote to override was 231–191, short of the necessary two-thirds majority. See 135 *Cong. Rec.* H7482-95 (daily ed. Oct. 25, 1989).

Abortion on Demand Has No Constitutional or Moral Justification

James Bopp, Jr., and Richard E. Coleson

I. THE ABSENCE OF A CONSTITUTIONAL RIGHT TO ABORTION

Abortion is not mentioned in the United States Constitution. Yet, in *Roe v. Wade*,[1] the United States Supreme Court held that there is a constitutional right to abortion.

How could the Court justify such a decision? Actually, it never did. The Court simply *asserted* that the "right of privacy . . . is broad enough to encompass a woman's decision whether or not to terminate her pregnancy."[2] Leading constitutional scholars were outraged at the Court's action in *Roe* and vigorously argued that the Court had no constitutional power to create new constitutional rights in this fashion.[3] And, of course, many people were incensed that a whole class of innocent human beings—those awaiting birth—was stripped of all rights, including the right to life itself.

Why does it matter whether abortion is found in the Constitution? Why shouldn't the United States Supreme Court be free to create new constitutional rights whenever it chooses? The answers lie in the carefully designed structure of our democracy, whose blueprints were drawn over two centuries ago by the framers of the Constitution and ratified by the People. This design is explained below as the foundation for rejecting abortion on demand on a constitutional basis.

But what of abortion on demand as a legislative issue? Even if there is no constitutional right to abortion, how much should state legislatures restrict abortion? The answer lies in the states' compelling interest in protecting innocent human life, born or preborn. This interest is given scant attention by abortion rights advocates. Rather, they envision an extreme abortion-on-demand regime; but their societal vision is overwhelmingly rejected by public opinion. As shown below, the states constitutionally may and morally should limit abortion on demand.

A. The People Have Created a Constitutional Democracy With Certain Matters Reserved to Democratic Control and Other Matters Constitutionally Protected

The United States Constitution begins with the words "We the People of the United States . . . do ordain and establish this Constitution for the United States of America."[4]

James Bopp, Jr. is an attorney in the law firm of Bopp, Coleson, & Bostrom, Terre Haute, Indiana, and general counsel to the National Right to Life Committee, Inc. Richard E. Coleson is an associate with Bopp, Coleson, & Bostrom and general counsel, Indiana Citizens for Life, Inc. This article was written especially for Points of View *in 1992.*

Thus, our Republic is founded on the cornerstone of democratic self-governance—all authority to govern is granted by the People.[5] The only legitimate form of government is that authorized by the People; the only rightful authority is that which the People have granted to the institutions of government.[6]

The People have chosen to authorize a regime governed by the rule of law, rather than rule by persons.[7] The supreme law of the land is the Constitution,[8] the charter by which the People conferred authority to govern and created the governing institutions. Thus, the only legitimate form and authority for governance are found in the Constitution.

The constitutional grant of governing authority was not a general grant but one carefully measured, balanced, and limited. Three fundamental principles underlie the Constitution: (1) the People have removed certain matters from simple majority rule by making them constitutional rights but have retained other matters to be democratically controlled through their elected representatives;[9] (2) the People have distributed governmental powers among three branches of government, with each limited to its own sphere of power;[10] and (3) the People have established a federal system in which the power to regulate certain matters is granted to the national government and all remaining power is retained by the states or by the People themselves.[11]

Because these fundamental principles were violated by the Supreme Court in *Roe v. Wade,*[12] leading constitutional scholars condemned the decision. Law professors and dissenting Supreme Court Justices declared that the Court had seized power not granted to it in the Constitution, because (1) it had created new constitutional rights, which power only the People have,[13] (2) it had acted as a legislature rather than as a court,[14] and (3) it had trespassed into an area governed by the states for over two centuries.[15] The scholarly rejection of *Roe v. Wade* continues to the present.[16]

Although the Court's power grab in *Roe* was a seizure less obvious to the public than tanks in the street, it has nevertheless been rightly characterized as a "limited *coup d'état.*"[17] The Court seized from the People a matter they had left to their own democratic governance by declaring a constitutional right to abortion without establishing any connection between the Constitution and a right to abortion. Richard Epstein attacked the Court's *Roe* decision thus, "*Roe* . . . is symptomatic of the analytical poverty possible in constitutional litigation."[18] He concluded: "[W]e must criticize both Mr. Justice Blackmun in *Roe v. Wade* . . . and the entire method of constitutional interpretation that allows the Supreme Court . . . both to 'define' and to 'balance' interests on the major social and political issues of our time."[19]

B. To Determine Which Matters Are Constitutionally Removed from Democratic Control, the Supreme Court Has Developed Tests to Determine Fundamental Rights

The Court did not violate the Constitution in *Roe* simply because there is no *express* mention of abortion in the Constitution. There are matters which the Constitution does not *expressly* mention which the Supreme Court has legitimately found to be within some express constitutional protection. But where the Court employs such constitutional analysis, it must clearly demonstrate that the newly recognized constitutional right properly falls within the scope of an express right. This requires a careful examination and explanation of what the People intended when they ratified the particular constitutional provision in question. It was the *Roe* Court's failure to provide this logical connection between the Constitution and a claimed right to abortion which elicited scholarly outrage.

Under the Supreme Court's own tests, the Court had to find that the claimed right to abortion was a "fundamental" right in order to extend constitutional protection to it under the Fourteenth Amendment, the constitutional provision in which the Court claimed to have found a right to abortion.[20] The Fourteenth Amendment guarantees that no "State [shall] deprive any person of life, liberty, or property, without due process of law."[21] While the provision on its face seems to guarantee only proper legal proceedings before a state may impose capital punishment, imprisonment, or a fine, the Court has assumed the authority to examine activities asserted as constitutional rights to determine whether—in the Court's opinion—they fall within the concept of "liberty."[22] The notion that the Court may create new constitutional rights at will by reading them into the "liberty" clause of the Fourteenth Amendment could readily lead to a rejection of the foundational constitutional premise of the rule of law, not of persons. If a handful of Justices can place whatever matters they wish under the umbrella of the Constitution—totally bypassing the People and their elected representatives—then these Justices have constituted themselves as Platonic guardians,[23] thereby rejecting the rule of law for the rule of persons. What would prevent a majority of the Supreme Court from declaring that there is a constitutional right to practice, e.g., infanticide or polygamy (matters which the states have historically governed)?

This danger has caused many scholars to reject the sort of analysis which allows five Justices (a majority of the Court) to read new constitutional rights into the "liberty" clause.[24] It led the Court in earlier years to forcefully repudiate the sort of analysis the Court used in *Roe v. Wade.*[25] This danger has caused the current Court to establish more rigorous tests for what constitutes a constitutional right to prevent the Supreme Court from "roaming at large in the constitutional field."[26] These tests had been established at the time of *Roe,* but were ignored in that case.[27]

The Court has developed two tests for determining whether a new constitutional right should be recognized. The first test asks whether an asserted fundamental right is "implicit in the concept of ordered liberty."[28] The second test—a historical test—is whether the right asserted as "fundamental" is "so rooted in the traditions and conscience of our people as to be ranked as fundamental."[29] The historical test is the one now primarily relied upon by the Court.

C. Applying the Proper Test for Determining Constitutional Rights Reveals That Abortion Is Not a Constitutional Right

In *Roe,* the Court should have determined whether or not there is a constitutional right to abortion by asking whether it has historically been treated as "implicit in the concept of ordered liberty" in this nation or whether it has been "deeply rooted [as a right] in this Nation's history and tradition."

The *Roe* opinion itself recounted how abortion had been regulated by the states by statutory law for over a century and before that it had been regulated by the judge-made common law inherited from England.[30] In fact, the period from 1860 to 1880—the Fourteenth Amendment was ratified in 1868[31]—saw "the most important burst of anti-abortion legislation in the nation's history."[32] Therefore, the framers of the Fourteenth Amendment and the People who ratified it clearly did not intend for the Amendment to protect the right to abortion, which was considered a crime at the time.

Now Chief Justice Rehnquist stated well the case against *Roe*'s right to abortion in his 1973 dissent to that decision:

> To reach its result, the Court necessarily has had to find within the scope of the Four-teenth Amendment a right that was apparently completely unknown to the drafters of the Amendment. As early as 1821, the first state law dealing directly with abortion was enacted by the Connecticut Legislature. By the time of the adoption of the Fourteenth Amendment in 1868, there were at least 36 laws enacted by state or territorial legisla-tures limiting abortion. While many states have amended or updated their laws, 21 of the laws on the books in 1968 remain in effect today. Indeed, the Texas statute struck down today was, as the majority notes, first enacted in 1857 and has remained sub-stantially unchanged to the present time.
>
> There apparently was no question concerning the validity of this provision or of any of the other state statutes when the Fourteenth Amendment was adopted. The only conclusion possible from this history is that the drafters did not intend to have the Four-teenth Amendment withdraw from the states the power to legislate with respect to this matter.[33]

Thus, applying the Court's own tests, it is clear that there is no constitutional right to abortion. As a result, the Supreme Court has simply arbitrarily declared one by say-ing that the right of privacy—previously found by the Court in the "liberty" clause—"is broad enough to encompass a woman's decision whether or not to terminate her pregnancy."[34] In so doing, the Court brushed aside the restraints placed on it by the Con-stitution, seized power from the People, and placed within the protections of the Con-stitution an abortion right that does not properly belong there.

One thing is clear from this nation's abortion debate: abortion advocates do not trust the People to decide how abortion should be regulated.[35] However, in rejecting the voice of the People, abortion partisans also reject the very foundation of our democratic Republic and seek to install an oligarchy—with the Court governing the nation—a sys-tem of government rejected by our Constitution.

II. THE INTEREST IN PROTECTING INNOCENT HUMAN LIFE

Abortion rights advocates generally ignore one key fact about abortion: abortion re-quires the willful taking of innocent human life. Abortion involves not merely the issue of what a woman may do with her body. Rather, abortion also involves the question of what may the woman do with the body of another, the unborn child.

A. The People Have an Interest in Protecting Preborn Human Life

The fact that human life begins at conception was well-known at the time the Fourteenth Amendment was ratified in 1868. In fact it was precisely during the time when this Amendment was adopted that the medical profession was carrying the news of the discovery of cell biology and its implications into the legislatures of the states and territories. Prior to that time, science had followed the view of Aristotle that the unborn child became a human being (i.e., received a human soul) at some point after conception (40 days for males and 80–90 days for females).[36] This flawed scientific view became the basis for the "quickening" (greater legal protection was provided to the unborn from abortion after the mother felt movement in the womb than before) distinction in the common law received from England, which imposed lesser penalties for abortions performed prior to "quickening." With the scientific discovery of cell biology, however, the legislatures acted promptly to alter abortion laws to reflect the newly established scientific fact that individual human life begins at conception.

Victor Rosenblum summarized the history well:

> Only in the second quarter of the nineteenth century did biological research advance to the extent of understanding the actual mechanism of human reproduction and of what truly comprised the onset of gestational development. The nineteenth century saw a gradual but profoundly influential revolution in the scientific understanding of the beginning of individual mammalian life. Although sperm had been discovered in 1677, the mammalian egg was not identified until 1827. The cell was first recognized as the structural unit of organisms in 1839, and the egg and sperm were recognized as cells in the next two decades. These developments were brought to the attention of the American state legislatures and public by those professionals most familiar with their unfolding import—physicians. It was the new research findings which persuaded doctors that the old "quickening" distinction embodied in the common and some statutory law was unscientific and indefensible.[37]

About 1857, the American Medical Association led the "physicians' crusade," a successful campaign to push the legal protection provided for the unborn by abortion laws from quickening to conception.[38]

What science discovered over a century before *Roe v. Wade* was true in 1973 (when *Roe* was decided) and still holds true today. For example, a recent textbook on human embryology declared:

> It is the penetration of the ovum by a spermatozoon and the resultant mingling of the nuclear material each brings to the union that constitutes the culmination of the process of *fertilization* and *marks the initiation of the life of a new individual*.[39]

However, abortion rights advocates attempt to obscure the scientific evidence that individual human life begins at conception by the claiming that conception is a "complex" process and by confusing contraception with abortion.[40]

The complexity of the process of conception does not change the fact that it marks the certain beginning of individual human life.[41] Moreover, the complex process of conception occurs in a very brief time at the beginning of pregnancy.[42]

Furthermore, the fact that some so-called "contraceptives" actually act after conception and would be more correctly termed "abortifacients" (substances or devices causing
abortion, i.e., acting to abort a pregnancy already begun at conception) does nothing to
blur the line at which individual human life begins. It only indicates that some so-called
"contraceptives" have been mislabelled.[43] Such mislabelling misleads women, who have
a right to know whether they are receiving a contraceptive or are having an abortion.

The "spin"[44] which abortion advocates place on the redefinition of "contraception"
is deceptive in two respects. First, there is a clear distinction between devices and substances which act before conception and those which act after conception. This was admitted by Planned Parenthood itself (before it became involved in advocating, referring
for, and performing abortions) in a 1963 pamphlet entitled *Plan Your Children:* "An
abortion kills the life of a baby after it has begun. . . . Birth control merely postpones
the beginning of life."[45]

Second, even if there were no "bright physiological line . . . between the moments
before and after conception"[46] this does not mean there can be no constitutional line.[47]
At *some point* early in pregnancy, scientific truth compels the conclusion that individual human life has begun. If the indistinction is the real problem, then abortion advocates should be joining prolife supporters in protecting unborn life from a time when
there is certitude.[48] However, abortion partisans are not really interested in protecting
unborn human life from the time when it may be certain that it exists. They are seeking
to justify absolute, on-demand abortion throughout pregnancy.

B. Abortion Rights Advocates Envision an Abortion-on-Demand Regime Unsupported by the People

Abortion rights proponents often argue that our democratic Republic must sanction
abortion on demand lest women resort to dangerous "back-alley" abortions. The claims
of abortion advocates that thousands of women died each year when abortion was illegal are groundless fabrications created for polemical purposes.[49] In reality, the Surgeon
General of the United States has estimated that only a handful of deaths occurred each
year in the United States due to illegal abortions.[50] Even since *Roe,* there are still maternal deaths from legal abortions.[51] As tragic as the death of any person is, it must be
acknowledged that women who obtain illegal abortions do so by choice and most
women will choose to abide by the law. In contrast, preborn human beings are
destroyed—without having a choice—at the rate of about 1.5 million per year in the
United States alone.[52]

Abortion supporters also resort to the practice of personally attacking prolifers and
making false charges about them.[53] A founding member of what is now called the
National Abortion Rights Action League (NARAL) chronicles how prolifers were
purposely portrayed as Catholics whenever possible, in an attempt to appeal to latent
(and sometimes overt) anti-Catholic sentiment in certain communities.[54] It is also
routinely claimed that opposition to abortion is really an attempt to "keep women in
their place"[55]—to subjugate them—as if requiring fathers to support their children
subjugates them. And prolifers are depicted as forcing what are merely their religious
views upon society,[56] despite the fact that the United States Supreme Court has held that

opposition to abortion "is as much a reflection of 'traditionalist' values towards abortion, as it is an embodiment of the views of any particular religion."[57] Those attempting so to "poison the well," by attacking prolife supporters with untruthful allegations, ignore the fact that polls consistently show that abortion opinion is rather evenly divided in our country within all major demographic groups. For example, women are roughly equally divided on the subject, as are whites, non-whites, Republicans and Democrats.[58] Abortion advocates also ignore the fact that most prolifers simply are opposed to the taking of what they consider (and science demonstrates) to be innocent human life.

Of even greater risk than the risk to a few women who might choose to obtain illegal abortions is the effect of abortion on demand—for any or no reason—on society. Abortion cheapens the value of human life, promotes the idea that it is permissible to solve one's problems at the expense of another, even to the taking of the other's life, legitimizes violence (which abortion is against the unborn) as an appropriate solution for problems, and exposes a whole class of human beings (those preborn) to discrimination on the basis of their age or place of residence (or sometimes their race, gender, or disability).

The regime which abortion-on-demand advocates envision for our society is a radical one. Their ideal society is one where abortions may be obtained for any reason, including simply because the child is the wrong sex; where a husband need not be given any consideration in (or even notice of) an abortion decision involving a child which he fathered; where fathers are shut out even when the child to be aborted might be the only one a man could ever have; where parents could remain ignorant of their daughter's abortion, even when she is persuaded to abort by counselors at an abortion mill whose practitioners care only about financial gain, practice their trade dangerously, and never bother to follow up with their patients; where abortion may be used as a means of birth control; where abortionists do not offer neutral, scientific information about fetal development (and about resources for choosing alternatives to abortion) to women considering abortion; where women are not given adequate time to consider whether they really want an abortion; where abortion is available right up to the time of birth; and where our taxes are used to pay for abortion on demand.[59]

The American People reject such a regime. In fact, polls show that an overwhelming majority would ban well over 90 percent of all abortions that are performed.[60] For example a *Boston Globe* national poll . . . revealed that:

> Most Americans would ban the vast majority of abortions performed in this country.
> . . .
>
> While 78 percent of the nation would keep abortion legal in limited circumstances, according to the poll, those circumstances account for a tiny percentage of the reasons cited by women having abortions.
>
> When pregnancy results from rape or incest, when the mother's physical health is endangered and when there is likely to be a genetic deformity in the fetus, those queried strongly approve of legal abortion.
>
> But when pregnancy poses financial or emotional strain, or when the woman is alone or a teen-ager—the reasons given by most women seeking abortions—an overwhelming majority of Americans believes abortion should be illegal, the poll shows.[61]

Yet *Family Planning Perspectives,* a publication of the Alan Guttmacher Institute, which is a research arm of the Planned Parenthood Federation, reveals that these are precisely the reasons why over 90 percent of abortions are performed.[62]

Thus, it is little wonder that the Supreme Court's effort to settle the abortion question with its decision in *Roe v. Wade* has utterly failed. That there is not an even greater groundswell of public opposition to abortion must be attributed to the fact that many Americans are not aware that *Roe* requires virtual abortion on demand for the full nine months of pregnancy.[63] Many people still believe that abortion is only available in the earliest weeks of pregnancy and that abortions are usually obtained for grave reasons, such as rape and incest, which abortion rights advocates always talk about in abortion debates. Of course, such "hard" cases make up only a tiny fraction of all abortions, and many state abortion laws, even before *Roe,* allowed abortions for such grave reasons. It is clear, therefore, that the People reject the radical abortion-on-demand regime promoted by abortion rights advocates.

III. CONCLUSION: STATES CONSTITUTIONALLY MAY AND MORALLY SHOULD LIMIT ABORTION ON DEMAND

One of the principles underlying our liberal democratic Republic is that we as a People choose to give the maximum freedom possible to members of our society. John Stuart Mill's essay *On Liberty,*[64] a ubiquitous source on the subject, is often cited for the principle that people ought to be granted maximum liberty—almost to the degree of license. Yet, Mill himself set limits on liberty relevant to the abortion debate. Mill wrote his essay *On Liberty* to assert "one very simple principle," namely, "[t]hat the only purpose for which power can be rightfully exercised over any member of a civilized community, against his will, is to prevent harm to others."[65] Thus, under Mill's principles, abortion should go unrestricted only if it does no harm to another. But that, of course, is precisely the core of the abortion debate. If a fetus is not really an individual human being until he or she is born, then the moral issue is reduced to what duty is owed to potential life (which is still a significant moral issue). If however, a fetus is an individual human being from the moment of conception (or at least some time shortly thereafter), then the unborn are entitled to legal protection. Ironically, the United States Supreme Court neglected this key determination—when human life begins—in its *Roe* decision.[66]

Science, of course, has provided the answer to us for well over a hundred years. Indeed, modern science and technological advances have impressed upon us more fully the humanity and individuality of each unborn person. As Dr. Liley has said:

> Another fallacy that modern obstetrics discards is the idea that the pregnant woman can be treated as a patient alone. No problem in fetal health or disease can any longer be considered in isolation. At the very least two people are involved, the mother and her child.[67]

In fact, since *Roe,* the technology for improving fetal therapy is advancing exponentially.[68] In sum, modern science has shown us that:

The fetus as patient is becoming more of a reality each year. New medical therapies and surgical technology increasingly offer parents a new choice when a fetus has a particular disorder. Recently, the only choices were abortion, early delivery, vaginal versus a cesarean delivery, or no intervention. We are now able to offer medical and/or surgical intervention as a viable alternative to a number of infants. With advancing technologies, it is clearly evident that many new and exciting therapies lie just ahead for the fetus.[69]

Because all civilized moral codes limit the liberty of individuals where the exercise of liberty would result in the taking of innocent human life, arguments that abortion is necessary to prevent the subjugation of women must also be rejected.[70] It cannot logically be considered the subjugation of anyone to prevent him or her from taking innocent human life; otherwise, society could not prevent infanticide, homicide, or involuntary euthanasia. No civilized society could exist if the unjustified killing of one citizen by another could not be prosecuted.

Nor do abortion restrictions deny women equality by denying them the same freedom which men have. Men do not have the right to kill their children, nor may they force women to do so. Thus, abortion rights advocates are really arguing for a right that men don't have, and, indeed, no one should have—the right to take innocent human life.

Society has recognized that in some situations men and women should be treated differently, because they are biologically different and are, therefore, not similarly situated for constitutional purposes. For example, the Supreme Court decided in 1981 that a statute that permitted only men to be drafted was not unconstitutional because "[m]en and women . . . are simply not similarly situated for purposes of a draft or registration for a draft."[71] The same principle, however, made constitutional a Navy policy which allowed women a longer period of time for promotion prior to mandatory discharge than was allowed for men.[72] The Supreme Court in this case found that "the different treatment of men and women naval officers . . . reflects, not archaic and overbroad generalizations, but, instead, the demonstrable fact that male and female line officers . . . are not similarly situated."[73] Because men and women are not similarly situated—by the dictates of nature rather than by society or the law—with respect to pregnancy, it is neither a denial of equality to women nor the subjugation of women to provide legal protection for unborn human beings.[74]

It is essential to a civilized society to limit liberties where reasonably necessary to protect others. Thus, government has required involuntary vaccination to prevent a plague from decimating the community,[75] military conscription to prevent annihilation of the populace by enemies,[76] and the imposition of child support—for 18 years—upon fathers unwilling to support their children.[77] These and other limits on freedom are not the subjugation of citizens, but are the essence of life in a community.

In sum, the states constitutionally may and morally should limit abortion on demand.

NOTES

1. 410 U.S. 113 (1973).
2. *Id.* at 153.

3. See *infra,* notes 13–19 and accompanying text.

4. U.S. Const., preamble.

5. In the landmark case of *Marbury v. Madison,* 1 Cranch 137, 176 (1803), the United States Supreme Court explained, "That the people have an original right to establish, for their future government, such principles, as, in their own opinion, shall most conduce to their own happiness is the basis on which the whole American fabric has been erected. See also The Declaration of Independence, para. 2 (U.S. 1776); *The Federalist,* No. 49 (J. Madison).

6. *Marbury,* 1 Cranch at 176 ("The original and supreme will [of the People] organizes the government, and assigns to different departments their respective powers. It may either stop here, or establish certain limits not to be transcended by those departments. The government of the United States is of the latter description.").

7. See, e.g., *id.* at 163 ("The government of the United States has been emphatically termed a government of laws, and not of men."); *Akron v. Akron Center for Reproductive Health,* 462 U.S. 416, 419–20 (1983) (We are a "society governed by the rule of law.").

8. *Marbury,* 1 Cranch at 177 ("Certainly all those who have framed written constitutions contemplate them as forming the fundamental and paramount law of the nation. . . ."); *id.* at 179 ("[T]he constitution of the United States confirms and strengthens the principle, supposed to be essential to all written constitutions, that a law repugnant to the constitution is void; and that courts, as well as other departments, are bound by that instrument.").

9. The Constitution enumerates certain rights; the creation of additional constitutionally protected rights is through amending the Constitution, which depends upon establishing public support for such a right by a supermajority of the People acting through their elected representatives. U.S. Const., art. V. Cf. Bork, "Neutral Principles and Some First Amendment Problems," 47 *Ind. L.J.* 1, 3 (1971).

10. U.S. Const., art. I, § 1, art. II, § 1, art. III, § 1.

11. U.S. Const., amend. IX ("The enumeration in the Constitution, of certain rights, shall not be construed to deny or disparage others retained by the people."), amend. X ("The powers not delegated to the United States by the Constitution, nor prohibited by it to the States, are reserved to the States respectively, or to the people.").

12. 410 U.S. 113.

13. Ely, "The Wages of Crying Wolf: A Comment on *Roe v. Wade,*" 82 *Yale L.J.* 920, 947 (1973) (*Roe* was "a very bad decision. Not because it [would] perceptibly weaken the Court . . . and not because it conflict[ed] with [his] idea of progress. . . . It [was] bad because it [was] bad constitutional law, or rather because it [was] *not* constitutional law and [gave] almost no sense of an obligation to try to be.") (emphasis in the original). *Doe v. Bolton,* 410 U.S. 179, 222 (1973) (White, J., dissenting in this companion case to *Roe*) (The Court's action is "an exercise of raw judicial power. . . . This issue, for the most part, should be left with the people and to the political processes the people have devised to govern their affairs.").

14. The *Michigan Law Review,* in an edition devoted to abortion jurisprudence, contained two passages which summarize the scholarly critiques well. In the first, Richard Morgan wrote:

Rarely does the Supreme Court invite critical outrage as it did in *Roe* by offering so little explanation for a decision that requires so much. The stark inadequacy of the Court's attempt to justify its conclusions . . . suggests to some scholars that the Court, finding no justification at all in the Constitution, unabashedly usurped the legislative function.

Morgan, "*Roe v. Wade* and the Lesson of the Pre-*Roe* Case Law," 77 *Mich. L. Rev.* 1724, 1724 (1979). The editors of the journal concluded from their survey of the literature on *Roe,* "[T]he consensus among legal academics seems to be that, whatever one thinks of the holding, the opinion is unsatisfying." "Editor's Preface," 77 *Mich. L. Rev.* (no number) (1979).

15. *Roe,* 400 U.S. at 174–77 (Rehnquist, J., dissenting).
16. See, e.g., Wardle, " 'Time Enough': *Webster v. Reproductive Health Services* and the Prudent Pace of Justice," 41 *Fla. L. Rev.* 881, 927–49 (1989); Bopp & Coleson, "The Right to Abortion: Anomalous, Absolute, and Ripe for Reversal," 3 *B.Y.U. J. Pub. L.* 181, 185–92 (1989) (cataloging critiques of *Roe* in yet another critique of *Roe*).
17. Bork, *supra* note 9, at 6.
18. Epstein, "Substantive Due Process by Any Other Name: The Abortion Cases," 1973 *Sup. Ct. Rv.* 159, 184.
19. *Id.* at 185.
20. The Court acknowledged this duty in Roe itself, but failed to apply the usual tests for determining what rights are rightfully deemed "fundamental." *Roe,* 410 U.S. at 152.
21. U.S. Const., amend. XIV, § 1, cl. 3.
22. *Roe v. Wade,* 410 U.S. 113, revived this sort of "substantive due process" analysis in recent years.
23. The Greek philosopher Plato advocated rule by a class of philosopher-guardians as the ideal form of government. A. Bloom, *The Republic of Plato,* 376c, lines 4–5, 412b–427d (1968).
24. See, e.g., Ely, *supra* note 13; Bork, *supra* note 9.
25. In repudiating an earlier line of "substantive due process" (i.e., finding new rights in the "liberty" clause of the Fourteenth Amendment) cases symbolized by *Lochner v. New York,* 198 U.S. 45 (1905), the Supreme Court declared that the doctrine "that due process authorizes courts to hold laws unconstitutional when they believe the legislature has acted unwisely, has been discarded." *Ferguson v. Skrupa,* 372 U.S. 726, 730 (1963). The Court concluded in *Ferguson,* "We have returned to the original constitutional proposition that courts do not substitute their social and economic beliefs for the judgment of legislative bodies, who are elected to pass laws." *Id.*
26. *Griswold v. Connecticut,* 381 U.S. 479, 502 (1965) (Harlan, J., concurring.)
27. *Cf. Duncan v. Louisiana,* 391 U.S. 145, 149–50 n.14 (1968), with *Roe v. Wade,* 410 U.S. at 152, and *Moore v. City of East Cleveland,* 431 U.S. 494, 503–04 n.12 (1977). See also Ely, *supra* note 13, at 931 n.79 (The *Palko* test was of "questionable contemporary vitality" when *Roe* was decided).
28. *Roe,* 410 U.S. at 152 (quoting *Palko v. Connecticut,* 302 U.S. 319, 325 (1937)) (quotation marks omitted).

29. *Palko,* 302 U.S., at 325 (quoting *Snyder v. Massachusetts,* 291 U.S. 97, 105 (1934)) (quotation marks omitted).
30. *Roe,* 410 U.S. at 139.
31. *Black's Law Dictionary,* 1500 (5th ed. 1979).
32. J. Mohr, *Abortion in America: The Origins and Evolution of National Policy 1800–1900,* 200 (1978). These laws were clearly aimed at protecting preborn human beings and not just maternal health, *id.* at 35–36, so that medical improvements bringing more maternal safety to abortions do not undercut the foundations of these laws, as *Roe* alleged. *Roe,* 410 U.S. at 151–52.
33. *Roe,* 410 U.S. at 174–77 (Rehnquist, J., dissenting) (citations and quotation marks omitted).
34. *Id.* at 153.
35. *Cf.* Estrich & Sullivan, "Abortion Politics: Writing for an Audience of One," 138 *U. Pa. L. Rev.* 119, 150–55 (1989), with *Webster v. Reproductive Health Services,* 109 S. Ct. 3040, 3058 (1989) (plurality opinion). In *Webster,* the plurality opinion declared:

> The goal of constitutional adjudication is to hold true the balance between that which the Constitution puts beyond the reach of the democratic process and that which it does not. We think we have done that today. The dissent's suggestion that legislative bodies, in a Nation where more than half of our population is women, will treat our decision today as an invitation to enact abortion regulation reminiscent of the dark ages not only misreads our views but does scant justice to those who serve in such bodies and the people who elect them.

Id. (citation omitted).
36. *Roe,* 410 U.S. at 133 n.22.
37. *The Human Life Bill: Hearings on S. 158 Before the Subcomm. on Separation of Powers of the Senate Comm. on the Judiciary,* 97th Cong., 1st Sess. 474 (statement of Victor Rosenblum). See also Dellapenna, "The History of Abortion: Technology, Morality, and Law," 40 *U. Pitt. L. Rev.* 359, 402–04 (1979).
38. J. Mohr, *supra* note 32, at 147–70. This 19th-century legislation was designed to protect the unborn as stated explicitly by 11 state court decisions interpreting these statutes and implicitly by 9 others. Gorby, "The 'Right' to an Abortion, the Scope of Fourteenth Amendment 'Personhood,' and the Supreme Court's Birth Requirement," 1979 S. *Ill, U.L.J.* 1, 16–17. Twenty-six of the 36 states had laws against abortion as early as 1865, the end of the Civil War, as did six of the ten territories. Dellapenna, *supra* note 37, at 429.
39. B. Patten, *Human Embryology,* 43 (3rd ed. 1969) (emphasis added). See also L. Arey, *Developmental Anatomy,* 55 (7th ed. 1974); W. Hamilton & H. Mossman, *Human Embryology,* 1, 14 (4th ed. 1972); K. Moore, *The Developing Human: Clinically Oriented Embryology,* 1, 12, 24 (2nd ed. 1977); *Human Reproduction, Conception and Contraception,* 461 (Hafez ed., 2nd ed. 1980); J. Greenhill & E. Friedman, *Biological Principles and Modern Practice of Obstetrics,* 17, 23 (1974); D. Reid, K. Ryan & K. Benirschke, *Principles and Management of Human Reproduction,* 176 (1972).

40. See, e.g., Estrich & Sullivan, *supra* note 35, at 128–29. While a complete discussion of cell biology, genetics and fetology is beyond the scope of this brief writing, the standard reference works cited by Estrich & Sullivan verify the fact that individual human life begins at conception.
41. *Supra,* note 39.
42. *Id.*
43. By its etymology (*contra + conception,* i.e., against conception) and traditional and common usage, the term *"contraception"* properly refers to "[t]he prevention of conception or impregnation." Dorland's *Illustrated Medical Dictionary,* 339 (24th ed. 1965) or a "deliberate prevention of conception or impregnation," *Webster's Ninth New Collegiate Dictionary,* 284 (1985).
44. Estrich & Sullivan, *supra* note 35, at 1.
45. Planned Parenthood International, *Plan Your Children* (1963).
46. Estrich & Sullivan, *supra* note 35, at 129.
47. At oral arguments in *Webster v. Reproductive Health Services,* 109 S. Ct. 3040 (1989), Justice Antonin Scalia could see a distinction between contraception and abortion, remarking, "I don't see why a court that can draw that line [between the first, second, and third trimesters of pregnancy] cannot separate abortion from birth control quite readily."
48. For example, the West German Constitutional Court in 1975 set aside a federal abortion statute which was too permissive, for it "did not sufficiently protect unborn life." M. Glendon, *Abortion and Divorce in Western Law,* 33 (1987). The West German court began with the presumption that "at least after the fourteenth day, developing human life is at stake." *Id.* at 34.
49. B. Nathanson, *Aborting America,* 193 (1979). Nathanson, a former abortionist and early, organizing member of the National Association for the Repeal of Abortion Laws (NARAL, now known as the National Abortion Rights Action League), says:

    In N.A.R.A.L. . . . . it was always "5,000 to 10,000 deaths a year [from illegal abortion]." I confess that I knew the figures were totally false. . . . In 1967, with moderate A.L.I.-type laws in three states, the federal government listed only 160 deaths from illegal abortion. In the last year before the [*Roe*] era began, 1972, the total was only 39 deaths. Christopher Tietze estimated 1,000 maternal deaths as the outside possibility in an average year before legalization; the actual total was probably closer to 500.

    Id. at 193. Nathanson adds that even this limited "carnage" argument must now be dismissed "because technology has eliminated it." *Id.* at 194 (referring to the fact that even abortions made illegal by more restrictive abortion laws will generally be performed with modern techniques providing greater safety, and antibiotics now resolve most complications).
50. U.S. Dept. of Health and Human Services, *Centers for Disease Control Abortion Surveillance,* 61 (annual summary 1978, issued Nov. 1980) (finding that there were 39 maternal deaths due to illegal abortion in 1972, the last year before *Roe*).
51. Deaths from legally induced abortions were as follows: 1972 = 24, 1973 = 26, 1974 = 26, 1975 = 31, 1976 = 11, 1977 = 17, 1978 = 11. *Id.* During the same period,

deaths from illegal abortions continued as follows: 1972 = 39, 1973 = 19, 1974 = 6, 1975 = 4, 1976 = 2, 1977 = 4, 1978 = 7. *Id.*

52. See, e.g., Henshaw, Forrest & Van Vort, "Abortion Services in the United States, 1984 and 1985," 19 *Fam. Plan. Persps.* 64, table 1 (1987) (at the rate of roughly 1.5 million abortions per year for the 18 years from 1973 to 1990, there have been about 27 million abortions in the U.S.A.).

53. Estrich & Sullivan, *supra* note 35, at 152–54.

54. B. Nathanson, *The Abortion Papers: Inside the Abortion Mentality,* 177–209 (1983).

55. Estrich & Sullivan, *supra* note 35, at 152–54.

56. See, e.g., *id.* at 153 n.132.

57. *Harris v. McRae,* 448 U.S. 297, 319 (1980).

58. See generally R. Adamek, *Abortion and Public Opinion in the United States* (1989).

59. These are some of the radical positions urged by abortion rights partisans in cases such as *Roe v. Wade,* 410 U.S. 113, *Planned Parenthood of Central Missouri v. Danforth,* 428 U.S. 52 (1976), and *Thornburgh v. American College of Obstetricians and Gynecologists,* 476 U.S. 747 (1986).

60. "Most in US favor ban on majority of abortions, poll finds," *Boston Globe,* March 31, 1989, at 1, col. 2–4.

61. *Id.*

62. Torres & Forrest, "Why Do Women Have Abortions?" 20 *Fam. Plan. Persps.,* 169 (1988). Table 1 of this article reveals the following reasons and percentages of women giving their most important reason for choosing abortion: 16% said they were concerned about how having a baby would change their life; 21% said they couldn't afford a baby now; 12% said they had problems with a relationship and wanted to avoid single parenthood; 21% said they were unready for responsibility; 1% said they didn't want others to know they had sex or were pregnant; 11% said they were not mature enough or were too young to have a child; 8% said they had all the children they wanted or had all grown-up children; 1% said their husband wanted them to have an abortion; 3% said the fetus had possible health problems; 3% said they had a health problem; less than .5% said their parents wanted them to have an abortion; 1% said they were a victim of rape or incest; and 3% gave another, unspecified reason. (Figures total more than 100% due to rounding off of numbers.) It is significant to note, also, that 39% of all abortions are repeat abortions. Henshaw, "Characteristics of U.S. Women Having Abortions, 1982–1983," 19 *Fam. Plan. Persps.* 1, 6 (1987).

63. *Roe* held that a state may prohibit abortion after fetal viability, but that it may not do so where the mother's "life or health" would be at risk. 410 U.S. at 165. In the companion case to *Roe, Doe v. Bolton,* the Supreme Court construed "health" in an extremely broad fashion to include "all factors—physical, emotional, psychological, familial, and the woman's age—relevant to the well-being of the patient." 410 U.S. 179, 195 (1973). The breadth of these factors makes a "health" reason for an abortion extremely easy to establish, so that we have virtual abortion on demand

for all nine months of pregnancy in America. Moreover, there are physicians who declare that if a woman simply seeks an abortion she *ipso facto* has a "health" reason and the abortion may be performed. *McRae v. Califano,* No. 76-C-1804 (E.D.N.Y. Transcript, August 3, 1977, pp. 99–101) (Testimony of Dr. Jane Hodgson) (Dr. Hodgson testified that she felt that there was a medical indication to abort a pregnancy if it "is not wanted by the patient.").

64. J. Mill, *On Liberty* (Atlantic Monthly Press edition 1921).

65. *Id.* at 13. It should be noted that Mill's contention that society should never use its power to protect the individual from the actions of himself or herself is hotly disputed. See, e.g., J. Stephen, *Liberty, Equality, Fraternity* (R. White ed. 1967) (the 1873 classic response to Mill); P. Devlin, *The Enforcement of Morals* (1974).

66. *Roe,* 410 U.S. at 159 ("We need not resolve the difficult question of when life begins.").

67. H. Liley, *Modern Motherhood* 207 (1969).

68. "Technology for Improving Fetal Therapy Advancing Exponentially," *Ob. Gyn. News,* Aug. 1–14, 1987, at 31.

69. P. Williams, "Medical and Surgical Treatment for the Unborn Child," in *Human Life and Health Care Ethics,* 77 (J. Bopp ed. 1985).

70. Estrich & Sullivan, *supra* note 35, at 152–54. In legal terms, this argument is an equal protection one. See *id.* at 124 n.10. However, equal protection of the laws is only constitutionally guaranteed to those who are equally situated, and the Supreme Court has held that treating pregnancy differently from other matters does not constitute gender-based discrimination. *Geduldig v. Aiello,* 417 U.S. 484, 496–97 n.20 (1974). For a further discussion of this point, see Bopp, "Will There Be a Constitutional Right to Abortion After the Reconsideration of *Roe v. Wade?*" 15 *J. Contemp. L.* 131, 136–41 (1989). See also Smolin, "Why Abortion Rights Are Not Justified by Reference to Gender Equality: A Response to Professor Tribe," 23 *John Marshall L. Rev.* 621 (1990).

71. *Rostker v. Goldberg,* 453 U.S. 57 (1981).

72. *Schlesinger v. Ballard,* 419 U.S. 498 (1975).

73. *Id.* at 508.

74. Bopp, "Is Equal Protection a Shelter for the Right to Abortion?" in *Abortion, Medicine and the Law* (4th ed. 1991) (in press).

75. *Jacobson v. Massachusetts,* 197 U.S. 11 (1905).

76. The Selective Service Draft Law Cases, 245 U.S. 366 (1918).

77. See, e.g., *Sistare v. Sistare,* 218 U.S. 1 (1910). All states have recognized this obligation by passage of the Uniform Reciprocal Enforcement of Support Act. See Fox, "The Uniform Reciprocal Enforcement of Support Act," 12 *Fam. L.Q.* 113, 113–14 (1978).